In Custer's Shadow:
Major Marcus Reno

The harrowing sight of the dead bodies crowning the height on which Custer fell, and which will remain vividly in my memory until death, is too recent for me not to ask the good people of this country whether a policy that sets opposing parties in the field armed, clothed, and equipped by one and the same government should not be abolished.

Reno's Report, July 5, 1876

Major Marcus Albert Reno
(Glen Swanson Collection)

In Custer's Shadow: Major Marcus Reno

by

Ronald H. Nichols

Introduction by
Brian C. Pohanka

University of Oklahoma Press

Norman

ISBN 0-8061-3281-7

The paper in this book meets the guidelines for permanence and durability of the Committee on Production Guidelines for Book Longevity of the Council on Library Resources, Inc. ∞

In Custer's Shadow originally was published in 1999 by the Old Army Press.

Oklahoma Paperbacks edition published by the University of Oklahoma Press, Norman,
Publishing Division of the University. Manufactured in the U.S.A. First edition, 1999.
First printing of the University of Oklahoma Press edition, 2000.

1 2 3 4 5 6 7 8 9 10

• Contents •

• Preface •

Controversy over the Little Big Horn battle began almost before the fighting ended in 1876. Since then, numerous books have been written about the battle and the 7th U.S. Cavalry's colorful leader, George Armstrong Custer. Probably the first was Frederick Whittaker's, *A Popular Life of Gen. George A. Custer*, published before the end of 1876. Looking to assign blame for Custer's defeat, Whittaker found his scapegoats in Major Marcus Reno and Captain Frederick Benteen. The results of the 1879 Court of Inquiry into Reno's conduct at the Little Big Horn did little to stem the controversy. However, it did provide the only official testimony from a number of officers and men who had participated in the battle.

The Court of Inquiry's official transcript did not become available until 1951 when Colonel William Graham produced just 125 copies. By the time I became interested in the battle in 1975, the transcript's high cost and lack of availability made it difficult to obtain a copy. I did have Colonel Graham's *Abstract of the Reno Court of Inquiry* but knew that he had provided only selected portions of the testimony. In 1981, I finally obtained a retyped copy of the full official version from which I made a photocopy of all 700-plus pages. That same year, while attending the Little Big Horn Associates conference in San Antonio, Texas, I had my first opportunity to talk to Charles Reno, great-nephew of Marcus Reno.

About that same time, I had the opportunity to read John Upton Terrell's and Colonel George Walton's book *Faint the Trumpet Sounds*. In stark contrast to Whittaker's book, it stated it was "the full story of Major Marcus Reno — man and soldier" and certainly placed a different slant on the role Reno played at the Little Big Horn. But I read the book with some skepticism when the authors listed Reno's middle name as "Alfred" instead of "Albert." What other errors did the book contain and how accurate a biography was it?

Reading the official testimony of the court of inquiry in detail gave me a different perspective on the battle — and the role played by its main participants, especially Reno the soldier and his actions at the battle. Certainly a more compelling and accurate biography of this beleaguered individual seemed appropriate. That provided the impetus for me to undertake the task of producing such a manuscript.

i

During numerous trips to Washington, D.C., I spent considerable time at the National Archives. With the help of Michael E. Pilgrim, archivist, Military Service Branch, I found more information available on Reno than I expected. Many more visits followed over the next several years.

In late 1984, I again contacted Charles Reno and asked him for any material he might have on Marcus or his family, including letters, diaries and photographs. Charles provided some information that suggested where other material might be found.

Early 1985 took me to my next stop in my quest for information, the Military Academy Library at West Point. With the help of Marie Capps and Kenneth Rapp (both now deceased), I obtained a fairly complete picture of Reno's six years as a cadet. I was disappointed to find that only two members of the Class of 1857 apparently had not had their graduation pictures taken — and Reno was one of them. Later that year, I spent several days in Spartanburg, S.C., where Reno was stationed in 1871-1872. The assistance of Curtis E. Hinkle of the Spartanburg County Library and Herbert Hucks Jr., archivist at Wofford College's Sandor Teszler Library, provided much data about Spartanburg following the Civil War and the conflict with the Ku Klux Klan.

My next stop on my search took me to the U.S. Army Military History Institute, Carlisle Barracks, Penna. With the help of John J. Slonaker, Chief, Historical Reference Branch, I found the history of the 1st U.S. Cavalry during the Civil War and other files related to individuals who were at the Little Big Horn.

On March 17, 1986, during the first of my three visits to Harrisburg, Penna., I was fortunate to meet the man who contributed more material for this book than any other individual. At the Dauphin County Records Office, I was looking for information about Reno's marriage to a local woman, Mary Hannah Ross, when another researcher, Gene R. Boak, asked if he could help. He suggested I might find information on Mary Hannah in the state library genealogical files, especially since her mother was Mary Haldeman Ross and her Haldeman grandparents were well-known in the area. I spent several hours in that library but was unable to locate the material I wanted. In April 1986, I wrote to Gene, and over the next three years, I came to respect his talents as one of the best researchers I have been privileged to know. Gene became so interested in my Reno project that he traveled, at his own expense, to Philadelphia, Washington, New Orleans, Carrollton, Ill., and Nashville and uncovered a wealth of information on Reno. Gene's contributions to this book can not be underestimated — his assistance is greatly appreciated.

Also in 1986, I received help in my research from several other people, including Brian Pohanka, whom I have known for many years. His knowledge of events and personalities of both the Civil War and Indian Wars is phenomenal. During his own research, whenever he would find a fact about Reno, he would send it to me. Brian also reviewed many of the photographs I obtained for the book and he was able to identify not only the individuals in them, but where and probably when the images were taken. His overall understanding of the participants in the Little Big Horn battle and his expertise on the entire Indian Wars period made him the obvious choice to write the introduction to this tome. He also reviewed the manuscript itself. Thanks again Brian for all your effort.

Over the years I've attended a number of meetings of several organizations: Custer Battlefield Historical & Museum Association, Little Big Horn Associates and the Order of the Indian Wars. I've met a number of folks who also had a strong interest in the Indian Wars period. When they learned I was preparing a Reno biography, they would often send me articles from newspapers and magazines that mentioned him. Any attempt on my part to name them all would inevitably leave someone off the list, so I'll take the easy way out and say thanks to all of you who have sent me information for my book.

During my many visits to the battlefield between 1980-1987, I was received most courteously by Superintendent Jim Court and Chief Historian Neil Mangum, both of whom allowed me access to the battlefield library and photo collection where I obtained much additional data on Reno.

In 1988, while at the battlefield I took the opportunity to pause, as I had done a countless times before, at the Reno gravesite in the cemetery. As they say, sometimes "you can't see the forest for the trees" — Reno's gravestone bore the wrong date of his death! It stated he had died March 29, 1889, but the actual date was March 30. An April 24, 1988, letter to the new superintendent, Dennis Ditmanson, brought almost immediate results. On June 10, Ditmanson wrote to me that I was "the proud 'parent' of a bouncing 215 pound headstone," and "indeed the correct date for the demise of the good Major" was March 30, 1889. He ordered a new headstone which was installed that summer.

In 1991, I contacted Philip B. Alfeld of Alton, Ill., who had written a paper for the English Westerners Society entitled, "Major Reno and His Family in Illinois." It covered Reno's early life in Carrollton, Ill. I asked him for copies of the research material he had obtained from the Greene County Courthouse in Carrollton. He suggested I meet him there. Our visit would not happen until early 1993, when we spent a full day going over important county records and visiting the two cemeteries in Carrollton where Marcus' parents and grandparents were buried. Phil's help has been very valuable.

A couple of other people have contributed greatly to this project. The first is Sandy Barnard, associate professor of journalism at Indiana State University, Terre Haute. Sandy and I were working on biographies at the same time:

Sandy's was on Mark Kellogg, the *Bismarck Tribune* reporter who accompanied Custer to his demise at the Little Big Horn. Both of us procrastinated on the actual task of writing a manuscript but Sandy received an offer from the *Bismarck Tribune* that he couldn't refuse. His book, *I Go With Custer, The Life and Death of Reporter Mark Kellogg*, was published in 1996. His encouragement has greatly contributed to my final effort to wrap up this project. Sandy also edited my final manuscript for this book which has significantly improved its readability.

Another person instrumental in compelling me to complete this manuscript was Mike Koury of Old Army Press, Fort Collins, Colo. Mike has never been timid about his criticisms of Reno's action at the Little Big Horn or in expressing them to me. The depth of research I did to provide a full picture of Reno the man and the soldier was directly related to what I knew would be a thorough review of my efforts by Mike. His experience and knowledge have proved invaluable and I thank him for his effort.

In the last few years, I have had to acquire a number of photographs of Little Big Horn participants. Photographs have come from many sources but the largest number were provided by Kitty Belle Deernose of the Little Bighorn Battlefield National Monument. Her assistance will be evident in the many images of individuals who participated in the Little Big Horn battle — thanks Kitty.

Besides Brian, Sandy and Mike, several other friends have reviewed my manuscript. Joe Sills, Jr., of Baltimore, Md., possesses phenomenal knowledge and insight into events of the battle. Joe wrote the introduction for Kenneth Hammer's *Men With Custer: Biographies of the 7th Cavalry*, which I edited, so I knew his input on the battle would be accurate. He saved me a couple of times from making serious mistakes in the timing and sequence of battle events. After writing the two chapters dealing with the Little Big Horn battle itself, I again asked Joe to review them. His efforts have assisted in assuring the book's accuracy.

Two other reviewers were Jeff Broome of Golden, Colo., and Jim Brust of San Pedro, Calif. Jeff peered over the manuscript in minute detail and taught me a few things about writing, especially punctuation. His contributions certainly improved the flow of the text. Jim, a tireless researcher who has written numerous articles about early battlefield photographs, provided tidbits of Reno information that he discovered during his own research at the Huntington Library in San Marino, Calif.

Finally, I must acknowledge the contributions of one more person who has had as much to do with this book as I have — my wife, Joyce. She has managed to live with Reno as a house guest for more than 15 years. She has listened to countless hours of discussions about Reno's life, from cradle to grave — and even after! We have spent many hours walking the battlefield together, even though she didn't like the possibility of running into rattlesnakes. Her continuing encouragement has enabled me finally to see this project through to completion. Thanks Joyce. I hope it has been worth it.

One final note — errors in facts, composition, details, punctuation or interpretation, are mine alone. Every effort has been made to provide the reader with what I think is a fair and accurate picture of a truly complex 19th century soldier — Marcus Albert Reno.

Ron Nichols
Costa Mesa, California
January 1999

• Introduction •

Custer battle historian Fred Dustin made a pointed observation when he wrote of Marcus Reno, "His Civil War and previous record was very creditable, but whiskey-drinking got him into trouble as it usually does with whiskey-drinkers, and his personality was not very attractive, and personality goes a long ways, and carries a man over very rough places where lack of it may be the cause of much unearned criticism." In that assessment Dustin, a fervent Reno partisan and posthumous defender of the hapless major, offered some thoughts that are well worth considering.

Unquestionably Reno's Civil War career was creditable, even distinguished, as the testimony of his superior officers makes abundantly clear. In the clash at Kelly's Ford, where Reno was unhorsed and injured leading a small brigade of Regulars, General William Averell reported the captain "handled his men gallantly and steadily." General Alfred Torbert, on whose staff Reno served in the grueling 1864 campaigns for Richmond and the Shenandoah Valley, praised Reno's "coolness, bravery and good judgment," and urged his promotion — an opinion seconded by that most demanding of Federal cavalry commanders, Philip Sheridan, who characterized Reno as "full of energy and ability." Concluding his wartime service as colonel of the 12th Pennsylvania Cavalry, Reno received the brevet rank of brigadier general for "meritorious service."

As for "whiskey-drinking," doubtless Reno did on occasion imbibe to excess as early as his tenure at West Point. Cyrus Comstock, a fellow cadet in the Class of 1855, once noted in his diary that Reno was "pretty tight." But Reno was hardly exceptional in that regard, and no evidence suggests Reno's Civil War career was impaired by alcohol. On the contrary, the official record shows him to have been a solid, dependable soldier. As for Reno's service with the 7th Cavalry prior to Little Big Horn, Lieutenant Winfield Scott Edgerly, who served under Reno on the Northern Boundary Surveys, characterized his superior as "a moderate drinker," and noted "I never saw him drunk." It is certain that a fair amount of liquor was consumed by Reno, Weir, Keogh and other officers during their expedition on the Canadian border, but it does not seem to have been anything out of the ordinary.

But Dustin's observation is clearly applicable to the last decade of Major Reno's life. In the years following Little Big Horn, "whiskey-drinking" did get Marcus Reno "into trouble" and accelerated his downhill slide to ignominy and an early grave. Again, he was not alone in that regard, as alcohol ruined the lives of at least two other prominent figures in the battle of Little Big Horn — Captains Thomas B. Weir and Thomas H. French, both of whom died earlier than Reno — and in French's case, resulted in court martial and disgrace. Each of those men was tragically affected by the events of June 1876, and each waged an ultimately losing battle with their personal demons.

In remarking that Reno's "personality was not very attractive" and citing the potential harm that might entail, I think Dustin touched on an intangible but nonetheless essential ingredient in Reno's tragedy. Long before the fateful summer of 1876, Cyrus Comstock wrote of his West Point classmate, "Reno is not very popular." Comstock did not elaborate, and while his view may in part have stemmed from Reno's involvement in a particularly nasty fight with another cadet, in fact, something in the personal makeup of Marcus A. Reno seems to have prevented him from ever fitting into the hail-fellow-well-met camaraderie of the Regular Army officer corps. An introvert, by nature reserved, even dour, he must have appeared colorless by comparison with the swashbuckling bravado affected by so many cavalry officers. Reno had his defenders, but never, apparently, a wide circle of friends.

As is often the case in affairs of the heart, Reno married a woman whose personality was, in many respects, quite different from his own. By all accounts Mary Hannah Ross was genteel, outgoing, vivacious, fun-loving and popular. Within the narrow social confines of a frontier army post, her presence must have been a professional as well as emotional blessing to her soldier husband — and her early death a blow from which he never fully recovered. Along with the obvious emotional pain and the concerns of raising a young child whose absence with Mary Hannah's relations must have been a constant regret, the loss of his wife likely furthered Reno's withdrawal into military routine, the performance of duty for duty's sake that made him something of a martinet.

Of course, Reno's personality — complex and elusive as it was — would be of little interest to historians were it not for his crucial and disputed role in the battle of Little Big Horn. Whatever one may think of his judgment and command decisions during the fight, it is hard not to pity Reno for the merciless criticism he was subjected to, often by those (like Thomas Rosser and Frederick Whittaker) whose passionate and public excoriation of Custer's second in command belied their absence from the event itself. Those who saw Custer as martyr needed a scapegoat, and Reno easily fit that role. His later misconduct — those unfortunate, almost grotesquely self-destructive imbroglios he became involved in — seemed to validate his tormentors and further fueled the fires of his inner demons.

For all the ink that has been spilled on the life, times and deeds of George Armstrong Custer, Reno remains something of a cipher even to the most dedicated student of Little Big Horn. One can examine and debate his actions during the valley fight and subsequent siege atop the bluffs, poring over every word and implication of the Reno Court of Inquiry and sifting through the letters, memoirs and recollections of the battle's survivors. But precious little has been written of Reno the man, and the events of his life that preceded and followed those bloody June days, and most of what has been written tends to be sketchy, biased and poorly documented.

Fortunately, thanks to the dedicated scholarship of Ron Nichols whose 15 years of research comes to fruition in this volume, students of the battle of Little Big Horn finally have a detailed biography of Marcus Reno. Eagerly awaited by those of us so compellingly drawn to the never-ending quest for the historical truth of Little Big Horn, *In Custer's Shadow* will illuminate — and I believe help us to better understand and empathize with — a man whose life was destroyed in that battle as surely as those who fell to arrow or bullet.

Brian C. Pohanka
Alexandria, Virginia

• Prologue •

"A Scene of Sickening, Ghastly Horror"

Early on the morning of June 27, 1876, troopers of the 7th U.S. Cavalry Regiment watched as a dust cloud, created by a large number of men on horseback, moved slowly up the Little Big Horn Valley. Major Marcus Reno sent two Arikara scouts out with a message and told them to go as near the approaching column as was safe to determine whether they were white men or Indians. If they were soldiers, the scouts were told to return at once, and if they were Indians, attempt to go around them and push on for help.

Reno and the survivors of the 7th Cavalry had just spent two terrifying days besieged on the hot, dusty bluffs above the Little Big Horn River. They had faced an overwhelming force of Sioux and Northern Cheyenne warriors who were determined to protect their families and their way of life.

A career Army officer, Reno was graduated in 1857 from West Point and had served capably and with little controversy for 19 years. On June 25, 1876, he found himself second in command to Lieutenant Colonel George Armstrong Custer as the 7th Cavalry moved toward a long expected fight with hostile Indians. Custer directed him to cross the Little Big Horn River and lead the attack on the Indian village. Reno, with his battalion of three companies, anticipated fierce resistance as they approached the village. He dismounted his troops and formed a skirmish line on the open prairie. Met by a substantial number of Indian warriors, the soldiers were soon compelled to take refuge in a nearby stand of timber. Reno's decision to leave the woods resulted in a disastrous retreat with heavy casualties. Crossing the river, Reno's command finally established a defensive position on the high eastern bluffs. Following the arrival of Captain Frederick Benteen with three companies and the pack train with one reinforced company, an abortive attempt was made to follow Custer's trail. Driven into a defensive position, Reno and his men braced themselves for an extended fight.

With a number of men killed and wounded, Reno and his troopers fought the Indians under the most adverse conditions. Indians swarmed about their position, firing at them from every side and trooper casualties continued to mount. They possessed few tools for digging entrenchments, the heat and dust were oppressive, and thirst quickly became an important concern for the wounded. They finally obtained water on the second day only by heroic dashes to the river by soldiers who frantically filled canteens and cooking pots before scurrying back to cover under intense Indian fire.

For two days that seemed like an eternity, the troopers held their ground. Finally, on the second afternoon, the men watched the Indians break their huge camp and proceed south toward the Big Horn Mountains. Reno and the survivors of his seven companies waited atop the hill caring for their wounded. They wondered what had become of Custer and the five companies that had accompanied him, last seen just before Reno charged the Indian village the previous day. Had they been abandoned by Custer to the mercy of the hostiles?

With their safety finally assured by the approach of a relief column, Reno could take pride in the accomplishment of saving a substantial number of his men against staggering odds. But they were to receive a shock that would match the terror of what they had lived through during the previous two days — Custer and every man in the five companies under his command lay dead on the hills above the Little Big Horn River just three and a half miles from where Reno and his men had fought.

As he viewed the "scene of sickening, ghastly horror" on Custer's field on the morning of June 28, perhaps Reno sensed what lay ahead for him. The mutilated bodies of his fellow soldiers were discolored and bloated from the hot sun. Reno had his men bury their comrades as best they could, but nothing was going to prevent the shock that would soon go through the entire nation. The enthusiastic celebrations of the country's 100th birthday would be dampened by disbelief that so many men of one of the Army's elite cavalry regiments, led by one of its most famous and dashing soldiers, could be slaughtered in this fashion.

It was inevitable that the search for the culprits of the tragedy would eventually lead directly toward Major Marcus Reno. The relief Reno felt as he moved off the bluffs along the Little Big Horn River was to quickly disappear — he would soon discover what a profound effect the battle would have on his army career — and his life.

• 1 •

Growing Up in Southern Illinois

The American frontier had expanded well into the Mississippi Valley by the 1820s, and migration to the rich fertile lands in the Midwest had increased significantly after Illinois gained statehood in 1818. By 1830, much of southern Indiana and Illinois had been settled, most of the new immigrants coming from the South where the growth of the plantations had forced them to move. The "Gateway to the West," St. Louis, had been incorporated as a city in 1822, providing an additional opportunity for families to move west.

Greene County, located in southwest Illinois, was organized in 1821 and named for General Nathaniel Greene, a military hero from the Revolutionary period. As the population of Greene County increased, four "large" towns came into existence. The first of these was Carrollton in 1821, which became the county seat. The new town attracted settlers from the east and south, and by 1832 it would boast of a population of 300.

Aaron and Nancy Reno (original surname "Reynaud"), a family of farmers, lived briefly in Tennessee and Alabama before they were attracted to Greene County by the rich and inexpensive land. Moving there in early 1827, they purchased a farm outside the town of Carrollton.[1] James Reno, born in Tennessee on Sept. 7, 1801, the second of six sons of Aaron and Nancy Reno, moved with his parents to Greene County.

James quickly abandoned farming and moved to Carrollton, then the largest of the Greene County settlements. James was assimilated into the community quickly. On June 3, 1827, he married Charlotte Hinton Miller, 28, a divorcee with a young daughter, Harriet Cordelia. The marriage would eventually produce six children: Eliza, Leonard, Cornelia, Marcus, Sophronia and Henry. James' profession for the next several years is unclear but he probably was employed in some form of mercantile trade.[2] In the next three years, James bought 12 real estate lots in Carrollton and may have operated a tavern or hotel as early as 1831.[3]

Carrollton was at the center of commerce for the area. A stage line ran from the town to St. Louis and it enjoyed frequent communication with boats on the nearby Illinois River. These outside contacts introduced a disastrous

1

Reno Hotel, circa 1896
Photo by C. Reime, Carrollton, Ill. (In Author's collection)

cholera epidemic in 1832 — every adult in town was either ill or caring for the sick.[4] More than 30 died, but the Reno family was spared.

James quickly adapted to Carrollton's business environment, becoming an influential citizen in the community. After the incorporation of Carrollton Aug. 15, 1833, he was one of five men elected as village trustees. These individuals were considered "substantial citizens and heads of well known families."[5]

The birth of their fourth child, Marcus Albert, occurred Nov. 15, 1834, adding to the family of two sisters, a brother, and a half-sister. James bought the recently constructed Union Hotel on the west side of the Carrollton square on June 13, 1836, and moved his family into these comfortable quarters. The hotel, located on the main road to Alton and St. Louis, served as a stagecoach stop and was said to have an excellent tavern. James was also involved with his brother Aaron Jr. and his brother-in-law Alfred Hinton in other business

2

RENO HOTEL, 1996
(IN AUTHOR'S COLLECTION)

enterprises.[6] He was appointed postmaster of Carrollton in 1837, a position he held for several years.

The "Panic of 1837" almost totally destroyed James Reno financially, along with many others, and he sold the Union Hotel in March 1840 to his brother-in-law, Alfred Hinton. To pay his remaining debts, James was forced by the courts to sell his personal property. An agreement signed July 31, 1840, between Hinton and Reno provided that Hinton would "agree to employ the said James Reno and family to superintend and keep the Tavern Establishment." Hinton agreed to pay Reno $600 a year and Reno agreed to "keep the said establishment in a neat and orderly manner, according to the best of his ability."[7] James and his family lived in and managed the hotel for the next four years. After the depression, James purchased the hotel back from Hinton on Feb. 5, 1844.[8]

3

During this period opportunities for formal education in the Carrollton area were rare. Only a low proportion of children attended school even for a short time in any year. For the Reno children education was limited to a local one-room school house staffed mainly with itinerant teachers. Their mother Charlotte also devoted much of her time teaching the younger Reno children. Lessons typically taught in the local school included "reading in the English reader, writing from copy set by the master or mistress, spelling out of Noah Webster's spelling book, arithmetic from Pike's book, and grammar as laid down by [Lindley] Murray."[9] Cornelia, Marcus' sister, later commented that he "assisted his father in the general merchandise business and attended the schools of Carrollton. Here he gained the reputation of being an excellent scholar and a quiet, unobtrusive lad particularly fond of serious literature. He grew to young manhood with the desire of entering military life."[10]

By 1847, James had become financially stable, and in January became partners with his step-son-in-law, Dr. James French Simpson, whose deceased first wife had been Marcus' half-sister, Harriet Cordelia Miller. The business was located on the square in Carrollton and according to newspapers ads, "Reno & Simpson" sold "Drugs, Medicines, Paints, Oils, Dye Stuffs, Glass Ware…Dry Goods, Groceries, Hardware…Boots, Caps."[11] Young Marcus helped his father stock the shelves and make deliveries to the local citizens. During this time Marcus became a proficient horseman — a talent that would serve him well in later years.

Tragedy struck the Reno family on the morning of June 25, 1848, when Charlotte Reno died after an extended illness. The local newspaper reported, "Mrs. Reno had been afflicted for several years; and for the last three years of her life seemed to know of her approaching dissolution."[12] She was buried in the Carrollton City Cemetery.

Following Charlotte's death, James leased the Union Hotel to Robert Hance, husband of his daughter Cornelia, for a period of one year and moved to White Hall, about 10 miles north of Carrollton. Forming a partnership with his brother Aaron Jr., "J. & A. Reno" soon became the largest dry goods and drug store in the northern part of Greene County.[13]

Four Reno children, Leonard, Marcus, Sophronia and Henry, remained at the Union Hotel with their sister Cornelia and her husband Robert Hance. However less than seven months after their mother's death, their father died of smallpox Jan. 11, 1849.[14] James was buried beside his wife in the Carrollton City Cemetery.

A year later, on Jan. 15, 1850, Robert Hance was appointed legal guardian of "Sophronia Reno, Marcus Albert Reno and Henry Clinton Reno minor heirs of James Reno late of Greene County, Illinois, deceased."[15] Sophronia and Henry stayed with the Hances at the hotel while Marcus moved to the home of Doctor Simpson, James Reno's former business partner. Marcus had been working for Simpson as a clerk in his drug store prior to this time, and continued to do so.

Marcus was now 15 and had to decide about his future. He would require further education to establish himself in the community but any hope of being able to afford college was slim. The potential of a military career was appealing, especially if he could get into West Point. Although he was not aware of the physical and education requirements of the military academy, he was determined to find out if he could qualify. On Oct. 1, 1850, he wrote directly to Secretary of War C. M. Conrad:

> Sir, I have the honor to request of you information, in relation to the qualifications of a candidate for admission to the U.S. Military Academy and especially that in regard to age and physical qualification. My reason for making inquiry on this subject is that I desire to receive an appointment as Cadet at the Military Academy. As my Father and Mother are both dead and it is not within my power to obtain an education at my own expense. I can give the required recommendation in regard to moral character and intellectual capacity.
>
> I have the honor, Sir to be,
> Your obe. servant
> Marcus A. Reno[16]

The qualifications for entrance to West Point as stated by the United States Military Academy Regulations of 1832 indicated that:

> [C]andidates must be over sixteen and under twenty-one years of age at the time of entrance into the Military Academy, must be at least five feet in height, and free from any deformity, disease, or infirmity, which would render them unfit for the military service, and from any disorder of an infectious or immoral character. They must be able to read and write well, and perform with facility and accuracy the various operations of the four ground rules of Arithmetic, of Reduction, of simple and compound Proportion, and of vulgar and decimal Fractions.

Reno was in good health, physically sound, solidly built, and weighed about 145 pounds. He was about 5 foot 8 inches tall, with dark hair, brown eyes and a dark complexion. If accepted as a cadet, he would be required to pass an entrance examination. Although his formal education was limited, he could certainly read and write well, and because of his employment as a clerk in Mr. Simpson's drug store, knew the fundamentals of mathematics. He possessed natural perseverance and tenacity, and was not willing to accept defeat easily.

Getting into West Point would not be easy. An 1843 law allowed each representative to select only one candidate from his home district. William Alexander Richardson was the Congressman from the district in which Reno lived, and had, on occasion, stayed at the Union Hotel in Carrollton. He had known James Reno and knew both Alfred Hinton, Marcus' legal guardian, and Doctor Simpson. However, Richardson had already offered the appointment for the next West Point class to another young man in his district, Andrew J. Markley, a judge's son. But fate seemed to be on Marcus' side. On May 30, 1851, Richardson wrote to Secretary of War Conrad:

> Sir, I understand that the young Gent Andrew J. Markley I recommended for a cadet appointment at West Point declines the appointment, if so I recommend Marcus A. Reno, of Carrolton (sic) Greene County Ill. as a suitable young Gent for the place.
>
> I received a short time since a letter from Judge Markley saying that his son would decline the place for reasons not necessary to specify. I requested him to inform the Dept. over which you preside of the fact which I presume he has done.[17]

Reno received a letter from Secretary Conrad, dated June 11, 1851, stating that he would receive the appointment to the next West Point class starting in September. Marcus was elated and responded July 10, 1851:

> Sir, I have the honor to acknowledge the receipt of your communication of the 11th of June informing me that the President had conferred upon me a conditional appointment of Cadet in the service of the Untied States, and to inform you of my acceptance of the same.[18]

He underscored his elation with his flourishing signature. Reno, only 16 years old at this time, required a release from his guardian. Alfred Hinton signed the letter, which stated the youth "has my full permission to sign articles by which he will bind himself to serve the United States, eight years."[19]

Candidates, furnished with their official appointment, were required to report in person to the superintendent of the Military Academy at West Point between June 1-20. If an unavoidable reason prevented reporting by that date, the candidate could delay his arrival until Aug. 28.[20] Marcus received his notification of the appointment after the June 20 date so he made arrangements to leave Carrollton in early August which would provide him sufficient time to arrive at West Point by Aug. 28. He was about to embark on a career that would span 29 years.

Endnotes

[1] Philip L. Alfield, *Major Reno and His Family in Illinois* (The English Westerners' Brand Book, Volume 13, No. 4, July 1971, London), p. 4.

[2] Alfield, p. 4.

[3] Alfield, p. 5.

[4] *History of Greene County, Illinois, Its Past and Present* (Donnelley, Gassette & Loyd, Publishers, Chicago, 1879), p. 335.

[5] Greene County, Ill., *The Patriot*, March 1, 1907.

[6] Alfield, p. 5.

[7] Articles of Agreement, July 31, 1840, Records, Greene County, Ill.

[8] Alfield, p. 5.

[9] Milo Milton Quaife, editor, *Growing Up with Southern Illinois, 1820-1861* (The Lakeside Press, R.R. Donnelley & Sons Co., Chicago, 1944), p. 36.

[10] *The Rushville Times and Schuyler County Herald*, Rushville, Ill., Wednesday, July 13, 1927.

[11] Alfield, p. 6.

[12] *Carrollton, Ill., Gazette,* July 1, 1848.

[13] Alfield, p. 6.

[14] *Carrollton, Ill., Gazette,* Jan. 20, 1849.

[15] Guardian Bonds - 1850-68, Jan. 15, 1850, Records of Greene County, Ill.

[16] Reno's personal file, National Archives & Records Administration (NARA), Washington, D.C. Hereafter, "Reno File."

[17] Reno File.

[18] Reno File.

[19] Reno File.

[20] Captain Edward C. Boynton, *History of West Point, and the Military Importance During the American Revolution: and the Origin and Progress of the United States Military Academy* (D. Van Nostrand, New York, 1863), p. 267.

• 2 •

Long Gray Line

Being accepted at the West Point Military Academy in New York was one thing, getting there was another. For a young man who had never ventured more than 50 or 60 miles from his home in Carrollton, soon-to-be Cadet Marcus Reno would embark on a trip of 1,000 miles. It would be a slow and tedious trip, using stage coaches, railroad trains and steam ships. In 1851, the railroads, just starting their westward expansion, had not reached either Chicago or St. Louis. One of the longest completed section of railway was from Buffalo to Albany and New York City, but only short sections had been completed west of Buffalo. Illinois in 1850 had only two short lines, one running west of Chicago, and the other west of Springfield — a total of 111 miles track.[1] Only Ohio, of the "western" states, had more than 500 miles of railroad in 1850.[2]

Young Reno took the stagecoach from Carrollton to a point well east of Chicago, and then alternated between the railroad and stagecoach until finally reaching Buffalo. The train ride from Buffalo directly to Albany would be the most comfortable part of the journey. Finally, a steam ship took him down the Hudson to the South Dock of West Point. It had taken him more than a week to journey from the farming country of Illinois to West Point, and the start of his long military career.

Cadets landing at the South Dock were met by a sentry who sent them up the long road to the "Plain." From there the new cadet saw "the almost unbelievable natural beauty which is West Point's back-drop — sundrenched field, dipping elms, indigo hills, and deep blue water between steep granite banks."[3] Reno reported on arrival, as required, to the post adjutant, 1st Lieutenant Seth Williams, 1st Artillery, and provided him with his name, address, parents' names and other pertinent information. Prior to taking the entrance examinations, Reno was assigned a room in the recently completed cadet's barracks on the south side of the Plain. It was "the most imposing structure at the Institution…built of stone, with fire-proof rooms, castellated and corniced with red sandstone, in the Elizabethan style…. [T]he building contains 176 rooms, of which 136 are Cadets' quarters, 14 x 22 feet…and the base-

9

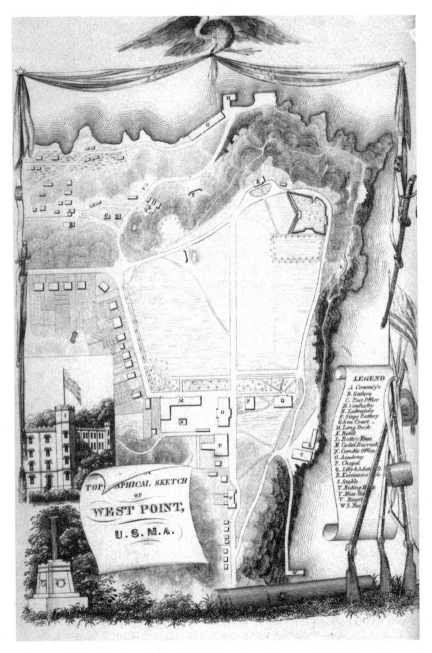

TOPOGRAPHICAL SKETCH OF U.S. MILITARY ACADEMY AT WEST POINT
(U.S. MILITARY ACADEMY LIBRARY, SPECIAL COLLECTIONS)

1851 Cadet Barracks, West Point
(U.S. Military Academy Library, Special Collections)

ment contains a profusion of bathing-rooms."[4] Cadets were assigned two, three, and sometimes, four to a room. Reporting to the quartermaster, the new cadet obtained the required furniture and equipment needed for his stay in the barracks. That included two blankets, a chair, arithmetic text, slate, bucket, broom, tin or coconut dipper, tin wash basin, lump of soap, candlestick, tallow candles, and a supply of stationery.[5]

Reno passed his physical and academic examinations, as reflected in Special Orders 87, issued Sept. 1:

> The following named individuals, having been duly examined by the Academic and Medical Boards, and found qualified for admission into the Military Academy are hereby Conditionally admitted as Cadets, to rank as such, from the dates set opposite their respective names...Marcus A. Reno, September 1, 1851.[6]

He was ranked as a member of the lowest, or Fourth Class. His pay would be $24 a month, from which he would pay for his uniforms, equipment, text books, and any other services he received while at West Point. Any money he had on arrival would be turned over to the academy treasurer, and in return he received an account book as cadets were not permitted to handle cash while at the academy.[7]

The Military Academy at West Point was established July 4, 1802, to develop technical officers for the Corps of Engineers. During the administration of Major Sylvanus Thayer (1817-1833), the academy became a source of army officers trained for military leadership instead of just training army engineers. Captain Henry Brewerton, Corps of Engineers, was the academy superintendent at the time of Reno's arrival.

Class standings, which would eventually affect a cadet's placement in the Regular Army, were not only based on the cadet's performance in class, but also his standing in conduct. The academy employed an elaborate system of delinquencies and punishments to control the corps of cadets. Delinquencies in the form of demerits were actually grades in conduct, while punishment included loss of privileges, incarceration, extra duty and expulsion. Accumulation of 200 demerits by a cadet in any class year resulted in the Academic Board recommending to the secretary of war that the cadet be discharged for deficiency in conduct.[8]

A cadet's day, starting at dawn, included nine to ten hours of classes and studying, three hours of drills, two hours of recreation, and two hours at meals. The day ended with "Taps" at 10 p.m.[9] Reno's classes for his first year included mathematics, French and English studies. Among his classmates were William Woods Averell, Cyrus B. Comstock, William Babcock Hazen and Alfred Thomas A. Torbert. The Class of 1855 saw 71 cadets admitted but only 60 would remain by the completion of the first year. The passage of the January examinations completed the term of probation for each new cadet. He then received his warrant and was sworn into U.S. service for eight years. Reno's warrant was signed Feb. 7, 1852.[10]

Reno accumulated 128 demerits during his year as a Fourth Classman. His first delinquency occurred Sept. 23: "Making & allowing to be made unnecessary noise during call to quarters to annoyance of occupants of a neighboring room," for which he received three demerits and "One extra tour of Sunday guard duty."[11] Getting up early appeared to be difficult for the new cadet as he was cited six time for being either "absent" or "late" at reveille. Two other types of delinquencies seem to have plagued young Reno that first year — inattention in class, during drill or on guard duty (nine times), and smoking or chewing tobacco (three times). His most serious offense occurred June 15, 1852, when, as a sentinel, he was given eight demerits for "entering room on his post unnecessarily."[12] During that first year, punishment included nine extra tours of guard duty and twice being confined to his room for one week and once for two days. This record placed Reno 35th in the general order of merit in a class of 60 with French being his best subject.[13]

On completion of final examination, cadets would move to their summer encampment on the Plain. For the cadets this was the practical phase of their professional military training. They would live in tents for the entire summer where Fourth Class members learned and practiced the duties of privates. The Third Classman performed the duties of non-commissioned officers and the First Classman those of lieutenants and captains. The Second Classman were on furlough, the only extended leave of absence granted cadets in their four years at West Point.[14] Due to Reno's late arrival at the academy in August 1851, he did not participate in the summer exercises of that year. As a Third Classman, he would practice the duties of a non-commissioned officer.

That summer of 1852 would not be easy for Reno as he accumulated 64 demerits for various delinquencies. On July 29, he was given six demerits for "insubordinate conduct, appearing at morning drill with a musket not his own, after he had been expressly ordered the previous day to carry his own musket." Punishment was "confined to the grounds of his company two weeks, and to perform two extra tours of camp guard duty."[15] But Aug. 22 would prove to be the single worst day of his still short cadet career. First, he was caught at 1 p.m. standing on his guard duty post instead of walking it as required (two demerits), and later that same day he was collared for ripping the bark off a tree (eight demerits). This last offense resulted in his arrest and confinement to quarters. Special Orders No. 133, dated Aug. 31, provided the rest of the story; "Cadet Reno, is released from arrest, and will return to duty. He will perform four extra tours of Sunday guard duty 'for breach of trust as sentinel, on the 22nd instant, wantonly destroying a shade tree which it was his duty to protect.' "[16]

On Aug. 28 Reno wrote a letter to Captain Bradford R. Alden, commanding the Corps of Cadets:

> Sir: Upon the 22nd instant I was reported for a breach of trust, as sentinel, wantonly destroying a shade tree which it was my duty to protect. As I made no explanation of my report at the time I was placed in arrest and being one of very serious character, I thought that the Commandant might think it was intentional.
>
> The circumstances which led to my report are as follows: the tree had been slightly chipped by someone and in a fit of thoughtlessness I merely tore the bark, some few inches, which I do not think at all injured the tree.

Cadet's Barracks Room
(Drawn by a cadet - U.S. Military Academy Library, Special Collections)

Cadet's Barracks Room(Opposite Side)
(Drawn by a cadet - U.S. Military Academy Library, Special Collections)

If I may be permitted to differ with the reporting officer, I think the report is couched in terms rather too severe for my offense. I have never received any orders in regard to the trees therefore it cannot be considered a breach of trust, strictly speaking. As to my wantonly destroying the tree I beg leave to state that such was not my intention for indeed at the time I committed the offense I had not intention of doing anything wrong or even had an idea of what I was doing. Thoughtlessness in regard to the safety of anything entrusted to my care is a defect in my character which I cannot correct. My offense is one which I acknowledge is sufficient to bring censure upon me by my superior officers; but if the Commandant will give my case a serious thought and take into consideration that the offense was committed in a thoughtless moment, he will doubtless give me a more moderate report.

I wish also to bring to the attention of the Commandant to the fact that several offenses of a similar kind have occurred during the encampment and that none of the offenders were arrested and besides I did not use my bayonet as has been the case in several instances, and that I have been confined to my tent the whole encampment with the exception of two or three weeks.

In conclusion I beg the Commandant will consider all the circumstances attending my case and respectfully petition to be released from arrest.[17]

The tone of the letter indicates Reno was either feeling sorry for himself, or more probable, sorry for being caught doing something that other cadets did but for which they hadn't been caught — but at least he hadn't used his bayonet.

Superintendent Henry Brewerton was reassigned as of Sept. 1, 1852. His replacement was Captain Robert E. Lee, Corps of Engineers, who was a graduate of West Point (Class of 1820) and had been brevetted colonel for gallant and meritorious conduct at Chapultepec.[18] He would serve as the academy's superintendent until April 1, 1855. Lee would revitalize the curriculum and form close relationships with many of his students.

Reno's classes as a Third Classman would include mathematics, drawing and French. When the year ended in June 1853, only 48 cadets of the original 71 in the Class of 1855 remained at the academy. Again French would be Reno's strongest subject with a standing of 19th, and drawing would be his worst, 40th. He was 32nd in the General Order of Merit, and had accumulated 125 demerits (plus 20 penalty demerits) for the school year.[19] This was a significant improvement over the rate at which he received them during the summer encampment. He was still having problems of being late (nine times), absent (seven times), and using tobacco (three times). However, his worst offense occurred Jan. 10, 1853, when he was given six demerits for "making loud & irrelevant remarks concerning guard at Guard Meeting." Total punishments since the summer amounted to only four extra tours of Sunday guard duty which was a significant improvement over the 12 extra tours he pulled during the summer of 1852. Reno's reading habits during his year as a Third Classman included the popular novels of the time. He read 18 Cooper's novels and 11 Waverley novels in less than five months.[20]

With the completion of their second year at the Academy, all the cadets eagerly looked forward to their only extended furlough. Cyrus Comstock, Reno's classmate, described it well: "June 17. Last night order was read for our being relieved at 7 a.m. today, 'Sweet Home' was played & furlough men were generally in ecstasies.... Hurrah for furlough."[21] Special Order No. 68 provided this leave with an admonishment from Superintendent Lee:

> Leave of absence from 7 o'clock a.m. tomorrow, until 2 o'clock p.m. on the 28th of August next, is granted the following named Cadets...Allen...Nicholls...Reno.... The Superintendent places full reliance upon the deportment of the Cadets now granted a leave of absence, and trust that while away from the Academy, they will be guilty of no act calculated to reflect discredit upon themselves, or the Institution of which they are members.[22]

The cadets headed for home, but not without celebrating first. Arriving in New York, Comstock noted that several other cadets and he "had a splendid dinner at Delmonico's."[23] Some of the other cadets apparently started their celebrations earlier: "The fellows coming down the river behaved very well although Reno and [Charles T.] Larned were pretty tight and they had some high singing as we entered N.Y."[24]

The trip back to Carrollton was not as tedious as it had been in 1851. The railroads had expanded their rail lines through to Chicago and St. Louis, and only the final segment of the trip, into Carrollton itself, had to be made by stage coach. Reno was proud to wear his cadet uniform around his home town square and spent time with his brothers and sisters as well as the Hintons and Simpsons. To earn spending money he was again employed by Doctor Simpson in the local drug store. The summer passed quickly and Reno departed in mid-August for his return to West Point.

Reno's start into the next academic year as a Second Classman would not begin well. Reporting to the academy Aug. 28, he took only one day to earn his first delinquencies of the new class year. Cited for "using profane language 6 1/2 a.m.," he earned eight demerits and two extra tours of Sunday guard duty.[25] September would not prove to be any better when he earned 53 demerits for the month. All were relatively minor, earning him four demerits per offense or less, except on Sept. 10, when he missed the evening parade which cost him six demerits. At that rate Reno would break the 200 barrier and be dismissed by the end of the calendar year. He managed to settle down and during the remainder of the school year (eight months) accumulated another 100 demerits. In 10 months, he walked 12 extra tours of guard duty as punishment. He was cited for being late 10 times and absent four times and received four demerits for "unbecoming conduct sleeping or apparently sleeping in church."[26]

Courses as a Third Classman included philosophy, chemistry and drawing. By the end of the academic year, the class size had decreased from 48 to 42. Reno's best course was philosophy where he stood 25th, his worst still being drawing at 35th. A total of 205 demerits for the year (154 delinquency demerits and 51 penalty demerits) placed him 29th in General Order of Merit. Although he exceeded the 200 demerit limit, no action was taken to dismiss him, because of his adequate performance in classroom activities and because he only exceeded the limit due to the penalty demerits.

Reno began his year as a First Classman with high expectations. In just one year, he would graduate and take his place as an officer in the U.S. Army. Unfortunately, that was not to be.

The 1854 summer encampment on the Plain did not start well for Reno. As First Classmen, his classmates and he would fulfill the role of officers for the Fourth and Third Classmen. But Reno had difficulty controlling his own temper and actions. July 2 and 3 would be a disaster for the young cadet. On the morning of July 2, he was late for breakfast roll call which cost him one demerit, and later that same morning he was caught twice, once at 9 a.m. and again at 10 a.m., using "profane" language. This brought eight demerits and a punishment of "confined to the limits of his tent for one week when not on duty."[27] July 3 would not prove to be much better. Following tattoo (drum call to quarters at 9:30 p.m.), Reno managed to wander off and not return to his tent until after taps but not without getting caught. "Absent from tent and camp from tattoo until 10:10 p.m." resulted in another eight demerits and "four extra tours of camp guard duty as a sentinel."[28] By the end of August, he had accumulated 65 demerits.

Academically, classes for a First Classman were challenging: engineering, ethics, mineralogy and geology, infantry tactics, cavalry tactics and artillery. Reno earned acceptable grades in his classes and was working at improving his conduct. He collected only 39 more demerits during the remainder of the first half year, giving him an even 100 as of Dec. 29. Many were for being late somewhere, at parade, dinner, reveille or roll call. As a First Classman, he received penalty demerits that would add another 50 to this total. This would allow him only an additional 34 for the entire second half of the year if he wanted to stay under the 200 dismissal number.

Reno tried to control his conduct, but the demerits continued to mount, 27 by the end of January 1855, and 41 by the end of February. He was in trouble and became sensitive about acquiring additional delinquencies. On March 12, he was cited for "rising before command at breakfast," which cost him one demerit. That evening he went to the room of Cadet Edward L. Hartz and challenged him to a fight. In a diary entry for March 13, Cyrus Comstock relates the incident:

> Hartz & Reno had a fight last night. They are not on good terms & Reno persists in walking around the mess hall and Hartz reported him. Reno went to Hartz room last night and told Hartz that he though him a d-d [damned] pusillanimous coward, or something of that kind, and Hartz rushed at him. Reno got the worst of it & got his thumb bitten badly, as he put it up in H[artz] face apparently for the purpose of gouging. Reno is not very popular.[29]

The bite apparently was painful enough for Reno to report to the post hospital on both March 14 and 15 where he was treated for the injury.[30] He also went to the hospital on March 18, 19 and 20 for the same injury.[31] No record reveals what he told the post surgeon about how the injury occurred, and no delinquencies are recorded for Reno for this incident.

On March 27, 1855, Reno received what would be a fatal blow to his expectations to graduate with the Class of 1855. Secretary of War Jefferson Davis had changed the 1853 West Point Regulations, and now, instead of a limit of 200 demerits for one class year, anyone having just 100 demerits before Jan. 1, 1855, would be declared "deficient in conduct" and be suspended until July 1. Reno had accumulated 100 delinquency demerits plus an additional 50 penalty demerits in the specified period. But Davis also specified that the suspended cadet would be allowed to join the next class at the same level which would allow Reno to return as a First Classman. Comstock noted, "[Francis L.] Vinton & Reno have orders to that effect and there are half a dozen in the other classes. It is very hard. And within two months of graduation, too. It is just about as bad as dismissal."[32] Reno left the academy March 28, 1855.

The furlough Reno had taken during the summer of 1853 had been well planned in advance and the cost of the long trip anticipated. This was not the case with his sudden dismissal. He had no funds to make the trip back to Carrollton, and besides, he would probably have difficulty explaining to his brothers and sisters exactly why he was home again. He decided to stay in the immediate area and work until he could report back to the academy July 1. Although not officially a cadet during this period, he had access to the post hospital and checked himself in for four days, apparently for a head injury, starting June 8.[33]

Reno eagerly waited for the opportunity to return to the academy and complete his final year. He checked in with the post adjutant, 1st Lieutenant James B. Fry, from Carrollton, Ill., on June 30, 1855, and was immediately sent to the summer encampment on the Plain as a First Classman and now a seasoned veteran of the summer camps. During Reno's absence, Superintendent Lee had been reassigned to the cavalry and would serve in Texas for several years. The new superintendent was Captain Jonathan G. Barnard, Corps of Engineers, who had been brevetted major May 30, 1848, for "meritorious conduct while serving in the enemy's country [Mexico]."[34]

Reno was now acutely aware that it would take only 100 demerits (delinquency and penalty) during the next six months to get him dismissed again, and this time probably permanently. His start was not promising. On July 1, he was absent from tattoo roll call, and on July 2, missed both reveille and breakfast roll calls for which he received a total of nine demerits. By the end of July, his total numbered 23. August also was not a good month as the delinquencies continued to grow. Reno earned eight demerits Aug. 18 for "highly unmilitary conduct — deserting ranks at drill (on the 14th)" and a punishment of two extra tours of Sunday guard duty. "Chewing tobacco in ranks 5 p.m." on Aug. 28 cost him another six demerits and four extra tours of guard duty.[35] He was late on eight separate occasions, and his total delinquencies climbed to 60 by the end of August.

Getting back to the classroom routine was beneficial to Reno's conduct. He acquired only two demerits in September, 13 in October, none in November and only one in December. The new cutoff date was Dec. 15, and with the removal of 10 demerits for valid excuses, Reno had a total of 66, and even with the penalty demerits, he only had 88 total which was sufficiently under the 100 dismissal number.[36] Academically, he continued to do well in his classes, and while he knew it would take some effort, he looked forward to graduation in June.

The morning of Jan. 23, 1856, would shatter that expectation. As a sentinel on post in the cadet's barracks, he was required to walk his post in a military fashion and follow military protocol. With graduation only five months

away, Reno showed his exuberance by starting to sing. He realized that singing while on guard was not considered proper military conduct, but he was
happy and didn't see any harm in it. Unfortunately, he was overheard by one
of the instructors. When challenged by 1st Lieutenant William H. Wood, 3rd
Infantry, an assistant instructor of tactics, to stop singing, Reno replied that
he had a right to sing on post. Wood obviously didn't agree and brought Reno
up on a charge of "conduct to the prejudice of good order and military discipline," with the specification that "said Cadet Marcus A. Reno…being a sentinel on post in Cadet's Barracks and being ordered by his superior officer…to
stop singing on post did reply to said officer in a contemptuous and disre-
spectful manner that he…had a right to sing on post or words to that effect."[37]

A general court-martial was held in early February with Colonel Joseph
Plympton, 1st Infantry, acting as president of the court. Reno pleaded "Not
Guilty" to the charge and specification. The court wasted little time. The
findings and sentence of the court stated:

> The court having maturely considered the evidence adduced
> find the accused as follows: of the Specification "Guilty" except
> the word "Contemptuous," and "Guilty" of the charge and so
> therefore sentences him, Cadet Marcus A. Reno of the U.S. Mili-
> tary Academy, "to be suspended from the U.S. Military Academy
> until the 1st of July 1856, with the privilege of then entering the
> First Class of the Corps of Cadets.[38]

Once again Reno found himself packing his kit, and once again he had no
funds to return to Illinois. He remained in the area and worked for the next
four months. Where or how he was employed is not known, but the post
hospital records would soon reveal how he spent at least part of his leisure
time. Reporting to the post adjutant in late June, he was assigned to summer
encampment as of July 1, 1856, his third tour of duty in summer camp as a
First Classman. An entry on the Post Hospital log, dated July 5, noted that
Reno had reported to the hospital and was diagnosed with syphilis, a serious,
health threatening venereal disease.[39] He probably acquired the disease, as did a
number of other cadets, at a bordello in New York City before returning to
the academy. He was treated and released that same day.

The 1853 Regulations for West Point cadets were modified and a First
Classman in the Class of 1857 would receive only one-third penalty demerits
for delinquencies instead of one-half. The maximum of 100 demerits, including both delinquencies and penalty, for each half-year, would remain the same.
It was now a little easier to stay under the limits. Reno did reasonably well that

summer, receiving only 28 demerits. On Aug. 10, he was cited for "highly unsoldierlike conduct imitating a drunken man on the company parade ground by singing & staggering 12 & 1 PM," and on Aug. 15, he earned four demerits for "not rising or saluting the Superintendent on his approach to visit the exercise of Practical Engineering (on 14th)."[40] The punishment for the Aug. 10 incident was rather severe: "Two extra tours of camp guard duty as sentinel and confined to camp during the remainder of the encampment."[41]

Returning to the classroom Sept. 1, Reno put forth a concentrated effort on both his studies and his conduct. While his class standings improved, his conduct was still a problem. By December 1856, he had accumulated a total of 98 demerits (74 delinquency demerits and 24 penalty demerits) which again put him at the edge of disaster. Most of the delinquencies were minor and he did not have to walk any extra tours of guard duty. He made some improvement in the second term and accumulated only 81 demerits total (delinquency and penalty) for a total of 179 for the year. He earned a number of delinquencies for his chronic problems which included either being late (19 times) or absent (eight times). His worst single offense was for "chewing tobacco in church," which earned him six demerits.[42]

However, his extra effort in the classroom was obvious and he stood 20th in a class of 38 in general order of merit when he completed the year as a First Classman. Surprisingly his best standing was in artillery (eighth) and ethics (11th). His lowest standing was in infantry tactics (22nd). Given his choice of infantry, artillery or cavalry, he decided it was better to ride than to walk and chose the cavalry branch of the Army.

A new superintendent, Major Richard Delafield, Corps of Engineers, had been assigned Sept. 8, 1856, replacing Major Barnard. Delafield had been the academy superintendent from 1838 to 1845. Delafield, with Adjutant Fry by his side, presented Cadet Reno with his diploma on a warm day in June 1857. Reno was appointed brevet 2nd lieutenant as of July 1, 1857, and would receive his permanent 2nd lieutenant commission at a later date. The number of cavalry officers was fixed by Congress and until an opening occurred at the grade of 2nd lieutenant, no West Point graduate could be appointed to that rank. Although it had taken him almost six years to get through West Point, his tenacity had finally paid off. He would, at last, begin his career as an Army officer.

Endnotes

[1] John F. Stover, *Iron Road to the West: American Railroads in the 1850s* (Columbia University Press, New York, 1978), p. 116.

[2] Stover, p. 115.

3 Mary Elizabeth Sergent, *They Lie Forgotten, the United States Military Academy, 1856-1861* (The Prior King Press, Middletown, N.Y., 1986), p. 15.

4 Captain Edward C. Boynton, *History of West Point and the Military Importance During the American Revolution: and the Origin and Progress of the United States Military Academy* (D. Van Nostrand, New York, 1863), p. 261.

5 John C. Tidball, Papers, Manuscript Collection, U.S. Military Academy, West Point, N.Y., Chapter I, pp. 15-16.

6 West Point Military Academy Post Orders No. 3, Special Orders No. 87, Sept. 1, 1851.

7 Boynton, p. 268.

8 Regulations for the U.S. Military Academy at West Point, 1832, pp. 20-21.

9 James L. Morrison, Jr., *The United States Military Academy, 1833-1866: Years of Progress and Turmoil* (University Microfilms, Inc., Ann Arbor, Michigan, 1971), pp. 116-117.

10 Record Group 94, Marcus A. Reno, Military File, National Archives & Records Administration (NARA), Washington, D.C.; Boynton, p. 273.

11 Register of Delinquencies, 1851-1852, U.S. Military Academy, West Point, N.Y.; Register of Punishments, No. 2, Sep. 1847-Oct. 1857, U.S. Military Academy, West Point, N.Y.

12 Register of Delinquencies, 1852-1853, U.S. Military Academy, West Point, N.Y.

13 Academic Record of Cadets at the United States Military Academy, West Point, N.Y., 1851 to 1857, as extracted from the *Official Register of the Officers and Cadets of the United States Military Academy, June 1852-1857.*

14 Morrison, p. 108.

15 Register of Punishments, No. 2.

16 Post Orders, 1852, West Point Military Academy Post Orders No. 4, Special Orders No. 133, Aug. 31, 1852.

17 Register of Punishments, No. 2.

18 James B. Fry, *The History and Legal Effect of Brevets in the Armies of Great Britain and the United States* (D. Van Nostrand, Publisher, New York, 1877), p. 439.

19 The 1853 Regulations of the United States Military Academy at West Point, provided in Section 71., 4th. "For each year (after the first) a Cadet may be a member of the Institution, his offences (sic) shall be made to count more, by adding to the number expressing his demerit one sixth for his second, one third for his third, and one half for his fourth year." Reno's accumulation of 125 demerits resulted in 20 penalty demerits being added to the total, thus a total of 145 for the year.

20 U.S. Military Academy Library Circulation Records, 1852-1855.

21 Merlin E. Sumner (Ed.), *The Diary of Cyrus B. Comstock* (Morningside House, Inc., Dayton, Ohio, 1987), p. 119.

22 West Point Military Academy Post Orders No. 5, Special Orders No. 68, June 16, 1853.

23 Sumner, p. 119.

24 Sumner, p. 119.

25 Register of Delinquencies, 1853-1854, U.S. Military Academy, West Point, N.Y.

26 Register of Delinquencies, 1854-1855, U.S. Military Academy, West Point, N.Y.

27 Register of Delinquencies, 1854-1855; Register of Punishment No. 2.

28 Register of Delinquencies, 1854-1855; Register of Punishment No. 2.

29 Sumner, p. 183.

30 Record Group 94, NARA, New York Hospital Register, Post (Cadets) Hospital, U.S. Military Academy, West Point, N.Y, Volume 609, Jan. 1, 1854-Dec. 27, 1860, page 50, Case No. 88.

31 Hospital Register, page 51, Case No. 114.

32 Sumner, p. 186-87. Vinton returned on July 1, 1855, and graduated with the Class of 1856 with a class standing of 10 out of 49.

33 Hospital Register, p. 63, Case No. 19, June 8-11, 1855.

34 Fry, p. 308.

35 Register of Delinquencies, 1855-1856; Register of Punishment No. 2.

36 It is interesting to note that in the official Register of Delinquencies for Marcus Reno, 1855-1856, they gave him 22 penalty demerits, or one-third. The academy had gone to a five-year program and cadets in their "fourth" year were given one-third penalty demerits instead of what had formerly been prescribed one-half for First Classman. The number "1/3" is marked on the records. The total demerits, including the penalty, shown on the records is 88.

37 Special Orders No. 12, War Department, Adjutant General's Officer, Washington, D.C., Feb. 9, 1856, NARA.

38 Special Orders No. 12.

39 Hospital Register, p. 109, Case No. 18, July 5, 1856. Syphilis is an infectious, chronic venereal disease which, if left untreated, can cause serious health complications. The disease was sometimes called "the great imitator" as it could lead to a variety of later health problems. Reno was probably treated with Mercuric Chloride, a common compound of mercury used as a topical antiseptic, or Mercuric Oxide, a powder used in ointments as an antibacterial agent. The incubation period for syphilis is two to six weeks, so it is apparent Reno contracted the disease while he was working during the spring and early summer of 1856 prior to his return to the Academy.
The first sign of the disease is a sore or "chancre" on the genitals and this probably was what Reno was treated for initially in July 1856. He was treated again for syphilis on Oct. 28, 1856, (p. 121, Case No. 123). The lesions probably healed in two to six weeks following the July 5 treatment. However, the disease was just going through its usual brief latent period of six to eight weeks. The reappearance of the disease on Oct. 28, which would include a generalized rash all over the body, would therefore not be unusual, and Reno was probably again treated with Mercuric Chloride or Mercuric Oxide, and released.
Following the reappearance and treatment, the disease will undergo spontaneous cure in one-third of the cases, remain in a latent phase without symptoms in another one-third, and develop serious complications in the remaining one-third. There is no indication that Reno ever had a recurrence of the disease.
The third stage of the disease, if it occurs, is the dreaded tertiary syphilis which is usually delayed 20 years or more, the attacks the brain and other vital organs with disastrous results.

[40] Register of Delinquencies, 1856-1857.
[41] Register of Punishment No. 2.
[42] Register of Delinquencies, 1856-1857.

• 3 •

First Duty

Following graduation exercises at the West Point Military Academy in June 1857, Marcus Reno made plans for a leave of absence that would extend through the summer. Graduating 20th in a class of 38, he received his choice of duty types and was assigned to the Army's cavalry branch. At the time of his graduation he had not received his official orders to join his first command. He applied for active service with the 2nd Regiment of U.S. Dragoons but did not know where he would be assigned before he left the academy in late June.[1]

Awaiting orders, Reno left West Point and took the steam packet up the Hudson to Albany on the first leg of the trip to Carrollton. Most of his brothers and sisters still lived in Carrollton and he would visit with them until he received word of his first duty station assignment. During his journey back home, he decided to stay with a friend in Delaware, Ohio, for a short period.

It would be a leisurely summer for the young Reno and marked the last occasion he would spend any considerable time in his home town of Carrollton. Finally, his long awaited orders arrived. Instead of the 2nd Regiment of Dragoons, he was assigned to the 1st Regiment as a brevet 2nd lieutenant. He was ordered to report for temporary duty at Carlisle Barracks, Penna. (12 miles west of Harrisburg), by Oct. 1, 1857, to await a permanent assignment. In his response to the Adjutant General, written Aug. 14, 1857, from Carrollton, Reno accepted his appointment as brevet second lieutenant, 1st Regiment Dragoons, and noted, "I have not reported to Commdg. officer of the regt. as I am not acquainted with his station."[2] However, Reno must have determined the location of his new duty station for a notation in the Carlisle Barracks Post Returns for the month of Oct. 1857 states: "Marcus A. Reno, Brevet 2nd Lieut., First Dragoons — joined Oct. 1, 1857 per Gen'l. Order No. 9."[3]

Carlisle Barracks, established in 1838 as a cavalry recruit training depot, was, from time to time, almost totally abandoned with only a caretaker detachment present. A series of fires in early 1857 destroyed the large stables on the depot as well as buildings used for officers' quarters and barracks.[4] A fire in August destroyed another large building. By the time Reno reported for duty in October there were only a total of 74 personnel, officers and enlisted, on station.

Crowded conditions were the way of life, especially when the number of recruits increased significantly during the next few months. Dropping to a low of 51 personnel in November 1857, the depot's population increased to 172 in December, 294 in January 1858, and 374 in February.[5] Reno was involved with training these recruits for cavalry service, a difficult task as most of them were Easterners with little or no experience on horseback. In addition, the large number of recruits had access to a limited number of serviceable horses which resulted in short riding time for each recruit. Everyone lived under crowded conditions — it was a less than enjoyable way to spend the first days of their enlistments. As they completed their training, most of the new soldiers were shipped west to garrison frontier forts and to replace soldiers who had completed their enlistments. Reno was looking forward to orders assigning him to his regiment somewhere in the West.

In December 1856, the regimental headquarters of the 1st Dragoons had been moved to Fort Tejon, Calif., and two companies were stationed in the northwest: Company E at Fort Walla Walla, Washington Territory, and Company C at Fort Yamhill, Oregon Territory. By early 1858, two additional companies were moved to the northwest: Company I to Fort Walla Walla and Company H to Fort Vancouver. Company C was moved from Fort Yamhill to Fort Walla Walla in mid-1858.

In March 1858, Reno finally received orders to join his regiment at Fort Walla Walla, Washington Territory, via Jefferson Barracks, Missouri, and Fort Leavenworth, Kansas Territory. Leaving Carlisle Barracks with a group of new recruits March 22, he traveled to Jefferson Barracks, remaining there only until April 24 before moving northwest to Fort Leavenworth. Waiting for the weather to improve for the journey westward over the Oregon Trail, Reno continued his training of recruits for their assignments to western posts.

Leaving Fort Leavenworth June 21, Reno was part of a larger contingent of military personnel proceeding over the Oregon Trail via Forts Kearny (Nebraska Territory), Laramie, Bridger, Hall, and into Fort Walla Walla in southeastern Washington Territory. The name "Marcus A. Reno, Bvt. 2nd Lieut." appears for the first time on the September 1858, Post Return for Fort Walla Walla.[6]

Troops on permanent assignment to Walla Walla were in the field when Reno arrived in September. They returned from field service Oct. 5 and Reno reported to Company E which was under the temporary command of 1st Lieutenant Nelson B. Sweitzer. The company's assigned captain was Lucius B. Northrop, but according to the muster roll of Company E for October, Northrop was on "Sick leave Oct. 6, 1839. Not joined since transferred to company."[7] Typical of the army of that period, promotions came slowly. Only retirement, dismissal, promotion or death of a more senior officer afforded a junior officer an opportunity to advance in rank. Although Northrop had not joined his company for more than 19 years, he was still carried on the muster roll as company commander.

With the death of 2nd Lieutenant William F. Gaston on May 16, 1858, at the battle of To-hoto-nim-me Creek, an opening existed in the company for a 2nd lieutenant. Reno received the promotion, effective June 14, 1858, and joined his company at that rank Dec. 1.[8] Company E consisted of more than 100 enlisted men and was one of three companies of 1st Dragoons stationed at Fort Walla Walla under the command of Captain (Brevet Major) William N. Grier. Six of the regiment's companies were stationed in California and New Mexico, while its remaining company was at Fort Vancouver, Washington Territory. During this period the regiment was commanded by Colonel Thomas T. Fauntleroy, whose headquarters was at Fort Tejon, Calif.

Expeditions by the 1st Dragoons from Fort Walla Walla during the late fall and into the winter of 1859 were limited. However, certain military duties were still necessary and Reno was assigned to serve on his first general courts-martial board by an order signed by Acting Assistant Adjutant General Alfred Pleasonton.[9] The trial of 1st Lieutenant Hugh B. Fleming, 9th Infantry, began Feb. 7, 1859; he was charged with "intentional disrespect to his commanding officer." After the court found him guilty, he was confined to the limits of the military reservation for three months and reprimanded by the commanding officer of the department. Nine enlisted men also appeared before the board, seven being found guilty and two not guilty. Punishment for the enlisted men ranged from one to six months hard labor and loss of pay.

Reno assumed command of Company E on March 1, while Sweitzer was on detached service at Fort Vancouver, and relinquished command when Sweitzer returned April 1. On April 2, Reno was again assigned to a general courts-martial board, this time to try various enlisted men on a variety of charges, including disobedience of orders, desertion, conduct to the prejudice of good order and military discipline, sleeping on post, theft, and drunkenness on duty.[10] At the conclusion of the courts-martial, and in addition to his regular assignment to company duty, Reno was also appointed post adjutant.

Although peace treaties had been signed with many of the tribes, renegade Indian factions continued to harass settlers and travelers throughout the area. A special order from Headquarters, Department of Oregon, Fort Vancouver, stated the Army's intent to maintain a safe road to the Oregon and Washington territories:

> To increase the facilities of communication between the Co-
> lumbia River and the valley of the Great Salt Lake, in connection
> with the overland route to the frontiers of the Western States the
> following command will be organized at Fort Dalles to move from
> that point by the 1st of June next for the purpose of opening a
> good wagon road to the Snake River in the vicinity of the mouth
> of the Malheur River [near present day Payette, Idaho] and from
> thence to a point called City Rocks at the junction of the road
> from Forts Laramie and Bridger with the road from Fort Hall to
> the Salt Lake City, viz; Companies E and H of the 1st Dragoons;
> Company H, 4th Infantry; and Detachment of Engineers, Com-
> pany A. Captain Henry D. Wallen, 4th Infantry commanding.[11]

As part of this "Wagon Road Expedition," Company E, under Lieutenant Sweitzer's command, planned to meet the main column near Fort Dalles, Oregon, sometime prior to the June 1 deadline. The company left Fort Walla Walla May 19, 1859, and arrived at Three Mile Creek May 29 after marching 173 miles.[12] Joining the main group, the command left the Three Mile Creek area June 4 and reached Crooked River June 27, establishing a camp at that point. The troopers had covered another 172 miles and remained at a spot dubbed "Camp Seperation" until July 1. The strength of Company E remained at about 85 officers and men during the expedition. In July, Reno was appointed acting assistant quartermaster and acting assistant commissary of subsistence for the expedition.[13]

The command left Camp Seperation July 1, marched to a camp on the Salmon Falls River on July 31, and reached Raft Creek Aug. 7, where a supply depot was established under Reno's command by a detachment of Company E troopers. The remainder of the company accompanied Captain Wallen and proceeded to the Great Salt Lake Valley, arriving at Camp Floyd Aug. 16 and remaining there four days before retracing their route. On Aug. 31, they reached Swamp Creek, where Reno had moved the supply depot.

The expedition left Swamp Creek Sept. 3 and set up camp Sept. 16 on the Owyhee River three miles from Fort Boise. The main portion of the command remained at the Owyhee camp while a detachment of Company E backtracked almost 50 miles in an attempt to recover horses reportedly stolen by the Indians from a group of emigrants. Neither Indians nor horses were found, and the detachment returned to the Owyhee camp. The entire command left camp on the 24th and proceeded northward, reaching Grande Ronde Valley, Oregon, Oct. 3. Company E then split from Wallen's command and headed to Fort Walla Walla, while Reno continued with Captain Wallen to Fort Dalles. Company E arrived at Fort Walla Walla Oct. 7, having covered

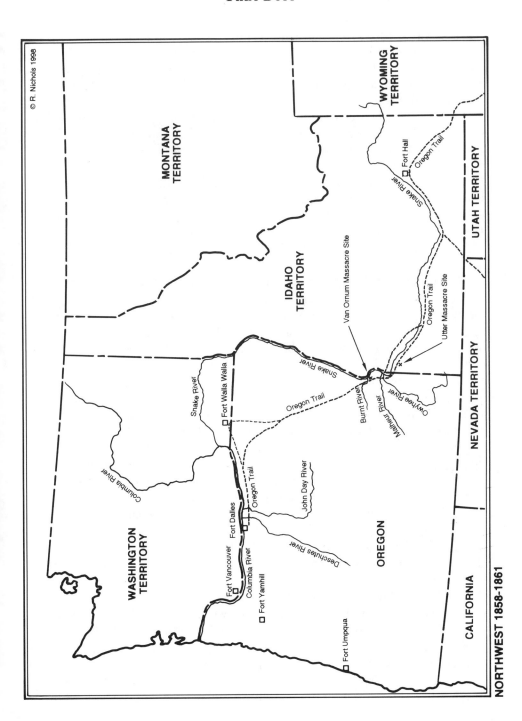

NORTHWEST 1858-1861

© R. Nichols 1998

more than 1,900 miles without reporting a single incident with Indians.[14] Reno, with Wallen's command, arrived at Fort Dalles Oct. 9. He was again assigned as a member of a general courts-martial board to try various cases against enlisted men beginning Nov. 14.[15] The court president was Captain Frederick Dent.

As acting assistant commissary of subsistence for the recently completed expedition, Reno was accountable for the stores and supplies used by the troops while in the field. A question arose as to the loss of certain subsistence stores, and Reno, in a letter of Nov. 28, requested a board of survey be held at Fort Vancouver to investigate any irregularities.[16] An order was issued to assemble a board Nov. 29.[17] Expedition records were presented to the board which concluded the loss of the subsistence stores for which Reno had been accountable was acceptable, and no further action would be required.[18] Reno, with a detachment of recruits for the 9th Infantry, returned to Fort Walla Walla Dec. 23.[19]

The winter of 1859-1860 proved quiet for the regiment with only limited activities outside the fort. Garrison duty at isolated western frontier forts in the winter was generally boring and depressing. An occasional dance or party by the married officers broke the daily routine, but for bachelor officers, gambling and drinking appeared to be the acceptable pastime. Reno certainly participated in both activities. In January 1860, he was again assigned to a general courts-martial board with Colonel George Wright as president.[20]

Lieutenant Sweitzer took a leave of absence in mid-February and Reno assumed command of Company E for a week. During the winter, the strength of the companies stationed at Fort Walla Walla declined, and by February, Company E had only about 65 enlisted personnel. Factors contributing to this decline included the lack of new recruits, completion of enlistments and desertions. The latter was a problem which would continue to plague the army for years at isolated posts throughout the West.

In May, Reno assumed command of the company when Sweitzer was assigned to recruiting service and was not scheduled to return for an extended period.[21] The shortage of officers at Fort Walla Walla was evident as Reno was also assigned to two general courts-martial boards, one in early May and another in mid-June.[22]

On July 6, 1860, the Department of Oregon issued orders directing Captain (Brevet Major) William N. Grier and two companies of the 1st Dragoons, Company I and Reno's Company E, to march from Fort Walla Walla to Fort Boise over the Emigrant Road.[23] The expedition was to meet and protect emigrants on the Oregon Trail from hostile Indians.

The command left July 18 and moved eastward, arriving at a point on the Owyhee River opposite Fort Boise on July 31 after marching 211 miles. On

Aug. 4, the command moved its bivouac to a point 12 miles up the Emigrant Road. The following day Grier sent Reno with a scouting party another 10 miles "in advance…to march rapidly back on Owyhee River with a view to draw the Indians from the mountains, or surprise any small party that might be lurking in my rear." Reno returned with "information that there were no 'signs' of Indians in advance," and Grier decided the Indians "seemed desirous to avoid an engagement with my troops."[24] Grier's command joined an emigrant train headed to Washington Territory Aug. 6 and started back to Fort Walla Walla, arriving there Aug. 30 after marching 289 miles. Grier's command had covered 500 miles in six weeks without a single encounter with the Indians.[25] As a result of the expedition, Colonel George Wright declared the Oregon Trail open and safe from Indian attacks — a proclamation that soon would have tragic results.[26]

Reno returned to his normal duties as company commander and on September 15 was assigned to a general courts-martial board under the presidency of Captain Andrew J. Smith, 1st Dragoons.[27] Various cases would come before the board involving infractions by enlisted personnel, two primary offenses being drunk on duty and failure to obey orders.

About this same time, in another part of the country, a situation developed that would parallel the tragedy of the ill-fated Donner party. While attempting to cross the mountains into California in late 1846, the Donner party was caught by early snow storms in the Sierras, and survivors had resorted to cannibalism before finally being rescued. An incident at Sinker Creek, Idaho Territory, in 1860 would have similar results.

In May 1860, a small train of eight ox-drawn wagons, four families and a number of single men left Wisconsin, heading west toward Oregon country. The wagonmaster, Elijah P. Utter, was accompanied by his wife Abagel, and their 10 children ranging in age from 9 months to 23. Accompanying the train were the Joseph Myers family of eight, the Daniel Chase family of five, the Alexis Van Ornum family of seven, and 12 single men including two brothers, Jacob and Joseph Reith, for a total of 44.[28] Alexis Van Ornum was the assistant wagonmaster. The wagons reached Council Bluffs, Iowa, by the end of May. This small train, which was to be the last of the season, moved over the Oregon Trail, pausing briefly at Fort Kearny, Nebraska Territory, and Fort Laramie, Wyoming Territory, to restock their supplies, and arrived at Fort Hall, Idaho Territory, on the evening of Aug. 21. During the previous three months, they had made their way through Shoshone Indian country without incident. The emigrants were pleased to be at Fort Hall — the end of the trail was not too far ahead.

At the fort, located in Snake and Bannock Indian country, Utter and Van Ornum heard about Indian problems in the area and requested a military escort to protect the wagon train. Although Colonel Wright had declared the Emigrant Road open, small bands of renegades had been attacking travelers and settlers in the area. A small escort of 22 troopers was assigned to the train and would accompany it for six days through the most dangerous territory. The train left Fort Hall Aug. 23, and met the military escort seven miles west of the fort. When the escort left the train Aug. 29, the emigrants were told they were now past the worst danger and it was unlikely the train would be attacked as long as they kept the Indians away from the wagons.[29] With the escort gone, small groups of Indians started visiting the wagons over the next several days and appeared to be friendly.

When the wagons reached Three Island Crossing of the Snake River Sept. 4, Utter and Van Ornum decided the train should leave the main Oregon Trail and take the alternate "dry route" south of, but parallel to, the Snake River. Although more difficult, that route was thought to provide better forage for the animals, and to be safer from the Indians — an unfortunate assumption. On Sept. 8, the wagons reached Castle Creek 22 miles west of the Bruneau River.

The following day, after proceeding several miles northwest of Castle Creek, Utter stopped the train when he saw a large dust cloud on the trail ahead. Within the hour the wagons were set upon by about 100 shouting Shoshone or Bannocks waving blankets and buffalo robes in an attempt to stampede the stock. When this tactic proved unsuccessful, the Indians decided to make peace with the emigrants and requested food. Utter agreed to give them food, and after being fed, the Indians rode away, apparently satisfied.[30] After completing a noon meal, the wagon train had just started on the trail when it was again attacked by the same Indians, only this time instead of waving blankets, the Indians came firing their guns. After a lengthy battle lasting into the night and most of the following day, the emigrants, despite suffering heavy losses, continued to hold off the Indian attacks. Finally, the Indians agreed to a truce which would allow the emigrants to leave with four of their eight wagons. The families were placed in the four wagons and the reduced train left the corral, but they were almost immediately attacked by the Indians. Still attempting to escape, the emigrants continued fighting. It was soon evident the entire party was in danger of being massacred so the wagons were finally abandoned. Total emigrant losses at the end of the second day were 11 killed, including Utter, his wife and four of their children.[31] Four of the single men had escaped earlier, and the two brothers, Joseph and Jacob Reith, set out to seek help several hundred miles to the north and west.

The emigrant party, now numbering 27 including 18 children, carried what they could — weapons, ammunition and little food. For the next week, the survivors moved northward, traveling only at night. The small cache of

Captain Marcus Reno
First known
photograph
(From the collection of
Bill Armstrong, June
1988)

Captain Marcus Reno
Obviously taken at
the same time as the
above photograph
(From the collection
of Roger D. Hunt)

food was quickly consumed, and by the end of the week, the women and children, suffering hunger and weakness, could continue no longer. They set up a camp of wickiups near the Owyhee River while the stronger survivors spent their time searching for food.

After the first week, two of the survivors, 10-year-old Christopher Trimble and Goodsel Munson, left the camp to find help. They traveled 25 miles and arrived at the Malheur River Hot Springs where they met the Reith brothers and one of the men, Lucius Chaffee, who had earlier escaped the massacre.[32] Munson informed the brothers about the location of the survivors' camp and decided to join Chaffee and the Reith brothers rather than return to the camp. Chaffee still had the horse with which he had escaped. After understanding the situation at the Owyhee camp, Chaffee killed the horse and gave much of the meat to Trimble to take back to the survivors. Trimble returned to Owyhee camp with the most-welcomed food and told the survivors that the Reichs, Munson and Chaffee were going for help.

During the next several weeks berries, lizards and fish bartered from local friendly Indians barely sustained the group. The Indians finally stole most of the guns from the survivors and Alexis Van Ornum was convinced the Indians would kill them all. He decided to take his wife and family and leave the camp. Accompanied by another man and two of the orphaned Utter children, the small group of 10 made their way northwestward and finally reached a plateau near the Burnt River where they were attacked by Indians. The three adults and three children were killed, and the remaining four children were taken captive by the Indians.

Back at the Owyhee camp the survivors grew desperate. Hunger dominated their every thought and they fought over the smallest scrap of food brought in by those still strong enough to do so. Daniel Chase had died on the day the Van Ornums left camp and soon hunger began to take its toll on the rest of the survivors. Ten days after Chase's death, the first of the younger children died. Within the next eight days, three more children died from starvation.[33] Survivors appeared to have little hope.

The Reith brothers, who had left the emigrant party Sept. 10, finally arrived at the Umatilla Indian reservation in Washington Territory Oct. 2, after traveling more than 250 miles. Chaffee and Munson could not keep up and had remained at Burnt River. The reservation was just 25 miles south of Fort Walla Walla. An employee at the agency, Byran N. Dawes, immediately dispatched a messenger to Fort Walla Walla and also sent two well mounted men with a heavily provisioned mule in the direction of the Owyhee camp. Once the information reached army headquarters at Fort Vancouver, Colonel Wright issued orders, dated Oct. 4, 1860:

A detachment of troops from Fort Walla Walla will proceed immediately under Capt. Dent, 9th Infantry, to the scene of the reported massacre of emigrants in the vicinity of the Salmon Falls of the Snake River to obtain any survivors there may prove to be in the hands of the Indians and if season and opportunity permit, to punish the aggressors. The detachment will be composed of Co. E, 1st Dragoons, and a detail from Co. I, 1st Dragoons, sufficient to make a total of 60 Dragoons, and a subaltern and 40 enlisted men to be selected for the service by Capt. Dent from Co. B and E, 9th Infantry. The Infantry will be mounted on mules. Forty days rations and an ample supply of ammunition will be taken with the command.[34]

The detachment of dragoons and infantry left Fort Walla Walla on their rescue mission Oct. 11, with Reno commanding the 40 men of Company E and the detachment of 20 men of Company I.[35] On the evening of Oct. 19, Reno found the nearly starved Chaffee and Munson on a small branch of the Burnt River. After providing them with clothing and food, Reno assigned 10 men and a corporal to remain with them while he took the remainder of his command in search for more survivors. Heading eastward, he arrived at the Burnt River where he put 25 of his men into camp. Reno then took five men and a guide, William Craig, and continued to scout to the Malheur River in search of the emigrant families. He found no sign of the survivors and started back to the camp he had established at Burnt River. On the emigrant road between the Malheur and Burnt Rivers, he found fairly fresh tracks of women and children. Although evening was approaching, Reno continued the search and about two miles from camp discovered the badly beaten bodies of Alexis Van Ornum, his wife Abigail, their 16-year-old son Mark, their companion, Samuel Gleason, and the two Utter children, Charles and Henry.

> The arms of Mrs. Van Ornum were tied; she had been whipped, scalped, and otherwise abused by her murderers.... Charles and Henry Utter had been killed by arrows.... Mr. Van Ornum, Mark, and Gleason had their throats cut, and besides were pierced by numerous arrows. They appeared to have been dead from four to six days.[36]

Reno's men buried them where they were found, returning to camp only long enough to get fresh horses. With 10 men and the guide, Reno followed what he thought was the trail of the Indians and possibly some Van Ornum survivors as he had found a small barefoot track among the moccasin tracks.

35

Continuing his search to the Snake River, which was deep and rapid, but having no way to cross, Reno returned to camp. Captain Dent had arrived at Reno's camp and "deemed it best not to pursue the trail at that time, as I [Dent] had learned from Mr. Munson during that day that on Snake River, some fifteen miles beyond Owyhee, he had parted with the Van Ornums...and some of the Trimble and Otter [Utter] families.... I therefore determined to push forward with all haste."[37]

At the encampment on the Owyhee, the emigrant survivors had made a quiet and fateful decision. The four dead children still lay unburied as no one possessed the strength to bury them. On Oct. 21, the survivors decided that for any of them to survive it would be necessary to use the only food source available — the dead bodies. Over the next few days, the unburied bodies were consumed, and when Dent rode into the Owyhee camp on Oct. 25, he found that the survivors had also exhumed and eaten the remains of Daniel Chase who had been buried Oct. 5.[38]

Dent started back to Fort Walla Walla immediately with the emigrant survivors, arriving there Oct. 31. Reno's detachment came into the fort Nov. 7 after continuing to search the area along the Oregon Trail for hostile Indians.[39] Dent's report, filed after returning to Fort Walla Walla, provides an ample description of the survivors: "Those who were still alive were skeletons with life in them. Their frantic cries for food rang unceasingly in our ears. Food was given them every hour in small quantities; but for days the cries for food were kept up by the children."[40] A total of 15 emigrants survived the ordeal.

A report filed Nov. 22, 1860, by Colonel Wright concerning the rescue of survivors of the massacre on the immigrant route, related that "Lt. Reno...with the noncom officers and men of the Expedition are deserving of praise for the zeal and energy which characterized the discharge of their duty in this service."[41]

Following the rescue of the emigrants, Colonel Wright was still concerned about the four missing children who had been with Van Ornum when his party was attacked and killed by the Indians. In a letter to John Whiteaker, governor of Oregon, dated Jan. 3, 1861, Wright stated, "Messengers dispatched by Major Steen, commanding the troops at Fort Walla Walla, and Mr. Cain, the Indian agent in that neighborhood, have been sent into the Snake country to ascertain if there be any children captives there." He also indicated, "If the children be alive, they are, if possible, to obtain them by negotiation forthwith."[42] No trace of the children was ever found, and likely they were murdered by the Indians prior to returning to their camp.

Colonel Wright was now convinced that something had to be done about the Snake Indians and determined "an energetic campaign against the Snakes, to be commenced early and continued late" would be undertaken.[43] In a message to Major Enoch Steen, commanding Fort Walla Walla, Wright wanted a detachment of dragoons sent into the field to apprehend Indians that were committing "depredations" in the area. He also wanted swift justice for those caught. He directed "that should any of the guilty be captured, instant and summary punishment is to be had upon them, that their fate may be a warning to others."[44]

Anticipating Wright's order, Major Steen had already sent Major Grier and Lieutenant Reno into the field Feb. 9 in an attempt to capture the renegades. In his report dated Feb. 18, Steen noted, "Lieutenant Reno executed his orders with an energy and zeal which gives me the greatest satisfaction."[45] Reno's report, dated Feb. 14, 1861, provides the results of the expedition:

> I have the honor to report that in obedience to instructions I left this post [Fort Walla Walla] February 9, 1861, with Company E, 1st Dragoons, and proceeded to the Columbia River, encamping near the place where the Indians of whom I was in pursuit had been last seen. Immediately upon my arrival I sent out scouts to discover, if possible, any clue which would enable me to capture them. About 9 o'clock that night I received information that they were some miles below my camp on the river. I started with a small party and, proceeding rapidly, succeeded in surprising their camp. I found but two of the Indians who had been committing depredations in that vicinity. After a short but severe struggle, in which but my first sergeant, Private Moran, and myself were engaged for a short time, I succeeded in securing them and bringing them to my camp. They were immediately recognized as desperate characters, having been punished in the guard-house and whipped by Colonel Wright. Early next morning and in presence of the whole tribe with whom they had been living I had them hung, telling their tribe at the same time that any future harboring of such murderers and thieves would be interpreted as hostility to the whites, and punished accordingly. I have particularly to recommend the zeal and activity of Lieutenant Kellogg, First Sergt. Daniel Coleman, and Private Moran, of Company E, 1st Dragoons.[46]

The Company E muster roll for the period ending April 30 indicates that Captain Northrop was finally dropped as the company commander after 21 years.[47] A new captain, William T. Magruder, was appointed as commander of Company E though he had not joined his new company since being promoted. Reno was promoted to first lieutenant as of April 25, and in Magruder's absence, continued as company commander.

As winter gave way to spring, the Indians continued their hit and run tactics, usually operating in small bands seldom exceeding 10 or 12 warriors. When headquarters suggested that Major Steen plan for an extensive summer expedition along the emigrant trails to protect the anticipated travelers, he responded:

> The subjugation of the Snakes, so effectually as to bring them to sue for peace, would require a large and expensive force, perhaps ten or twelve companies, necessarily requiring a large number of citizen employees as packers, herders, guides, etc., and the result would not be certain, as their country affords great facilities for concealment and escape.... The remaining squadron of dragoons [Companies E and I], with a company of infantry from this post [Fort Walla Walla], would keep the Indians from their fisheries all summer and afford ample protection to whatever emigrants may come across.[48]

Steen's plan was for troops stationed at Fort Walla Walla to operate in the immediate vicinity of the fort. The lack of sufficient troops to provide control of the Indians in the field and still provide protection for the fort dictated this strategy. Some protection could still be given to the large emigrant wagon trains expected later in the summer.

The first shots of the Civil War had been heard in the east, and the effects of the attack on Fort Sumter were soon felt in the west. Colonel Fauntleroy, who had served as the colonel of the 1st Dragoon regiment since 1850, resigned May 13 to join the Confederacy. He was succeeded by Lieutenant Colonel Benjamin L. Beall. Major Henry H. Sibley and nine other 1st Dragoon officers also resigned their commissions to join the South. Even though Reno had been born in Illinois, his family, especially on his father's side, had strong ties with the South. However, with both of his parents dead, and having had little contact with his family over the past 10 years, Reno decided to remain loyal to the Union and retain his commission in the cavalry.

Dragoon and infantry companies were being ordered to proceed toward debarkation points for transportation east. On June 14, 1861, Colonel Wright ordered eight companies of troops to proceed to San Francisco, noting that he was "compelled to withdraw the troops entirely from Forts Cascades, Yamhill, and Townsend, as well as Camps Pickett and Chehalis."[49]

By midsummer 1861, many officers of the cavalry and infantry units were resigning to join up with the Confederacy. Of the more than 900 officers in the Union Army at the time, 313, including 184 West Point graduates, resigned their commissions that summer. Of those who resigned, 182 were to attain the rank of general in the Confederate Army in the next four years.[50]

Major Steen remained concerned about the travelers and miners moving over the Oregon Trail:

> We have this summer, in addition to the disturbed state of the country at home, which has withdrawn a portion of the troops from Oregon, a mining excitement which is pouring all the restless and loose portion of the community into the Nez Perce country, and upon the very land which was promised them as their own exclusive soil.... [There is the] prospect also of a large emigration this summer via Fort Hall, and unless troops be on the road from this post to keep it clear of the Snakes, there will a repetition of last year's massacre at Salmon Falls, an occurrence too horrible almost to contemplate.[51]

Few incidents with the Indians were reported for the summer of 1861, but the potential for serious conflict was evident. Steen, in a letter dated July 30, still thought that there was "danger of Indian troubles in the vicinity before winter. A large portion of the Nez Perces refused to come into council and receive their annuities, and it is expected they will shortly join the Snakes, and unless I am re-enforced by a company of infantry and another of dragoons, I shall be unable to do anything beyond taking care of the post." Steen also reported troubles with the Indians in the immediate vicinity of the fort; "the Snakes have been in the valley already within fifteen miles of the post."[52]

The loss of officers and troops to the east was being severely felt, and Steen was obviously feeling frustrated:

> They [the Snakes and Nez Perce] are roving all over the country in defiance of treaty, law, or remonstrance, and must take care of themselves. I would send Lieutenant Reno with his company at once to reinforce Captain Smith [at the Nez Perce reservation], if I only had Company H here to render my garrison sufficiently strong.[53]

The emigrants were also on Steen's mind: "There has been no news from the emigrant road, no parties having come in yet, but that there will be trouble if the emigrants break up into small parties there can be no doubt. They must be keeping together, and perhaps have an escort, or we should have heard from them before this."[54]

Company H of the 1st Dragoons, garrisoned at Fort Dalles, lacked its full complement of officers, e.g., a first lieutenant, and accordingly, Reno was assigned to that company as of July 18. But as noted in the regimental muster roll for September, he was on "detached service at Fort Walla Walla...commanding Company E, 1st Cavalry."[55] Captain W. T. Magruder finally reported for duty at Fort Walla Walla and assumed command of Company E Sept. 6.

The lack of a commanding officer of Company C at Fort Walla Walla resulted in Reno being assigned as its temporary commanding officer Sept. 7.[56] On Nov. 16, Companies C, E and I of the regiment, a total of 190 soldiers, having received orders to transfer to the "Atlantic States," left the fort and marched to Fort Dalles, arriving there Nov. 23.[57] Leaving almost immediately, the command arrived at Fort Vancouver Nov. 26 and boarded the coastal steamer *Ortes* for San Francisco Dec. 3, arriving there several days later.[58] Eight companies of the regiment were assembled at San Francisco preparing for travel to the east coast.

Indian troubles would continue in the Department of Oregon for years to come but, at least temporarily, troops of the U.S. Army would not be used to resolve the problems. During the next three and one-half years, the 1st Cavalry would see action, not against the Indians, but against the soldiers of the newly formed Confederate States of America.

Endnotes

[1] Letter, Marcus A. Reno to Colonel S. Cooper, July 1, 1857, Microcopy M-1064, Roll 208, National Archives & Record Administration (NARA).

[2] Letter, Marcus A. Reno to Colonel S. Cooper, Adjutant General, Aug. 14, 1857, Microcopy M-1064, Roll 208, NARA.

[3] Post Return of the Cavalry Depot at Carlisle Barracks, Penna., Microcopy M-617, Roll 183, NARA.

[4] Lt. Col. Thomas G. Tousey, M.C., *Military History of Carlisle and Carlisle Barracks* (The Dietz Press, Richmond, 1939), pages 213-214.

[5] Post Return of the Cavalry Depot at Carlisle Barracks, Penna., Microcopy M-617, Roll 184, NARA.

[6] Post Return for Fort Walla Walla, Washington Territory, September 1858, Microcopy M-617, Roll 1343, NARA. Hereinafter PRFWW.

[7] Company E Muster Roll, First Dragoons, Oct. 31, 1858-Dec. 31, 1858, Record Group 94, NARA. Hereinafter CEMR.

[8] CEMR.

[9] General & Specials Orders Issued, Dept. of Oregon, 1859-1861, Volume 1, Series 3576, Special Order No. 8, dated Jan. 19, 1859, Record Group 393, NARA. Hereinafter GSO.

[10] GSO, Special Order No. 30, dated April 2, 1859.

[11] GSO, Special Order No. 40, dated April 27, 1859.

[12] Information concerning the Wagon Road Expedition came from two main sources: CEMR and Regimental Returns, 1st Dragoons, Microcopy M-744, Roll 4, NARA.

[13] Wagon Road Expedition information.

[14] Wagon Road Expedition information.

[15] GSO, Special Order No. 112, dated Oct. 28, 1859.

[16] Department of Oregon, Letters Received, 1858-1861, Volume I, Series 3573, 1 or 2, Record Group 393, NARA, p. 296.

[17] GSO, Special Order No. 127, dated Nov. 28, 1859.

[18] GSO, Special Order No. 128, dated Dec. 1, 1859.

[19] GSO, special Orders No. 125 & 126, dated Nov. 24, 1859, and Nov. 26, 1859, respectively.

[20] GSO, Special Order No. 9, dated Jan. 19, 1860.

[21] CEMR, April 30, 1860-June 30, 1860.

[22] GSO, special Orders No. 55 and 72, dated May 9, 1860, and June 19, 1860, respectively.

[23] GSO, Special Order No. 82, dated July 6, 1860.

[24] Report of Captain Grier dated September 2, 1860, Fort Walla Walla, W.T., to the Department Commander.

[25] CEMR, June 30, 1860-Aug. 31, 1860.

[26] A. R. Leichner, "Horror on the Owyhee," *The West Magazine*, March 1971.

[27] GSO, Special Order No. 100, dated Sept. 15, 1860.

[28] Donald H. Shannon, *The Utter Disaster on the Oregon Trail* (Snake Country Publishing, Caldwell, Idaho, 1993), pp. 12-13. Other information on the Sinker Creek tragedy is contained in two articles: A. R. Leichner, "Horror on the Owyhee," *The West Magazine*, March 1971, and Kelsie Ramey Osboren, "Cannibalism on the Oregon Trail," *The Sunday Oregorian Magazine*, Aug. 31, 1952. While there are discrepancies between the two articles they are, in general, reasonably accurate and tie-in with the available military data.

[29] Shannon, p. 27.

[30] Shannon, pp. 35-38.

[31] Shannon, pp. 43-44.

[32] Shannon, p. 59.

[33] Shannon, p. 72.

[34] GSO, Special Order No. 105, dated Oct. 4, 1860.

[35] Regimental Returns, 1st Dragoons, Microcopy M-744, Roll 4, NARA, October 1860.

[36] Frederick T. Dent, Report of Nov. 8, 1860, Fort Walla Walla, 36th Congress, 2nd Session, House, *Ex. Doc. No. 29.*

[37] Dent Report, Nov. 8, 1860.

[38] Shannon, p. 74.

[39] MRCE, October 20, 1860-Dec. 31, 1860.

[40] Kelsie Ramey Osborne, "Cannibalism on the Oregon Trail," *The Sunday Oregonian Magazine*, Aug. 31, 1952, p. 9. Colonel George Wright also reported this incident to the Secretary of War. Executive Document No. 29, 36th Congress, 2nd Session, House of Representatives, *Indian Depredations in Washington and Oregon*, pp. 79-80.

[41] Department of Oregon, Letters Sent, 1858-1861, Record Group 393, Volume I, Series 3570, Report No. 13, dated Nov. 22, 1860, NARA.

[42] U.S. War Department., *The War of the Rebellion: A Compilation of the Official Records of the Union and Confederate Armies*, 128 Volumes, Washington, D.C., Government Printing Office, 1880-1901. Volume 50, Part I, pp. 430-431. Unless otherwise indicated all citations are Series I. Hereinafter OR.

[43] *OR*, Volume L, Part I, pp. 430-431.

[44] *OR*, Volume L, Part I, p. 442, letter to Major Steen from Colonel Wright, dated Feb. 10,1861.

[45] *OR*, Volume L, Part I, pp. 446-447, letter to Captain James A. Hardie from Major E. Steen, dated Feb. 18, 1861.

[46] *OR*, Volume L, Part I, Report of Lieutenant Marcus A. Reno, 2nd Dragoons, dated Feb. 14, 1861.

[47] MRCE, February 28, 1861-April 30, 1861.

[48] *OR*, Volume L, Part I, p. 465, letter from Major E. Steen to Major W. W. Mackall, dated April 16, 1861.

[49] *OR*, Volume L, Part I, p. 514, letter from Colonel G. Wright to Major D. C. Buell, dated June 14, 1861.

[50] Robert M. Utley, *Frontiersmen in Blue, The United States Army and the Indian, 1848-1865* (University of Nebraska Press, Lincoln, Nebraska), p. 212, footnote 3.

[51] *OR*, Volume L, Part I, pp. 516-517, letter from Major E. Steen to Colonel L Thomas, dated June 14, 1861.

[52] *OR*, Volume L, Part I, pp. 547-548, letter from Major E. Steen to Major D. C. Buell, dated July 30, 1861.

[53] *OR*, Volume L. Part I, p. 575, letter from Major E. Steen to Lieutenant A. C. Wildrick, dated Aug. 19,1861.

[54] *OR*, Volume L, Part I, p. 575.

[55] Post Return for Fort Dalles, Oregon, September 1861, Microcopy M-617, roll 285, NARA. On Aug. 3, 1861, an Act of Congress designated the First Regiment of Dragoons as the First U.S. Cavalry—one of six regular regiments that would be used throughout the Civil War.

[56] PRFWW, October 1861.

[57] PRFWW, November 1861.

[58] Post Returns, Fort Vancouver, Washington Territory, December 1861, Microcopy M-617, Roll 1316, NARA. 1st Cavalry Muster Rolls, Troop H, RG 94, 31 Oct. 61 - 31 Dec. 61.

• 4 •

"The Late Unpleasantry Between the States"

The shots fired at Fort Sumter April 12, 1861, would start the bloodiest war in America's history, but it would also be viewed as a great adventure by professional soldiers, especially early in the war. The major concern these soldiers had in 1861 was that the war might be over before they had an opportunity to participate. Few Union officers thought the South had sufficient resources for an extended war and 1st Lieutenant Marcus Reno was no exception.

The first major engagement of the war at Bull Run (Manassas) July 21, 1861, proved to be a disaster for the Federal troops. President Abraham Lincoln appointed General George B. McClellan to revamp the Federal troops demoralized at Bull Run and to provide the army with the leadership necessary to move against the Confederacy. Regular U.S. infantry, cavalry and artillery units would be the core groups about which McClellan could fashion a formidable army.

Units of the 1st U.S. Cavalry stationed in New Mexico, California and the Pacific Northwest, had assembled in San Francisco in November 1861 awaiting transportation east. The recent completion of the railroad across the Isthmus of Panama would significantly reduce the time required to move troops from the west to port cities on the east coast. Finally, eight companies of the 1st Cavalry, including Company E which was under the temporary command of Lieutenant Reno, were ready for the journey east. The companies embarked on a coastal steamer Dec. 11, 1861, en route to New York.[1]

Sailing down the coast of California and Mexico to Panama, the troops disembarked, moved across the Isthmus on the new railroad, and re-embarked on another coastal steamer. Arriving in New York City Jan. 3, 1862, Reno's Company E was part of a group moved to Camp Sprague near Washington, D.C., arriving there Jan. 7. There Reno learned of his promotion to captain, effective Nov. 12, 1861. On Jan. 19, the new captain was assigned Company H, 1st U.S. Cavalry, and the next two months would be spent in the defense of Washington where his troopers were mainly employed as couriers, pickets and escorts.[2]

McClellan continued to reorganize the Army of the Potomac but it appeared "Little Mac" was reluctant to move against the Confederate army. In early March 1862, Lincoln made the decision to have McClellan take his army to Richmond. The Army of the Potomac would be moved to Fortress Monroe, Va., just 70 miles from Richmond, and move up the peninsula formed between the James and York Rivers. On March 17, troops started to board a variety of ships for the movement to Monroe.

McClellan had five army corps under his command but his cavalry forces were widely scattered throughout the five corps rather than being concentrated as a single unit. The cavalry was not used to advantage in the early stages of the war. Finally, a separate unit, the "Cavalry Reserve" under the command of General Philip St. George Cooke, was formed and contained units of the 6th Pennsylvania Cavalry, 6th U.S. Cavalry, four companies of the 1st U.S. Cavalry, including Reno's H Company, and four companies of the 5th U.S. Cavalry.

Reno moved his company from Camp Sprague March 30, arriving at Alexandria, Va., the same day. On April 2, Reno loaded his company on one of the flotilla of ships bound for Fortress Monroe, arriving at Hampton Roads on the 4th and setting up camp at Kentucky Farm on the 6th.

McClellan's army, with its five corps and more than 100,000 men, had started moving up the peninsula April 4. Two days later, his army approached Yorktown and encountered a series of Confederate fortifications. McClellan was extremely popular with his soldiers but was slow to act. Although possessing a vastly superior force, he made no attempt to storm the line and instead began a siege operation that would last four weeks. The Confederate forces were under the command of General Joseph E. Johnston.

Reno's Company H was assigned to Colonel George A. H. Blake's 2nd Brigade of Cooke's Cavalry Reserve. Blake's brigade consisted of four companies (two squadrons) of the 1st U.S. Cavalry commanded by Lieutenant Colonel William N. Grier, and the provost guard of the division under the command of Lieutenant Stephen S. Balk, 6th U.S. Cavalry.[3] Blake's brigade left Kentucky Farm April 10, moved to Ship Point, remaining there for two weeks, and finally set up camp on the 24th near Cheeseman's Creek, about six miles southeast of Yorktown.

By the time McClellan was ready to attack Yorktown, the Confederates had quietly slipped away and moved their forces up the peninsula to Williamsburg. McClellan approached it cautiously and on May 4-5, the Federals, including Blake's brigade, attacked. Although the battle of Williamsburg was a hard fought and bloody affair, losses on both sides were relatively light. Following the battle the Confederates were again able to slip away and move their forces from Williamsburg into positions around Richmond. The cavalry's

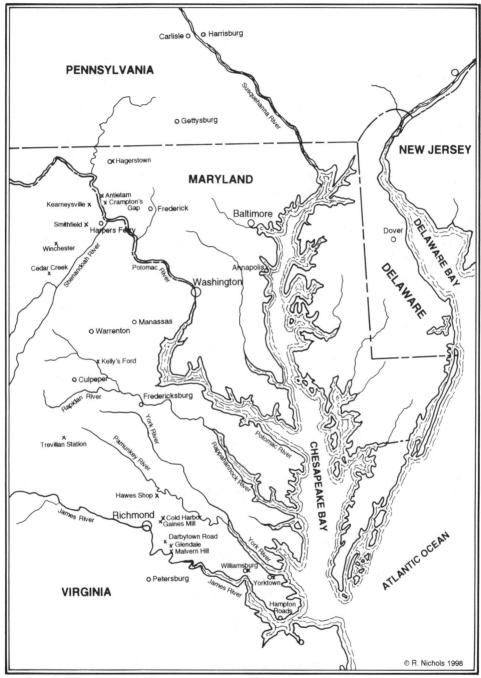

CIVIL WAR 1861-1865

part in the attack on Williamsburg was not significant and Blake's brigade camped near the town until May 11. A series of moves up the peninsula occurred over the next several weeks — camps were established near West Point, New Kent, St. Peter's Church, Tunstall's Station, and finally within seven miles of Richmond.[4] The brigade would spend much of June either on reconnaissance patrols or acting as pickets and escorts.

McClellan's forces, within sight of Richmond, were attacked May 31 by the Confederates under Johnston at Seven Pines. Lack of coordination between Confederate units finally forced them to retreat June 1. Johnston was severely wounded during the battle May 31, and following the battle, was replaced by General Robert E. Lee. Lee quickly reorganized his troops into the Army of Northern Virginia and reinforced the field fortifications around Richmond.

Blake's brigade remained north of the Chickahominy and made repeated sorties into the field to determine the whereabouts of Confederate cavalry. Reno commanded a squadron (two companies) under Grier and acted as an advance guard for the 1st Cavalry. His squadron was constantly on the move and many of the scouting marches occurred at night. Brigadier General John F. Reynolds reported moving his brigade to Tunstall's Station and relied on scouting reports to establish the enemy's presence; "About 2 o'clock [a.m.] General Emory arrived with Rush's Lancers [6th Pennsylvania Cavalry], and at daylight [June 14] Captain Reno, with a squadron of the 1st Cavalry, reached Tunstall's."[5] Lee assumed the offensive and attacked the Union forces on the morning of June 26 to open the "Seven Day's Battle."

Late on the 26th, Blake's brigade was informed of the approach of the Confederates and about midnight marched to Cold Harbor where they remained for the night. The following morning the brigade, consisting of two squadrons of about 125 enlisted men, with Reno commanding one squadron and Lieutenant Josiah H. Kellogg commanding the other, resumed the march and proceeded to General FitzJohn Porter's V Corps headquarters near Gaines' Mill.[6] Shortly before noon, the brigade first encountered the Confederates and was engaged in skirmishes throughout the day. Late in the evening, the cavalry pulled back when the Union infantry was forced to retreat before overwhelming numbers of Confederate infantry.

The brigade was ordered to act as reserve to the 5th Cavalry during what proved to be a disastrous charge. Confederate fire was intense and the command was forced to fall back. Returning to the front, the brigade acted as a support to a body of infantry that had rallied and were holding the enemy in check. Blake finally was ordered to retire and pulled his brigade back north across the Chickahominy near Savage Station.[7] Reno's company had two enlisted men die from wounds suffered during the battle. Grier noted in his

June 28 report: "During the afternoon's engagement the squadrons were subjected to a heavy fire from the enemy, which was met with coolness and steadiness by officers and men."[8] Colonel Blake, in his report of July 3 noted that he was "indebted to Lieutenant-Colonel Grier, Captain Reno, Captain Kellogg...for the prompt and cheerful assistance given me on the field."[9] The brigade set up camp near Turkey Ridge on the 30th.

On June 30, Union troops fell back to a position at Malvern Hill where, after severe fighting and heavy losses on both sides, the Confederates were eventually repulsed. By July 2, the entire Army of the Potomac had reached Harrison's Landing and cavalry reconnaissance patrols were sent out to assess the position and strength of the enemy. On July 3, Reno led his company on a reconnaissance and found a Confederate artillery position firing into General Philip Kearny's camp. The artillery was protected by a force of cavalry and infantry considerably stronger than Reno's small company so he wisely withdrew to Union lines.[10]

Union forces remained at Harrison's Landing during the month of July while McClellan argued for additional men to continue the campaign against Richmond. Individual companies from the Cavalry Reserve continued to be used for picket, escort and reconnaissance duty.

McClellan was ordered to evacuate the peninsula and join General John Pope's "Army of Virginia" in Northern Virginia. Withdrawal from the peninsula proceeded slowly. The main portion of McClellan's army left Harrison's Landing between Aug. 13 and 16. Cooke's Cavalry Reserve with Reno's Company H left the area Aug. 8, encamped at Waxalls for 10 days, and finally moved on to Yorktown on the 20th. Embarking Aug. 31, Cooke's group proceeded to Alexandria, arriving there Sept. 3.

During McClellan's withdrawal from the peninsula, Pope's Army of Virginia attacked the Confederates commanded by General Thomas J. "Stonewall" Jackson at Gainesville and Manassas Junction, Va., on Aug. 28. On the 30th, Pope mounted a major offensive and was badly mauled. Discouraged by a second Union loss at Bull Run, Lincoln relieved Pope of his command and combined his army with the Army of the Potomac under McClellan. By early September, Federal troops were safely back in the defenses of Washington. Lee decided to move into the Cumberland Valley of Maryland and between Sept. 4-7 had his army cross the Potomac near Leesburg.

In camp near Fort Albany Sept. 3, Brigadier General Alfred Pleasonton, commanding the Cavalry Division, waited for the arrival of four 1st U.S. Cavalry companies, including Reno's Company H, to complete his 2nd Brigade.[11] After he arrived, Reno was assigned a squadron of two companies of the 1st Cavalry and was immediately dispatched into the field on reconnaissance duty. On Sept. 6, Reno's squadron entered Mechanicsville but reported no enemy there.[12]

On Sept. 10, Reno lead his squadron on a reconnaissance to Hyattstown and reported to Pleasonton that he had been fired upon by the Confederates with one piece of artillery. Reno also reported Confederate cavalry entering the town and that the enemy had cavalry, infantry and artillery in the area. Pleasonton instructed Reno, if pressed, to fall back to Rockville. Pleasonton concluded from Reno's report that the Confederates were supporting their position on Sugar Loaf Mountain.[13]

Following his reconnaissance to Hyattstown, Reno was assigned all four companies of the 1st Cavalry under Pleasonton. While shown on the organization chart as the "Quartermaster's Guard" reporting to General Headquarters, in reality Reno's command, two squadrons, was engaged in reconnaissance patrols, escorts and the support of artillery batteries for General William B. Franklin's VI Corps.[14]

The Confederates under Jackson surrounded Harpers Ferry on Sept. 13 and Union forces surrendered on the 15th. McClellan, already in pursuit of Lee's forces, ordered Franklin's VI Corps to move through Crampton's Gap toward Sharpsburg while his remaining four corps were to cross the Blue Ridge six miles north at Turner's Gap. Reno's two squadrons of the 1st Cavalry accompanied the VI Corps and provided protection for the corp's artillery. In bitter fighting Franklin finally was able to penetrate through the gap by the evening of Sept. 14. General Jesse Lee Reno, commanding McClellan's IX Corps, was killed in the early evening of the 14th while attempting to push the Confederates from Fox's Gap near South Mountain.[15]

McClellan's Army of the Potomac halted east of Sharpsburg along Antietam Creek on the 16th. The battle of Antietam on the 17th resulted in the war's single bloodiest day — the casualties for both sides totaled more than 23,000 including 6,000 killed. Neither side could claim victory and the two armies remained facing each other throughout the 18th. McClellan was hesitant to attack — he was not willing to again risk the enormous losses of the previous day.

Reno's two squadrons continued support and protection of Franklin's artillery on the right wing of the army. Franklin's VI Corps was held in reserve during most of the battle. Cavalry casualties were light due the continued ineffective use of cavalry in the early years of the war.[16]

On Sept. 18 Reno's squadrons returned to Pleasonton's command and during the night of Sept. 18-19 pursued portions of Lee's army as he withdrew south of the Potomac.[17] Pleasonton, pleased with the effort of the cavalry under his command, noted in his Sept. 19 report, "A portion of the First Regular Cavalry were under my command in the pursuit of the enemy to the

CAPTAIN MARCUS RENO AND LT. COLONEL JOSEPH HANCOCK TAYLOR
AT THE ANTIETAM BATTLEFIELD, SEPTEMBER OR OCTOBER 1862
(GLEN SWANSON COLLECTION)

river, and did good service under Captain Marcus A. Reno...."[18] Harpers Ferry was evacuated by the Confederates on the 20th.

For the next four weeks the 1st Cavalry under Reno's command would participate in picket and escort duty with an occasional reconnaissance patrol to determine the location of Confederate cavalry. Pleasonton then sent Reno's cavalry for duty to the 1st Division of the II Corps, commanded by Brigadier General Winfield S. Hancock. An expedition was made by Hancock's Division on Oct. 16 from Harpers Ferry to Charlestown, W. Va., and included cavalry under the command of Major Charles J. Whiting, 2nd U.S. Cavalry. Reno's command, under Whiting, consisted of four companies but contained only 120 men.[19]

The expedition encountered the enemy on the high ground near Charlestown. The horse artillery battery, supported by Reno's 1st Cavalry, engaged the Confederates with fire from their five guns. The enemy fell back and the town of Charlestown was captured. Reno's cavalry then made a reconnaissance of several miles but the Confederates had left the area. Hancock's Division returned to Harpers Ferry on the 18th.

General Hancock's report of Oct. 22, 1862, indicated that "The officer and troops behaved well.... Captain M. A. Reno, First Regiment Cavalry, commanding the supports to the horse artillery...[and five other officers]...are the only officers whom it is thought deserve special mention."[20]

The cavalry and artillery units of the Army of the Potomac had suffered enormous losses of horses during several months of hard campaigning. Many of McClellan's surviving horses were broken down and sick with a hoof-rot disease. On Oct. 20, Reno and several other officers were dispatched to Harrisburg, Pittsburgh and other locations to acquire 2,000 horses. Reno was directed to use specific individuals as agents to procure the horses.[21] It was expected that the horses could be provided to the Army in about 10 days.[22] This assignment also would prove to be one of the most fateful of Reno's career.

Harrisburg's residents were well aware of its proximity to the South and of its desirability as a military objective. Not only was it the state capital, but it was also the center of railroad, wagon, and canal boat transportation for that area of Pennsylvania. Newspaper reports from the time give a seamy picture of the city:

> The great influx of soldiers and strangers for many months past has brought with it a corresponding increase of crime and disorder. Professional thieves of every description seem to have congregated. They have shown themselves ever on the alert to entice the unsuspecting soldier into the grog shops, houses of ill fame, low theaters, and gambling saloons, which disgrace our city, and there rob them.[23]

Another point of view, however, painted a somewhat brighter picture:

> The war has benefited Harrisburg. It has given impetus to her business; it has thronged her public places. Harrisburg is brisker and wealthier today, than she ever was before. At the Pennsylvania Central Railroad Depot thousands of soldiers are coming into the city on their way to Camp Curtin on the edge the city.[24]

Women from some of the best families in the city worked with the Ladies Union Relief Association in the local hospitals to ease the wounded soldiers' lives.[25] Sanford's Opera House and Brant's Hall were two of the places Harrisburg society went for some of their entertainment. The Harrisburg *Pennsylvania Daily Telegraph* announced in its Nov. 21 edition, "The First Ball of the Season — the first grand military and citizens dress ball this season will come off at Brant's Hall on next Wednesday evening, the 26th November."

But residents also feared an attack from the South: "The city was full of rumors all day (Nov. 21) on the subject of anticipated invasion of Pennsylvania and the contemplated capture of the State Capital by the Confederates. The public would do well to discountenance all such exaggerations."[26]

Reno arrived in Harrisburg in late October to buy horses. His contact for the large number of horses required was William Calder who had been established as the official purchasing agent for the local area. Calder bought horses from farms throughout the area and many of the prominent families of Harrisburg owned farms outside of the city.

Two of the most prominent families of Harrisburg were the Haldemans and the Rosses. The patriarch of the Haldeman family was Jacob M. Haldeman who built a significant fortune in farms and real estate before settling in Harrisburg in 1830. Jacob was one of the founders and a large stockholder in the Harrisburg National Bank.[27] He married Elizabeth E. Jacobs in 1810 and between 1812 and 1831 they had six children. Their second child, Mary Ewing, born in 1814, married Robert James Ross of Harrisburg in 1833. Ross, a native of Londonderry, Ireland, moved to Harrisburg in the 1830s and became the cashier at the Dauplin Deposit Bank, a position he held until his death in 1861. He was successful in various enterprises in the Harrisburg and Philadelphia area and owned R. J. Ross & Co, a brokerage-banking firm in Philadelphia.[28] He accumulated considerable wealth from his interests, including several farms in the Harrisburg area.[29]

The marriage between Robert Ross and Mary Ewing Haldeman produced six children. Their fourth child and second daughter, Mary Hannah, was born Nov. 16, 1843. Mary Hannah, a well-educated young lady, attended the Pennsylvania Female College, described as "an institution for the liberal education of young ladies." Monthly reports were forwarded to her parents which, it was hoped, "will be the means of inciting the students to honorable and lady-like deportment, and preserving industry."[30]

Some of the horses being procured for the government by William Calder were purchased from the farms owed by Mrs. Elizabeth E. Haldeman, Jacob's widow, and Mary Ewing Ross, Robert's widow. Through introductions by Reno's friend, Captain Henry M. Baldwin, on duty in Harrisburg as a recruiting officer, and as a courtesy to the army officers sent to Harrisburg on assignment, the prominent families would include these officers in the social events of the day. Reno and Baldwin were invited to the Elizabeth Haldeman home at 27 N. Front St., Harrisburg, on several occasions for dinner parties. Invited guests also included Elizabeth's daughter, Mary Ewing Ross and her granddaughter, Mary Hannah Ross.

Reno, now a mature 28, soon found himself attracted to this enchanting, pretty and charming 18-year-old young woman. Stories of his adventures in

the northwest fighting Indians and McClellan's peninsula campaign enter-
tained the family for hours. Since Mary Hannah's father had died the year
before, Reno had to obtain permission from her mother before he could "officially" court Mary Hannah. With permission granted, Reno started his courtship of Mary Hannah. However, his detached service in Harrisburg was soon
completed, and he had to return to duty with the Army of the Potomac.

McClellan had finally moved his army across the Potomac and marched
south to near Warrenton, Va. On Nov. 5, Lincoln, having convinced himself
that McClellan had no intention of moving rapidly on the Confederates, relieved him of his command, replacing him with Major General Ambrose E.
Burnside.

Returning to the Army of the Potomac in late November, Reno was assigned a detachment of 1st Cavalry encamped at Belle Plain, Va. On Nov. 26,
he sent an application to Brigadier General Lorenzo Thomas requesting a
position in the Adjutant General's Department. No action was taken on his
request.[31]

Reno's 1st Cavalry detachment, the Oneida (New York) Cavalry and two
companies of the 4th U.S. Cavalry, were assigned to escort duty for Burnside's
army headquarters.[32] Burnside, under pressure from Washington to attack,
decided to take his Army of the Potomac across the Rappahannock and take
Fredericksburg. Approaching Fredericksburg Nov. 17, Burnside waited for
pontoon bridges to cross the Rappahannock, delaying his crossing until Dec.
9. The long delay allowed Lee to significantly fortify Fredericksburg. Burnside's
forces made repeated attempts to take the town between Dec. 11 and 15, but
was finally forced to pull his command back across the Rappahannock on the
15th. Reno's cavalry saw little combat during the five days of action near
Fredericksburg — his cavalry was again mainly used as escorts or pickets, or
on reconnaissance patrols.

Units of the 1st Cavalry, including Reno's Company H, encamped near
Falmouth, Va., until Dec. 31, when they moved to Warrenton, arriving there
that same day. The weather permitted only limited activity for the cavalry
during the winter of 1862-63 and Reno's command was used only as escorts
or on picket duty during this time. The inactivity allowed many officers and
men to take leave and Reno received a leave of absence from Jan. 24 to March
2, his longest leave since entering the army in July 1857. His destination was,
of course, Harrisburg where he could continue courting Mary Hannah — life
had suddenly become much more interesting.

Following his leave, where much attention was given to his courtship of
Mary Hannah, Reno returned to the Army of the Potomac and helped prepare for a spring campaign against the Confederates. Burnside, having failed
against the Confederates at Fredericksburg, had been relieved by Lincoln on

Jan. 26, 1863, and replaced by General Joseph "Fighting Joe" Hooker. Brigadier General George Stoneman, commanding the Cavalry Corps of the Army of the Potomac, directed Brigadier General William W. Averell, commanding the 2nd Division of the Cavalry Corps, to pursue the Confederate cavalry forces under the command of General Fitzhugh Lee. Averell had more than 3,000 cavalry and six pieces of artillery, including 760 men from the Reserve Brigade under Reno's command which consisted of companies from the 1st and 5th U.S. Cavalry.

Fitzhugh Lee was reported in the vicinity of Culpeper Court House, Va., and Averell decided to cross the Rappahannock at Kelly's Ford — it presented the shortest way to the Confederate camps. The ford was crossed about 9 a.m. March 17 after brisk fighting. About noon, after reforming, Averell's division moved toward Culpeper and was soon engaged in heavy fighting. Reno, with three squadrons, was sent in support of the 1st Brigade and drove the enemy from the battlefield. The Confederates continually regrouped and attacked but were repulsed. Fighting continued most of the afternoon with steady gains being made by Averell's command. The enemy retired to entrenched positions, making further advance by Averell's brigades extremely hazardous. At 5:30 p.m. he decided to withdraw his command back across the Rappahannock. The fight at Kelly's Ford would be the beginning of the renewed confidence and ability of the Federal Cavalry — so long outfought by the Confederates.[33]

Averell's March 20 report on the fighting at Kelly's Ford noted, "Captain Reno, whose horse was wounded under him, handled his men gallantly and steadily."[34] What his report did not say was that when Reno's horse went down, he suffered a hernia and was in considerable pain on the march back across the Rappahannock. As a result of his "gallant and meritorious service" action at Kelly's Ford, he was brevetted Major, U.S. Army.[35] Due to his injury, he was granted 30 days sick leave, starting March 18, and he returned to Harrisburg to recuperate.

While recuperation in Harrisburg with Mary Hannah in close attention was certainly more enjoyable than spending time in a local military hospital, Reno's recovery was slower than anticipated. A physical examination by Army Surgeon J. P. Nelson April 17 indicated that Reno was "unfit for duty" for an additional 10 days due to an "inflammation of the glands of the groin, caused by the irritation of a truss."[36] After a re-examination by the same doctor April 29, Reno requested another 10 days of sick leave to "prevent permanent disability."[37] A letter written the same day by Reno suggested that he might not be able to return to his regiment for two or three months and requested that he be assigned to Harrisburg as a recruiting officer. He wrote, "The 9 months men [volunteers] will soon be mustered out from this state and I think many recruits could be made."[38] Another examination in Philadelphia May 9 granted him an additional 15 days of sick leave.[39]

Special orders issued in Washington, D.C., May 7, 1863, assigned Reno on detached service as a recruiting, mustering and disbursing officer at Harrisburg.[40] Reno was pleased with the new assignment which would keep him near Mary Hannah. The relationship between the two had developed to where they planned to marry. They had opted for an early July wedding in Harrisburg — a fashionable wedding with the prominent families of Harrisburg in attendance. The wedding would take place at the Pine Street Presbyterian Church and the ceremony would be performed by the Rev. W. C. Cattell.

Although his sick leave was not scheduled to end until May 24, Reno joined his new temporary command at Carlisle May 16 and the recruiting station staff at Harrisburg on the 19th. In the meantime, "Fighting Joe" Hooker had withdrawn his troops across the Rappahannock after an abortive offensive against Lee at Chancellorsville May 1-6. Lee decided that an invasion of the north by his Army of Northern Virginia might significantly shorten the war, so he ordered his generals to prepare for an invasion into Pennsylvania.

The possibility of a Confederate intrusion into the north brought panic to the areas of southern Pennsylvania. With the Confederates on the move, it was decided to use as many experienced officers as were available to pull together the existing scattered forces of militia in that area of Pennsylvania. On May 20, Reno was transferred from recruiting duty in Harrisburg to chief of staff for Brigadier General William F. "Baldy" Smith at Carlisle. Smith was assigned to command all the troops of the Department of the Susquehanna on the south side of the Susquehanna River in the vicinity of Harrisburg.[41] His command consisted of 11 New York National Guard regiments, five Pennsylvania emergency infantry regiments, two companies of Pennsylvania emergency cavalry and two batteries of Pennsylvania artillery — about 7,000 men.

Confederate Lieutenant General Richard S. Ewell's II Army Corps crossed the Potomac June 15 and moved into Pennsylvania toward Chambersburg and Carlisle. Hooker's Army of the Potomac finally started in pursuit and moved behind Lee and Ewell as they progressed north.[42] Amid great excitement in Harrisburg, many people feared that the capitol and city would be burned. Thousands of refugees from the Cumberland Valley poured into the city.[43] To add to the confusion, farmers drove their herds of cattle through the city's streets. Plans for a July Reno-Ross church wedding in Harrisburg were quickly abandoned. Before the Confederates reached Carlisle on the 28th, the Haldeman and Ross families hurriedly left Harrisburg by train for New York City.

By June 27, Lee had established the headquarters of the Army of Northern Virginia at Chambersburg. As the Confederates moved north, Union soldiers and civilians were busily engaged in strengthening the defenses opposite the city of Harrisburg. A series of entrenchments were constructed from which the soldiers thought they could defend the state capital. That same day, Smith's troops were forced to fall back from Carlisle toward Harrisburg, just 12 miles to the east. Ewell spent part of the 28th at Carlisle Barracks raising the Confederate flag while some of his troops scouted the fortifications at Harrisburg.

While no match for Ewell's 22,000 troops, Smith's "volunteers" were ready to defend the capital and expected an attack on either the 29th or 30th. Fate, however, intervened and on the 29th, Ewell was ordered to provide support to Robert E. Lee's Army of Northern Virginia farther to the south. During the night of June 29-30, Ewell abandoned his positions at Carlisle and marched south. With the abandonment of Carlisle and the danger to Harrisburg considerably reduced, Reno received permission for a short leave of absence. Reno, aware that the situation could change momentarily, telegraphed Mary Hannah in New York that he would be arriving there late in the evening of the 30th. Reno remained in Harrisburg only long enough to invite the Reverend Cattell to accompany him on the trip to New York.

Arriving late Tuesday evening, he quickly made plans for a small wedding to be performed the following morning. On Wednesday, July 1, 1863, Captain Marcus Albert Reno and Mary Hannah Ross were married at the exclusive Astor House hotel in New York by Reverend Cattell.[44] The wedding was attended by members of the Haldeman and Ross families and a few of Mary Hannah's closest friends. Marcus and Mary Hannah had no opportunity for a honeymoon following the wedding — he departed almost immediately from New York and joined Smith later that same night.

When Smith learned of Ewell's departure, he proceeded toward Carlisle, occupied the city on July 1, and by early evening had 2,000 men and a battery of artillery in and around Carlisle.[45] Later that night, a brigade of General James E. B. "Jeb" Stuart's cavalry division, under the command of General Fitzhugh Lee, surrounded Carlisle. Lee issued an ultimatum to Smith to surrender the town or evacuate the women and children — Smith chose to send out the women and children. Again Lee demanded Smith's surrender, and again Smith refused. Confederate artillery fired on the town until about 1 a.m. but abandoned their attempt to take the town early the next morning — Robert E. Lee needed their help at Gettysburg.

Prior to their departure, the Confederates burned the barracks at Carlisle to the ground. This was a sad event for both Fitzhugh Lee and Reno as both had served there together following their graduation from West Point — Lee in 1856 and Reno in 1857. In a story published in 1886, Reno reported:

"When I reported I found Fitz Lee there...your readers can imagine my feelings in seeing from the village where I was the flames arising from the very buildings Fitz Lee and I had occupied as quarters before the war."[46]

At Carlisle, Reno learned that Smith had received orders from General Darius N. Couch to move his command toward Gettysburg and harass Lee's left flank. Heavy weather and untrained troops prevented Smith from moving rapidly toward the Confederates. On July 5, Smith's 1st New York Cavalry attacked one of Lee's wagon trains near Greencastle and captured 653 prisoners and a considerable number of wagons, horses, mules, and one piece of artillery.[47] Logistical difficulties continued to impede the progress of Smith's command — straggling and desertions became common.

Arriving at Waynesborough July 8, Smith was exasperated: "My command is an incoherent mass, and, if it is to join the Army of the Potomac, I would suggest that the brigades, five in number, be attached to old divisions, and thus disperse the greenness."[48] Following a meeting with General George G. Meade (who had replaced Hooker as commander of the Army of the Potomac June 28), Smith was reinforced by a division from the Army of the Potomac under the command of General Thomas H. Neill. Smith was ordered in pursuit of Lee and marched toward Hagerstown, Md., but had only arrived at Leitersburg, Md., when most of Lee's army made their final escape to the south. Minor skirmishes took place July 10 between troops of Smith's command and remnants of Lee's army in the area of Hagerstown but casualties were light on both sides. Reno later reported:

> [A]bout dusk we went into camp. I was very tired, and had been some time rolled up in blankets on the ground, when I was awakened by an orderly, who told me General Smith wanted to see me. At once I went to his tent, and he told me that General Neill's division had been recalled, and as the militia were within rifle range of Lee's army we must make for the mountains, and for me to issue orders for all the command to move out on the road to the mountains at daylight. I did this, and by the time the sun shone out we were several miles to the rear.

By July 12, with Smith's state militia units soon to be disbanded, the need for Regular Army officers to assist Smith ended and Reno was ordered back to recruiting duty at Harrisburg. In his report of July 18, 1863, Smith noted: "I am much indebted to Captain M. A. Reno, U. S. Cavalry, who acted as my chief of staff."[49]

For Reno the next two and half months would probably be the most enjoyable period of his life. His new bride and he took up residence at the home of Mary Hannah's mother, Mary Ross, at 227 N. Front St., Harrisburg. With the threat of a Southern invasion over, residents of Harrisburg returned to normal living. For the town's society it meant a return to a busy social schedule. Captain and Mrs. Reno enjoyed the new social life during the warm summer months and attended dances and other functions. By the time Reno received orders to return to his 1st Cavalry unit with the Army of the Potomac, Mary Hannah knew she was pregnant.

Reno returned Oct. 8 to the 1st Cavalry, then encamped near Camp Buford, Md. He again commanded two squadrons of the 1st Cavalry consisting of four companies, including his own Company H. His unit was part of the Cavalry Corp's Reserve Brigade under the command of Brigadier General Wesley Merritt containing units of the 1st, 2nd, and 5th U.S. Cavalry and the 6th Pennsylvania Cavalry. Merritt reported directly to Major General Alfred Pleasonton.

The Reserve Brigade remained in the vicinity of Washington, D.C., until Oct. 11, when it rejoined the Army of the Potomac camped along the Rappahannock River. The Union and Confederate armies had faced each other on the Rappahannock line since mid-September with little movement by either side. Merritt's command moved to Centreville on the 15th. On the 16th, Reno's two squadrons of 1st Cavalry went on a reconnaissance to Bull Run Creek. On Oct. 17, the brigade moved to Manassas Junction, and on the 18th, pushed on to Bristoe Station where the Confederates were found to be in considerable force with two batteries of artillery.[50] Light skirmishing with the enemy was reported by Reno's command at Catlett's Station on the 19th.[51]

Merritt remained in the vicinity of Manassas Junction for several days while elements of his brigade conducted reconnaissance throughout the area. On Nov. 8, Reno's command crossed the Rappahannock at Sulfur Springs and marched to within two miles of Culpeper, Va.[52] During a reconnaissance toward the Rapidan on the 11th, Reno found Confederate pickets and drove them across the river. The next several weeks found Reno's squadrons on picket duty, night patrols and reconnaissance. On the 26th, the brigade marched to Stevensburg. The next day, it proceeded to Ely's and Culpeper Fords to protect the supply trains at these points and guard river fords from Germanna down to the mouth of the Rapidan and Richards' Ford.[53] On Nov. 28-29, Reno's 1st Cavalry squadron provided an escort for the V Corp's supply train from the Rapidan to Robertson's Tavern and back. No encounters with the Confederates were reported.

Camping in the vicinity of Culpeper, Va., Dec. 2, Reno's command would be on almost continuous picket duty for the next three weeks. The hard marches, cold wet weather and long hours of duty were taking a heavy toll on both men and horses. By Christmas eve, Reno had developed a severe case of lumbago and sciatica and was in no condition to continue on active duty. Given a 15-day sick leave, he left Culpeper Dec. 26 and reported to a military hospital in Washington, D.C. Examined there again Jan. 11, 1864, he was found still to be "unfit for active service" and his leave of absence was extended an additional 20 days.[54] Mary Hannah added to his concerns as she was starting her seventh month of pregnancy. On Feb. 3, he was finally released from the hospital for active duty.

Returning to the Merritt's Reserve Brigade near Culpeper, Va., Reno was again in command of several squadrons of 1st Cavalry. On Feb. 6, a reconnaissance in force was made to several points along the Rapidan to attract the attention of the Confederates while other army units moved in adjacent areas. The force was comprised of several corps and the Reserve Brigade. Confederate troops were confronted at Culpeper and Barnett's fords, and the Federals took some prisoners while suffering only light casualties.[55]

Close camaraderie existed among the officers of the various Reserve Brigade units. On Feb. 15, officers of the 6th Pennsylvania Cavalry gave a dinner for General Merritt which included, "Captains Sweitzer and Reno, of the First, Captain Arnold, of the Fifth, and Captains Norris, Gordon, myself [Theo. F. Rodenbough], of the Second, were the guests, in addition to the General, and one staff officer, who, together with the officers of the Sixth Pennsylvania, made up a jolly party of eighteen. The dinner was excellent, and nicely served...two or three hours slipped away rapidly under the combined influences of music, tobacco, and an occasional toast...we all went away convinced that among so many gentlemen...there can be no difficulty in keeping up that esprit de corps so desirable, and yet so seldom found in the army as it is."[56]

Another reconnaissance was made Feb. 27 and Confederate pickets were encountered about three miles from Charlottesville, Va. The pickets were quickly driven off. When Reno's command returned from its scout, they destroyed a bridge crossing the Ravina River and burned several grist mills. They encamped in the woods three or four miles from Stannardsville, Va.[57]

Cold, wet weather continued to take their toll on both men and horses, and on March 8, Reno was ordered to report for duty in the Cavalry Bureau in Washington, D.C.[58] Because of his previous experience in procuring horses for the cavalry, he was assigned as an inspector of horses at Elmira, N.Y. This duty allowed him to occasionally visit Harrisburg which was only several hours away by train. Mary Hannah was in her final month of pregnancy and was not well. The birth of their son, Robert Ross, occurred in late April, and for Mary Hannah it was a difficult delivery. Recovery was slower than expected and she remained ill for several weeks. Receiving orders to return to the Cavalry Bureau in Washington May 1, Reno requested a delay of a "few days" to remain in Harrisburg.[59]

Finally returning to Washington in early May, Reno was assigned as the acting assistant inspector general, 1st Division, Cavalry Corps, Army of the Potomac, and his duties included visits to its various brigades to inspect the conditions of the horses and the unit's readiness for cavalry service. He was also assigned the duty of superintending the shipment of men and horses of the division.

After General Ulysses S. Grant took command of the armies March 9, 1864, the cavalry of the Army of the Potomac was finally organized into a full corps with three divisions. General Philip H. Sheridan commanded the Cavalry Corps, and his divisions were commanded by Generals Alfred T. A. Torbert, David McM. Gregg and James H. Wilson. Torbert had been appointed brigadier general of volunteers Nov. 29, 1862, and had earned brevets to major and lieutenant colonel in the Regular Army for gallant and meritorious service at Gettysburg and Hawes' Shop.

Following the battle of the Wilderness May 5-6, the Cavalry Corps carried out a series of raids behind Confederate lines and was pursued by "Jeb" Stuart's Cavalry Corps. Stuart's troops were defeated May 11 at Yellow Tavern and Stuart was killed. Sheridan remained south of the Rappahannock and continued to push toward Richmond. Because of his position as acting assistant inspector general, Reno had the opportunity to serve with the 1st Division during field operations and accompanied Torbert's division in a skirmish at Hawes Shop, Va., May 28.

The Cavalry Corps continued its movement toward the James River where it was engaged in heavy fighting near Cold Harbor, Va., May 31-June 1. On the morning of May 31, units of Lee's Army of Northern Virginia attacked Sheridan's Corps but Sheridan was able to hold off the attackers until General Horatio G. Wright's VI Corps arrived as reinforcements. In two days of bitter fighting, both sides suffered heavy casualties, and Grant was finally forced to withdraw his army to temporary fortifications. Following Cold Harbor, Sheridan moved west with the purpose of cutting the railroads to Richmond, thus reducing the means of transportation for supplies to Lee's army. The decision was to cut the line at Gordonsville, Va., and Sheridan moved in that direction June 8.

The Cavalry Corps approached Trevillian Station June 10 and a two-day battle began the following morning. Brigadier General George A. Custer, commander of Torbert's 1st Brigade, 1st Division, attacked the rear of Wade Hampton's division and captured 350 prisoners, a large number of horses, wagons, and other equipment. However, Custer soon found himself surrounded on three sides and lost all the captured booty before being rescued by the rest of Torbert's 1st Division.[60] Torbert's Reserve Brigade, commanded by Merritt, was having a hard fight to hold its own late in the afternoon of the 11th and Reno was sent by Torbert to assess the situation. Reno later described the episode as he went in search of Merritt:

> I can say it was a hot place. Reaching the line I asked for Merritt, and was told at his headquarters that he was with [Captain] Williston [3rd Artillery]. I galloped there with all haste, and found but two guns. The men from the other guns had all been killed or wounded, and I found Merritt, wearing the uniform coat of a Brigadier-General, aiding Captain Williston in loading and firing the single gun of the battery that was serviceable. None had been captured, however. This one gun had a flank fire upon Breckinridge's infantry, and saved Custer and the day. The fire of this gun made itself felt, and I was ordered to carry an order to Custer to advance. He had not much trouble in doing so, and the railroad was in our possession. Some time was spent in destroying it.[61]

Returning from Trevillian Station, the Cavalry Corps moved east and could see the dust from Hampton and Fitzhugh Lee moving on a road parallel to the Corps but no significant battles ensued. Camp was set up near White House, Va., where for the first time Reno saw Negro troops in the field. They were returning from a brief skirmish with the Confederates and were part of a colored division commanded by General Edward Ferrero. The Corps remained only briefly at White House and then resumed its march across the Peninsula toward the Army of the Potomac at City Point. On June 24, Torbert's division, escorting a wagon convoy, approached the pontoon bridge across the James River when it was attacked by a brigade of Hampton's cavalry and forced to retreat back to Charles City Court House. Gregg's 2nd Division came to the rescue and finally drove off the Confederates.

The Army of the Potomac had left Cold Harbor June 12, crossed the James on June 15-16 and had begun siege operations around the city of Petersburg. Crossing the James, the Cavalry Corps moved along the rear of the Army of the Potomac and made camp in the vicinity of Lee's Mills. For most of the next month, the cavalry would be used for picket, escort and reconnaissance duty.

On July 9, Torbert wrote to Secretary of War Stanton:

> Sir — I take pleasure in recommending 'to your favorable consideration,' Captain Marcus A. Reno, 1st U.S. Cavalry, for

promotion to the rank of Brig. Gen'l.... [H]e has served on my staff as Inspector General during the active campaign of this year, and distinguished himself at the battles of Coal (sic) Harbor and Trevillian Station for coolness, bravery, and good judgment. I know him to be fully competent to fill the position.

An endorsement by Sheridan July 10 stated:

The recommendation of Brig. Genl. Torbert is highly approved. The cavalry service has no better officer than Capt. Reno. He is full of energy and ability, has been in all the cavalry engagements of present campaign. He is one of the most promising young cavalry officers of this army, and will do great credit to the position for which he is recommended.[62]

No action was taken on Torbert's recommendation.

In late July, the Cavalry Corps, with General Hancock's II Corps, made an expedition north of the James and confronted the Confederates east of Richmond near Darbytown July 28. Defeating the Confederates in a series of hot skirmishes, Sheridan pulled his command back across the James and returned to his original camp near Lee's Mills.[63]

On the 30th, Torbert received orders to march the 1st Division to City Point for transportation to Washington, D.C. Embarking July 31, the command moved to Washington and then on to Harpers Ferry, arriving Aug. 8-9. Sheridan appointed Torbert Chief of Cavalry for the Middle Military Division of the Cavalry Corps and he immediately appointed Reno as his chief of staff. Torbert's division included the 1st Division of Cavalry from the Army of the Potomac under Merritt, and the 1st and 2nd Divisions of the West Virginia Cavalry commanded by Averell and Brigadier General Alfred N. Duffié, respectively.[64]

In his position as chief of staff, Reno had significant influence over the activities of both division and brigade commanders. Commanding one of Merritt's brigades was Brigadier General George Custer, who had been advanced four grades from captain to brigadier general of volunteers prior to the Battle of Gettysburg.[65] It was during this period that Reno and Custer had their first opportunity to meet.

Torbert remained at Harpers Ferry, Va., until Aug. 10 and then proceeded down the Shenandoah Valley in the direction of Berryville and Winchester. Confederate cavalry and infantry units were engaged during the next several days with only minor casualties on both sides. On the 16th, pickets of Merritt's 1st and 2nd brigades were attacked by two brigades of Confederate infantry and one brigade of cavalry near Cedarville. Merritt met the attack, and after a severe engagement, he totally routed the Confederates and drove them back across the Shenandoah River, killing and wounding about 300 men, capturing nearly 300 prisoners and two battle flags with a loss of only 60 men.[66]

Moving north toward Kearneysville Aug. 25 with Merritt's 1st Division and Brigadier General James H. Wilson's 3rd Division, Torbert encountered increasing resistance from Confederate troops. A strong attack by Federal cavalrymen overwhelmed the Confederates and forced them to retreat with a loss of 250 killed and wounded. Reconnaissance patrols indicated the approach of Confederate General John C. Breckinridge's Corps near Kearneysville so Torbert decided to fall back while the opportunity was available. Crossing the Potomac at Harpers Ferry, most of the Cavalry Corps encamped near Boonsborough, Md., on the evening of the 25th.[67] On the 28th, several of Torbert's divisions recrossed the Potomac and moved in the direction of Leetown, Va., where they met the Confederate cavalry in force and drove them "with the saber" through Smithfield and across Opequon Creek. Merritt's 1st Division was attacked by a strong force of Confederate cavalry at Smithfield on the 29th and was driven back about a mile. Receiving reinforcements from the 3rd Division, VI Corps, Merritt was finally able to drive the Confederates off and across Opequon Creek.[68]

During these skirmishes and engagements with Confederate forces, Chief of Staff Reno formulated and issued orders in the name of Torbert and accompanied him into the battle areas. This duty was at times hazardous — Torbert's chief surgeon was killed at his side Aug. 29.

For the next three weeks, the cavalry remained in the areas of Berryville, Smithfield and Charlestown, Va., and on numerous occasions sent out a reconnaissance in force to find the Confederates and bring them to battle. An entire infantry regiment (the 8th South Carolina) was captured Sept. 13 — officers, men, and colors — and was marched into camp.[69] On the 19th, Merritt's division, in a battle near Winchester, captured 775 prisoners, about 70 officers, seven battle flags and two pieces of artillery. Torbert's cavalry continued to pursue the Confederates for several more weeks and in a series of skirmishes seized a significant number of Confederate prisoners and equipment.[70] Custer replaced Wilson as commander of the 3rd Division on Sept. 30.

Reno was encouraged by Torbert to apply for a volunteer command. Because of his marriage the previous year to Mary Hannah Ross, Reno, although not born in Pennsylvania, was able to apply to Governor Andrew Curtin for command of a Pennsylvania cavalry regiment. The governor, dissatisfied with the performance and leadership of the 12th Pennsylvania Regiment of Cavalry (113th Regiment of Pennsylvania Volunteers), indicated he would con-

General A. T. A. Torbert & Staff

Torbert bottom row center -- Reno bottom row, under flag, facing left. (Brady Collection, Library of Congress)

sider Reno's appointment as colonel of the unit. Torbert wrote to Governor Curtin Oct. 7:

> Permit me to recommend for your favorable consideration Capt. M. A. Reno, 1st U.S. Cavalry for the Colonelcy of the 12th Penna. Regiment of Cavalry. Capt. Reno is an officer tried and long experienced in this branch of the service and will do credit to the State and Regiment. The Regiment needs a good head very much and unless it has a competent man to take charge of it, it will have to be dismounted. Let me urge your immediate action in this matter.

Endorsements were made by Sheridan and General William H. Emory, Late Chief of Cavalry:

> Sheridan: "I think so much of Capt. Reno that I heretofore recommended him for the appointment of Brig. General.... [Y]our Excellency will make no mistake in making this appointment."

> Emory: "I consider him one of the best and most faithful cavalry officers...and recommend him to your Excellency as imminently qualified for the command to which he is nominated."[71]

On Oct. 9, Torbert received orders from Sheridan to "whip the Rebel cavalry or get whipped" — Torbert wisely choose to attempt the former.[72] At a confrontation on the 10th at Tom's Brook, Merritt engaged a sizable Confederate force. After a battle lasting two hours, the Confederates were driven at what was described "a perfect rout" for 20 miles.[73] But the Confederate forces quickly recovered and on the 13th launched an infantry attack that forced the Union cavalry pickets across Cedar Creek.

As part of the nomination process for Reno to become the colonel of the 12th Pennsylvania Cavalry, an interview with Governor Curtin was required. Reno received a short leave of absence from his duties as Torbert's chief of staff and on Oct. 14 traveled to Harrisburg for the interview. He writes on Oct. 15, "Have just had an interview with the governor in reference to the 12th Pa Cav.... [T]he governor will, I think, give me the Regt."[74]

Reno returned to duty with Torbert on the 17th. Torbert had encamped along Cedar Creek for several days with Merritt's 1st Division and Custer's 3rd Division. Between the two divisions of cavalry was a large contingent of infantry, consisting of General George Crook's Department of West Virginia, General Wright's VI Army Corps, and two divisions of Emory's XIX Army

Corps. At daylight Oct. 19, Confederate General John B. Gordon's division, having forded the Shenandoah during the night, attacked Crook's divisions and routed them, sending thousands of men in flight to the rear. Torbert's cavalry held until 3 p.m. while most of the infantry was reforming. Sheridan, who had gone to Washington prior to the battle, arrived to direct movements of the troops. The Confederates had succeeded in crossing infantry and cavalry over Cedar Creek but about 4 o'clock, a general advance was made by the Union infantry and cavalry. The Confederates were soon driven across Cedar Creek in confusion, and late in the evening the cavalry, sweeping on both flanks, charged and broke the last line the enemy attempted to form. Torbert thought that darkness alone saved the greater part of the Confederate army from capture.[75]

In Torbert's November 1864 report, he stated:

> I will take this occasion to recommend to the favorable consideration of the proper authorities the following members of my staff, as fit recipients of higher honors than lay in my power to bestow, for gallantry and courage displayed upon this and several other occasions during the campaign; braver and more efficient staff officers never drew rein or saber, viz:...Capt. M. A. Reno, First U.S. Cavalry, chief of staff.[76]

For his "gallant and meritorious service at the Battle of Cedar Creek, Va., Oct. 19, 1864," Reno was brevetted Lieutenant Colonel, U.S. Army. By now, Reno's reputation was well known throughout the Cavalry Corps. General J. H. Wilson, writing from the Cavalry Corps Headquarters of the Military Division of the Mississippi Oct. 26, stated, "I have already asked General Grant twice by telegraph for General Upton and Colonel Mackenzie...Custer, Pennington, and Reno. Custer I don't expect to get, but...Reno, now captain of regular cavalry...[has] been recommended, ought to be promoted."[77]

In late October, Reno received a leave of absence and returned to Harrisburg to spend time with his new family. He also waited for the expected promotion to colonel of the 12th Pennsylvania Cavalry. The 12th Pennsylvania, assigned to the area around Charlestown, Va., was ordered to keep John Mosby's guerrillas out of the area. Sheridan was not pleased with the services of the 12th Cavalry and on Nov. 23 stated: "If the Twelfth Pennsylvania Cavalry cannot keep that country clear of guerrillas, I will take the shoulder straps off every officer belonging to the regiment and dismount the regiment in disgrace."[78] Governor Curtin finally took action and on Dec. 15, removed L. B. Pierce as the colonel of the 12th Pennsylvania for incompetence. On Dec. 20, Reno received the appointment to the vacant colonelcy position. On that day he sent a telegram to the Adjutant General requesting a leave of absence until "further orders" to accept the colonelcy of the 12th Pennsylvania.[79] Orders were issued Dec. 28 by the Adjutant General's office granting his request.[80]

The 12th Pennsylvania Cavalry, part of Brigadier General John D. Stevenson's 3rd Division, Department of West Virginia, was encamped several miles from Charlestown, W. Va. Its assignment was to guard the Baltimore and Ohio Railroad from Harpers Ferry to Winchester. Colonel Reno arrived in camp Jan. 6, 1865, and was mustered into the regiment Jan. 9.[81] General Order No. 12 was immediately issued to the effect that "all rules and regulations for the government of the command will remain in force until otherwise ordered."[82] The reputation of the regiment had suffered under Pierce's leadership and Reno was determined to bring the regiment up to a first line unit:

> I do think…I am going to have one of the finest regiments in the Cavalry Corps. Some of the officers are going out as their terms expire, and I'm sincerely glad, as I can find infinitely better material in the ranks than they ever were.[83]

The regiment was ordered to move Jan. 17 via the Berryville road to as near to Charlestown as possible and establish a suitable camping ground. Reno was authorized to "use lumber from secessionists farms, as to make his men comfortable."[84] On the 18th, Confederate guerrillas, dressed in Union uniforms, derailed a train on the Baltimore and Ohio Railroad near Duffield's, and Reno was ordered to send out a scout to determine where the Confederates had come from and where they had gone. He was ordered to establish a system of patrolling from Charlestown to the Baltimore and Ohio Railroad as far up as Kearneysville, and to "clear out one of these parties of raiders, which would perhaps cure the evil."[85] Reno reported that the Confederates were part of General John Mosby's command and had crossed the Shenandoah, passing between Charlestown and Halltown, and had then torn up the railroad tracks near Duffield's. They had recrossed the river at Snicker's Ferry and Reno had received the information too late to intercept them.[86]

Reno continued to try to improve his officer staff, requesting a number of promotions and new commissions. On Jan. 20, he wrote, "I hope my wishes will be fulfilled in these appointments as they embrace the best material in the Regiment. I would also request immediate action on them."[87]

On the 25th, Sheridan ordered the 12th to "destroy all ferry-boats on the Shenandoah from Berry's Ferry down to Harpers Ferry."[88] By Jan. 27, Reno had not received a response to his Jan. 20 letter and he wrote asking "have the recommendations sent in by me been acted upon? I am very anxious to set the officers up who come from the ranks...excuse me, please, but I have every interest in the speedy organisation (sic) of the Regiment."[89] Two days later he wrote: "The Regiment is coming on famously 'tho' I say it as shouldn't [it]. The inspecting officer yesterday congratulated me heartily and said that any requisitions for the benefit of the men that had my name to it would secure immediate attention — excuse this little professional vanity and believe me."[90]

Major James A. Congdon wrote: "Colonel Reno is taking the best steps to make the 12th an excellent regiment."[91] While Reno believed the regiment was making progress, the evening of Jan. 31 proved he still had a long way to go — Confederate guerrillas attacked several of the regiment's outpost pickets and threw the unit into confusion. "The attempt made last night by the guerrillas has shown the Commanding Officer the helpless condition of the command under such circumstances."[92]

On Feb. 3, a band of Confederate guerrillas crossed the Shenandoah at Keyes' Ford and derailed another train on the Baltimore and Ohio line.[93] Reno immediately sent out two scouting parties in different directions with orders to overtake and attack the guerrillas. One of the scouting parties, not following orders, changed direction and ended up being fired on by the other scouting party, wounding one man. The guerrillas recrossed the Shenandoah and escaped. On the 4th, Reno dismissed the officer who disobeyed his orders.[94] That same day he received a message directly from Sheridan:

> The country in your vicinity and out for a distance of ten miles is full of Confederate soldiers. With a regiment as strong as yours you should be able to capture many of them, and I will look to you to do so. At every house where you make a capture drive off all stock except one milch cow, and notify the people that I will put them out of my lines and let their Rebel friends take care of them.[95]

Reno was to still take the heat for the Feb. 3 incident — General John D. Stevenson, forwarding Reno's report to Sheridan, noted: "I forwarded you yesterday Colonel Reno's report of the party and the way in which he did not catch him."[96]

The 12th continued to patrol the area around Charlestown and attempted to discourage Confederate bands from attacking the Baltimore and Ohio Railroad. On Feb. 9, Reno received orders to send a force to determine if a band of 150 to 200 guerrillas were in the area of Kabletown.[97] By the time Reno's men arrived in the area, the Confederate irregulars had vanished. But the 12th was soon to again receive a visit from the guerrillas. On Feb. 13, Major Adolphus E. Richards of Mosby's command captured two stragglers from the

12th and forced them to act as guides. Richards, with 15 men, using the countersigns provided by his captives, rode in among the sleeping soldiers of Reno's command. They seized about 40 horses and, deciding to give the troopers a parting shot, rode among the tents, firing their weapons until finally driven off by the now awakened soldiers. Richards had only one man wounded but finally got away with only six horses. The following day Reno censured his men for allowing the attack and made the statement, "With such men as Mosby's I could go anywhere."[98] Reno's orders for the remainder of February were to "take charge of the country from Charlestown to Halltown, etc. Watch the Shenandoah well and patrol well towards Berryville. For the present you cannot be too vigilant."[99]

General Winfield S. Hancock assumed command of the Department of West Virginia Feb. 26, 1865, temporarily relieving Sheridan. On March 3, Lieutenant Colonel Charles Bird's 1st Regiment, 1st Veteran Reserve Corps, was ordered to relieve part of Reno's cavalry so Reno could extend his lines toward Leetown. Between Reno and Bird, the line between Charlestown and Harpers Ferry was strong enough to significantly reduce the amount of guerrilla activity in the area.[100] Reno was ordered on the 4th to send a small force to take and hold a bridge near Smithfield, and to arrest unarmed citizens who were unable to properly account for themselves.[101] The main part of the regiment remained encamped at Charlestown, and on the night of the 4th was again attacked by a band of guerrillas. The reaction of the regiment to the attack was not to Reno's liking. The following morning Reno issued a circular which stated:

> The alarm last night demonstrated to the Commanding Officer the utter helplessness of this command to their shame be it said many of the men were found in rear of camp skulking behind trees, the members of the guard were found absent and worse than all, officers who were required for duty were found absent from camp.[102]

Reno reported on March 8 that Mosby, with about 300 men, had crossed the Shenandoah at Snicker's Ferry and was moving toward White Post. General Stevenson wanted a cavalry force that could be sent in pursuit of Mosby and drive him from the country, but he believed the 12th was still not a reliable regiment to do the job.[103] Stevenson's assessment of the 12th Cavalry appeared to be in conflict with the report of Major Elmer Otis, Special Inspector of Cavalry, filed March 12:

I have previous to Colonel Reno taking command of the Regiment inspected it three times, I found it in very bad condition.... [S]ince Colonel Reno has taken command the Regiment has improved vastly. Should fair (sic) to be one of the best regiments in the cavalry service. The regiment is being thoroughly drilled and disciplined and...I cannot conceive that any officer could have done better in bringing it up to the standards of a good regiment than Colonel Reno has done since...January 1865.[104]

On the evening of March 13, a party of guerrillas attacked one of Reno's picket posts, killing one man and wounding two others. Reno reported on the 15th that a party of nine guerrillas had crossed the Shenandoah where they were attacked by seven men of the 12th Cavalry with the Confederates losing two killed and Reno losing one killed and one captured.

The regiment was not at the officer strength that Reno desired, and he had still been unable to get the promotions and commissions he had requested. On the 17th, he decided to take a short leave of absence and go to Harrisburg to determine why his recommendations were not being approved. This would also be the first time since mustering into the 12th that Reno would have an opportunity to see Mary Hannah and his young son.

He returned to Charlestown March 19 and was immediately ordered to take command of three regiments: Bird's 1st Regiment of the 1st Veterans Reserve Corps, the 12th Pennsylvania Cavalry placed under the command of Captain William H. McAllaster, and the Loudonn County (Virginia) Rangers, under the command of Captain James W. Grubb. The total strength of Reno's force was about 700 infantry and 300 cavalry. His orders were to lead an expedition across the Blue Ridge Mountains and proceed south to Upperville to destroy Confederate supplies that were supposed to be stored there. On March 20, Reno's command crossed the Shenandoah at Harpers Ferry and on the 22nd engaged Mosby's troops at Hamilton where the Confederates succeeded in throwing the cavalry into some confusion but were driven away by a volley from the infantry. Reno followed Mosby until dark and then encamped at Goose Creek. His losses were nine killed and 12 wounded, and he estimated Confederate losses at about the same. Moving on toward Upperville, he destroyed the supplies and forage he found there and had minor skirmishes with the Confederates all day on the 23rd. He returned with his command to Charlestown via Harpers Ferry on the 25th.[105] General Hancock was not overly impressed with the results of the trek: "The expedition returned having accomplished much less than I had expected it to do."[106]

On April 5, the 12th Pennsylvania Cavalry marched to Winchester, Va., and on the 7th, the regiment was transferred from the Department of West

Virginia to the Army of the Shenandoah under the command of General Torbert. Reno was given the Cavalry Brigade under Brigadier General Samuel S. Carroll's 4th Provisional Division. Reno's command consisted of the 5th and 22nd New York Cavalry, 12th and 18th Pennsylvania Cavalry, 1st Rhode Island Cavalry, 2nd U.S. Cavalry, and a detachment of 1st U.S. Artillery.[107]

Reno was ordered to make a reconnaissance in force to Lynchburg but following a skirmish with the Confederates at Edinboro, it was learned that Lee had surrendered, which included all of the troops in the Shenandoah

Brevet Brigadier General Marcus Reno
U.S. Volunteers (circa 1865)
(Library of Congress)

Valley. The command, then encamped near Mount Jackson, was charged with stopping and paroling all soldiers of Lee's army returning through that part of the country. By April 22, Reno had paroled about 1,200 to 1,500 men.[108] In late April, the brigade moved back to Winchester and remained there until mid-July. On June 16, Reno was informed that he had been brevetted brigadier general, Volunteers, and colonel, U.S. Army, as of March 13, 1865, for "Gallant and Meritorious Service during the Rebellion." Reno and the 12th Pennsylvania Cavalry returned to Philadelphia July 20, and the regiment was mustered out of volunteer service as of that date. Colonel Reno, now Brevet Brigadier General Reno, reverted to his regular rank of captain on the same day.

Endnotes

[1] Record Group 94, 1st U.S. Cavalry Muster Roll, Troop H, National Archives & Records Administration (NARA); hereinafter Troop H Muster.

[2] Troop H Muster.

[3] *War of the Rebellion: Official Records of the Union and Confederate Armies*; Volume 11, Part II, p. 44; hereinafter *OR*.

[4] Troop H Muster.

[5] *OR*, Volume 11, Part I, p. 1029.

[6] *OR*, Volume 11, Part II, p. 45.

[7] *OR*, Volume 11, Part II, p. 44.

[8] *OR*, Volume 11, Part II, p. 46.

[9] *OR*, Volume 11, Part II, p. 44.

[10] *OR*, Volume 11, Part II, pp. 921-22.

[11] *OR*, Volume 19, Part II, p. 172.

[12] *OR*, Volume 19, Part II, p. 172.

[13] *OR*, Volume, 19, Part II, p. 238.

[14] *OR*, Volume 19, Part I, pp. 169-170, p. 34.

[15] General Jesse Lee Reno was not related to Marcus Reno.

[16] Stephen Z. Starr, *The Union Cavalry in the Civil War* (Louisiana State University Press, Baton Rouge and London, 1979), Volume I, p. 317; hereinafter Union Cavalry.

[17] *OR*, Volume 51, Part I, p. 848.

[18] *OR*, Volume 19, Part I, p. 213.

[19] *OR*, Volume 19, Part II, p. 96.

[20] *OR*, Volume 19, Part II, pp. 91-93.

[21] Luther Reily Kelker, *History of Dauphin County Pennsylvania* (The Lewis Publishing Company, New York, 1907), Volume III. One was William Calder of Harrisburg, Pennsylvania. During entire period of the Civil War he furnished the Union Army with 42,000 horses and 67,000 mules, besides thousands of tons of hay.

[22] *OR*, Volume 19, Part II, p. 451.

[23] *Pennsylvania Daily Telegraph*, Harrisburg, Penna., Nov. 21, 1862.

[24] *Pennsylvania Daily Telegraph*, Oct. 25, 1862.

[25] *Pennsylvania Daily Telegraph*, Oct. 22, 1862.

[26] *Pennsylvania Daily Telegraph*, Nov. 12, 1862.

[27] Gilbert W. Beckley, *New Cumberland Frontier*, 1973.

[28] Account Ledger, R. J. Ross & Co., Dauphin County Historical Society, Harrisburg, Penna.

[29] *Biographical Encyclopedia of Dauphin County, Penna.*, (J. M. Runk & Company, 1896).

[30] *Pennsylvania Female College at Harrisburg Circular*, (Stephen Miller & Co., Harrisburg, Penna., 1855).

[31] Reno File, Letter dated Nov. 26, 1862, signed by M. A. Reno.

[32] *OR*, Volume 21, p. 48.

[33] Sources for the battle at Kelly's Ford include *Ten Years in the Saddle: The Memoir of William Woods Averell*, edited by Edward K. Eckert and Nicholas J. Amato (Presidio Press, San Rafael, CA, 1978), and *Fighting Rebels and Redskins: Experiences in Army Life of Colonel George B. Sanford 1861-1892*, edited by E. R. Hagemann (University of Oklahoma Press, Norman, Ok., 1969).

[34] OR, Volume 25, Part I, pp. 47-53.

[35] Brevets, or honor, ranks were usually given for gallant action or meritorious service, and were ranks above an officer's ordinary rank. Army Regulations indicated an officer could function at his brevet rank on special assignment to other corps commands, or when on court-martial duty with officers of other corps commands. Pay was then based on the brevet rank when serving in this capacity.

[36] Reno File, Letter dated April 17, 1863, signed by J. P. Nelson.

[37] Reno File, Letter dated April 29, 1863, signed by J. P. Nelson.

[38] Reno File, Letter dated April 29, 1863, signed by M. A. Reno.

[39] Reno File, Letter dated May 9, 1863, signed by Surgeon John J. Milhan.

[40] Special Orders No. 209, dated May 7, 1863, Post Returns, Carlisle Barracks, May 1863.

[41] OR, Volume 27, Part III, p. 330.

[42] R. Ernest Dupuy and Trevor N. Dupuy, Military Heritage of America (McGraw-Hill Book Company, Inc. New York, 1956), p. 265.

[43] The Daily Telegraph, Harrisburg, Penna., June 15, 1863, & June 17, 1863.

[44] The New York Herald, New York, July 1, 1863, p. 8; The Press, Philadelphia, Penna., July 3, 1863.

[45] John M. Coleman, Editor, Pennsylvania History, Volume XXV, January-February, 1958.

[46] National Tribune, Washington, D.C., April 29, 1886.

[47] Journal of the Lancaster County (Pennsylvania) Historical Society, Volume 66, 1962, p. 39.

[48] OR, Volume 27, Part II, p. 611.

[49] OR, Volume 27, Part II, p. 223.

[50] OR, Volume 29, Part I, p. 353; Troop H Muster.

[51] Troop H Muster.

[52] Troop H Muster.

[53] OR, Volume 29, Part I, p. 806.

[54] Reno File, Letter dated Jan. 11, 1864.

[55] Theo. F. Rodenbough, Editor, Everglades to Canon with the Second Dragoons (D. Van Nostrand, New York, 1875), p. 533.

[56] Rodenbough, p. 534.

[57] Troop H Muster.

[58] Reno File, War Department letter dated March 8, 1864.

[59] Reno File, Telegram dated May 2, 1864.

[60] Richard O'Connor, Sheridan the Inevitable (The Bobbs-Merrill Company, Inc., Indianapolis-New York, 1953), p. 181.

[61] National Tribune, Washington, D.C., April 29, 1886.

[62] Reno Military File, letters dated July 9 and 10, 1864.

[63] National Tribune, Washington, D.C., April 29, 1886.

[64] OR, Volume 43, Part I, p. 421-437.

[65] Edward J. Stackpole, Sheridan in the Shenandoah (The Stackpole Company, Harrisburg, Penna., 1961), p. 152.

[66] *OR*, Volume 43, Part I, p. 423.

[67] *OR*, Volume 43, Part I, p. 425.

[68] *OR*, Volume 43, Part I, p. 426.

[69] *OR*, Volume 43, Part I, p. 427.

[70] *OR*, Volume 43, Part I, p. 429.

[71] Records of the 113th Regiment (12th Cavalry), Pennsylvania, State Archives, Harrisburg, Penna., Folder #27; hereinafter PA Records.

[72] *OR*, Volume 43, Part I, p. 431.

[73] *OR*, Volume 43, Part I, p. 431.

[74] James A. Congdon Correspondence, The Historical Society of Pennsylvania, Philadelphia, Penna., File F-5; hereinafter Congdon.

[75] *OR*, Volume 43, Part I, pp. 433-435.

[76] *OR*, Volume 43, Part I, p. 435.

[77] *OR*, Volume 39, Part III, p. 444.

[78] *Military Operations in Jefferson County, Virginia, 1861-1865*; Jefferson County Camp, p. 34.

[79] Reno File, Telegram signed by M. A. Reno, dated Dec. 20, 1864.

[80] Special Orders No. 471, War Department, Adjutant General's Office, Dec. 28, 1864.

[81] Congdon, Letter dated Jan. 8, 1865, F-6.

[82] Record Group 94, Regimental & Company Books, 12th PA Cavalry; hereinafter RC Books.

[83] PA Records, Letter dated Jan. 15, 1865.

[84] *OR*, Volume 46, Part II, pp. 167-168.

[85] *OR*, Volume 46, Part II, pp. 182-183.

[86] *OR*, Volume 46, Part II, p. 189.

[87] PA Records, Letter dated Jan. 20, 1865, Folder #26.

[88] *OR*, Volume 46, Part II, p. 265.

[89] PA Records, Letter dated Jan. 27, 1865, Folder #26.

[90] PA Records, Letter dated Jan. 29, 1865.

[91] Congdon, Letter dated Jan. 31, 1865, F-6.

[92] RC Books.

[93] Millard Kessler Bushong, Ph.D., *Historic Jefferson County* (Carr Publishing Company, Inc., Boyce, Va., 1972), p. 245.

[94] *OR*, Volume 46, Part I, p. 455.

[95] *OR*, Volume 46, Part II, p. 387.

[96] *OR*, Volume 46, Part II, p. 411.

[97] *OR*, Volume 46, Part II, p. 504.

[98] Major John Scott, *Partisan Life with Col. John S. Mosby* (Harper & Brothers, Publishers, New York, 1867), pp. 445-446.

[99] Scott, p. 726.

[100] Scott, p. 822.

[101] Scott, p. 839.

[102] RC Books.

[103] Scott, p. 898.

[104] PA Records, Letter dated March 12, 1865, Folders #26 and #27.

[105] *OR*, Volume 46, Part I, pp. 535-536.

[106] *OR*, Volume 46, Part I, p. 526.

[107] *OR*, Volume 46, Part III, pp. 1047-1048.

[108] *OR*, Volume 46, Part III, p. 897.

• 5 •

West Point, New Orleans and Oregon

It was a long step from provisional brigade commander to company commander, but with the end of the Civil War and the Volunteer Forces, officers reverted to their permanent army ranks. Marcus Reno was no exception. He was listed on the books of the 1st U.S. Cavalry Regiment as the captain of Company H. Returning to Harrisburg from Philadelphia where the 12th Pennsylvania Cavalry had been mustered out of service July 20, Reno notified the Adjutant General, Lorenzo Thomas, on July 24, 1865:

> I have the honor to report myself mustered out of the Volunteer Force and awaiting orders at this place.[1]

Reunited with his family, Reno was ready to settle down for a well deserved rest before being assigned to a new duty station. However, it would be only a short time before he received his orders. The superintendent of the Mounted Recruiting Service at Carlisle Barracks, Penna., applied for two additional officers and recommended that Captain Marcus Reno be ordered to report in person to him "at once" for assignment of duty.[2] Carlisle Barracks, now partially rebuilt, was only 12 miles west of Harrisburg and would be an excellent duty station for the captain — Mary Hannah and young Ross could stay at the house on Front Street and be near her family. The War Department approved the request Aug. 4 and Reno was duly notified.

Reno was pleased to return to Carlisle Barracks where he had started his military career eight years before. His new assignment would fit in well with both his cavalry and recruiting experience. Most duty assignments were for two years so he could enjoy the comfort of good quarters and a robust social life in Harrisburg. Alas, it was to be a short-lived assignment.

Although the War Department had approved the request for Reno's services at Carlisle Barracks Aug. 4, special orders were cut that same day detailing him for duty at the U.S. Military Academy at West Point.[3] When notified that he was being relieved from Mounted Recruiting Service duty and ordered to report in person to the superintendent of the Military Academy, he was confused and requested clarification. New orders were cut Aug. 17, again relieving him from the Mounted Recruiting Service and ordering him to report in person to the West Point superintendent. Reno received the orders about Aug. 25 and made immediate plans to depart for West Point.

Although an assignment at West Point was a prestigious appointment, one sought after by many Army officers, to Reno it was not as acceptable as the potential personal benefits of a duty assignment at Carlisle Barracks. Reno realized the Military Academy assignment could be beneficial to his Army career and it would to be to his advantage to accept the duty at West Point, not as a lowly cadet, but as an instructor who held three brevet ranks in the Regular Army as well as a brevet of brigadier general in the Volunteers. However, it would also mean moving his family away from Harrisburg.

Reno followed his orders, and Mary Hannah, Ross and he arrived at West Point's South Dock in late August 1865. This was the point from which he started the long and arduous task to complete cadet training almost exactly 14 years before. Here, at least, would be the opportunity for him and Mary Hannah to establish their first real home in the adequate quarters assigned to Academy instructors. He reported to the superintendent, Lieutenant Colonel George W. Cullum, Corps of Engineers, and informed the War Department Aug. 30 he had "the honor to report myself on duty at this post."[4]

Almost immediately he was disillusioned with his new duty station. First was his disappointment in the assigned family quarters — a converted barracks building. The academy's growth during the war years greatly outstripped available funding, and cramped, make-shift quarters were all that were available to newly assigned instructors. Second was the expectation to be assigned as an assistant instructor of cavalry tactics — his assignment was in tactics, but infantry, not cavalry. His entire military career had been in the cavalry — his knowledge of infantry tactics was limited to what he had learned as a West Point cadet.

Reno wasted little time in filing two protests with Superintendent Cullum — one about his living quarters and the other about his academic assignment. On Sept. 1, 1865, Reno's protests were forwarded to the Adjutant General's office for disposition.[5] What he wanted was better quarters and an assignment as a cavalry tactics instructor. However, what he got was unexpected. After a review by the chief engineer of the Army and the approval of Secretary of War Edwin M. Stanton, orders were prepared Sept. 29 to have him "relieved from duty at West Point, and ordered to join his regiment at Headquarters, Military Division of the Gulf."[6] His new duty station would be in New Orleans, La. — even farther from Harrisburg.

Having waited four weeks for a response to his protests, Reno had difficulty understanding his new orders. Why had he been so quickly relieved from recruiting duty at Carlisle Barracks and reassigned to West Point only to be moved again? Also, was there still the original need for an officer at Carlisle Barracks? He thought he deserved some answers and on Oct. 2, he telegraphed the Adjutant General's office in Washington, asking, "Can I delay sufficient time to visit Washington?"[7] The reply to Reno from the Adjutant General Oct. 3 informed him that "he should state the nature of his business in this city, before his application could be considered."[8] Reno replied immediately:

> [T]hat my reason for my application was that I could make a verbal explanation to the War Dept. in reference to my protest, and also, that I might ask if my detail for Recg. [Recruiting] service was necessarily superseded. I have private reasons for making this request & which I think would obtain [acceptance] at the War Dept. were I permitted to submit them. I shall be at Harrisburg on Saturday enroute to the South, & will await at that point the answer to this comm[unication]."[9]

A telegram was sent to Reno Oct. 10, rejecting his request to stop in Washington and indicating he should proceed immediately to his new duty station. The matter was settled — he would not be allowed to explain to the War Department the reasons for his protests and there would be no reconsideration for assignment to Carlisle Barracks. Reno and his family prepared for the move to New Orleans.

Following the Civil War, the U.S. Government had to decide how to handle the defeated states and determine the status of the emancipated Negroes. The situation was described as "an atmosphere of hate, created by decades of sectional bitterness and four years of fighting."[10] The North did not want any of the four million newly released slaves in the South. They formed a potentially dangerous multitude of displaced people, and in Louisiana former slaves constituted almost half the state's residents.[11] On March 3, 1865, Congress created the Freedmen's Bureau, which was an "agency of refugees, freedmen, and abandoned lands," and General Ulysses S. Grant recommended the bureau's work be carried out by military officers.[12] Major General Oliver Otis Howard was named commissioner of the bureau. The agency's purpose was primarily social and economic in nature, and its functions included issuing supplies to the destitute, maintaining freedmen's schools, supervising labor contracts between black employees and white employers, attending to the disposition of confiscated or abandoned lands and property, and providing assistance in collecting taxes.

Thomas W. Conway had been appointed assistant commissioner for Louisiana in June 1865 and immediately adopted measures that angered local civil officials and included special courts for freedmen and the confiscation of

"Rebel" property for Negro use. Howard removed Conway in September but an adversarial relationship had been established between the local residents and the Freedmen's Bureau. Conway was replaced Oct. 16, 1865, by General Absalom Baird. Reno arrived in New Orleans in late October and on the 30th was assigned duty as judge advocate, Military Commission, Headquarters, Department of Louisiana, governing the city of New Orleans. Although lacking formal legal training, he would serve the next month as a legal adviser to the military commission.

Captured by General Benjamin Butler May 1, 1862, New Orleans was a devastated and bankrupt city. The city was described as having only four paved streets, and "the slaughter-houses were so located that all of their offal and filth were poured into the Mississippi river, just above the mains that supplied the people with their drinking water." The city was overrun with gamblers, prostitutes and thugs; ruled by corrupt and ignorant officials; and was "a dirty, impoverished, and hopeless place," and epidemics of yellow fever and malaria occurred every year.[13] This was the city to which Reno brought his family in October 1865.

On Dec. 2, 1865, General Baird sent a letter to General Philip H. Sheridan: "Since speaking to you on the subject of the detail of Brv.[Brevet] Colonel Reno, 1st U.S. Cavalry for duty in this Bureau, I have seen him and he expresses a willingness to accept the position [of Provost marshal].... I request that Colonel Reno may be ordered to report to me as soon as convenient."[14] Reno was relieved from duty Dec. 4 as judge advocate and appointed provost marshal general of the Freedmen's Bureau on the 6th.[15] Reno's provost marshal duties would include investigating atrocities against blacks, reuniting black families when possible, assuring blacks were treated in a humane matter, making certain labor contracts with freedmen were honored, overseeing special tax collections, and supervising the military police of the command. His job would not be easy and he was directed to reduce the cost of his operations by "hiring out from day to day, such vagrants or other disorderly persons as may be arrested by your patrols or otherwise come in your possession for such wages as you can obtain to be appropriated towards defraying some of the expenses of your office."[16] Reno also reviewed the tax collection receipts and found deficiencies in the accounts from various military officers in several parishes in the vicinity of New Orleans — he wanted explanations immediately.[17]

Baird was impressed with Reno's performance as provost marshal but knew Reno's regiment had sailed from New Orleans for the Pacific Coast Dec. 29, 1865. Normally Reno would have departed with his regiment except Baird requested him to remain. On Jan. 3, 1866, Baird wrote to General Howard:

Through the indulgence of Major General Sheridan commanding the Military Division of the Gulf, I have been able to secure the assistance of two or three officers of the old regular Army of known character and capacity. One is my Inspector General…and Brvt. Colonel M. A. Reno 1st Cavalry is another. These officers being entirely free from local interest and local prejudices, have been able to inspire confidence in all with whom they have had to do business, and the character of the Bureau has thereby greatly improved.

The policy of employing everywhere the best officers is the only one that can keep up the reputation of our establishment.

Colonel Reno is now occupying the position of Provost Marshal General and his duties are very important; his regiment however has just been sent to the Pacific Coast and he in common with other officers who did not go with it has been ordered to Carlisle Barracks for the winter.

Could we not have him regularly transferred to the Bureau with a view to his remaining here. I will be greatly embarrassed if I lose him.[18]

On Jan. 4, Sheridan forwarded his recommendation to the Adjutant General's office:

Since the assignment of General Baird as Commissioner of Freedmen for the State of L'a, and the assignment of…Col. Reno as Provost Marshal Gen'l., all officers of strong character, I have noticed a very great improvement in the condition of the freedmen in the state. The white people have confidence in these gentlemen, and freedmen have also, and know that the money received for their benefit is safe, and under their control, will be legitimately expended for the improvement of the Bureau.

Respectfully request that Col. Reno be relieved from compliance with Special Order No. 648, Hdqts. of the Army, dated Dec. 20, 1865, and permitted to remain in his present position.[19]

The Adjutant General's Office didn't agree and on Jan. 17 submitted a request to Lieutenant General Grant: "It would seem that Brevet Colonel M. A. Reno…should have sailed with his regiment, which left New Orleans for the Pacific Coast, Dec. 29, 1865.… The services of Capt. Reno are much needed with his regiment."[20] Grant did not concur and Reno was permitted to remain as the provost marshal for the Freedmen's Bureau.

Among his many duties as provost marshal, Reno was required to assist the military commission with the collection of taxes. This was a onerous task as the locals resented the "Yankees" for supplying the force needed in many instances to collect unpopular taxes. On April 2, Reno sent a secret circular to his subordinates telling them to complete the collection of a tax levied by the Department of the Gulf on the local population by April 20.

Social life for Union forces in New Orleans during this period was limited. The only Southerners who would associate with the army officers were the local politicians, and this provided a small but enthusiastic nucleus for all Union activities. They basically formed their own society and their wives and daughters sewed Union flags, organized "promenade concerts," and held elaborate receptions to which were invited military and administrative personnel. Little contact was made with the general populace on a social basis, and therefore the attitudes of the Union officers tended to sympathize more with the white point of view.

In June, a group of political radicals, whose goal was to enfranchise the blacks for party purposes, planned a session of delegates of the Constitutional Convention of 1864. Although strongly opposed by the governor, General Baird did not attempt to stop the meeting but did place his troops on alert. Reno, as provost marshal, had the duty to muster the necessary forces to protect the army and the citizens of New Orleans against violence. The night before the convention was scheduled, July 30, thousands of blacks paraded through the streets without a major incidence.

The following day, although the Army had been alerted, Baird misunderstood the proposed meeting time — he thought the meeting was to start at 6 in the evening while the Radicals intended it to start at noon. A black crowd, marching to the convention's opening, was met by a white mob at the meeting hall. In the ensuing riot the heavily armed police fired on the blacks. More than 100 blacks were killed and many more injured before Army troops arrived to clear the streets.

Following the riots, New Orleans was an unsettled city: "You know that we union and military men live here rather insecurely in this rebellious riotous city, constantly exposed to the bullet or danger of the assassin."[21]

On Aug. 7, 1866, Baird signed orders relieving Reno from duty at the Freedmen Bureau, and ordering him to report at once to General Howard in Washington, D.C. He was then to await orders which would return him to his regiment on the Pacific Coast.[22] Reno was pleased to be able to move his family away from a city where danger seemed to be constant. Proceeding first to Washington and then to Harrisburg, Reno waited for his new orders. On Aug. 22, he sent a letter to the Adjutant General's Office reporting he was awaiting orders and requested a delay for 90 days. He made the request "on the grounds that I did not receive the delay granted to officers of the Regular Army mustered out of the Volunteer Service, and that I desire to await the result of the reorganization of the Army."[23] Reno received orders granting him 60 days leave before he would join his regiment.

Reno wanted to make good use of his leave. While Mary Hannah and son Ross enjoyed the much quieter and safer life in Harrisburg, Reno visited Washington in hopes of enhancing his military career. He was aware that other Regular Army officers had received promotions in the army's reorganization (Captain George A. Custer had recently been appointed lieutenant colonel of the newly formed 7th U.S. Cavalry) while he was still a captain, a permanent rank he had held for almost five years. Reno arranged an interview with Brigadier General Benjamin Brice, paymaster general of the Army, and was informed several positions were open in the paymaster department which would lead to a promotion to the rank of major.

On Oct. 18, Reno sent a letter to the Adjutant General, stating, "I have the honor to apply for promotion to fill the first vacancy in the Regular Pay Department."[24] On Oct. 25, Brice endorsed the application "the appointment of Bvt. Col. Reno will be entirely satisfactory to me."[25] Reno returned to Harrisburg to await the decision of the secretary of war, but on Nov. 2, he was issued new orders to "report to Brevet Brigadier General Geier, Superintendent Mounted Recruiting Service, Carlisle Barracks, Penna. to accompany a detachment of recruits ordered to the Eighth U.S. Cavalry (by steamer of 21st inst.) to California."

Reno had not received an answer to his transfer request and was unwilling to give up the opportunity for promotion easily. He returned to Washington Nov. 10 and applied "for a further delay of forty days starting to join my Reg't. At this season of the year it will be unpracticable to reach my post (Camp C. F. Smith in Oregon) before the 1st of March."[26] He was granted permission to delay joining his regiment until Dec. 21, 1866.

Returning to Harrisburg, Reno contacted Pennsylvania Governor A. G. Curtin and requested his endorsement for the new position. Curtin wrote directly to the president Dec. 1, stating:

> Understanding that the name of Bvt. Brig. Genl. Marcus A. Reno, has been submitted to your Excellency for appointment in the Pay Dep't. of the Government, I must cheerfully commend him to your favorable consideration as a most worthy gentleman, and gallant soldier — during the late Rebellion he commanded the 12th Regt. Penna. Cavalry, with great credit to himself & efficiency to the Service.[27]

On Dec. 4, Reno wrote directly to the president: "I have served 10 years in the army...5 years in the war — occupying...positions of Company, Regimental, and Brigade Commander. My responsibility financially will be vouched for by the firm of Jay Cooke & Co., my field service by Gen. Grant & my fitness for the position I desire by Gen. Brice, Paymaster Gen."[28] He also solicited an endorsement from former Illinois governor and now Senator Richard Yates. Writing to Secretary of War Stanton, Yates stated: "I respectfully urge upon you the present consideration of this case, and earnestly recommend that his request be granted. I assure you that this mark of favor, which seems justified by the General's distinguished services during the war, will give great satisfaction to a large circle of admiring friends in Illinois, his native state."[29]

It was apparent to Reno that his request for promotion might not be acted on before he was to report to New York for embarkation to the Pacific coast Dec. 21. He requested a delay of another 40 days and on Dec. 12, received permission to wait until Feb. 1, 1867. He would at least enjoy the Christmas holidays with his family in Harrisburg instead of being confined to a steamer making its way toward Panama.

As for the potential promotion in the paymaster's office, Reno was fighting a losing battle. The position would have to be filled by a staff officer and Reno was a line officer. Even a transfer from line to staff, a request made by Senator Yates, would not make him eligible for promotion in the Pay Department. The position would go to the most senior staff captain who had the required knowledge and experience — and Reno could not meet those requirements. In early January 1867, he was informed he was "not eligible for Paymaster."[30]

On Jan. 28, knowing he would now have to return to his regiment, Reno requested new orders from the Adjutant General. Orders were issued Feb. 2 to "report in person to Gen. Butterfield for duty to accompany U.S. detachment of 2nd Artillery recruits to California after which you will join your regiment."[31] Instead of reporting as ordered, Reno telegraphed Butterfield Feb. 6, explaining he wanted to be with his wife who had met with a serious accident and requested a delay until the 17th. The response to his request was not sympathetic — he could delay until the scheduled embarkation in New York of the artillery recruit detachment bound for California.[32]

The coastal steamer for Panama left New York in late February with Reno, Mary Hannah and young son Robert Ross, along with the 2nd Artillery recruits. It was a difficult departure for Mary, just recovering from an accident and again leaving her childhood home for the far reaches of Washington Territory. While the trip to Panama was not necessarily hazardous, it was tedious, especially with a young child. This was the reverse of the trip Reno had made just over five years before.

Reaching Panama in early March and taking the train across the isthmus, Reno and his family boarded another coastal steamer for the trip to San Francisco. There the new recruits would join their regiment, and Reno and his family would await transportation north to Fort Vancouver. Almost a month would be spent in San Francisco before the Pacific mail ship headed north, finally arriving in early May at Fort Vancouver. The fort was located on the north bank of the Columbia River, six miles above its junction with the Willamette River, and about 100 miles from its mouth. Portland was located almost directly across the river and served as a point-of-entry for goods to both the state of Oregon and the territory of Washington.

Portland was described in 1864, as a town where "there is but little in this place yet but in anticipation. It is a sea port town and will in the near future be a great commercial city."[33] By the time the Renos arrived at Fort Vancouver, Portland had grown to about 4,500 and could provide for the needs of the soldiers in both goods and services. While not up to the standards of many eastern towns, Portland offered an active social life for the officers and their wives.

Reno reported to his new duty station May 6, 1867, but because of a recent fire at the fort, he was temporarily housed at one of the small hotels in Portland. He requested quarters at Fort Vancouver and on July 1 received the authorization: "[Y]ou are entitled to quarters at Fort Vancouver, W.T. You are authorized to repair to these quarters whenever in your discretion the interests of the service demand your personal attendance."[34]

The 1st U.S. Cavalry Regiment was commanded by Colonel George A. H. Blake, whom Reno had served with during the Civil War, and Lieutenant Colonel Washington S. Elliott. The regiment had a strength of about 800 men in May 1867.

Instead of joining the regiment, then in the field, Reno was placed on detached service May 9 to serve on a general courts-martial board. He was relieved from the board June 10, and was appointed acting assistant inspector general (AAIG), Department of Columbia, June 22.[35] This was a duty Reno knew he would enjoy — it would give him the opportunity to travel through Oregon and the territories of Washington and Idaho inspecting the facilities, troops and equipment of the Department of Columbia.

Reno made his first extended inspection tour in July to Fort Walla Walla, a fort where he had been stationed six years before. He was back in Portland inspecting mules for the army in August. In October, he began an extended inspection tour with visits to Forts Boise and Lyon, and Camp Three, Fort Owyhee, Idaho Territory.

Reno took his job seriously and prepared reports of his findings for Colonel (Brevet Major General) Frederick Steele, commanding the Department of Columbia. The results of his reports were not always appreciated by the officers where the inspections took place. On Nov. 16, 1867, Captain George K. Brady, 23rd Infantry, stationed at Camp Three, Fort Owyhee, Idaho Territory, filed charges and specifications against Reno. The charge was "Conduct unbecoming an officer and gentleman," with two specifications:

> 1st Reno...did in an official report...[state] that at an inspection...of Camp Three...on or about the ninth day of October 1867, he had asked 1st Lieut. L. R. Shele, Company E...to drill said company in skirmish drill when he...[Reno]...positively knew that he had not asked Lt. L. R. Shele...to do so.
>
> 2nd Reno...did in an official report...[state that he] observed that "none of the officers took any active part in drill," or words to that effect, which statement he knew positively to be false.[36]

Colonel Steele reviewed the report and dismissed the charge.

Continuing in his duty as AAIG, Reno inspected Fort Steilacoom and Camp Steele in November and returned to inspect Fort Vancouver Dec. 17. Although winters were mild in the Northwest, military activity was limited mainly to the areas of the forts. Reno's inspections continued but at a reduced pace. In March 1868, he performed inspections of Forts Stevens, Steele, Disappointment and Vancouver, and on April 27, he was appointed to a general courts-martial board under Lieutenant Colonel (Brevet Colonel) Elwell S. Otis, 22nd Infantry.

Even while stationed in the remote Northwest, Reno still had friends in Illinois who tried to get him promoted. On June 1, 1868, Congressman Ebon C. Ingersoll of Illinois wrote to Secretary of War J. M. Schofield, requesting "that Brevet Colonel M. A. Reno, U.S.A., now on duty at Portland, Oregon, be promoted to the rank of Brigadier General by brevet, U.S.A. Col. Reno is a graduate of West Point and served through the late war with distinction. I refer you to his record in the War Department. He holds the rank of Brigadier General by brevet in the volunteer service."[37] Promotion by brevet, widely used during the Civil War, had fallen into disfavor at this time because of inequities in the system. Only specially established boards could confer brevets and almost no brevets were awarded after 1867.[38] No action was taken on Ingersoll's request.

For the next year Reno would continue his tours of inspection throughout Oregon and the territories of Washington and Idaho. In early February 1869, he was notified that when weather permitted, probably in May, he would proceed to Sitka, Alaska, for general courts-martial duty. Alaska had been formally transferred from Russia to the United States Oct. 18, 1867, in Sitka, and the Army would control the area until replaced by a civil government in 1877. The location of troops in the area required the formation of courts-martial boards from time to time to try the most serious cases.

An event occurred Dec. 26, 1868, at Fort Leavenworth, Kan., that affected Reno's life and military career. Forty-four year old Major (Brevet Major General) Alfred Gibbs, 7th U.S. Cavalry, died, leaving a majority open for the most senior line captain — Captain Marcus Reno. Adjutant General E. D. Townsend wrote April 27, 1869: "Request that as Col. Reno has been promoted Major, vice Gibbs, 7th Cavalry, he be relieved from his present duties and ordered to join his new regiment."[39] A telegram had been sent May 31 from the Adjutant General's office in San Francisco, informing Reno of his promotion and ordering him to report to the Department of the Missouri.[40]

Reno proceeded to Sitka in May, via San Juan Island and Vancouver, W.T., on the steamer *Wright*. He would return to Fort Vancouver in early June and make preparations for his transfer to the 7th Cavalry. Mary Hannah was not overly thrilled by the transfer. Leaving the comforts of decent weather and an active social life at Fort Vancouver and Portland for the hot summer and cold winter of the Kansas plains, with continuing Indian problems, was not exactly what she had in mind for her husband's next duty station.

Endnotes

[1] Record Group 94, Marcus A. Reno, Military File, R314 CB 1865, National Archives & Records Administration (NARA), Washington, DC, Letter from Reno to Thomas, dated July 24, 1865.

[2] Reno Military File, Summary 684 R. 1865.

[3] Reno Military File, Summary 856 R. 1865; Summary 327 R. 1866, Special Orders No. 419, Adjutant General's Office, Aug. 4, 1865.

[4] Reno Military File, Letter to Adjutant General L. Thomas from Reno dated Aug. 20, 1865.

[5] Reno Military File, Summary 856 R. 1865.

[6] Reno Military File, Summary 327 R. 1866, Special Orders 519, Adjutant General's Office, Sept. 29, 1865.

[7] Reno Military File, Summary 856 R. 1865.

[8] Reno Military File, Summary 856 R. 1865

[9] Reno Military File, Letter to Major R. Williams, Assistant Adjutant General, from Reno, dated Oct. 3, 1865.

[10] Howard A. White, *The Freedmen's Bureau in Louisiana* (Louisiana State University Press, Baton Rouge, 1970), p. 3.

[11] White, p. 6.

[12] Senate Executive Documents, 39th Congress, 1st Session, No. 2, pp. 106-08.

[13] Ted Tunnell, *Crucible of Reconstruction, War, Radicalism and Race in Louisiana, 1865-1877* (Louisiana State University Press, Baton Rouge and London), pp. 152-53.

[14] Letter to Major General P. H. Sheridan from A. Baird, dated Dec. 2, 1865, Microcode M1027, Freedmen's Bureau, Louisiana, 1865-66, NARA.

[15] Special Orders No. 122, Extract 14, Headquarters, Military Division of the Gulf, and Circular No. 30 dated Dec. 6.

[16] Microcode M1027, Letter to Reno from General Baird, dated Dec. 26, 1865, NARA.

[17] Record Group No. 105, Record Identification 1344, Letters Sent, 2 Volumes, Numbers 126 and 127.

[18] Letter to Major General O. O. Howard from A. Baird, dated Jan. 3, 1866, Microcopy M1027, Freedmen's Bureau, Louisiana, 1865-66, NARA.

[19] Reno Military File, Summary 22 R. 1866.

[20] Reno Military File, Summary 22 R. 1866.

[21] James E. Sefton, *The United States Army and Reconstruction, 1865-1877* (Louisiana State University Press, Baton Rouge), p. 89. Quote is from quartermaster Captain William B. Armstrong.

[22] Special Orders No. 98, Headquarters, Bureau of Refugees, Freedmen and Abandoned Lands, State of Louisiana, New Orleans, Aug. 7, 1866.

[23] Reno Military File, Special Orders No. 123, Bureau of Refugees, Freedmen and Abandoned Lands, Washington, D.C., dated Aug. 17, 1866; and letter from Reno to the Adjutant General, dated Aug. 22, 1866.

[24] Reno Military File, Summary 491 R. 1866.

[25] Reno Military File, Summary 491 R. 1866.

[26] Reno Military File, Letter from Reno to Assistant Adjutant General, dated Nov. 10, 1866.

[27] Reno Military File, Letter to President Andrew Johnson from Governor A. G. Curtin, dated Dec. 1, 1866.

[28] Reno Military File, Letter to President Andrew Johnson from Reno, dated Dec. 4, 1866.

[29] Reno Military File, Letter to Secretary of War Edwin Stanton from Senator Richard Yates, dated Dec. 8, 1866.

[30] "Not eligible for Paymaster" note in Reno Military File, Executive Summary, dated Oct. 30, 1866.

[31] Reno Military File, Summary 27 R. 1867.

[32] Reno Military File, Summary 44 R. 1867.

[33] Kenneth L. Holmes (ed.), *Covered Wagon Women: Diaries & Letters from the Western Trails 1840-1890*, Volume VIII, 1862-1865 (The Arthur H. Clark Company, Spokane, Wash., 1989), p. 161.

[34] Record Group 393, Volume I, Entry 704, Department of the Columbia, Letters Sent 1866-1869, p. 304.

[35] NARA Record Group 94, 1st U.S. Cavalry Regimental Returns, June 1867, Microcopy M744, Roll 6.

[36] Record Group 393, Volume I, Entry 714, Register of Letters Received, 1866-1902, Department of the Columbia, letter B3, dated Nov. 16, 1867.

[37] Reno Military File, Letter from E. C. Ingersoll to Secretary of War J. M. Schofield, dated June 1, 1868.

[38] James B. Fry, *The History and Legal Effect of Brevets* (D. Van Nostrand, Publisher, New York, 1877), pp. 223-234.

[39] Record Group 393, Volume I, Entry 714, letter A17, dated April 27, 1869.

[40] Record Group 393, Volume I, Entry 714, telegram P56, dated May 31, 1869.

• 6 •

Joining the 7th Cavalry

Following the Civil War the Federal Government became increasingly concerned about the situation developing on the Western frontier. During the war, while the Regular Army was involved with fighting in the East, Indians in the West had taken advantage of the lack of control and dominated many areas. Attacks by the Sioux were common in Minnesota and the Dakotas, the Apaches were the scourge of the Arizona and New Mexico territories, Utes and Bannocks plundered in Idaho territory, Comanches operated freely in the Texas area, and even the normally quiet Navajos were on the warpath in New Mexico.

The small detachments of army personnel stationed along the western frontier had little chance of controlling the Indians and in many cases were not even able to prevent attacks upon themselves. The duty of the Army was to protect the immigrants and settlers on the western plains and the need for additional troops to be stationed in the West, especially cavalry units, was obvious.

When the Civil War began, Congress had authorized only six regular U.S. Army cavalry regiments — the 1st through the 6th. During the war the cavalry's role had been mainly fulfilled by volunteer regiments from various states. When these units were mustered out following Appomattox, Congress recognized the need for additional cavalry units and under the Act of July 28, 1866, authorized four new cavalry regiments — the 7th through the 10th. The 7th and 8th U.S. Cavalry regiments were to be composed of white soldiers, the 9th and 10th by Negro soldiers with white officers.

Under orders from the Military Department of the Missouri and the War Department, the organization of the 7th U. S. Cavalry began in September 1866, at Fort Riley, Kan.[1] By the end of September, the enlisted strength of the regiment was 882. The regiment's senior major, Major (Brevet Major General) Alfred Gibbs, was the first officer to report to Fort Riley and Lieutenant Colonel (Brevet Major General) George A. Custer joined Nov. 3, 1866. The commanding officer, Colonel (Brevet Major General) Andrew J. Smith, reported Nov. 26, 1866. By late November, the regiment was scattered over a wide area of Colorado and Kansas — companies were stationed at Forts Lyon and Morgan in Colorado Territory and Forts Riley, Hays, Harker, Wallace and Dodge in Kansas.[2]

Most of the regiment was in the field in 1867 under command of Lieutenant Colonel Custer. Frequent scouting expeditions were made in an attempt to maintain peace in an area of Kansas where marauding bands of Sioux and Cheyenne were known to be operating. Running fights with the Indians were recorded throughout the summer without significant results.

Various skirmishes between the Indians and detachments of the 7th Cavalry occurred during 1868. The most significant fight occurred Nov. 27, when the entire regiment, under the command of Custer, attacked the Cheyenne village of Black Kettle, located on the Washita River in Indian Territory in what is now northwest Oklahoma. The 7th Cavalry lost 21 men and the Indian losses were more than 100 killed and 53 captured.

The winter campaign against the Indians continued into early 1869 when elements of the regiment pursued bands of Cheyenne throughout Indian Territory.[3] Months in the field and cold weather took their toll on the men during this period and by the time the regiment returned to their winter stations in April, almost two-thirds of the soldiers were dismounted.[4] The regiment's effective strength was diminished considerably but the campaign was considered successful. The Cheyennes had returned to their reservation and continued expeditions by the 7th Cavalry into Indian Territory were no longer necessary. No further regimental operations took place during the rest of the year, but each of the companies conducted scouting expeditions to protect settlers in western Kansas.

Reno completed his duties as the acting assistant inspector general for the Department of the Columbia at Portland, Oregon, June 15, 1869. He had been ordered to report to Headquarters, Department of the Missouri at Fort Leavenworth, Kan., and his permanent duty station would be at Fort Hays. Reno received 30 days leave, starting June 18, and proceeded with Mary Hannah and son Ross to his new duty station.

Using both his leave and travel time, Reno reported to Fort Leavenworth July 28 and received verbal permission to delay at that post until Aug. 23. Even before officially joining the 7th Cavalry, Reno found himself in a conflict with one of the regiments officers, Major (Brevet Colonel) Lewis Merrill. The controversy was a result of both men wanting an apparently available staff assignment in the Adjutant General's Office in Washington. Major Samuel F. Chalfin, assigned to the Adjutant General's office, had proposed to resign, and both Merrill and Reno wrote to the adjutant general, General Edward D. Townsend, suggesting that each be allowed to transfer to the staff position before Chalfin's resignation. The law provided that if no one were assigned to the position prior to Chalfin's resignation, it would disappear. Reno suggested that "the position should not be vacated permanently as it would be were he [Chalfin] to resign but that a transfer would save an officer to the Department."[5] Conflict between the two officers continued for a month before Townsend finally decided that neither man would receive the transfer and the position disappeared when Chalfin resigned. This produced a strained relationship between the two that would be further aggravated in their next assignments.

On Aug. 23, Reno was assigned to detached service at

Major Marcus Reno
Joining the 7th Cavalry (circa 1870)

Santa Fe, New Mexico Territory, to serve on a general courts-martial board.[6] Again Reno and his family were on the move without sufficient time to get settled at any one location. Getting his family settled in Santa Fe would also prove to be difficult. Reno had not served at any post in the Department of Missouri since reporting and therefore was unable to draw commutations of fuel and quarters. In September, he wrote to Townsend asking him to resolve the situation.[7] Reno was finally assigned quarters and his family remained with him in Santa Fe while he served on the courts-martial board.

The general courts-martial board met Sept. 10 under its president, Colonel (Brevet Major General) George W. Getty, 3rd U.S. Infantry. The judge advocate was the 7th Cavalry officer with whom Reno had recently developed an adversarial relationship — Major Lewis Merrill. Ten cases were brought before the board during the next several months. One would cause controversy for years and would produce infighting among 7th Cavalry officers, including Custer, Reno, Merrill and Colonel (Brevet Major General) Samuel D. Sturgis.[8] The controversial case concerned Captain Samuel B. Lauffer's conduct at Fort Wingate, New Mexico Territory, in July 1869, while Lauffer was the assistant quartermaster at that post. Lauffer was accused of using a false affidavit concerning the loss of an Army mule for which he had responsibility. The affidavit, from a government employee, supposedly explained the loss of the mule. Lauffer's commanding officer, Major (Brevet Colonel) Andrew W. Evans, 3rd Cavalry, thought otherwise and had Lauffer arrested and brought charges against him.

Lauffer was judged not guilty by the court of the charges and specifications but a question arose after the trial as to whether Merrill had been paid by Lauffer to not prosecute the case vigorously. Later Lauffer accused Merrill of accepting money from him and, although he pursued his allegations at length, no further action was ever taken. Reno also indicated later that "the prosecution was not prosecuted with energy & that documentary evidence in the case was suppressed by Maj. Merrill."[9]

Members of the court completed their tasks by Nov. 28, at which time Reno received a 20-day leave before reporting to Fort Hays. This provided him with sufficient time to again move his family the almost 500 miles to his new post. On Dec. 19, Reno reported to the post that would be his permanent duty station for the next 16 months. His family would finally have a opportunity to settle down for at least a short period of time.

Fort Hays had been established June 22, 1867, in central Kansas, about a quarter of a mile from Big Creek, a branch of the Smoky Hill fork of the Kansas River. Hays City, which was a half mile from the fort, contained a post office, telegraph office, railroad station (Kansas Pacific Railroad), and various commercial enterprises, including the ever present saloons. Fort Leavenworth was 289 miles to the east by railroad from Hays City.

The surrounding country was not very adaptable for farming and most attempts to raise crops had been unsuccessful. Timber, consisting mainly of elm and cottonwood, proved to be scarce and was found only along the water courses. The climate for that part of Kansas was "dry, and very changeable, with extremes of heat and cold; strong winds prevail the greater part of the year. Average temperature about 48 degrees Fahrenheit."[10]

The commanding officer of Fort Hays when Reno arrived was Major (Brevet Lieutenant Colonel) George Gibson, 5th U.S. Infantry. Two companies of the 7th Cavalry were in winter quarters there: Company G under the command of 1st Lieutenant Edward Law, and Company H under the command of Captain (Brevet Colonel) Frederick W. Benteen. Companies E and G of the 5th Infantry and Company D of the 3rd Infantry were also stationed at Hays for the winter. A total of 358 men were on station as of the end of December 1869.[11]

Constant military action in the field for the previous year and a half had significantly reduced the threat of major Indian attacks. Scattered bands of Indians operated along the Solomon, Saline and Lower Republican Rivers, and settlements in those area were constantly threatened. In 1870, most of the companies of the 7th Cavalry would be used in the field independently and operations by the full regiment would not be necessary. Field service of this type was extremely difficult for the troopers. Long, weary marches were made in pursuit of Indians with the results being either a minor skirmish lasting only long enough for the Indians to escape or, as was the majority of cases, no Indians being sighted at all.

On Feb. 4, 1870, Colorado Governor Edward M. McCook wrote to Major General John M. Schofield at St. Louis, Mo., requesting "at least one battalion of four companies of Cavalry be stationed in this Territory during the coming Spring."[12] In McCook's opinion, the companies stationed there in 1869 had "preserved peace within the borders of Colorado; the first peace we have had for ten years."[13] The governor wanted the troops early in the spring and he reflected the feeling of many settlers in the area when he stated that if the Indians "do make any difficulty the War may be short, sharp and decisive, and that those who make trouble, may learn a lesson which will not be forgotten by their tribe in this generation."[14] On Feb. 8, Kansas Governor James M. Harvey reflected similar thoughts in a letter to General Schofield: "[S]end some troops to the frontier, and urge upon the president the adoption of the Indian policy we talked of last summer — i.e., forcing them, dismounted and disarmed, upon their reservations, and holding them there by military power" and "the troops be sent out now."[15] The governor was concerned about settlers along the frontier, for he saw the Indians as "roving bands who are ever watching an opportunity for the perpetration of their horrible deeds."[16]

The Kansas Pacific Railroad, which had been completed to Kit Carson, Colorado Territory, the previous fall, wanted to continue laying track toward Denver and to complete the 150 miles between Kit Carson and Denver by September. KPRR General Superintendent A. Anderson was aware of the dangers of Indian attacks along the rail line and requested 10,000 rounds of .58 caliber Springfield Rifle ammunition from General Schofield for issuance to the railway employees.[17] Anderson also requested 100 breech loading rifles and 5,000 rounds of ammunition for use by the command of General William J. Palmer at Sheridan, Kan. He wanted the rifles for "protection of the men engaged in building and taking care of the track of the KPRR west of

Sheridan." Anderson thought the arms would "be returned within thirty days."[18] The short duration of conflict that Anderson expected was to drag on throughout the summer of 1870.

On Feb. 18, Company G, under the command of 2nd Lieutenant Charles DeRudio, left Fort Hays to establish a camp on the South Fork of the Solomon River. Other 7th Cavalry companies were in the field during this period scouting for Indians but no encounters were recorded.[19]

Orders were issued from Schofield's headquarters to provide arms to the employees of the KPRR from Fort Harker, Kan., for defense against the Indians. Small infantry detachments would be used to protect working parties, and other measures of defense would be taken.[20]

At Fort Hays, Reno had not given up hopes of being transferred to the Adjutant General's Office in Washington. Duty in that city would certainly be more comfortable than Fort Hays and Mary Hannah and young Ross would be able to visit her parents and relatives regularly in Harrisburg. Reno wrote to General Townsend March 13, "to recall that I am an applicant for a position in your Department fearing that my application may have passed from your mind."[21] Reno was aware that a bill had been introduced in Congress which would provide additional openings on the Adjutant General's staff. However, the bill failed and no transfers were available.

Crowded housing conditions continued at Fort Hays and Reno was concerned with what might happen to his family's living quarters while he was on service in the field. In a letter to Colonel William G. Mitchell, acting assistant adjutant general, Department of the Missouri, Reno requested that the policy concerning families of officers on detached service be clarified, i.e., would the officer's family be able to "hold their quarters, draw fuel, etc." or would they be forced to move and be "at the mercy of a momentary whim of a Commanding Officer."[22] Assistant Adjutant General George L. Hartsuff, replying for Lieutenant General Sheridan, provided the policy: "Service in the field during the summer season by either cavalry or infantry must be considered as detached and special. The post they go from are their permanent post. All the rights and privileges pertaining to a permanent garrison are theirs while so detached."[23]

Reno assumed command of Fort Hays March 15, 1870, when Major Gibson went on leave. Gibson returned April 1, but was sent to a court of inquiry at Fort Harker April 20, and Reno again commanded the post. Sometime during this period, Reno had a confrontation with Benteen at the fort's trading post. Both men were normally moderate drinkers, but had been drinking heavily, and apparently Reno attempted to "bully" Benteen. Benteen defiantly addressed his superior as a "dirty SOB" and offered him further "satisfaction" which Reno declined. No further action occurred and, although the

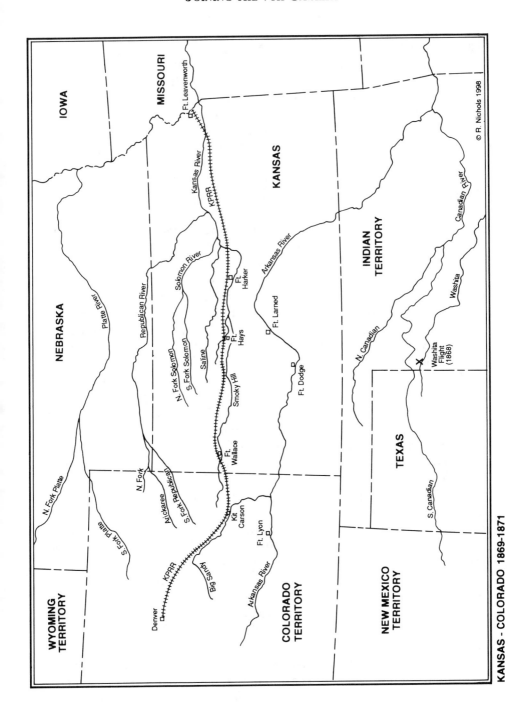

KANSAS - COLORADO 1869-1871

two men were never good friends, they at least maintained a formal military relationship while on duty. Following this tour of duty, their paths would not cross again until Fort Lincoln, Dakota Territory, in late 1875.[24]

By mid-April, Indian activities had increased significantly and settlements along the Kansas frontier were being threatened. A May 2 telegram from Reno, still commanding Fort Hays, to Colonel (Brevet Major General) Nelson A. Miles at Fort Harker informed Miles that a dispatch had been received from Kansas Governor Harvey, stating "great numbers of Indians reported on Solomon above Asheville threatening the settlement. Inform Tilford [Major (Brevet Lieutenant Colonel) Joseph G. Tilford]."[25] Reno replied to Harvey, "Dispatch received and sent to Col. Tilford commanding on Solomon. All the cavalry sent from this post."[26] Remaining at Hays were Companies E and G, 5th Infantry, and a small detachment of men from Company H, 7th Cavalry.

In mid-May, Custer, moving from his winter quarters at Fort Leavenworth, established a cavalry camp of six companies on Big Creek, about two miles from Fort Hays. He assumed command of Fort Hays from Reno and during the next several weeks dispatched detachments to the extreme settlements along the Saline, Solomon, and Lower Republican Rivers. The detachments made numerous scouts from their camps along the river courses, forcing most of the Indians out of the area and reestablishing peace along the Kansas frontier.

During this same period Colorado Governor McCook again wrote to General Schofield (McCook was not aware that General Pope had taken over the Department of the Missouri as of April 15) requesting a squadron or battalion of cavalry be sent into Colorado to protect the settlements. Indians were raiding working parties along the KPRR. The road was being graded and rail laid west of Kit Carson and a large force of laborers were distributed along the line.

On May 14, Lieutenant Colonel (Brevet Brigadier General) Charles R. Woods, 5th Infantry, commanding Fort Wallace, received a dispatch from the president of the Kansas Pacific Railroad: "Indians two hundred strong attacked train four miles east of Lake Station [C.T.]." Twelve men were killed in this raid and more than 300 head of stock driven off by the Indians. Woods immediately ordered Company E, 7th Cavalry, which was already in the field in Colorado, to pursue the attackers, and dispatched Company C, 7th Cavalry, by rail from Fort Wallace to Kit Carson. On the 15th, Woods telegraphed General Pope at departmental headquarters in St. Louis, informing him of the action he had taken.

Following another Indian attack May 15, at a water tank five miles west of Kit Carson, Company C was sent toward the Republican River in pursuit of the attackers. They were not successful in catching the Indians responsible for the raid and returned to Fort Wallace May 31. Company E, also unsuccessful in capturing the Indians that perpetrated the May 14 attack, remained in the field and continued its scouting activities along the KPRR.

When the news of these raids reached Pope, he directed Woods to take charge of the region along the railroad from Fort Wallace to Denver and to transfer his headquarters to some point between those places. Woods was given the service of companies from Wallace, Lyon and Reynolds and was to be reinforced with two cavalry companies from Fort Hays and one infantry company from Fort Larned.[27] Woods maintained his headquarters temporarily at Fort Wallace and ordered his infantry force to maintain a presence along the line of the railroad between Fort Wallace and Kit Carson.

General Pope reported to the secretary of war he thought the May 14 "raid was no doubt due to the gross carelessness of the working parties along the railroad. They were distributed along forty miles of the road without arms or preparation of any kind and their...utter neglect of every precaution...offered an irresistible temptation to the Indians."[28] The arms and ammunition requested earlier by Superintendent Anderson were either not received by the railroad, or if received, were not distributed to the workers.

A local Denver newspaper expressed the feelings of many Colorado Territory residents in an article published May 18. Under the title "Troops on the March," the paper said in part, discussing the 7th Cavalry:

> The 7th is one of the finest regiments in the service, gained a gallant reputation at Washita, and will follow Indians to the death when let loose. Gen. Pope, the new commander of the department will take vigorous measures to pursue and punish those murdering copper-colored devils.[29]

This was also the feeling expressed by General Sherman in a telegram to Pope: "The most energetic measures possible should be made to hunt down and destroy that party of Indians that made the attack [May 15] on the Railroad on the Sandy [River]. No Indian should be allowed respite between the two Railroads."[30]

On May 23, Reno was ordered to report to Colonel Woods at Kit Carson where he had moved his field headquarters. Woods believed that the Indians responsible for the attacks on the railroad had their village somewhere on the headwaters of the Republican River. During the previous winter, whenever Indians would make their appearance on the line of the KPRR and were pursued by the Army, their trail always led in a northwest direction toward the headwaters of the Republican.[31]

Woods had sent Companies B, C and L, 7th Cavalry, to the area of the Republican where he suspected the Indian villages were located and hoped to be able to break them up and drive them from the country, or to at least keep them so busy that they would have no time to trouble the railroad. Woods wanted not only to punish the Indians but to recover the stock stolen by them during their raids.[32] Two companies (B & L) returned to Kit Carson May 28 and Company C returned to Fort Wallace May 31.[33] The expedition had been hindered by the lack of competent guides and was unable to find any Indian villages.

On June 1, Colonel Miles reported from Fort Harker:

> Guards stationed along the KPRR report that parties of Indians numbering from 50 to 300 have been seen crossing the track going north in the last 24 hours. Also that Indian trails leading in the same direction indicating that a considerable body of Indians have passed north, and are evidently in the vicinity of the Solomon and Republican Rivers.[34]

Reno had left Fort Hays early on the morning of May 25 and reported to Woods at Kit Carson later that same day. For the next week, he was active in gathering the necessary supplies for an extended expedition against the Indians. Woods reported:

> Col. Reno with three companies, "B," "H," and "L," 7th Cavalry, and one company of infantry to guard the train, left this point on Thursday the 2nd inst. for Headwaters of the Republican with 20 days rations and forage to last his command 30 days, if necessary. On Friday the 3rd inst. I sent Capt. Plummer with "C" Company, 7th Cavalry, to join Col. Reno. This will give Col. Reno four [companies] of cavalry and he can cut loose from his train at any time. All Indians that have crossed the R.R. seem to strike in the direction where Col. Reno's command now is, and I think he will be able to strike them, as his horses will be strong and in good condition, whilst the Indian ponies will be more or less jaded.[35]

Pope reported to General Hartsuff, "There are between two and three hundred Indians believed to be Cheyennes now on the Republican and headwaters of Saline and Solomon. Custer with six companies of cavalry is moving westward and Reno with four companies eastward along the courses of those streams, and must in a few days settle the question."[36]

Reno moved his command due north from Kit Carson and on June 5, struck the headwaters of the South Fork of the Republican River. A scouting party was sent up the South Fork but found no Indians. The command proceeded north to the Arickaree and found signs where Indians had camped several weeks before. A supply camp was established at the junction of the South Fork of the Republican and the Arickaree from which scouting parties could be sent. Reno moved his cavalry to Beaver Creek and saw many Indians signs and found the two-week-old remnants of a large village of 200 to 300 Indians.[37]

Reno's command did not have experienced guides or "trailers" and he had to depend on his own judgment and the ability of "green" soldiers to find the Indians. Numerous scouting parties were sent out in the Beaver Creek area trying to determine where the Indians had gone. On June 13, three Indians were discovered and pursued for more than 10 miles before they eluded the soldiers. Other Indians were sighted but were too far off to give chase. On the night of the 13th Reno's command camped on the Republican and at midnight he moved his command "silently" down the river hoping to strike the Indian camp — but was not successful.[38]

He remained in camp on the Republican and sent many scouting patrols to search for the Indian trail. A trail was discovered on the 15th and Reno immediately broke camp, and with two days rations, started at midnight in pursuit. The command marched more than 60 miles in 20 hours and passed many abandoned Indian camps, but was unable to catch the Indians. He was satisfied they were Cheyenne, Sioux and a few Arapahoes, who were aware he was chasing them. At the last camp, he found the Indians had abandoned their village only a short time before, leaving all of their lodge poles behind, and had moved toward the South Platte River. Reno determined that the Indians had the capability to move 50 miles in a single day when being pursued, and therefore his command had little chance of catching them before they crossed the Platte.[39]

On the 18th, Reno returned with his command to the supply camp that had been established on the Republican. Rations were getting short and the horses and mules required shoeing so he decided to return to Fort Wallace. In his opinion the morale of his officers and men was good and they "seemed anxious to be brought to within striking distance of the Indians and…that the endurance of horse & man was put to the utmost" in an attempt to bring the Indians to battle.[40] In Reno's opinion the lack of experienced guides and trailers with his command enabled the Indians to escape across the Platte. The command returned to Fort Wallace on the 22nd after covering more than 470 miles in 20 days of exploration.[41]

99

Indian attacks had continued near Kit Carson and on June 21, Woods ordered one company of cavalry from Reno's command to immediately move into his area. He planned to keep it near Kit Carson until the railroad reached Lake Station.[42] Woods also planned to have Reno's command refitted for further field service when the command returned to Fort Wallace.[43] He personally went to Wallace to expedite the fitting of Reno's companies, and he wanted to send the command first to Kit Carson, then to River Bend, and to use that location as a central staging point for the companies to protect the KPRR.[44] As of June 29, the KPRR had been completed to a point 27 miles west of Kit Carson, and 123 miles east of Denver.[45]

Reno's command, consisting of Companies B, H, and L, completing preparations for field service, marched out of Fort Wallace June 29 and moved down along the railroad line, arriving at Kit Carson July 2. His command was immediately dispatched by Woods along the KPRR line to Willow Springs, about 45 miles northwest of Kit Carson, and then to River Bend, 20 miles farther. They arrived at River Bend on the 6th and Companies H and L proceeded toward Denver, arriving there on the 12th. The local newspaper reported:

> A detachment...arrived here yesterday afternoon.... The officers of the command are Brevet Col. M. L. Reno (sic), Major 7th Cavalry commanding detachment; Brevet Col. F. W. Benteen, Captain commanding H Company; Lieut. H. H. Abell, commanding L Company.... The command is from River Bend here and is a part of the force which has been scouting the country about the head of the Republican. They will remain here until tomorrow. The 7th is a favorite regiment; has done gallant service on the plains, and its officers and men are always welcome to Denver.[46]

Returning to River Bend July 16, Reno set up a permanent supply camp from which scouting expeditions would be sent to guard the KPRR as rail was laid toward Denver. The railroad had been completed to Willow Springs July 11. Companies B, C and E were at River Bend when Reno returned with Companies H and L on the 16th, thus giving Reno command of five cavalry companies. All five companies continued scouting expeditions along the KPRR during the next six weeks and Indian activity was almost non-existent.[47]

Near Fort Hays, Custer retained six companies of the 7th Cavalry and everything remained so quiet along the Kansas frontier that Custer failed to file any reports with General Pope about the conditions in the vicinity of Fort Hays. In a long rambling letter dated July 14, Custer explains that he had made no reports "to you for the reason that there had been a lull in Indian movements and nothing has occurred deserving mention." Custer had apparently been reprimanded by Pope for not filing reports for he replied:

> I have earnestly endeavored at all times to keep you thoroughly informed of events transpiring within the limits of my command and I feel confident that I have neglected to report nothing which you would have desired to know.... I have endeavored to be particularly zealous and prompt regarding the transmission of all reliable Indian intelligence.... Hereafter I will forward, at least once a week, a report — by mail — of the situation embraced in my command, with special report — by telegraph — of anything urgent or particularly important.[48]

It was to be a leisurely summer for Mary Hannah and Ross. Although conditions were crowded at Fort Hays, Reno was the second ranking officer assigned there so the Renos at least enjoyed separate quarters. Other officers' wives provided the opportunity for Mary Hannah to socialize with women whose husbands were in the same situation — in the field chasing Indians. The women whose company Mary Hannah enjoyed that summer included Elizabeth Custer (the Custers maintained quarters both at the fort and the cavalry camp on Big Creek), Kate Benteen, Margaret Custer (who later would marry 1st Lieutenant James Calhoun), Sarah Brewster, Eliza DeRudio, Fannie Gibson, and Annie Gibson Roberts (who would later marry Captain George Yates). The women enjoyed talking, sewing and just each other's company — the opportunities to do much else were limited. Mary Hannah even participated in a buffalo hunt with the other women and some of the officers stationed in the area. Son Ross also attended and it is evident that he acted just like any 6-year-old boy — Annie Roberts described him as "enfant ter-r-rrible."[49] Although some of their husbands were not on the best of terms with each other, the wives apparently got along well together. Mary Hannah seemed to enjoy socializing with both Libbie Custer and Kate Benteen and there is no evidence of friction between them.[50]

In Colorado, scouting by troopers of Reno's command in the area of River Bend revealed no Indian activity along the railroad and progress continued on the line toward Denver. In August, the most excitement at River Bend was caused by a severe hailstorm on the 6th which scattered the mule herd and most of the horses of the three companies camped there, leaving only 10 horses in the whole command. It would be more than a week before the horses and mules were rounded up.

Without harassment from the Indians, the KPRR workers moved forward rapidly and, on Aug. 16, the railroad was completed to Denver from St. Louis. In the future, this line would facilitate the movement of the army in their continual conflict with renegade Indians in western Kansas and eastern Colorado.

On Aug. 9, orders were issued placing Reno on detached service at Fort Leavenworth.[51] He was ordered to report for duty on the Retirement Board by Aug. 25, which allowed him sufficient time to stop at Fort Hays for a few days to visit his family. Reno reported to Fort Leavenworth on the 25th but hardly had time to settle into his quarters before he was summoned back to River Bend to testify before a courts-martial board Sept. 7.[52] Following the court session, he returned to Leavenworth where he remained on detached service for the next five months. During his service on the retirement board, Reno was able to return occasionally to Fort Hays to visit his family.

Companies of the 7th Cavalry remained in the field for the next several months at River Bend and near Fort Hays with little Indian activity reported. This lack of activity was attributed to the continual presence of troops in the field, and many of the choice targets of Indian raiding parties had disappeared with the completion of the railroad. At year's end, the soldiers were in their winter quarters in Kansas at or near Forts Leavenworth (six companies), Harker (two companies), Wallace (one company), and Hays (two companies), and in Colorado Territory at Fort Lyon (one company).

Completing his detached service at Leavenworth Feb. 7, 1871, Reno returned to Fort Hays and took command of the two cavalry companies on station there: Company H commanded by Benteen, and Company M commanded by Captain Thomas H. French. Total number of cavalry troopers at the fort was 145.[53]

In early 1871, the 7th Cavalry was notified that it would be transferred from the Department of the Missouri to the Department of the South to enforce post-Civil War reconstruction laws. The regiment was to be scattered extensively over the south with smaller towns being occupied by detachments of troops to assist U.S. marshals in arresting law violators. The regiment would remain on this duty until the spring of 1873 when its companies would be reunited to participate in the Yellowstone Campaign of that year.

Company G, under command of 1st Lieutenant Donald McIntosh, arrived at Hays April 18, and Reno assumed command of Fort Hays April 29, 1871, with the departure of Major Gibson. Reno was also appointed acting assistant inspector general for the Department of the Missouri, an assignment which would be short lived. On May 24, Reno and the four companies of the 7th Cavalry left Fort Hays for their newly assigned posts in the Department of the South. Only two companies of the 5th Infantry remained at the post.[54]

Endnotes

[1] Special Order No. 2, Headquarters, Department of the Missouri, Aug. 27, 1866. General Order No. 92, War Department, Adjutant General's Office, Washington, Nov. 23, 1866.

[2] Melbourne C. Chandler, *Of Garry Owen in Glory, The History of the Seventh United States Cavalry Regiment* (The Turnpike Press, Inc., Annandale, Va., 1960), pp. 2-3.

[3] Chandler, p. 29; Troop L returned to Fort Lyon, Colorado Territory, on Feb. 19. It should also be noted here that cavalry "companies" became "troops" starting about October 1868. They would be redesignated "companies" prior to the 1876 campaign against the Sioux and Cheyenne Indians. However for consistency I've decided to use "companies" throughout the text.

[4] Chandler, p. 29.

[5] Letter from M. A. Reno to Gen. E. D. Townsend, Fort Leavenworth, Kan., Aug. 13, 1869, Reno File, National Archives & Records Administration (NARA).

[6] Special Orders No. 152; Headquarters Department of the Missouri, Fort Leavenworth, Kan., Aug. 23, 1869.

[7] Letter from M. A. Reno to Gen. E. D. Townsend, September 1869, Reno File, NARA.

[8] Colonel Andrew J. Smith was on detached service from Feb. 26, 1867, until his resignation on May 6, 1869. Sturgis was appointed colonel of the 7th Cavalry as of that date.

[9] For an excellent dissertation on this subject see: *Custer, Reno, Merrill and the Lauffer Case, Some Warfare in "The Fighting Seventh"* by Barry C. Johnson, The English Westerners' Society Brand Book for July 1970 (Vol. 12, No. 4) and October 1970 (Vol. 13, No. 1).

[10] *Outline Descriptions of the Posts in the Military Division of the Missouri; Headquarters Military Division of the Missouri*, Chicago, Illinois, 1876; pp. 127-130.

[11] Returns from U.S. Military Posts 1800-1916, Fort Hays, Kan., December 1870; Microcopy No. 617, Roll 469; NARA (Hereafter Post Returns).

[12] Letter from Governor Edward M. McCook to General J. W. Schofield, dated Feb. 4, 1870, Record Group 393, Volume 1, Series 2601, Department of the Missouri Letters Received, 1870, NARA. (Hereafter RG393 - Letters).

[13] McCook Letter.

[14] McCook Letter.

[15] Letter from Governor James M. Harvey to General J. M. Schofield, dated Feb. 8, 1870, RG393 - Letters.

[16] Harvey Letter; RG393 - Letters.

[17] Letter from A. Anderson to General J. M. Schofield, dated Feb. 22, 1870, RG393 - Letters.

[18] Letter from A. Anderson to General J. M. Schofield, dated Feb. 24, 1870, RG393 - Letters.

[19] Post Returns; Fort Hays, Kan., February 1870.

[20] *Rocky Mountain News*, Denver, Colo., March 2, 1870.

[21] Letter from Major M. A. Reno to General E. D. Townsend, dated March 13, 1870, Reno File, NARA.

[22] Letter from Major M. A. Reno to Colonel W. G. Mitchell, dated March 14, 1870, Reno File, NARA.

[23] Reno Letter.

[24] Charles K. Mills, *Harvest of Barren Regrets, The Army Career of Frederick William Benteen, 1834 - 1898* (The Arthur H. Clark Co., Glendale, Calif., 1985), pp. 196-199.

[25] Telegram from Major M. A. Reno to Colonel N. A. Miles, dated May 2, 1870, RG 393 - Letters.

[26] Telegram from Major M. A. Reno to Governor J. Harvey, dated May 2, 1870, Record Group 393, Letters Sent; Fort Hays, Kan., Part V, Vol. 2 of 18.

[27] Report of the Secretary of War, Report of General John Pope, Headquarters Department of the Missouri, Fort Leavenworth, Kan., Oct. 31, 1870.

[28] Report of General John Pope.

[29] *Rocky Mountain News*, Denver, Colo., May 18, 1870.

[30] Telegram from General W. T. Sherman to General John Pope, dated May 18, 1870, RG 393 - Letters.

[31] Letter to General John Pope from C. R. Woods, dated May 25, 1870, RG 393 - Letters.

[32] Pope Letter; RG 393 - Letters.

[33] Letter from C. R. Woods to Lieutenant Henry Jackson, dated May 28, 1870, RG 393 - Letters.

[34] Letter from Colonel Nelson A. Miles to the Asst. Adjutant General, Department of the Missouri, dated June 1, 1870, RG 393 - Letters.

[35] Letter from General Charles R. Woods to Lieutenant Henry Jackson, dated June 7, 1870, RG 393 - Letters.

[36] Letter from General John Pope to General George L. Hartsuff, dated June 6, 1870; Record Group 94, Microfile M619, Roll 802, Letters Received, Dept. of the Missouri, 1870, NARA.

[37] Letter from M. A. Reno to Lieut. J. M. Johnson, dated June 22, 1870, RG 393 - Letters. This letter is Reno's report on the entire scouting expedition from the time his command left Kit Carson on June 2 to his return to Fort Wallace on June 22.

[38] Reno scout.

[39] Reno scout.

[40] Reno scout.

[41] Reno scout.

[42] There are two letters from C. R. Woods to Lieutenant Henry Jackson, dated June 21, 1870 on this same subject, RG 393- Letters.

[43] Letter from C. R. Woods to Lieutenant Henry Jackson, dated June 17, 1870, RG 393 - Letters.

[44] Letter from C. R. Woods to Lieutenant Henry Jackson, dated June 23, 1870, RG 393 - Letters.

[45] *Rocky Mountain News*, Denver, Colo., June 29, 1870.

[46] *Rocky Mountain News*, Denver, Colo., July 13, 1870.

[47] *Rocky Mountain News*, Denver, Colo., Aug. 3, 1870.

[48] Letter from G. A. Custer to General Pope, dated July 14, 1870, RG 393 - Letters.

[49] Brian Pohanka, *A Summer on the Plains, 1870 - From the Diary of Annie Gibson Roberts* (J. M. Carroll & Co., Mattituck, N.Y., 1983), p. 30. This is an enjoyable book that provides a snapshot of life at Fort Hays during the summer of 1870.

[50] Pohanka, p. 24.

[51] Special Orders No. 194, Adjutant General's Office, Aug. 9, 1870, NARA.

[52] Letter from Lieutenant Charles Brewster to the Asst. Adjutant General, dated Sept. 13, 1870, RG 393 - Letters.

[53] Post Returns, Fort Hays, Kan., November 1870 to May 1871, NARA.

[54] Post Returns, Fort Hays, Kan., April 1871 to May 1871, NARA

The Army, the Klan and the Guns of '76

At the conclusion of the Civil War, the 11 former Confederate states awaited readmission to the Union. Resources for rebuilding in the South were limited and thousands of white refugees roamed the land along with almost 4 million displaced blacks. While the Southerners had an economic resource in land, they lacked the capital to work the land. Many southerners feared the displaced blacks would be unwilling to work and that would produce a continuing stagnate economy. This fear would soon be dispelled by the willingness of the blacks to return to fields, and while being employed under terms decided by the Southerners, at least some labor force was available. White Southerners were both apprehensive and displeased about the role the blacks would play in the rebuilding of the South. In South Carolina the state's General Assembly passed the "Black Code of 1865" which restricted the freedom of the former slaves.[1]

The process of restoration of the Confederate states to the Union was hotly debated in Congress during the spring and summer of 1865. President Andrew Johnson, having succeeded the assassinated Abraham Lincoln, was viewed as having more firm views than Lincoln about how the process should work. Johnson stated, "They must not only be punished, but their social power must be destroyed."[2] The next 12 years, known as the Period of Reconstruction, would bring harsh reprisals to those Southerners who, in the federal view, did not act accordingly to the rules of the newly established civil governments. Nothing more offended the conquered South than the sight of Union troops, especially black soldiers, occupying their cities and towns. The Army's presence and influence was considered "very pernicious everywhere, and without exception" — even worse than defeat in battle.[3]

Congress agreed with President Johnson and decided that the former states had to be punished for the insurrection, especially South Carolina, the first state to secede from the Union Dec. 20, 1860. The Reconstruction Act of 1867, proposed by radical Republicans, disenfranchised many of the best citizens of the state and enfranchised blacks without regard to their education or fitness to exercise the right of suffrage.[4] With about 60 percent of South

Carolina's population black, whites feared their way of life would be significantly changed and even considered that the recently emancipated slaves might retaliate against their former owners.[5] The election of carpetbagger Richard K. Scott as governor of South Carolina in 1867 was a foregone conclusion, as were many of the seats in the state legislature. Of the 124 members of the state's House of Representatives, 76 were black. In the Senate nine of the 33 members were black.[6] Many blacks were poorly educated and thus easily manipulated into passing laws that placed an onerous burden on the white population.

As reconstruction continued in the South, small groups organized to oppose policies of the federal government that permitted its intrusion into what they considered local issues. Whites felt the need to organize for the "instinct of self-protection" of the member's families from "radical" groups.[7] No regular organization of the Ku Klux Klan existed in South Carolina until the summer of 1867. At first the "raids" by the Klan were relatively quiet, just to let the radicals and blacks know that the whites had an organization and were ready to defend themselves and their families. In 1868, the Klan kept a reasonably low profile, issuing warnings to those who had become overly obnoxious in the Klan's view, backed up with an occasional flogging, but without murder.[8] An act passed by the legislature in March 1869, authorizing the governor to establish a militia would be the catalyst for serious trouble in the future.[9]

In the forthcoming 1870 election, Governor Scott knew a concerted effort would be made to remove him and his Radical administration. To forestall that possibility, Scott proceeded to organize 14 full regiments of black militia, armed with 10,000 new Winchester rifles and a million rounds of ammunition, at a cost of more than $400,000 to the state.[10] Whites were not permitted to form militia companies. The Klan had remained comparatively inactive until these black militia units took to the streets of their towns. This triggered the emergence of the more violent Klansmen. In November, the black militia "armed and equipped,...went about in groups or in regular formation, as if seeking a conflict."[11] One favorite practice was to march in a "company front" formation to occupy the entire street, driving the local population off the street.[12] A number of clashes between whites and blacks occurred during the campaign of 1870. News of these "riots" was transmitted over the country to produce the image that South Carolina was on the brink of insurrection.[13] By the time the election was held, more than 96,000 blacks were enrolled in the militia — almost the entire black male population of the state.[14] Fraud was rampant and Scott was easily re-elected.

In January 1871, the murder of a former Confederate soldier by black militiamen in Union County triggered the Klan into violent action. Thirteen militiamen were arrested for the murder and jailed awaiting trial. In two separate attacks on the jails the Klansmen removed the militiamen and killed 10. The Klan was now operating in nine counties of South Carolina and extensively in the Spartanburg area. Placing more U.S. troops in South Carolina was viewed by Washington as a necessity.

The 7th Cavalry, having served for almost five years on the central plains, was directed to join the Department of the South. From his Department of the Missouri headquarters at Fort Leavenworth, Kansas, Brigadier General John Pope issued General Order No. 4, March 8, 1871, which stated in part:

> It [the 7th Cavalry] has been engaged in many bloody combats with the Indians in which its valor has been thoroughly tried and proved.... The presently soldierly condition and high state of discipline of the regiment give assurance that in the new field to which it is ordered it will be distinguished for the same high qualities which have so justly earned for it its brilliant reputation in this command.[15]

By the end of March, only four companies of the 7th Cavalry remained in Kansas and Colorado Territory — Company G at Fort Lyon, Colorado Territory; Companies H and M at Fort Hays; and Company L at Fort Wallace. At Fort Hays, with Custer's departure, Reno assumed command of the remaining companies of the 7th Cavalry. Orders were issued to regroup the companies from Forts Lyon and Wallace at Fort Hays in preparation for the move to the Department of the South. Company G arrived at Fort Hays April 18, and on April 29, with the departure of Major George Gibson, 5th Infantry, Reno assumed command of the post. Company L arrived May 23 and all four companies departed immediately by rail, arriving at Louisville, Ky., May 28, 1871. After arriving in Louisville, Reno received orders to dispatch the four companies to various locations. Company G was ordered to proceed by rail to Columbia, S.C. Companies H and L left Louisville on the 31st for station at Ash Barracks, Nashville, Tenn., and Company M left that same day for duty at Darlington, S.C. Reno remained in Louisville for most of June before proceeding to his next duty station at Spartanburg, S.C.

Growing violence by the Ku Klux in York, Union and Spartanburg counties was becoming a major concern to the public. Officials met in all three counties to discuss how to stem the excesses. They believed one of the main causes of the unrest among the civilian population was the black militia and that the Klan was reacting to this continued threat. Scott, now safely in the governor's office after using the black militia to assure his victory, decided in late May that it was time to dissolve what was described as the "malodorous militia and constabulary."[16] Almost immediately, attacks by the Klan were reduced significantly. However, the outbreaks had already attracted the attention of President Grant and on March 24, 1871, he issued a proclamation to the people of South Carolina that:

> [C]ombinations of armed men, unauthorized by law, are now disturbing the peace and safety of the citizens of the State of South Carolina, and committing acts of violence in said State of a character and to an extent which render the power of the State and its officers unequal to the task of protecting life and property and securing public order therein.[17]

Grant directed that all armed men in South Carolina disperse within 20 days. On April 20, he signed into law the Ku Klux Act, which imposed penalties on those who violated the 14th Amendment and would "conspire or go in disguise" to deprive "any person or class of persons of the equal protection of the laws."[18] The U.S. Army would be used to enforce the new law.

The move to South Carolina was welcome news for Mary Hannah. She was happy to give up the hot summers and bitterly cold winters of Kansas for the more temperate climate of her husband's new duty station at Spartanburg. It would also allow her opportunity to visit her family in Harrisburg more often, especially since receiving word that her mother was not well. Mary Hannah packed up the family belongings and, with Ross in tow, left Fort Hays about the same time as the troopers. However, she would first visit Harrisburg before traveling to Spartanburg.

By the end of June, the 12 companies of the 7th Cavalry would be scattered over the South. Reno, from his post at Spartanburg, would have command of the companies in York, Union and Spartanburg counties. Company E, 7th Cavalry, was already stationed in Spartanburg, having arrived March 29. The *Carolina Spartan* reported:

> A company of about seventy-five United States Cavalry arrived in our town a few night's ago. We learn that one company has also arrived at Union [Company B] and one at York [Company K]. We hope those quartered here will find their stay among us to be agreeable and pleasant, and learn that our people are by no means disposed to be rebellious towards the government of the United States, for such is the fact.[19]

The Spartanburg encampment was located at what "was known as Twitty's Grove on Henry Street. The encampment fronted [on] Henry Street and the tents filled the grove and the adjoining old field."[20] The land was rented from the tenant farmer for $10 a month. Reno described Spartanburg as being "on the Eastern slope of the Blue Ridge mountains, which are plainly visible," and the country as "high, rolling, and very healthful."[21] He assumed command of the post July 21, 1871. Company D, 2nd Infantry, arrived at Spartanburg July 29 to assist the 7th Cavalry in reducing the attacks by the Klan.

Spartanburg was a pleasant small southern town untouched by the Civil War. Reno quickly established his presence by renting a house at the corner of West Henry and Spring for his family. Mary Hannah and Ross ar-

Major Marcus Reno
(circa 1872)

rived in early August and, with the arrival of their belongings from Fort Hays, set up her family in their newly rented house. Ross finally had an opportunity to do something that had been lacking when the Renos were stationed at Fort Hays — to play with other boys his own age.

In a personal recollection, E. E. Bomar, Jr., remembered that Reno "was married and had a little son about the age of my brother Paul. His name was Robert Ross Reno. He played with 'us boys,' and there were plenty of us.... His mother called him Ross. He was a dear little fellow, who still carried his baby habit of sucking his thumb. But he was game and stood up to other and larger boys in their play."[22]

Once when Robert was hit with a green peach, he ran home crying: "He was stung with pain so that he kept on crying. And then came louder yells as his mother punished him with a paddle.... His mother had whipped him for crying and sent him back to play with us."[23] Mary Hannah was described as "a lovely lady" and the major as a "short, thick set man inclined in fleshiness, [and] was also friendly."[24]

111

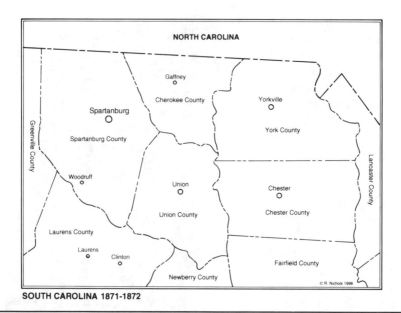

SOUTH CAROLINA 1871-1872

In July 1871, a sub-committee of the Congressional Investigating Committee, chaired by Senator John Scott of Pennsylvania, held a series of meetings in Columbia, Union, Spartanburg and Yorkville in "regards [to] the execution of the laws and safety of the lives and property of the citizens" of South Carolina.[25] On July 29, Scott sent a letter to the president describing what he considered "revolutionary conditions" and requested that action be taken immediately. This was disputed by a minority of the committee, and the citizens of Spartanburg believed the actual purpose of the committee hearings was to provide an excuse for Grant to increase the number of federal troops in South Carolina.[26]

Prior to Reno assuming command of the post at Spartanburg, 1st Lieutenant Thomas M. McDougall and men of his Company E had undertaken a number of scouts into the immediate area to find Klansmen and destroy illicit distilleries. While being moderately successful at finding and destroying a number of stills, McDougall had no success at capturing and arresting members of the Ku Klux. Other companies of the 7th Cavalry stationed in South Carolina had similar experiences. The reduction of the threat from the black militia had diminished the number of hit-and-run raids by the Klansmen who were always well back into their civilian, and innocent, attire by the time the cavalry arrived.

It was a rather pleasant summer for Reno and his family. The weather, while warm and muggy, was a welcome change from the harsh glaring heat of the Kansas plains. Mary Hannah frequently visited with her neighbors and enjoyed the social climate that had been lacking at Fort Hays.[27] Ross, like all 7-year-old boys, got into his normal share of trouble but there is no record of him breaking any bones. He and the other neighborhood boys liked to play "soldier" and even erected a make-shift camp with a flag pole. A bugler at the 7th Cavalry's camp sounded reveille and retreat each day for the raising and lowering of the U.S. flag. At the boy's camp they imitated the same sound with their mouths.[28]

Since Reno's arrival at Spartanburg in July, attacks by the Ku Klux had stopped almost completely. Reno thought it was "the active part taken

Captain Thomas M. McDougall

by some of the men of property, to show the folly of such deed & the harm it might bring the county."[29] However, the lack of violence in South Carolina didn't faze the bureaucrats in Washington. Under the act signed by Grant April 20, he could suspend the privileges of the writ of *habeas corpus* in any state whenever "combinations and conspiracies exist in such state...for the purpose of depriving any portion or class of the people...the rights, privileges, immunities and protection named in the Constitution," but he first had to make a proclamation commanding the insurgents to disperse. On Oct. 12, 1871, Grant issued such a proclamation, citing among other things:

> [T]hat such combinations and conspiracies did then exist in the Counties of Spartanburg, York...in the State of South Carolina, and commanding thereby all persons comprising such unlawful combinations and conspiracies, to disperse and retire peacefully to their homes within five days...[and] to deliver to the Marshal...or to any military officer...all arms, ammunition, uniforms, disguises and other means and implements used...for carrying out...unlawful purposes.[30]

Finally, on Oct. 20, the president suspended the writ of *habeas corpus* for nine counties of South Carolina, including Spartanburg.[31] Reno was ordered to begin wholesale arrests, without warrants, of anyone suspected of being a Klan member. The reaction of the local population was predictable:

> An insurrection at the South is needed to keep the Northern heart fired; and all the forms of suppressing one must be gone through with no matter how disastrous the consequences may be to the section of country selected for the enactment of the farce. Woe to the conquered has been the rule since the creation of the world. It would be idle for us to expect our fate to be better than that of other conquered people.[32]

Spartanburg was considered the heart of the Ku Klux conspiracy and the military had made a number of arrests even before the suspension of *habeas corpus*. The *Carolina Spartan* summed up the situation: "Many men, thus dragged from their distant homes and huddled in filthy pens, are not only innocent of any offense, but ignorant of the charges preferred against them. What a commentary on the boasted Republican freedom of the model Government!"[33]

Reno anticipated that a large number of arrests would still be necessary so he requested additional forces: "It will be understood that this command has very severe duty and it is of such a nature that the services of commissioned officers are indispensable." Reno added, "The town and county is in a state of the most intense excitement but I apprehend no violence."[34]

Three companies of the 7th Cavalry were transferred to Spartanburg to assist Company E: Company M, commanded by Captain Thomas H. French, on Oct. 18; Company G, commanded by 1st Lieutenant Donald McIntosh, on Nov. 4; and Company B, commanded by 1st Lieutenant Edward G. Mathey, on Nov. 9. Assisting McIntosh was 2nd Lieutenant Benjamin H. Hodgson. The cavalry companies were to assist local authorities in enforcing internal revenue laws (busting illicit stills) and arresting and guarding persons accused of being members of the Ku Klux. Over the next two months, hundreds of arrests were made by the cavalry, usually at night, without warrants, and many times without corroborating evidence.[35] The jail became so crowded that the upper floors of several stores had to be used to house prisoners. Many prisoners were not Klan members and were released on bail after several days or a week. Some did serve short prison terms, usually a few weeks to several months in Columbia, S.C. A few of the hard core members were bound over to trial.

Reno worked with the mayor of Spartanburg, John Earle Bomar, to determine who could be released with a promise to answer later summons.[36] The local newspaper, although critical of the arrests, praised Reno and the way he tried to handle the situation: "This county [Spartanburg] and York are the

2nd Lieutenant Benjamin H.
Hodgson

1st Lieutenant Donald McIntosh

Captain Thomas H. French

1st Lieutenant Edward G. Mathey

headquarters of United States soldiers, and here one sees any number of 'boys in blue,' under the command of Major Reno, who is said to be an energetic, considerate and mercifully disposed officer."[37] Working with the community leaders, he was able to gain their confidence: "Major Reno, the military commandant, is spoken of by all the white citizens as a courteous, high-toned gentleman."[38]

Trials were held in the November term of the U.S. Court in Columbia, and although hundreds were arrested and accused of being Klan members, fewer than 100 either pleaded guilty or were convicted. Sentences ranged from one month to five years, and fines ranged from $50 to $1,000.[39] Author Henry T. Thompson probably summarizes it correctly when he states:

> When it is remembered that the Federal Court was very hostile to the white people of South Carolina, and that its juries were tampered with and its witnesses suborned by the prosecutors, the fact that, of the large number of persons arrested upon Ku Klux charges, so few were convicted, one realizes the iniquity of these wholesale and indiscriminate arrests by the United States Army."[40]

By the end of 1871, only Companies B and G, 7th Cavalry, and Company D, 2nd Infantry, remained at the Spartanburg garrison. Activities of the Ku Klux had almost completely disappeared and the troops were being used to enforce internal revenue laws — back to busting the illicit distillers. In an article entitled "A Word About Soldiers," *The Carolina Spartan* said, "They are not so bad after all.... They are remarkably well behaved, and their officers gentlemen of culture and refinement."[41]

The reduced activities allowed Reno to spend more time with his family. They had been in Spartanburg for just over a year when Reno received orders to leave South Carolina and proceed to New York City on detached service. He was being assigned to the "Board for Selecting a Breech-System for Muskets and Carbines," to select a new weapon system for the army. Service in South Carolina had been a welcome change from his Kansas duty, and now the opportunity for a comfortable assignment presented itself in one of the most modern and fashionable cities — New York.

Reno welcomed the orders to join the evaluation board in New York. With the absence of Ku Klux activities in the Spartanburg area, Reno was ready to move on, especially if the new assignment included the opportunity for a fuller and more rewarding social life in the North. Relations with the civilians of Spartanburg, while cordial, were also strained at times when Reno was forced to follow his orders which meant arresting prominent citizens from the local area. He was ordered to leave his post Aug. 22, 1872, and to report to the board for its first meeting to be held Sept. 3.

Reno was given 10 days of travel time to move his family and belongings from Spartanburg to New York. Mary Hannah had kept close contact with her mother, Mary Haldeman Ross, while in Spartanburg, and most of the news was not promising. Her mother's health had continued to decline and the prognosis for recovery was not good. Marcus, Mary Hannah and Ross left Spartanburg by train Aug. 23 for Harrisburg. When the Renos reached Harrisburg, Mary Hannah found her mother in worse condition than expected and decided not to proceed to New York with her husband. Marcus left his wife and son Sept. 2 and checked into the Army and Navy Club in New York. It was not going to be as pleasant as he had planned.

During the American Civil War, a multitude of different firearms were used but the standard weapon for the military was a .58-inch caliber muzzle-loading rifle-musket. It was a cumbersome weapon that required at least 30 seconds to reload under the best of conditions. By the end of the war, firearms development had progressed to a point where breech-loading weapons became feasible and even repeating type breech-loaders made their appearance. The Spencer repeating carbine, capable of carrying seven rimfire copper cartridges in a metal tube loaded through the buttstock, saw limited use after 1863, mainly with the cavalry.

After the war, the need for a new weapon system to replace the old style rifle-musket was evident. The Ordnance Department received the assignment to standardize one rifle and cartridge design for the military service. This task would extend from 1865 into 1873 before such a system was selected. In March 1871, the Ordnance Department started field trials of three single-shot breech-loading weapons: the Springfield Model 1870 "trap door," the Remington Model 1870 "rolling block," and the Sharps Model 1870 with a vertically sliding breech block.[42] These weapons were distributed in 1871 in limited numbers to various cavalry units, mainly in the west, and reports were required each month as to how well the weapons performed and what problems were encountered with each design.

Five factors were considered in the Ordnance Department's decision to select a single-shot weapon over a repeating firearm system: manufacturing economy; ruggedness and reliability; preference of the field officers; the selection of a single-shot weapon system by major European countries; and the logistics of providing sufficient ammunition to the troops in the field, especially in the west.[43] Although repeating firearms had been successfully used during the Civil War, the Ordnance Department believed that to be practical a repeating rifle required an adequate ammunition supply. During the Civil War the ready availability of ammunition did not limit the use of weapons that could fire at a faster rate than the rifle-muskets. However, this would not be the case in the more remote regions of the western United States. All ammunition would have to be carried by the soldier, on his horse, in wagons or on pack mules. The total number of cartridges was therefore limited to that supply immediately at hand. Long campaigns into desolate areas meant the judicious use of ammunition — the expenditure of large amounts of ammunition in a serious fire fight with Indians, with only a limited supply available, could prove disastrous.

The Congressional Appropriations Act for the support of the Army for 1873 allocated $150,000 for the manufacture of arms at the National Armory in Springfield, Mass.[44] However, no expenditure of funds could occur until a weapon system was selected and adopted that would be used throughout the military service. The act called for the establishment of a board of officers to be selected by the secretary of war to evaluate various weapon systems and recommend one for adoption by the Ordnance Department. The selection board of officers was to consist of five officers: one general officer who would act as president, one ordnance officer, and one officer from each branch of the army — cavalry, infantry and artillery.[45] Brigadier General Alfred H. Terry was selected as president. General Order No. 58, War Department, Adjutant General's Office, Series of 1872, appointed the other board members: Colonel Peter V. Hagner, Ordnance Department; Colonel Henry B. Clitz, 10th Infantry; Captain La Rhett L. Livingston, 3rd Artillery; and Major Marcus A. Reno, 7th Cavalry. The recorder was 2nd Lieutenant Henry Metcalfe of the Ordnance Department.

The board, which would meet 105 times over eight months, gathered for the first time at the Army Building in New York Sept. 3, 1872. However, Terry missed a railroad connection and was unable to attend the opening session. After Terry's arrival, the board immediately established an agenda for selecting a breech-loading system. Notices placed in newspapers requested inventors and companies submit weapons to the board for evaluation. The board also developed rules for the reception of weapons and determined general tests for the arms presented for examination. Tests results would be evaluated and a recommendation would sent to the secretary of war. At the board's meeting Sept. 27, the members decided to reconvene Oct. 10 at the National Armory in Springfield, Mass., where the actual field trials would take place.

Taking advantage of the delay, Reno went to Harrisburg to visit his family and gravely ill mother-in-law. Her situation was serious and Mary Hannah asked her husband to postpone his departure for Springfield for several days but, under orders and unable to contact Terry, Reno was forced to leave Harrisburg as scheduled. At the board's meeting Oct. 10, Reno received permission to absent himself for a week. He immediately returned to Harrisburg but was present when the board met again Oct. 17.

Field trials began Oct. 22, and the tests for record would be conducted by teams of soldiers made up of both new recruits and Civil War veterans. Trials continued until Dec. 20, when the board adjourned until Jan. 6, 1873. Reno journeyed back to Harrisburg for the holiday season which was rather quiet because of the illness of Mary Hannah's mother. Returning to Springfield Jan. 6, Reno found himself and the recorder, Lieutenant Metcalfe, the only ones present — the rest of the board had been detained by a severe snow storm. The other board members appeared the next day, but General Terry would not rejoin the board until Jan. 10. The field tests continued until March 4 and were designed to determine which system would endure conditions expected in the field. A total of 89 rifles and carbines were eventually submitted for testing, which included rapid and continuous firing; firing the weapons after they had been subjected to prolonged exposure of water and dust; and firing them with both defective and excessively charged cartridges. The test program eliminated all but 21 weapons, which were then subjected to a series of supplementary, and more severe, tests. Six weapons were selected for final consideration. The board adjourned March 4, and Terry scheduled it to reconvene in New York on April 1. Reno left Springfield the following day and returned to Harrisburg to visit with his family.

Although Mary Hannah continued to care for her ill mother, the Renos had opportunities to participate in some local social affairs. Ross, now coming up on his 9th birthday, was having problems with his school work. The years of traveling from Oregon to Kansas to South Carolina and back to Pennsylvania had interrupted his schooling so he had trouble keeping up with his classmates. Mary Hannah provided the extra effort to help Ross with his lessons. On March 30, 1873, Reno returned to New York to resume his duties on the Breech-Loading Small-Arms Board.

Meeting April 1, the board found it difficult to make the final selection of the weapon system to be used by the military. Of the six potential candidates, each had certain advantages over the others and the board was divided. On April 28, Terry sent a telegram to Adjutant General Edward D. Townsend, stating, "The first vote taken in the board...develops great differences of opinion among the members of the board. May the board recommend two or three systems, and also recommend their trial in the field before final adoption?" Townsend's reply, received on the 29th, was explicit: "[T]he act contemplates one system and the guns can only be made after its adoption."[46]

On the same day Terry sent the telegram to Townsend, Reno received permission to be absent for three days. Mary Hannah traveled to New York to spend a pleasant reunion with her husband before returning to Harrisburg.

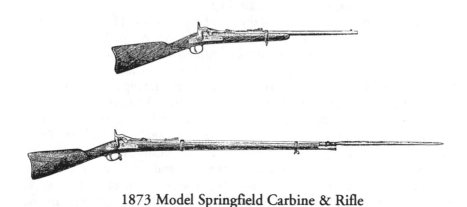

1873 Model Springfield Carbine & Rifle

At their May 3 meeting, board members discussed the form in which their opinions would be expressed in their final report to Secretary of War William W. Belknap. The board's final report of May 5, 1873, recommended "that the Springfield breech-loading system be adopted for the military service of the United States." The board also made several additional recommendations, including one written by Reno:

> Whereas the Elliot system [another breech-loading carbine] has exhibited remarkable facility of manipulation in requiring but one hand to work it, and therefore rendering it especially adapted to the mounted service...it be recommended that a limited number of carbines be made after this system for issue to the mounted service, for trial in the field.[47]

The board's final report was sent to Chief of Ordnance Alexander B. Dyer and on May 19 he made his recommendation to the secretary of war to adopt the Springfield system. He also stated, "The law prohibits the manufacture of the...Elliot gun for trial.... [W]ere it not for this prohibition the trial of [this] gun in the field would be recommended." Belknap approved the recommendation May 20.

By early spring 1876, all 12 companies of the 7th Cavalry were equipped with the new Springfield Carbine Model 1873. Its first real test would come June 25-26, 1876, at the Little Big Horn River in Montana Territory. The Model 1873 carbine would be the standard weapon for the army throughout the 1870s and 1880s and well into the 1890s.

Endnotes

[1] Lou Falkner Williams, *The Great South Carolina Ku Klux Klan Trials, 1871-1872* (University of Georgia Press, Athens, 1996), p. 3.
[2] John Hope Franklin, *Reconstruction After the Civil War* (University of Chicago Press, Chicago, 1961), p. 27.
[3] Franklin, p. 35.
[4] Stanley F. Horn, *Invisible Empire: The Story of the Ku Klux Klan 1866-1871* (Houghton Mifflin Co., Boston, 1939), p. 215.
[5] Williams, p. 3 & 7.
[6] Horn, p. 215.
[7] Franklin, p. 156.
[8] Horn, p. 217.
[9] Horn, p. 218.
[10] Horn, p. 218.
[11] John S. Reynolds, *Reconstruction in South Carolina, 1865-1877* (The State Co., Columbia S.C., 1905), p. 183.
[12] Reynolds, p. 183.
[13] Horn, p. 220.
[14] Henry T. Thompson, *Ousting the Carpetbagger from South Carolina* (R. L. Bryan Co., Columbia, S.C., 1926), p. 47.
[15] Lt. Col. Melbourne C. Chandler, *Of Garryowen in Glory: The History of the 7th U.S. Cavalry* (The Turnpike Press, Annandale, Va., 1960), p. 35.
[16] Horn, p. 232.
[17] Reynolds, p. 192.
[18] Reynolds, p. 193.
[19] *The Carolina Spartan*, Spartanburg, S.C., Thursday, April 6, 1871.
[20] E. E. Bomar, Jr., *What Happened When 'Yankees' Came to Town*, from the Spartanburg district office Federal Writers' Project, WPA, p. 1. Copy in the Spartanburg County Library, S-975.79-No. 18.
[21] Letter from Reno to Major J. H. Taylor, Sept. 16, 1871. Department of the South, Letters Received, 1871, Record Group 393, E4406, Vol. 1, NARA.
[22] Bomar, pp. 2-3.
[23] Bomar, p. 3.
[24] Bomar, p. 3.
[25] Reynolds, p. 194.
[26] *A History of Spartanburg County*, compiled by the Spartanburg Unit of the Writers' Program of the Work Project Administration (The Reprint Company, Spartanburg, S.C., 1976), p.157.
[27] Bomar, p. 3.
[28] Bomar, p. 2.
[29] Richard Zuczek, *State of Rebellion: Reconstruction in South Carolina* (University of South Carolina Press, Columbia, 1996), p. 106.
[30] *The Carolina Spartan*, Spartanburg, S.C., Thursday, Oct. 26, 1871.

[31] Although four cases challenging the constitutionality of this action were carried to the Supreme Court, they were all dismissed on technicalities before the court could rule.

[32] *The Carolina Spartan*, Oct. 26, 1871.

[33] *The Carolina Spartan*, Oct. 5, 1871.

[34] Letter from Reno to Major J. H. Taylor, Oct. 15, 1871. Department of the South, Letters Received, 1871, Record Group 393, E4406, Vol. 1, NARA.

[35] Thompson, pp. 56-57.

[36] Bomar, p. 6.

[37] *The Carolina Spartan*, Nov. 30, 1871.

[38] *The Carolina Spartan*, Nov. 30, 1871.

[39] Thompson, p. 57.

[40] Thompson, p. 58.

[41] *The Carolina Spartan*, April 4, 1872.

[42] David F. Butler, *United States Firearms, The First Century, 1776-1875* (Winchester Firearms Co., New York, 1971), pp. 184-185.

[43] Butler, pp. 189-190. European countries (France, Great Britain, Germany and Austria) had selected powerful single-shot rifles for their military services. They understood the need for a rugged and reliable weapon in the field and the need, from a logistical standpoint, to make efficient use of available ammunition. The preference of the field officers, in this author's opinion, was the reason why the Springfield system was selected and not a consideration as to why a single-shot system was desirable.

[44] Adopted June 6, 1872, and the Report of the Secretary of War to the Two Houses of Congress at the Beginning of the First Session of the 43rd Congress, Volume III, Washington, 1873.

[45] Ordnance Memoranda No. 15, Report of the Board of Officers. This memoranda contains the entire proceedings of the board from Sept. 3, 1872, to May 5, 1873.

[46] Ordnance Memoranda No. 15, p. 93.

[47] Ordnance Memoranda No. 15, p. 48.

• 8 •

Escort Commander & Personal Tragedy

The 49th parallel, which was recognized as the boundary between Canada and the United States from Lake of the Woods to the summit of the Rocky Mountains, had never been surveyed to determine its correct location. Hamilton Fish, secretary of state under President Grant, suggested that a joint survey be conducted with the British Government to mark the boundary. On Dec. 5, 1870, Grant recommended that Congress authorize an appropriation to fund the survey. However, it was not until March 1872 that funding was approved. A former army officer and West Point graduate (Class of 1835), Archibald Campbell was appointed U.S. commissioner for the survey in June 1872. Later that fall surveying began in the Red River area with the survey party being escorted by Company K of the 20th Infantry under the command of Captain Abram A. Harbach. The approach of winter curtailed further work for the year.

The area through which the survey would be performed during 1873 consisted of western Dakota Territory and into Montana Territory — a distance of more than 350 miles. The Sioux and Northern Cheyenne were active in these areas, which made unescorted survey parties prime targets for attack. General Phil Sheridan's Division of the Missouri, which included the military Department of Dakota under the command of General Alfred H. Terry, had the responsibility for protecting the survey commission. Terry had been assigned the position while still president of the Breech-Loading Small-Arms Board in New York. Sheridan realized that the survey commission would require more than a single infantry company for protection and appealed to the War Department for additional troops. Activities of the Ku Klux had virtually disappeared in the South and the War Department reassigned 10 companies of the 7th Cavalry under Custer to various Missouri River forts. The two remaining 7th Cavalry companies, D and I, and the headquarters staff were sent on temporary duty to Fort Snelling near St. Paul, Minn., headquarters for the Department of Dakota.

Completing his service on the Breech-Loading Small-Arms Board May 5, 1873, Reno was ordered by Terry to report to St. Paul where he would receive further orders. Reno received permission to delay for two weeks before reporting to St. Paul and returned to Harrisburg to be with Mary Hannah and Ross. The health of Mary's mother continued to decline and the doctors indicated it would be only a few months before the end. The situation left little doubt that Mary Hannah would not accompany her husband to St. Paul. Reno said good-bye to his family and left Harrisburg about May 20, arriving in St. Paul several days later.

Reporting to headquarters, he received verbal orders for temporary assignment in St. Paul. His orders were confirmed May 29: "The verbal order of the Department commander, of the 25th instant, assigning Major M. A. Reno, 7th Cavalry, to temporary special duty in this city, in connection with the supply and equipment of the command he is to assume, is hereby confirmed."[1] New orders were issued the following day:

> Major M. A. Reno, 7th Cavalry, is hereby relieved from the temporary special duty in this city...and is hereby assigned to command the squadron of his regiment for service as escort to the Northern Boundary Survey Commission, now at Fort Snelling, Minn., to which post Major Reno will proceed and report for duty with his command.[2]

Reno reported to Fort Snelling June 2 and received verbal orders to proceed with Companies D and I to Minneapolis June 5, where railroad transportation would be provided to Breckenridge, Minn. Two civilians of officer status, Junior Veterinary Surgeon John Tempany and Acting Assistant Surgeon Francis O. Nash, would accompany the command. Reno was also informed that Fort Totten, Dakota Territory, was designated as the winter quarters for the troops.[3]

Companies D and I assigned to Reno were commanded by Captains Thomas B. Weir and Myles W. Keogh, respectively. First Lieutenant James E. Porter was assigned as Reno's adjutant and 1st Lieutenant James M. Bell as the quartermaster and commissary officer. The 2nd lieutenants were Winfield Scott Edgerly (Company D) and Andrew H. Nave (Company I).

Weir, a graduate of the University of Michigan, served in the Civil War, and was breveted major for gallant and meritorious service at the battle of Farmington, Tenn., and lieutenant colonel for service in the engagement against Nathan Bedford Forrest near Ripley, Miss.

Keogh attended St. Patrick's College in Carlow, Ireland, and served in the Irish Battalion of the Army of Pope Pius IX. He also had an excellent record of service during the Civil War, being breveted major for gallant and meritorious service in the battle of Gettysburg, Penna., and lieutenant colonel for services in the battle of Dallas, Ga.

Captain Myles W. Keogh

Captain Thomas B. Weir

1st Lieutenant James E. Porter

2nd Lieutenant Winfield S. Edgerly

Neither man had served under Reno previously and both were thought to be heavy drinkers. Weir had come close to being released from the army in 1870 when Colonel Sturgis had recommended him for review by the "Benzine Board," indicating that Weir was "intemperate, and when dissipating becomes dissolute and abusive."[4] Captain Albert Barnitz wrote of Keogh's drinking in a letter to his wife: "Capt. [Lee P.] Gillette and Major [William M.] Beebe are confirmed inebriates, and the same may be said of Col. Keogh — they are seldom sober."[5]

A major dispute arose between Reno and Doctor Nash on the train to Breckenridge. Reno stated that Nash had "reported for duty...without having made any provision as to his support during the summer," and that the daily papers of Minneapolis and St. Paul "had detailed disgraceful conduct on his part at his hotel...and his bruised face gave every confirmation of it as a fact."[6] Reno considered relieving Nash of his duties as medical officer for the military escort.

Reno's command arrived at Breckenridge June 6 and immediately left for Fort Abercrombie, about 15 miles to the north. Remaining at Abercrombie several days, Reno decided that Nash was unfit to accompany his command and relieved him of duty, sending him back to St. Paul. Nash protested but left Reno's command and returned to departmental headquarters where he took his case to the department commander. Meanwhile, Reno and his command left Fort Abercrombie and headed north to Fort Pembina, arriving June 22. Both the American and British surveying parties had already moved westward from Fort Pembina, escorted by Captain Abram A. Harbach's Company K, 20th Infantry. Realizing he was in unfamiliar territory, Reno requested permission to enlist 20 Indian scouts for service with the escort. He received authorization June 25 but was unable to hire any scouts before leaving Fort Pembina.[7] Reno also received authority to hire two guides for use throughout the 1873 season.

As for Nash's appeal to the department commander, the assistant adjutant general, Major Oliver D. Greene, decided Reno had exceeded his authority and ordered Nash to return to the escort. On June 23, Reno received a telegraph from Greene:

> On his [Nash's] rejoining you will again place him on duty and submit in writing for the consideration of the Commanding General, the reasons governing in his relief by you. If these should appear satisfactory, upon examination, Dr. Nash's contract will at once be annulled and another medical officer sent you, if requisite.[8]

Nash rejoined the escort June 29 at Fort Pembina. The Nash problem was not the only difficulty Reno would face before leaving Fort Pembina. Dr. Elliott Coues, who had been appointed surgeon and naturalist to the Northern Boundary Commission, convinced the commander of Fort Pembina, under protest by Reno, to issue an order that would allow the escort's enlisted men to collect specimens for him during their free time.[9]

Leaving Fort Pembina July 2 and moving westward along the boundary line for about 145 miles, Reno's command established a supply depot July 10 at the western base of Turtle Mountain. U.S. chief astronomer, Captain William J. Twining, Corps of Engineers, arrived at the depot July 13, accompanied by Harbach's infantry company. Reno then assumed command of the entire military contingent, which consisted of 70 infantry and 160 cavalry soldiers. Commissioner Campbell arrived on the 18th with Coues and decided to move the supply depot about 75 miles farther west to "the 2nd crossing of the Souris River with the 49th Parallel."[10] The two cavalry companies broke camp July 20, Keogh's Company I escorting the supply train to the new depot while Reno, with Weir's Company D, went to Fort Stevenson to meet another supply train and escort it to the new Souris depot.[11]

The final confrontation between Reno and Nash took place July 24 at Fort Stevenson. Reno suspended Nash "from exercising the functions of attending Surgeon," and requested "the annulment of his contract, as he is no manner of use here."[12] Nash was ordered to remain at Fort Stevenson until a decision could be made by the department commander. Coues had endorsed Reno's July 24 statement and on Aug. 3, Terry ordered Nash to return to St. Paul.[13] When Nash returned to St. Paul, he mounted a vigorous defense of his actions and accused Reno of being a heavy drinker. Edgerly later wrote:

> I have been with Col. Reno for two summers '73-'74 on the Naschim (sic) boundary survey and knew him very intimately. He was, in those days when almost everybody drank, what was called a moderate drinker and I never saw him drunk.[14]

With Nash's dismissal, Reno asked Coues, still technically an army surgeon, to temporarily assume the duties of Nash until a new surgeon could be appointed. Coues refused, stating that he worked only for the boundary commission and would not attend to the medical needs of the soldiers. Coues was later reprimanded by the Surgeon General's Office for his cavalier attitude.[15]

Reno and Company D left Fort Stevenson with the new supplies July 30 and established the supply camp, appropriately named Camp Terry after the department commander, on Aug. 3, near present day Sherwood, N.D. The new camp would be the main supply depot for the remainder of the season.

For the next two months, duties of the infantry and cavalry would become routine — and boring. No Indian troubles were encountered during the long summer. Most of the Indian activity that summer was encountered by the main force of the 7th Cavalry, 10 companies, escorting General David S. Stanley's Yellowstone Expedition, in Montana Territory. Reno's escort troopers were used to gather stones and build the mounds which marked the 49th parallel. Reno was not particularly pleased with his military personnel being used as common laborers. In his 1873 field report Reno expressed his concern:

> I think it proper in this report that the attention of the Department Commander should be called to the uses made by the small parties, of the mounted men who were furnished as guard. The detachments were numerous, so that they were necessarily removed from the supervision (daily) of the officers, and they were used virtually as Assistants by the parties for which they were escorts...consuming that time that care and attention to grazing renders necessary, when the allowance of forage is reduced. The horses were seldom released from the saddle until too late to fill themselves with grass; and when through thieving and other means loss of forage occurred, the condition of the horses became very low.[16]

By the end of September, most of the commission's surveying had been completed only to be complicated by a furious snowstorm that lasted a week. Orders received Sept. 28 from St. Paul stated: "after placing his command in winter quarters at Fort Totten, Major M. A. Reno, 7th Cavalry, will repair to these headquarters and report to the Commanding General on public business."[17] Shortly after receiving his orders, Reno was informed that his mother-in-law, Mary Haldeman Ross, had died in Harrisburg Sept. 26 at age 59.

Finally, on Oct. 13, the last of the survey crews returned to the Souris depot. Twining and Harbach's infantry company had departed the depot for Fort Totten several days before. Reno's two companies of cavalry left Camp Terry Oct. 14 and marched to Fort Stevenson, arriving there on the 18th. The following day the command left Stevenson for its permanent winter quarters at Fort Totten, arriving there on the 22nd. It had been a grueling trip with prairie fires creating a fine dust and ash which, combined with strong east winds and snow, filled "the eyes, nose, and mouth with an irritating (sic), which bit and smarted with undying zeal."[18] On the return march to Fort Totten, Reno suffered a bad ankle sprain that caused him a great deal of pain when he attempted to walk. After attending to his troops and getting them settled, he applied for 30 days leave based on a surgeon's certificate of disability.[19] The leave was granted and Reno left for Harrisburg Oct. 26 with an intermediate stop in St. Paul. He spent only a short period in St. Paul before traveling to Harrisburg, arriving about Oct. 30.

The caring for and final loss of her mother had been a severe strain on Mary Hannah and her health had deteriorated considerably. Being home with his family was certainly a welcomed change for Reno from the rigors of field service along the border of Dakota Territory. Mary Hannah's health improved but the sprained ankle Reno suffered on the march to Fort Totten continued to hamper his movements. His sick leave was scheduled to terminate Nov. 26, and he was expected to return to duty on the 27th. He was still in considerable pain and decided to remain in Harrisburg on sick leave for the remainder of the year, but he knew that a certificate of disability would be required to justify the extended leave. No army surgeon was stationed in Harrisburg to issue the certificate so Reno issued it himself, sending copies to Fort Totten and headquarters in St. Paul. He later explained in a letter to the paymaster who had placed a stop against Reno's pay for being absent without leave for the period Nov. 27-Dec. 31, 1873, that "I was unable to do duty. I sent my own certificate to that effect.... Under Gen. Order No. 2, Series 1871, AGO, I was at liberty to assume myself 'absent sick' and so draw my pay."[20] The paymaster contended the certificates of disability were not on the correct forms and so he was justified in withholding the pay. The matter was finally settled by the Adjutant General's Office that decided "Under circumstances accept them for the time covered."[21]

Reno was aware that he would again be assigned to command the military escort to the Northern Boundary Survey Commission for the 1874 season. He was still concerned about Mary Hannah's health, and since the survey commission would undertake no major activity until May, he decided to take her to New York for further treatment. In New York it became apparent that treatment for Mary would extend into the new year and he was scheduled to report back for duty Dec. 31. On Dec. 27, he requested an additional four months regular leave of absence to begin Jan. 1, 1874. The request, received by the Adjutant General's Office Dec. 31, was not approved: "No action for the present. I have explained to Col. Reno."[22] Apparently the disapproval came from Division Commander Phil Sheridan, which sparked a quick response from Reno in a letter he wrote to the Adjutant General Jan. 2, 1874:

> Gen. Sheridan protests so strongly that I cannot hope to effect anything in the matter of my leave without seeing him. I shall start tonight for Chicago — I wrote you today & drop this

second note to say that the reference to my leave need not engage his attention — I only hope I can arrange matters so as not to resign.[23]

The quick trip to Chicago was partly successful for Reno — he was granted an extension of his certificate of disability for his ankle injury to Feb. 10.[24] Returning to New York, Reno informed the Adjutant General Jan. 6 that he would be staying at the Army and Navy Club for the month.[25]

Following his leave, Reno reported to St. Paul for temporary duty. He was granted another leave of absence Feb. 27 for seven days starting March 1.[26] Returning to Harrisburg March 3, Reno continued to be concerned about Mary Hannah's health, which apparently had not improved significantly. It was obvious some improvement would be necessary if she was to accompany her husband to his permanent duty station at Fort Totten. Reno received permission to extend his leave to May 1 to remain with Mary Hannah and Ross.[27] Mary's health prevented her from accompanying her husband when he left for St. Paul April 29.

Reporting to St. Paul May 1, Reno was assigned temporary duty at that station. He received new orders May 20 to "proceed without delay to Fort Totten, D.T., and report for duty with the battalion of his regiment now at that post."[28] As he had anticipated, he would command the military escort for the Northern Boundary Survey Commission for the 1874 field season. The danger of attack by hostile Indians would be significantly higher than the previous year. In 1873, the commission had confined its surveying to the northern boundary line of Dakota Territory while the activities of the Sioux were mainly directed against the Stanley expedition in Montana Territory. The surveying in 1874 would extend well into Montana Territory and would require a much larger military escort. Reno received orders May 23 that provided further evidence the 1874 season would be more dangerous:

> The escort for the Northern Boundary Survey Commission during the coming season's operations, will be composed as follows, viz: companies D and I, 7th Cavalry and Companies B, D, E, I, and K, 6th Infantry, the whole under the command of Major M. A. Reno, 7th Cavalry. The cavalry will be put en route overland without delay to Fort Buford. Companies B and K, 6th Infantry will be sent from Forts Abraham Lincoln and Stevenson respectively by first steamer to the same point.... After seeing the cavalry en route from Fort Totten, Major Reno will proceed via Bismarck and the Missouri River to Fort Buford for the purpose

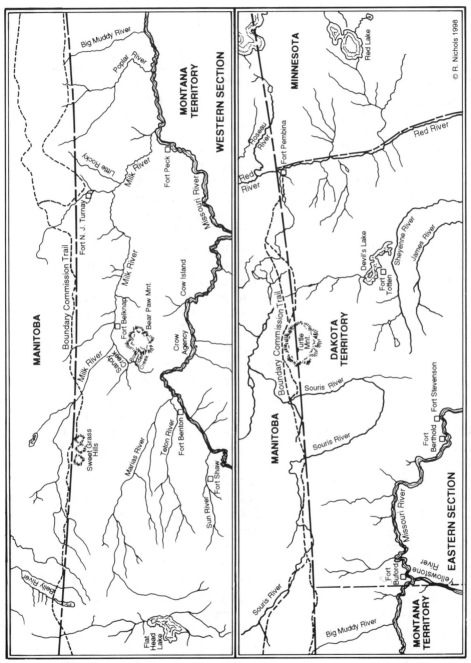

NORTHERN BOUNDARY SURVEY 1873-1874

© R. Nichols 1998

of organizing his command and arranging all necessary details connected therewith."[29]

Reno reported to Fort Totten May 25 and took temporary command of the post while the permanent post commander, Lieutenant Colonel Lewis C. Hunt, was on detached service on courts-martial duty.[30] He immediately set about organizing the two companies of the 7th Cavalry for field duty but apparently not at the speed headquarters desired, as a May 28 message indicated: "Let your cavalry move at once."[31]

The two 7th Cavalry companies were the same that had provided escort service the previous year, except Weir would now command the two-company squadron. Keogh had been given six months leave to return to Ireland and Companies D and I were each left with a single lieutenant: Winfield S. Edgerly, Company D, and Andrew H. Nave, Company I. The squadron was to escort the supply train on the march to Fort Buford. Reno thoroughly inspected the troops and train and found them in "tip top condition."[32] On May 30, the squadron, with 119 enlisted men, left Fort Totten with the supply train for Fort Stevenson and was expected to arrive at Fort Buford by June 15.[33] Reno and Lieutenant Porter, his adjutant, left Fort Totten June 1 and arrived at Bismarck on the 4th. After arranging for the remaining portion of his command, Reno met with Chief Astronomer Twining to discuss furnishing supplies to the survey party. Doctor Coues arrived in Bismarck June 5 and, still smarting from the reprimand he had received from the surgeon general, had "difficulty with Marcus A. Reno." The following day Coues challenged Reno to a duel — which never took place — and Coues left later that day on the steamboat *Fontenelle* for the trip to Fort Buford.[34] Boarding a steamboat the following day, Reno and Porter left Bismarck and traveled up the Missouri River to Fort Buford, arriving there June 11. With the arrival of the five companies of the 6th Infantry, Reno prepared to move his command into the field and requested an "ox train of capacity" be sent to Fort Benton, Montana Territory, to transport sufficient rations for "539 soldiers and half forage for 119 U.S. horses and 401 U.S. mules for 30 days and rations for 109 men and half forage for 142 animals belonging to Boundary Commission for 40 days."[35] The supplies would be at Fort Benton and Reno directed the ox train to then move to "Milk River at the mouth of Box Elder Creek" where he would have the mule train there to meet them. On June 17, Reno issued Special Orders No. 2 detailing which elements of his infantry and cavalry would provide escort to the various surveying crews.[36]

On June 20, Reno reported that "the companies designated to form the escort to NBS Commission have been organized and supplied, and will leave this post tomorrow morning."[37] He also reported he would reemploy the two guides used the previous year and that one guide would be paid $100 per month and the other $75 per month. Reno had much better luck in recruiting Indian scouts for the 1874 survey than he did in 1873. Second Lieutenant R. T. Jacob Jr., 6th Infantry, was given command of the detachment of 14 Indian scouts June 15, and they were equally divided between Companies E and I, 6th Infantry.[38] These companies would accompany 2nd Lieutenant Francis V. Greene, who was in charge of three topographical surveying groups, a tangent party and a mound-building party.

Leaving the camp near Fort Buford June 21, Reno and his entire command proceeded northwest in the direction of the Big Muddy River. Establishing a camp on the Big Muddy June 24, Reno informed headquarters that "official communications intended for the companies comprising the escort will reach them promptly via Fort Benton as it will be impracticable [for them] to keep up communication with Fort Buford after July 1st."[39] During the next two weeks the command traveled west along the Milk River valley and finally camped July 12 at the junction of Milk River and Box Elder Creek. The various survey parties, with their military escorts, continued to their assigned areas of operations. Company K, 6th Infantry, remained at the camp while the two cavalry companies moved about 70 miles farther northwest to establish a permanent supply depot in the Sweet Grass Hills. Reno had expected the ox supply train to be in the vicinity of the Box Elder Creek camp when he arrived. When it had not appeared as expected, he and Captain Twining, who had remained behind the survey parties which had moved into the field, decided to return to Fort Benton to determine why the supplies were late. Reno's plans would be abruptly changed.

While Reno and his command had been moving along the Milk River Valley, events occurred a thousand miles to the east that would have a serious effect on the remainder of Reno's life. Although she was only 30, Mary Hannah's health had taken a decided turn for the worse since Marcus' departure in late April. She was having symptoms of drowsiness, stupor and convulsions. Unable to care for herself, she temporarily moved to the home of her brother, Andrew Ross, in Fairview Township, York County, Penna. Early on Friday morning July 10, she had a seizure and died at 3 a.m. Death was attributed to "disease of the kidneys."[40] The funeral was held at the residence of her grandmother, Mrs. E. E. Haldeman, at the corner of Front and Walnut streets, Harrisburg, at 2 p.m. On Monday, July 13, Mary Hannah was buried in the Ross family plot in the Harrisburg Cemetery where her mother had been buried less than 10 months before. Robert Ross, now just 10, would be cared for by Mary's younger sister and brother-in-law, Bertie E. and J. Wilson Orth, until his father could return to assign a permanent guardian. Final settlement of Mary's sizable estate would also have to wait for Marcus' return as she had given him complete power-of-attorney over her affairs earlier that year.[41]

On the afternoon of July 10, Andrew Ross sent a telegram to Department of Dakota headquarters in St. Paul notifying it of the death of Reno's wife. The following day headquarters wired the District of Montana commanding officer: "Convey the news to Major Reno, 7th Cavalry, of the death of his wife at Harrisburg on the 10th instant."[42] A courier was immediately dispatched from Fort Benton to the Box Elder Creek camp, arriving there on the morning of the 13th. Reno, upon receiving the crushing news, hastily made plans to return to Harrisburg. He had the courier immediately return to Fort Benton with a quickly penned a message to Terry indicating he was leaving his command and that Weir would be in charge during his absence. Before leaving camp for Fort Benton, he wrote specific instructions for Captain Weir:

> Unforeseen circumstances imperatively demanding my departure and it being impossible that I can return before the completion of the seasons operation with the commission, I have the honor to transmit for your guidance instructions from the department commander regarding the return of the cavalry to Fort Totten, D.T. its designated winter quarters. You will consult with the Chief Astronomer and when in your opinion no trouble is anticipated from Indian depredations you will return with the cavalry at a sufficiently early date to secure the arrival of the battalion at its winter quarters on or before Oct. 10th.[43]

Reno left Box Elder Creek camp that same day and arrived at Fort Benton on the 15th. A telegram was then sent to department headquarters:

> Am starting home. Please authorize my leave. Command provided for. Wrote Gen. Terry regarding it before leaving camp. Answer.[44]

Adding to Reno's agony was the slow response from headquarters. The telegraph line directly to Fort Benton was apparently down but the line to Fort Shaw, Montana Territory, was open so the reply to Reno's request for leave came through Fort Shaw. The response, dated July 18, was not what Reno expected:

> While fully sympathizing with you in your affliction the Department Commander [Terry] feels it imperative to decline to grant you leave. You must return to your command.[45]

The emotional impact of losing his wife would have a profound effect on Reno and his Army career. Mary Hannah had been outgoing, warm and entertaining which, during their 11 years of marriage, had a soothing effect on Reno's somewhat cold and harsh personality. He was, by nature, introverted and aloof and, without Mary Hannah, he would find it difficult in future years to socialize in the close-knit society of the army post.

Although obviously depressed about the news of his wife's death, Reno had no choice but to continue with his army duties. He remained at Fort Benton for another week concerned that supplies required for his command in the field would not be available there because of the falling water level of the Missouri River. Supplies by steamboat could only reach Cow Island, a point almost 100 miles downstream. Reno received permission to obtain supplies for the escort from Fort Shaw.[46] Leaving Fort Benton July 25, Reno rejoined his command at the Sweet Grass Hills supply depot on the 29th. Before Reno's arrival, Weir, who had commanded the squadron since Reno's departure, reported July 23: "Everybody thinks the Indians will not interfere with the survey."[47]

In his report to department headquarters Aug. 2, Reno stated:

> The work has progressed with so much greater rapidity than was anticipated that no doubt now exists but that the survey will be completed before the end of September and our party will be out of the field by that time.... Under these circumstances I have decided to return with Companies B and K, 6th Infantry, and D and I, 7th Cavalry, on the 15th or 20th and leave the 3 companies of 6th Infantry belonging to [Fort] Buford to return under command of Captain Bryant after all parties are on their homeward march. The Engineering parties on their return march say they will not need escort being of sufficient strength and armed so they can protect themselves. No Indian troubles have occurred on the entire trip. The Yanktonnals (sic) Sioux only having exhibited infractions to one of the small parties under Captain Ames.[48]

However, still concerned about the continued rumors of potential Indian troubles for the survey crews, Reno left the Sweet Grass Hills depot Aug. 6 to conduct a reconnaissance to within 50 miles of the west end of the line in advance of the working parties. Returning on the 12th, he reported, "I met many Indians all of them very peaceably disposed." In the same report he states:

135

On Sept. 1st the work will be completed and the entire working force of the Commission will be concentrated on the 'West Butte' of Sweet Grass Hills. It is not deemed necessary by themselves that any escort will be necessary after leaving that point for Benton.... The two Companies of Cavalry and B and K, 6th Infantry, will proceed under my command to Buford reaching that post about Aug. 31st or Sept. 1st.[49]

Companies D and I, 7th Cavalry, and Company B, 6th Infantry, left the Sweet Grass Hills depot early on the afternoon of Aug. 14, camping later that day at Sage Creek. First Lieutenant D. H. Lee, Company K, 6th Infantry, was ordered to bring his company and join the rest of the command which would be camped near Fort Belknap Aug. 21.[50] Here Reno finally received approval of the leave of absence he had requested July 13: "Leave of absence for one month is hereby granted Major M. A. Reno, 7th Cavalry, with permission to apply at Headquarters...for an extension of one month, the leave to take effect when Major Reno's command is placed in winter quarters."[51] After Company K rejoined near Fort Belknap, Reno's command broke camp and continued east along the Milk River valley. Camping between Fort Peck and Fort Buford Aug. 31, Reno ordered the two infantry companies to board the steamboat *Josephine* the following day for their return to Forts Stevenson and Lincoln.[52] The two cavalry companies marched on to Fort Buford, arriving there Sept. 3. From there they proceeded to Fort Stevenson, camping near there on the 10th, and finally reached Fort Totten on the 14th to establish their winter camp. The command had marched more than 1,400 miles since leaving Fort Totten in late May.

Reno completed his final field report of the 1874 season Sept. 15 and left Fort Totten the following week, stopping at department headquarters in St. Paul before proceeding to Harrisburg. While at headquarters he requested an additional 30 days leave which was approved, "with permission to apply for a further extension of six months."[53] His leave started Sept. 22, and the return to Harrisburg was both emotional and strained. Mary Hannah's sister and brother-in-law had found it difficult to understand why Reno had not returned to Harrisburg shortly after Mary's death to provide comfort to his son. His explanation of Army procedures was not well accepted and the strained relationship that was created would extend into the future. The Orths had taken custody of Ross after his mother's death but Reno quickly reclaimed his son and decided to take him on an extended vacation. On Oct. 3, Reno requested an additional eight months leave and permission to visit Europe. The request was approved Oct. 5 by Sherman and Adjutant General Townsend.[54]

Reno and his son embarked on an ocean liner to France with a final destination of Paris, arriving there in early November 1874. Little is known of his stay in Europe except he did have an opportunity to visit his old field commander, Alfred T. A. Torbert, for whom he had served as chief of staff late in the Civil War. Torbert had been appointed the American consul general in Paris. Reno wrote to Adjutant General Townsend Feb. 1, 1875, requesting an additional three months extension of his leave. The extension was approved by Terry on Feb. 23, Sheridan on March 16, Sherman's office on March 19, and finally by the Adjutant General on March 24. He remained in France until April or May at which time he visited other countries — even outside Europe. A letter from Walter Scribner Schuyler to his father George Washington Schuyler, written in St. Petersburg, Russia, and dated June 29, July 11 and 12, 1875, recounts a meeting with Reno:

> After arriving at Petersburg we met an officer of our service (7" Cav'y) Major Reno, who has been travelling about since last November. He came here from Moscow, and not talking Russian would have been rather uncomfortable here, but for my having been about enough to learn the ropes. We went one day to the 'Abonkof' foundry where the great guns are cast, then to the Imperial porcelain works and the glass establishment.[55]

Finally Reno had to return to the United States to take care of Ross' guardianship and schooling and to settle his wife's estate. Reno was back in Harrisburg by mid-October and filed a petition Oct. 19 with the Orphan's Court of Dauphin County to appoint a guardian for "a minor child…under the age of fourteen years…and has no guardian to take care of his person and estate."[56] The court appointed John Andrew Bigler, who was married to Anna Mary Haldeman (Mary Hannah's cousin), as Robert's guardian. Mary Hannah had died "intestate" (without a will) and the division of her estate, determined by the inheritance laws in effect at the time of her death, gave one-half to Marcus and one-half to Ross. Reno acted as the administrator of the estate which contained several pieces of real estate that Mary had inherited from her mother. Ross and he shared two pieces of property, the house and land at 223 N. Front St. in Harrisburg, appraised at $12,000, and a farm in Lower Allen Township, Cumberland County, Penna., containing 185 acres, appraised at $27,853. Other assets gave Reno a total of more than $35,000 as his share of his wife's estate.[57]

With the settlement of his wife's estate and the appointment of a guardian for his son, Reno proceeded to department headquarters in St. Paul for his next duty assignment, arriving there Oct. 22. He was scheduled to return to his last command at Fort Totten but was delayed under verbal orders by the department commander while the subject of his future station was under consideration. Ordered to report to the commanding officer at Fort Abraham Lincoln, Dakota Territory, Reno arrived there Oct. 30, 1875. This assignment would eventually lead to the events that would end his long military career.

Endnotes

[1] Special Orders No. 114, St. Paul, Minn., May 29, 1873. Record Group 393, Volume I, Series 1191, Special Orders 1873-1874, Department of Dakota, NARA.

[2] Special Orders No. 115, St. Paul, Minn., May 30, 1873, RG 393.

[3] Special Orders No. 119, St. Paul, Minn., June 3, 1873, RG 393.

[4] Berry C. Johnson, "Reno as Escort Commander," *The Westerners Brand Book*, Volume XXIX, Number 7, Chicago, Sept. 1972, p. 50.

[5] Robert M. Utley, *Life in Custer's Cavalry* (Yale University Press, New Haven, Conn., 1977), p. 203. Letter from Albert Barnitz to his wife Jennie, dated Oct. 28, 1868.

[6] Reno to the Assistant Adjutant General, Dept. of Dakota, June 29, 1873.

[7] Special Orders No. 139, St. Paul, Minn., June 25, 1873, RG 393.

[8] O. D. Greene to Reno, June 23, 1873, Dr. Francis O. Nash's personal file, Record Group 94, NARA.

[9] Special Orders No. 68, War Department, March 31, 1873.

[10] Reno's Report 1873 in Letters Received, Division of the Missouri, Record Group 393, NARA.

[11] Official Report by Major Marcus A. Reno, 7th Cavalry, Civil War Branch, Record Group No. 98, M.D. Mo. 3194 (1873).

[12] Reno to Assistant Adjutant General, Department of Dakota, July 24, 1873.

[13] Upon final review of the case by the Surgeon General in Washington, Nash was placed on the "black list" and was not eligible to receive future contracts from the Medical Department.

[14] Colonel W. A. Graham, *The Custer Myth* (Stackpole Company, Harrisburg, Penna., 1953), p. 323.

[15] Paul R. Cutright and Michael J. Brodhead, *Elliott Coues: Naturalist and Frontier Historian* (University of Illinois Press, Urbana, 1981), pp. 161-162.

[16] Reno's Official Report 1873.

[17] Special Orders No. 215, St. Paul, Minn., Sept. 27, 1873, Record Group 393.

[18] State Department Report, "Reports upon the Survey of the Country between the Territory of the Untied States and the Possession of Great Britain," Washington: Government Printing Office, 1873.

[19] Special Orders No. 239, St. Paul, Minn., Oct. 26, 1873, Record Group 393.

[20] Letter from Reno to General E. D. Townsend, Adjutant General, dated May 17, 1874, Reno's personal file, R. 314, CB 1865, Record Group 94, NARA.

[21] Record 5083 ACP 1873 in Reno's personal file.

[22] Record 1959 ACP 1874 in Reno's personal file.

[23] Letter from Reno to General Townsend, dated Jan. 2, 1874, Reno's personal file.

[24] General Order No. 2, Department of Dakota, 7th Cavalry Regimental Returns, 1874.

[25] Letter from Reno to Adjutant General, dated Jan. 6, 1874, Reno's personal file.

[26] Special Orders No. 39, St. Paul, Minn., Feb. 27, 1874, RG 393.

[27] General Order No. 15, March 1, 1874, Department of Dakota, 7th Cavalry Regimental Returns, 1874.

[28] Special Orders No. 100, St. Paul, Minn., May 20, 1874, RG 393.

[29] Special Orders No. 103, St. Paul, Minn., May 23, 1874, RG 393.

[30] Larry Remele, editor, *Fort Totten* (State Historical Society of North Dakota, Bismarck, 1986), p. 15.

[31] Letter from Assistant Adjutant General O. D. Greene, to Reno, dated May 28, 1874. Record Group 393, Volume I, Series 1167, Letters Sent 1874-1875, Department of Dakota.

[32] Letter to O. D. Green from Reno, dated May 31, 1874, RG 393.

[33] Special Orders No. 1, Fort Totten, Dakota Territory, May 29, 1874, RG 393.

[34] Cutright, pp. 165-166.

[35] Letter to Commanding Officer, District of Montana, from Reno, dated June 14, 1874, Fort Buford, D.T., RG 393.

[36] Special Orders No. 2, June 17, 1874, Camp near Fort Buford, D.T. , RG 393.

[37] Letter to Assistant Adjutant General from Reno, dated June 20, 1874, Camp near Fort Buford, D.T., RG 393, Entry 1337, page 36.

[38] Special Orders No. 108, Headquarters, Fort Buford, D.T., June 15, 1874, and Special Orders No. 4 (extract), Headquarters, Northern Boundary Survey Commission, camp near Fort Buford, D.T., June 17, 1874.

[39] Letter to Major O. D. Green, Assistant Adjutant General, from Reno, dated June 24, 1874, Camp on the Big Muddy, RG 393.

[40] City of Harrisburg, Dauphin County, Penna., Affidavit of Death, signed by Andrew Ross, dated Oct. 3, 1874. Dauphin County Courthouse, Pennsylvania, Affidavit of Death 1-4. The cause of death was probably Bright's disease which is a common form of nephritis. A serious complication of the disease is the poisoning caused by the failure of the kidneys to remove the bodies waste material.

[41] Cumberland County Orphans Court Docket 20, page 183, Cumberland County Court House, Carlisle, Penna., Power of Attorney from Mary H. Reno to Marcus A. Reno, dated Feb. 3, 1874.

[42] Telegram from O. D. Greene, Assistant Adjutant General to District of Montana Commanding Officer, dated July 11, 1874, Record Group 393, Volume I, Series 1167, Letters Sent 1874-1875, Dept. of Dakota.

[43] Letter to Captain T. B. Weir from Reno, dated July 13, 1874, from Camp on Box Elder Creek, Montana Territory, RG 393, Part 1, Entry 1337, Letters Sent.

[44] Telegram No. 3, Fort Benton, July 13th, 1874, from Reno to Major O. D. Greene, A.A.G., Dept. of Dakota, RG 393, Letters Sent. A copy of Reno's July 13 instructions to Weir was probably sent to General Terry via the courier who had brought the news of Mary Hannah's death.

[45] O. D. Greene, A.A.G., to Reno, dated July 18, 1874, St. Paul, Minn., RG 393, Volume I, Series 1167, Letters Sent 1874-1875, Department of Dakota. There are possibly two explanations as to why Terry refused to allow Reno to return to Harrisburg: 1) It would have taken Reno at least 10 days to travel back to Harrisburg and he would not have arrived there until the end of July — almost three weeks after the funeral, and 2) Terry may not have had much trust in Weir to lead the military expedition — Weir was known to be a heavy drinker and had almost been released from the Army in 1870 by the "Benzine Board."

[46] Telegram No. 5, July 23, 1874, Fort Benton, Montana Territory, to O. D. Greene , A.A.G.,from Reno, and reply from O. D. Greene, date July 29, 1874, St. Paul, Minn., RG 393.

[47] Letter to O. D. Greene, A.A.G., from T. B. Weir, dated July 23, 1874, RG 393.

[48] Report to O. D. Greene, A.A.G., from Reno, Camp Near Sweet Grass Hills, M. T., dated Aug. 2, 1874, RG 393.

[49] Report to O. D. Greene, A.A.G., from Reno, Camp Near Sweet Grass Hills, M. T., dated Aug. 14, 1874, RG 393.

[50] Order to 1st Lieutenant D. H. Lee from Reno, In the Field Montana Territory, Aug. 19, 1874, RG 393.

[51] Special Orders No. 176, St. Paul, Minn., Aug. 17, 1874, from O. D. Greene, A.A.G., RG 393.

[52] Special Orders No. 23, Aug. 31, 1874, In the Field, Montana Territory, RG 393.

[53] Special Orders No. 75, Sept. 26, 1874, Headquarters Military Division of the Missouri, Chicago, Ill., RG 393.

[54] Letter from Reno to Adjutant General E. E. Townsend, New Cumberland, Penna., Oct. 3, 1874, and endorsement in Reno file 4015, R. 314, C. B. 65, NARA. Special Orders No. 217, Series 1874, same file.

[55] Letter is part of the Walter Scribner Schuyler papers at the Huntington Library in San Marino, Calif., identified as WS 85. My thanks to James Brust for finding this choice item.

[56] Petition in Orphan's Court Records, Dauphin County, Penna., File #70, Paper #2, Oct. 19, 1875.

[57] Estate information from Register's Index, Orphan's Court, Dauphin County, Penna., Oct. 20, 1875. The purchasing power of $35,000 in 1875 would be the same as $218,000 in 1998 at a conservative 1.5 percent annual cost of living increase over 123 years. At 2 percent annual increase, the amount would be $400,000, and at 2.5 percent, $729,000.

• 9 •

To the Little Big Horn

The expansion of the Northern Pacific Railroad west of Bismarck, Dakota Territory, required the use of military troops to protect the engineers, survey crews and work parties. In June 1872, a stockaded infantry post called Fort McKeen was built on the west bank of the Missouri River across from Bismarck. Later that summer, the stockade was moved about four miles south to the bluffs overlooking the confluence of the Heart and Missouri Rivers. The decision was made to expand the fort to include cavalry troops and on Nov. 19, 1872, the name of the post was changed to Fort Abraham Lincoln. The post was described in 1876 as surrounded "except on the river front, by ravines, broken and irregular bluffs, and hills."[1]

Ten companies of the 7th Cavalry, under the command of Lieutenant Colonel George A. Custer, arrived in Yankton, Dakota Territory, in April 1873. On May 7, 1873, they marched to Fort Rice, arriving there June 10 after traveling 495 miles. Two companies of the 7th Cavalry (D and I) had been assigned to Fort Snelling, Minn., for duty as the escort for the Northern Boundary Survey Commission. Custer and his command joined the Yellowstone Survey Expedition under General David S. Stanley during the summer of 1873 and returned to occupy the newly constructed Fort Abraham Lincoln in September. In his annual report Sheridan had recommended establishing a military post in the Black Hills area "to secure a strong foothold in the heart of the Sioux Country, and thereby exercise a controlling influence over these warlike people."[2] Ten companies of the 7th Cavalry, two infantry companies and a number of scouts and scientists were sent into the Black Hills during the summer of 1874 to explore the country and make recommendations to the War Department for the establishment of military posts. The discovery of gold in the Black Hills during the expedition, and the subsequent influx of prospectors, miners, settlers, farmers and fortune hunters during the next two years aggravated the already strained relationship between the Sioux and the whites.

Major Marcus Reno reported for duty Oct. 30, 1875, at Fort Lincoln. On Nov. 1, 1875, he assumed command of the 7th Cavalry and Fort Lincoln. The 7th Cavalry's colonel, Samuel D. Sturgis, its lieutenant colonel, George

Custer, and its two senior majors, Lewis Merrill and Joseph Greene Tilford, were either on detached service or leaves of absence. Custer and his wife Elizabeth (Libbie) had left Fort Lincoln Sept. 25 to vacation in New York and would not return until mid-March. Only five companies of the 7th Cavalry (A, C, D, F and I) were garrisoned at Fort Lincoln when Reno arrived. Six companies had been transferred to the Department of the Gulf in September 1874 and only three of those companies had returned to Dakota Territory by November 1875. Of the remaining seven companies, three (B, G and K) remained in the south, two (H and M) were stationed at Fort Rice and the remaining two (E and L) at Fort Totten. Also garrisoned at Fort Lincoln was one company of the 6th Infantry, two companies of the 17th Infantry, and a detachment of 32 Indian scouts. Total military personnel at the post was 527.[3] Reno's duties included the procurement of supplies and equipment and the training of personnel, especially new recruits who periodically arrived at the post. During the fall and winter of 1875-76, the troops performed normal garrison duty with occasional escort duty. The bitter Dakota winter allowed only limited duty outside of the immediate fort area.

Reno soon observed that two factions existed among the officers of the 7th — those who rallied around the charismatic Custer and those who belonged to an anti-Custer group. The latter group, in reality led by Captain Frederick W. Benteen, blamed Custer for abandoning Major Joel H. Elliot and 17 of his men at the Washita in 1868. Since joining the 7th Cavalry, Reno had served only a limited time directly with Custer — at Fort Hays in 1870 and 1871 — and while not among the "Custer favorites," he apparently did not belong to the "anti-Custer" group. The two officers he considered his friends were Captain Myles Moylan and 2nd Lieutenant Winfield S. Edgerly.

Moylan served with the 2nd Cavalry in the Civil War in actions at Forts Henry and Donelson, Shiloh, Beverly Ford, Snicker's Gap, and Gettysburg. He had been dismissed from the service in 1863 for being in Washington without permission, re-enlisted as Charles Thomas in the 4th Massachusetts Cavalry in December 1863 and was appointed captain in the regiment in December 1864. Mustered out Nov. 26, 1865, he enlisted as a private in the General Mounted Service in January 1866 as Myles Moylan. He transferred to the 7th Cavalry in August 1866, rising through the ranks to private, corporal, sergeant major, 1st lieutenant and finally captain, effective March 1, 1872. Moylan's Company A was on the Stanley Expedition in 1873 and the Black Hills Expedition in 1874. He was married to Charlotte Calhoun, 1st Lieutenant James Calhoun's sister.

Edgerly graduated from the West Point Military Academy with the class of 1870 and received his appointment as 2nd lieutenant, Company D, 7th Cavalry, June 15, 1870. He served with his company at various posts in the

Southern states and was with the military escort serving the Northern Boundary Survey Commission in 1873-74.

Both Moylan and Edgerly were married and had their wives with them at Fort Lincoln. Since the loss of Mary Hannah, Reno found comfort in socializing with Moylan and Edgerly. His duties as regimental commander kept him busy and he had little time to feel the total impact of his personal loss.

Outside of Fort Lincoln events were starting to take shape that would decide the fate of many 7th Cavalry troopers in the next year. Conditions on the Indian reservations had deteriorated and with the fraudulent practices of the Indian agents, Indians lacked sufficient food to feed their families. Supplies that were supposed to be issued to the Indians were actually sold to them at inflated prices, which few Indians could afford. Flour and grain sent to the reservations was mixed with sand and the meat was rotten.[4] While the military attempted to keep miners and prospectors out of the Black Hills, they were unsuccessful. When caught, escorted off the restricted lands, and turned over to local authorities, trespassers were immediately released, only to return to the restricted land. A confidential letter to General Terry from Sheridan stated:

> President Grant had a small conference in Washington on November 3rd, and that while the orders forbidding miners to go into the Black Hills should not be revoked, the troops should make no efforts to keep them out...therefore quietly cause the troops of your Department to assume such attitude as will meet the views of the President in this respect.[5]

Small groups of young men of the various Sioux tribes began to leave the reservations to hunt and to join bands of their brothers, designated hostiles, under the leadership of Sitting Bull. Sheridan wanted to take immediate action against the hostiles but the Interior Department, which administered Indian affairs, notified the secretary of war that the department would make one additional attempt to return the Indians to their reservations before military action was authorized. In November, Indian agents in Sioux and Cheyenne regions were told to notify the Indians living in unceded territory that they must return to their agencies by Jan. 31, 1876. If they failed to do so, they would all be classified as hostiles and the War Department would take action to force them to return to their reservations. Despite severe winter conditions of heavy snows and low temperatures, most of the hostile bands were notified by trusted Indian runners. Few, if any, of the hostiles returned to their reservations by the January deadline, not because of the weather, but because none of their chiefs took the order seriously.[6] On Feb. 1, 1876, the secretary of the interior officially notified the secretary of war "that the time given the hostile Indians having expired," he was formally turning the problem over to the military authorities for whatever action the secretary decided might be required.[7]

Prior to the deadline, preparation had already begun for a winter military expedition to return the Indians to their agencies. In December, General Crook had informed headquarters that his command could be ready to move immediately against the hostiles. General Terry also indicated he could move on short notice and that the five companies of the 7th Cavalry from Fort Lincoln plus two from Fort Rice would be sufficient to attack Sitting Bull's camp located at the mouth of the Little Missouri River. By the time the War Department issued authority to commence operations on Feb. 7, 1876, Sitting Bull had moved his camp to a new location 200 miles farther west. Sheridan developed a plan for a winter campaign by which three columns would move simultaneously against the Sioux and Cheyenne to catch them in their winter camps. Columns were to be dispatched from Forts Lincoln, Fetterman and Ellis in March with an anticipated meeting point in the area of the Big Horn or Little Horn Rivers.

At Fort Lincoln Reno began preparations for the expedition. Reports were received from various agents about Indian activities and on Feb. 22, Reno telegraphed the Adjutant General in St. Paul: "[C. W.] Darling, [U.S.] Indian Agent at Berthold, reports Sitting Bull and camp moving to Fort Peck."[8] On Feb. 23, he sent Lieutenant John A. Carland, 6th Infantry, to the Fort Berthold Agency to recruit Arikara scouts. Carland returned March 3 with only Charley Reynolds, considered one of the best scouts in Dakota Territory, and the half-Arikara, half-Sioux Bloody Knife. Carland also brought back additional information about Sitting Bull which Reno telegraphed to St. Paul March 3: "Sitting Bull is encamped on Tongue River but will be in Berthold this month to trade. A party of Gros Ventres, who went to camp of Sitting Bull, left there all the arms and ammunition they had."[9] Although Reno was unable to get scouts at that time, later attempts were more successful and by May 9, 30 Arikara scouts would be at Fort Lincoln.[10]

Sheridan and Terry recognized that a successful campaign against the Sioux and Cheyenne would require a significant military contingent to force the Indians back to their reservations. All 12 companies of the 7th Cavalry would be required and orders were issued to reassemble the entire regiment at Fort Lincoln. The regiment was widely scattered and with three companies still on duty in the Department of the Gulf, it would take considerable time to provide them the necessary transportation to Lincoln. Two companies each were stationed at Forts Totten and Rice. Bitter cold weather and heavy snows delayed the assembly of the regiment and the anticipated departure date of

Lt. Colonel George Armstrong Custer
(Photo taken in April 1876)

the Dakota Column slipped from March to early April. However, Crook's column was already in the field. Departing March 1 from Fort Fetterman in heavy snow, Crook's command consisted of five companies each of the 2nd and 3rd Cavalry regiments, two companies of the 4th Infantry, a large number of wagons and a pack train of 400 mules. On March 17, after an apparently successful attack by six companies of cavalry on a Cheyenne village on the Powder River, Colonel Joseph J. Reynolds inexplicably withdrew his command and allowed the Indians to retake their village and much of their possessions and pony herd. The loss of five men killed and six wounded discouraged Crook and he decided to return his exhausted command to Fort Fetterman for refitting. Reynolds was subsequently court-martialed by Crook and charged with destroying much needed supplies, abandoning the wounded, and permitting the recapture of the pony herd. Reynolds was found guilty, received a suspension (which was later remitted by Grant), and retired in 1877.

Custer, who had been on leave of absence until Feb. 15, requested an extension of his leave but Terry, expecting Custer to lead the column from Fort Lincoln, instead ordered him to temporary duty at St. Paul. Custer remained on detached service in St. Paul until early March when Terry ordered him to proceed to Fort Lincoln.[11] It was a difficult trip for the Custers who were forced to spend nearly a week aboard a snow-bound train 65 miles east of Bismarck. Finally arriving at Fort Lincoln on March 13, Custer assumed command of the post and regiment from Reno. He would not remain there long. While on leave, Custer, in discussions with friends, indicated that he knew something about the corruption in William W. Belknap's War Department concerning post traders. When Congressman Hiester Clymer learned that Custer might have some information concerning the post trader scandal, he decided the officer should testify before his committee in Washington on the subject. A summons was sent to Custer on March 15 requesting his presence back in Washington. Custer, concerned about being replaced if he was not present for the upcoming spring campaign, offered to testify at Fort Lincoln. On March 16, he wired Clymer:

> I am engaged upon an important expedition, intend to operate against the hostile Indians and I expect to take the field early in April. My presence here is deemed very necessary. In view of this, would it not be satisfactory for you to forward me such questions as may be necessary, allowing me to return my replies by mail?[12]

This was not acceptable to Clymer and a subpoena was telegraphed to Custer to return to Washington immediately. Custer left Fort Lincoln March 20, at which time Reno again assumed command of the post and regiment.

Bad weather continued to delay the departure of the Dakota Column past the early April date assigned to begin the campaign against the Sioux.[13] Two 7th Cavalry companies (E and L) arrived at Lincoln from Fort Totten April 17, and Company C, 17th Infantry arrived April 22. Two 7th Cavalry companies (H and M) were only a short distance away at Fort Rice, and the remaining three companies (B, G and K) were still on their way from the South.

The continued delay of the Dakota Column did not affect the start of the 1876 campaign against the Sioux. Five companies of the 7th Infantry left Fort Shaw March 17 on a 200-mile march to Fort Ellis, Montana Territory, arriving there March 28. By April 2, the Montana column, consisting of the five 7th Infantry companies and four 2nd Cavalry companies, under the command of Colonel John Gibbon, was in the field and proceeding east. The cavalry was commanded by Major James S. Brisbin.

As the committee hearings in Washington dragged on, Custer became concerned the regiment would leave on the campaign without him. But his own testimony was working against him. He accused, without proof, President Grant's brother, Orvil, of being involved with Belknap in the illegal selling of rights to military post traderships. Grant was not pleased with the news and directed the

Colonel John Gibbon

military operation against the Indians to begin without Custer.

The flurry of letters, telegrams and newspaper articles about Custer's problems in Washington suggesting he might not be allowed to go with the expedition provided an opportunity for Reno that he could not pass up. In command of the post at Fort Lincoln and the regiment for almost six months except for a short period in March, Reno had devoted all his time and effort in preparing the troops for the expedition and wanted, if Custer was not available, to command the regiment in the field. He telegraphed Terry:

> From Custer's telegrams and the papers it seems he will not soon be back. In the meantime the expedition here is making large expenses and Sitting Bull waiting on Little Missouri. Why not give me a chance as I feel I will do credit to the army?[14]

Terry's diplomatic reply: "I have not the slightest doubt that you would do the work admirably; but the question of rank would be troublesome, for two colonels are anxious to go. Besides I have little doubt that Custer will return very soon."[15] Although Terry had denied his request to lead the regiment, Reno still thought Custer might remain unavailable to take the regiment into the field. On April 16, bypassing the normal chain of command, he appealed directly to Sheridan:

Expedition ready when transportation from Abercrombie and cavalry companies from Rice arrive. Why not give me a chance, sending instructions what to do with Sitting Bull if I catch him. He is waiting for us on the Little Missouri.[16]

Reno received his answer the following day: "Your telegram received. Gen. Terry has entire charge of the expedition. I do not feel like interfering with him in his plans."[17] Reno was obviously disappointed but the issue had at least been resolved and he continued to prepare the regiment for the campaign.

In April, an incident occurred at Fort Lincoln while Reno was post commander which further stressed his already tense relationship with Weir. While on escort duty with the Northern Boundary Commission Survey, Reno had previously taken issue with Weir on his conduct, mainly concerning his drinking. On April 16, he brought formal charges against Weir for missing battalion drill on the 13th. Apparently Weir not only didn't attend the drill, but he also flaunted the fact before Reno. Instead of being at the dress parade ceremony, Weir appeared on the porch of the house occupied by Lieutenants Porter and Edgerly and then moved to the walk in front of the officers' quarters. From there he went and sat on the porch of the house occupied by Lieutenants W. W. Cooke and Henry J. Nowlan until the completion of the drill. Reno charged him with displaying insubordination before the enlisted men and being absent from his proper duties without having a legitimate excuse.[18] Apparently Terry didn't feel the incident warranted a court-martial and dismissed the charges.

Reno continued to receive information about Indian activities which he forwarded to Terry. On April 27, he reported: "Sioux scout from Standing Rock reports all young men are leaving reservation with best ponies. They report going to fight Crow Indians, but he says they are going to join Sitting Bull." On May 2, he wrote: "Twelve lodges of Uncpapas at Berthold, trading, report several hundred lodges between here and Yellowstone, waiting for expedition. Indians from camp attacked by Crook have joined Sitting Bull — fuller details in letter from Col. Huston by this mail."[19]

The three 7th Cavalry companies (B, G and K) that had been serving with the Department of the Gulf finally arrived at Fort Lincoln May 1, and the two companies from Fort Rice (H and M) arrived May 5. Fort Lincoln lacked quarters for the five recently arrived companies, so Reno had them camp two miles south of the post. For the first time since its formation in 1866, all 12 companies of the 7th Cavalry were garrisoned at one location. Reno immediately issued orders forming the regiment into three battalions, designated the 1st, 2nd and 3rd. The three senior captains present were assigned battalions (squadrons): Benteen, Companies A, D, H and K; Keogh, Companies B, G, I and M; and Yates, Companies C, E, F and L.[20]

Meanwhile in Washington, Custer was becoming desperate. He appealed to Sherman and to the president without success — he was not given an opportunity to explain his accusations directly with Grant. Leaving Washington May 2, he traveled to New York to appeal his case directly to Sherman but was refused an audience. He decided to return to St. Paul and boarded the night train to Chicago, arriving there the following day. Met by one of Sheridan's staff officers, Custer was notified he was under arrest for leaving Washington without permission and ordered to remain in Chicago to await further orders. Despite the order to remain in Chicago, Custer proceeded to St. Paul where he, following consultation with General Terry, sent a telegram May 6 to the Adjutant General, basically begging to be allowed to go on the expedition:

> I respectfully but most earnestly request that while not allowed to go in command of the expedition I may be permitted to serve with my regiment in the field. I appeal to you as a soldier to spare me the humiliation of seeing my regiment march to meet the enemy and I not share its dangers.

Terry endorsed the request, adding that Custer's "services would be very valuable with his regiment."[21] It was later reported that Custer "with tears in his eyes" actually "got down on his knees and begged Terry to get the orders changed."[22]

The situation with Custer was finally resolved May 8 when Sherman telegraphed Terry:

> The dispatch of General Sheridan enclosing yours of yesterday touching General Custer's urgent request to go under your command with his regiment, has been submitted to the President, who sends me word that, if you want General Custer along, he withdraws his objections. Advise Custer to be prudent and not to take along any newspapermen, who always work mischief, and to abstain from any personalities in the future.[23]

Terry and Custer left St. Paul that same day by train, arriving at Fort Lincoln late on the 11th. Custer relieved Reno the following day and assumed command of Fort Lincoln and the 7th Cavalry. One of his first actions was to change the regimental assignments made by Reno: "For service with the proposed expedition the Companies of this Regiment are hereby organized into four Battalions of three Companies each."[24] Captains Keogh, Yates, Weir and

Brigadier General
Alfred H. Terry

French were each assigned three company battalions; Keogh, Companies B, C and I; Yates, Companies E, F and L; Weir, Companies A, D and H; and French, Companies G, K and M. Keogh's and Yates' battalions were designated the "Right Wing" under command of Major Reno, and Weir's and French's battalions were designated the "Left Wing" under command of Captain Benteen. The quick countermanding of Reno's regimental assignments accomplished exactly what Custer wanted to show — that he was now in command, not Reno. On May 13, the seven companies still quartered at Fort Lincoln were moved to the camp south of the fort — the 7th Cavalry was finally ready to take to the field. The command's departure was scheduled for the 15th but again severe weather postponed the start until early on the morning of May 17.

At the end of May, all three columns were in the field. Crook's Wyoming Column left Fort Fetterman May 29 with 15 companies of cavalry and five companies of infantry, a force of 1,300 men; Gibbon's Montana Column continued their march east along the Yellowstone River with about 400 men; and Terry's Dakota Column included 12 cavalry companies, three and a half infantry companies, and a battery of Gatling guns for a total of about 900 soldiers.

For the next week the Dakota Column proceeded westward, marching into Montana Territory June 3 and crossing O'Fallon Creek on the 6th. On the morning of June 7, Custer, with one company of cavalry and the scouts, proceeded ahead of the main column to find a road to the Powder River while Reno commanded the main column and wagon train. Later that day, the column camped on the Powder River, 25 miles above its mouth. Terry left the camp the next morning with two cavalry companies and reached the confluence of the Powder and Yellowstone rivers later that day, where he found a party from Colonel Gibbon's command waiting for him on board the steamer *Far West*. The following morning the *Far West* proceeded up the Yellowstone to Gibbon's camp where Terry and Gibbon discussed campaign strategy. Returning to the mouth of the Powder in the afternoon, Terry immediately went to the Powder River camp, arriving there later that night.

The information Terry received from Gibbon and late arriving dispatches indicated significant Indian activity farther west, perhaps in the area of the Rosebud or Big Horn valleys. On June 10, Terry ordered a reconnaissance to determine whether the Sioux or Cheyenne were upstream on the Powder and Tongue rivers and possibly to establish communications with Crook's command. Reno was ordered to take the 7th Cavalry's Right Wing, consisting of Companies B, C, E, F, I and L, one gun from the Gatling battery, a detachment of Arikara scouts and 100 pack mules to:

> [M]ake a reconnaissance of Powder River from the present camp to the mouth of the Little Powder. From there he will cross to the headwaters of Mizpah Creek and descend it to its junction with the Powder. Thence he will cross to Pumpkin Creek and Tongue River and descend the Tongue to its junction with the Yellowstone, where he may expect to meet the remaining companies of the 7th Cavalry and supplies of subsistence and forage.
>
> Maj. Reno's command will be supplied with subsistence for twelve days and with forage for the same period at the rate of two pounds of grain a day for each animal. The guide, Mitch Boyer (sic), and eight Indians to be detailed by Lt. Col. Custer will report to Maj. Reno for duty with this column. Acting Assistant Surgeon H. R. Porter is detailed for duty with Maj. Reno.[25]

This was the first stage of Terry's plan to locate the recalcitrant Indians and force them back to their reservations. The second stage would use the information obtained from Reno's scout and put the 7th Cavalry and Gibbon's command in the field to complete the plan. Terry's dispatch of June 12 to his St. Paul headquarters outlined the plan:

1st Lieutenant James Calhoun
Company L

2nd Lieutenant Henry M. Harrington
Company C

1st Lieutenant Algernon E. Smith
Company E

Captain George W. Yates
Company F

No Indians east of Powder River. Reno with six companies of 7th Cavalry is now well up the river on his way to the Forks, whence he will cross to and down Mizpah Creek and thence by Pumpkin Creek to Tongue River, where I expect to meet him with the rest of the cavalry and fresh supplies. I intend then, if nothing new is developed, to send Custer with nine companies of his regiment upon the Tongue and thence across to and down the Rosebud, while the rest of the 7th will join Gibbon, who will move up the Rosebud.[26]

Reno's command left the Powder River camp at five o'clock on the afternoon of June 10 and encamped the first night eight miles above their previous camp site. The next day the scout continued south along the Powder, marching 26 miles before stopping. On the 12th the command proceeded, as ordered, in the direction of the fork of the Powder and Little Powder. After a march of 24 miles, they found the site of a week-old Indian camp, and although it was still early afternoon, Reno decided to set up camp for the night.

The command had been able to move fairly rapidly and was only slowed by the Gatling gun battery. Pulled by four condemned cavalry horses, the gun battery tended to upset when traveling over the rough terrain and, at times, had to be hauled by hand: "At some of the ravines had to unlimber guns (sic) and unhitch horses and haul over by hand."[27] Reno sent the scouts farther up the Powder Valley to examine the area where the Little Powder flowed into the Powder. The scouts reported nothing and Reno decided not to take the whole command to the fork.

On June 13, the detachment moved west to Mizpah Creek and then turned north, downstream, covering 24 miles before camping for the night. His scouts, returning from farther down the Mizpah, reported no recent activity there, and Reno learned from Bouyer that if they continued down the Mizpah as ordered, they would bypass the village Lieutenant James Bradley had seen on the Tongue in May. An inspection of the village site could provide information on the number of lodge sites and would not delay the command's return to the Yellowstone.

On the morning of the 14th, Reno made his first deviation from Terry's orders to "descend it [Mizpah Creek] to its junction with the Powder." Reno decided that continuing as ordered would bring Terry no new information on the location of the Indians or what direction they had taken, so he turned his command west toward Pumpkin Creek. After a march of 22 miles, the command reached Pumpkin Creek at a point about a mile below where the Little Pumpkin joined Pumpkin Creek. Crossing over the Pumpkin, Reno rode upstream to the confluence with the Little Pumpkin and ordered the detachment into camp about a mile up the Little Pumpkin.

The following day, June 15, the command proceeded west and then north, and after a march of 25 miles, arrived at the Tongue River where a campsite was established. It had been a difficult march, Private Peter Thompson later reported: "One day we made our way through some pine covered hills; the trail was so narrow that the horses were jostling and jamming one another all the time."[28]

The next day, the 16th, Reno again would deviate significantly from Terry's orders. Proceeding about eight miles down the Tongue, the command reached the village site that Bradley had discovered in May. The month-old site showed signs that it had contained about 400 lodges, and the scouts reported the Indians had moved farther west toward Rosebud Creek.[29] Bouyer told Reno he knew where the Indian encampment had been and suggested that the command cross over to the Rosebud Valley to determine if the Indians were still there. Reno was on the horns of a dilemma — he had already violated Terry's orders by not going down the Mizpah to the Tongue and now Bouyer was suggesting he further violate his orders by going to the Rosebud. Should he follow his specific orders and proceed down the Tongue to the Yellowstone and report he had found a month-old village, or should he scout into the Rosebud Valley and possibly locate the existing site of a larger Indian village? He would endure little censure if he choose the former option, but it would not provide any new information on the possible location of the Indians. The latter decision could entail significant risk in having the command discovered by the Indians and possibly exposing it to an attack, but perhaps the additional information on recent Indian activities might prove valuable for Terry to formulate his plans on how the campaign should continue. Reno decided on the latter and turned westward toward Rosebud Creek.

Traveling 19 miles in about five hours, Reno's command stopped four and one-half miles east of Rosebud Creek at two o'clock in the afternoon. Scouts were sent out to determine if the valley was clear of Indians. Returning to the detachment six hours later, the scouts reported the location of two old Indian encampments and a wide travois trail leading up the valley. Reno remounted his command and resumed the march to the Rosebud, arriving at the stream just after 9 p.m. He then turned south and marched up the valley for another three miles, camping at the site of another abandoned Indian village.[30]

On the morning of June 17, Reno had another critical decision — to go farther up the Rosebud Valley and follow the Indian trail, or turn north and go down the Rosebud to the Yellowstone. Again the risk of moving in the direction the Indians had taken would place his troops in danger of being discovered or even being attacked, but it might also provide information as to

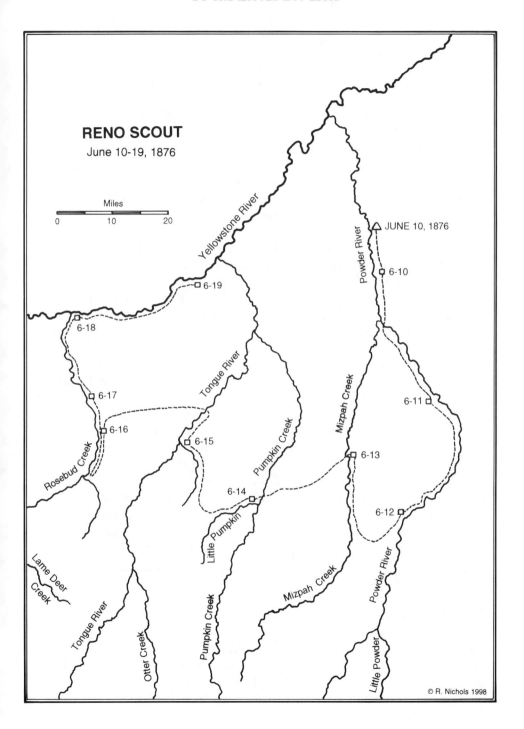

RENO SCOUT

June 10-19, 1876

Miles

0   10   20

Yellowstone River

Powder River

△ JUNE 10, 1876

6-10

6-19

6-18

6-11

Tongue River

6-17

Mizpah Creek

6-16

Pumpkin Creek

6-15

6-13

Rosebud Creek

6-14

6-12

Little Pumpkin

Lame Deer Creek

Tongue River

Otter Creek

Pumpkin Creek

Mizpah Creek

Powder River

Little Powder

© R. Nichols 1998

where the Indians were going. At this point, having already violated Terry's orders several times, Reno decided he had better gather as much information as possible about the Indian's movements, or he might have to face an angry Terry and attempt to explain his decisions. He took his command seven and a half miles farther south up the Rosebud Valley.

He halted his command at 10 o'clock on the site of another large abandoned Indian village. Scouts were sent from the campsite to explore the Indian trail, while he took extra precautions to prevent the command's discovery by the Indians. Private Peter Thompson recalled that "orders were given that no bugles be blown, no loud noises was (sic) to be made and double pickets were to be placed around our camp. Our scout, who was Mich Burey [Mitch Bouyer], was of the opinion that we could overtake the Indians in a day's march"[31]

The scouts, returning six hours later, reported they had found still another village site and that the Indians had continued to move in a southwesterly direction. Reno asked the senior Arikara scout Forked Horn, "What do you think of the trail?" Forked Horn replied: "If the Dakotas see us, the sun will not move very far before we are all killed, but you are leader and we will go on if you say so." Reno thought about it for only a minute before replying, "Custer told us to turn back if we found the trail, and we will return. These are our orders."[32] Reno left the abandoned village site at 4 o'clock in the afternoon and marched the command 15 miles down Rosebud Creek in the next four hours before establishing a camp.

The same morning Reno was moving upstream on the Rosebud, June 17, Crook's mule-mounted infantry left their campsite at 3 o'clock in the morning on a planned 50-mile march down the Rosebud Valley. The cavalry moved out several hours later, soon overtaking and passing the mule train. About 8 o'clock, Crook halted the cavalry and ordered the horses to be unsaddled and allowed to graze. A temporary camp was established in a small valley divided equally north and south by Rosebud Creek. Half an hour later, scattered firing was heard to the north and Shoshone scout Humpy and the Crow scouts all came galloping back into camp shouting "Lakota! Lakota!"[33] Sioux warriors chased the scouts almost into Crook's camp. More Sioux attacked the command and Crook was hard pressed to close up his scattered elements. Captain Anson Mills finally succeeded in taking eight companies of cavalry down the Rosebud for several miles with orders to take the Indian village Crook thought must be the source of the attack. However, he soon realized that because of the rough terrain, Mills could be marching into an ambush and sent a recall order. Crook believed his forces were outnumbered and began to withdraw his troops and form defensive positions. Fighting gradually ended by late afternoon and Crook had his command set up camp for the

Acting Assistant Surgeon
Henry R. Porter

Mitch Bouyer

night on the field. A careful retreat began the next morning and his base camp at Goose Creek was reached by the evening of the 19th. Crook's casualties were relatively light with 10 killed and 21 wounded.

The results of Crook's fight on the Rosebud and the withdrawal of his command from the campaign would remain unknown to Terry and Gibbon for several weeks. The Sioux, gaining confidence from their apparent victory over Crook, combined with the recent completion of their annual Sun Dance ceremony, proved to be an uncharacteristically aggressive foe at the battle which would take place in just eight days at the Little Big Horn.

Breaking camp early on the morning of June 18, Reno marched his command 19 miles down the Rosebud to the confluence of the Rosebud and Yellowstone. Here he turned his detachment east and moved along the south bank of the Yellowstone for another mile until he was opposite Gibbon's command camped on the north side of the river. Gibbon had expected Reno's reconnaissance to end near the mouth of the Tongue and was surprised to see them on the opposite bank. Establishing rudimentary communications with Reno, Gibbon wrote Terry:

> Col. Reno made his appearance at the mouth of the Rosebud today and I have communicated with him by signal and by scouts swimming the river. He had seen no Indians, but I gather from the conversations which the scouts had with Mitch Bowyer (sic) that they found signs of camps on Tongue River and Rosebud, and trails leading up the Rosebud. I presume the only remaining

chance of finding Indians now is in the direction of the headwaters of the Rosebud or Little Big Horn. I have been anxiously looking for the boat [*Far West*] and shall be glad to meet you or to hear of your future plans.[34]

Gibbon realized the information Reno had brought back from his scout would alter Terry's plan for a pincer movement to trap the Indians on the Rosebud — the Indians weren't on the Rosebud.

After Reno's departure June 10, Terry had moved his rest of his column to the mouth of the Powder on the 11th to establish a supply depot. On June 15, Custer led the left wing of the 7th Cavalry, pack train and Gatling gun battery, west along the Yellowstone to the mouth of the Tongue to await the arrival of Reno's command. Implementation of part two of Terry's plan could not occur until the wings of the 7th Cavalry were reunited. Custer became more frustrated as each day passed — he had been at the rendezvous point for four days with no signs of Reno.

On the morning of June 19, Reno left the camp across from Gibbon's command and marched his troopers east along the south bank of the Yellowstone in the direction of the Tongue. After traveling 33 miles, Reno established his camp about eight miles west of the planned rendezvous at the mouth of the Tongue. Reno sent Bouyer to Terry with his report and the note from Gibbon. Reno's brief report read:

> I am in camp about eight miles above you. I started this a.m. to reach your camp, but the country from the Rosebud here is simply awful and I had given orders to cache the gun, but Kinzie is coming in all right. I am sure you cannot take wagons to Rosebud without going some distance up Tongue River.
>
> I enclose you a note from Gibbon, whom I saw yesterday. I can tell you where the Indians are not, and much more information when I see you in the morning. I take it the Tongue River is not fordable at the mouth and I will necessarily have to camp on this side. I have had no accident, except breaking the tongue of Kinzie's gun carriage. My command is well. I will be on Tongue River opposite your camp about 8 a.m. My animals are leg weary and need shoeing. We have marched near to 250 miles.[35]

As expected, Terry was angry. In his June 19 diary entry, Terry wrote: "Lay in landing in afternoon received despatches (sic) from Major Reno informing me that he had been to Mouth of Rosebud. Also note from Gibbon. Sent

[Captain Robert P.] Hughes to meet Reno. Hughes returned at (?) Reno gave him no reason for his disobedience of orders."[36]

Reno's disobedience of orders was a fact. However, it also provided Terry with information he would not otherwise have had — the Indians were no longer on the Rosebud. He knew when he received Reno's report and Gibbon's note that part two of his plan to entrap the Indians with a pincer movement by Custer and Gibbon would have been an embarrassing failure and that he would have to change his plan. After receiving Reno's report, he dispatched Hughes to Reno's encampment with orders for the major to remain in camp and with the message that Custer, with the left wing, would join him the following morning. Hughes recalled:

> Terry learned through an Indian of the result of Reno's scout in the evening of June 19. That night I rode through to Reno's bivouac with orders for him to remain there and rest the next day, while Custer should bring up the remainder of the 7th, the scouts and Low's battery. After I returned to Terry that night with such information I had gathered, the maps were got out and the general field gone over.[37]

Issuing Special Field Orders No. 15 on the morning of June 20, Terry ordered Custer to proceed to Reno's bivouac and then to continue to the mouth of the Rosebud. Custer's command left the Tongue River encampment at 8 o'clock and reached Reno's encampment at just before noon. Custer was not pleased with the performance of his subordinate, and the first meeting between two since the beginning of Reno's scout was not a pleasant encounter for either man. The two apparently had a heated discussion about "Reno's movements" in violation of Terry's orders.[38] In a dispatch to the *New York Herald*, dated June 21, and published after his death, Custer wrote:

> The general impression is, and has been, that on the Rosebud and headwaters of the Little Big Horn rivers the "hostiles" would be found. It was under this impression that General Terry, in framing the orders which were to govern Major Reno's movements, explicitly and positively directed that officer to confine himself to his orders and instructions and particularly not to move in the direction of the Rosebud River.... Reno, instead of simply failing to accomplish any good results, has so misconducted his force as to embarrass, if not seriously and permanently to mar, all hopes of future success of the expedition. He had not only deliberately and without a shadow of excuse failed to obey his written

orders issued by General Terry's personal directions, but he had acted in positive disobedience to the strict injunction of the department commander.... Faint heart never won fair lady, neither did it ever pursue and overtake an Indian village. Had Reno, after first violating his orders, pursued and overtaken the Indians, his original disobedience of orders would have been overlooked, but his determination forsook him at that point, and instead of continuing the pursuit, and at least bringing the Indians to bay, he gave the order to countermarch, and faced to the rear.... The details of this affair will not bear investigation.... Few officers have ever had so fine an opportunity to make a successful and telling strike, and few ever so completely failed to improve their opportunity."[39]

Custer also wrote to Libbie:

The scouting-party has returned. They saw the trail and deserted camp of a village of three hundred and eighty (380) lodges. The trail was about one week old. The scouts reported that they could have overtaken the village in one day and a half. I am now going to take up the trail where the scouting party turned back. I fear their failure to follow up the Indians has imperiled our plans by giving the village an intimation of our presence. Think of the valuable time lost! But I feel hopeful of accomplishing great results.[40]

In a letter that Terry wrote to his sisters on the same day (June 21), he also displayed his apparent anger with Reno's performance:

Here we lay in idleness until Monday evening, when to my great surprise I received a note from Colonel Reno which informed me that he had flagrantly disobeyed my orders, and that instead of coming down the Tongue he had been to the Rosebud.... It appears that he had done this in defiance of my positive orders not to go to the Rosebud, in the belief that there were Indians on that stream, and that he could make a successful attack on them, which would cover up his disobedience.... He had not the supplies to enable him to go far and he returned without justification for his conduct, unless wearied horses and broken-down mules would be justification. Of course, this performance made a change in my plans necessary.[41]

Terry boarded the *Far West* on the afternoon of June 20 and the boat pushed off for Gibbon's camp near the Rosebud about 4 o'clock. About the same time, Custer's reunited command began its march on the south side of the Yellowstone toward the mouth of the Rosebud. The following morning the *Far West* arrived at the site of Gibbon's command and picked up Gibbon and Brisbin before continuing on toward the Rosebud. About noon on the 21st, Custer established a camp about two miles east of Rosebud Creek.

Earlier that same morning, Terry had established a preliminary plan of operations. He modified his original plan that had Custer proceeding up the Tongue and crossing over to the Rosebud and Gibbon moving up the Rosebud to trap the Indians in a pincer movement. Terry's new strategy, based on information obtained from Reno's scout, essentially moved the operation one river valley to the west. Reno's scout suggested that the Indians had continued in a southwesterly direction and were probably in the Big Horn Valley. Terry would have Custer proceed up Rosebud Creek and cross over into the Big Horn Valley while Gibbon would move west along the Yellowstone and then south up the Big Horn valley. Terry sent a dispatch to Sheridan with a summary of his new plan:

> No Indians have been met with as yet, but traces of a large and recent village have been discovered 20 or 30 miles up the Rosebud. Gibbon's column will move this morning on the north side of the Yellowstone for the mouth of the Big Horn, where it will be ferried across by the supply steamer, and whence it will proceed to the mouth of the Little Horn, and so on. Custer will go up the Rosebud tomorrow with his whole regiment and thence to the headwaters of the Little Horn, thence down the Little Horn. I only hope that one of the two columns will find the Indians. I go personally with Gibbon.[42]

Terry had the *Far West* return downriver to Custer's bivouac and that afternoon Terry, Gibbon, Brisbin and Custer held an on-board conference to discuss Terry's new plans for the expedition.[43] The conference lasted two hours during which Custer refused Brisbin's offer of additional companies of the 2nd Cavalry. When the conference aboard the *Far West* broke up about 4 o'clock, Custer hurried back to his regiment to prepare it to take the field the next day.

Gibbon had already anticipated Terry's plan and had started the Montana column, including Brisbin's 2nd Cavalry, moving westward along the north side of the Yellowstone. The column had rations for only six days, but because of its proposed route along the Yellowstone and up the Big Horn, it could be furnished with additional rations as required from the *Far West*. The 7th Cavalry, supported by the pack train, would be provided with 15 days rations which could extend its time in the field until July 6. On the morning of June 22, Terry provided written instructions for Custer's operation:

> The Brigadier General commanding directs that, as soon as your regiment can be made ready for the march, you will proceed up the Rosebud in pursuit of the Indians whose trail was discovered by Major Reno a few days since. It is, of course, impossible to give you any definite instructions in regard to this movement; and were it not impossible to do so, the department commander places too much confidence in your zeal, energy and ability to wish to impose upon you precise orders, which might hamper your action when nearly in contact with the enemy. He will, however, indicate to you his own views of what your action should be, and he desires that you should conform to them unless you shall see sufficient reason for departing from them.... The column of Colonel Gibbon is now in motion for the mouth of the Big Horn. As soon as it reaches that point it will cross the Yellowstone and move up at least as far as the forks of the Big and Little Horns. Of course its future movements must be controlled by circumstances as they arise; but it is hoped that the Indians, if upon the Little Horn, may be so nearly inclosed by the two columns that their escape will be impossible....[44]

While Terry may have been angry with Reno for disobeying his orders, he acknowledged in his instructions to Custer that the information from Reno's scout provided him with the intelligence necessary to formulate the campaign's strategy.

At noon June 22, the 7th Cavalry passed in review before Terry, Gibbon and Custer. The regiment had been given the privilege of making the main strike against the Indians and its morale ran high. Passing smartly before the reviewing officers, the 7th Cavalry, led by Reno, was staffed by 31 officers, 566 enlisted men, 35 scouts, 13 quartermaster employees, newspaperman Mark Kellogg, Custer's brother Boston Custer, and Custer's nephew Autie Reed. Colonel Gibbon later wrote of the departure:

> The bugles sounded the "boots and saddles," and Custer, after starting the advance, rode up and joined us. Together we sat on our horses and witnessed the approach of the command as it threaded its way through the rank sage brush which covered the

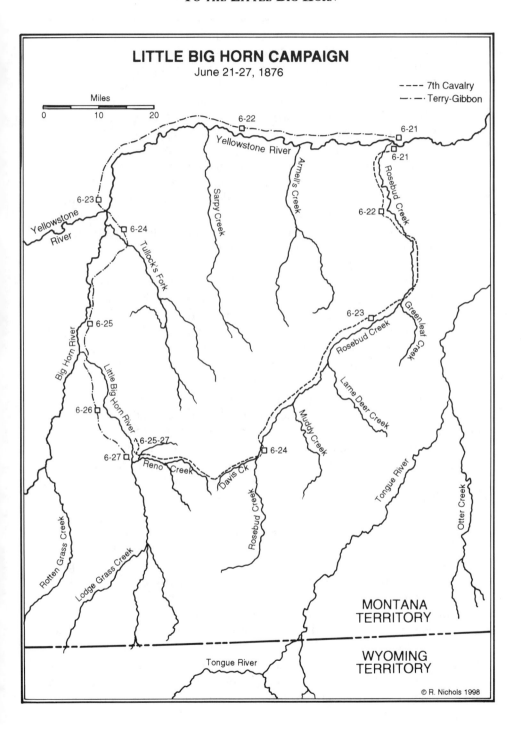

LITTLE BIG HORN CAMPAIGN
June 21-27, 1876

---- 7th Cavalry
—·— Terry-Gibbon

Miles

0   10   20

6-22

6-21

6-21

Yellowstone River

Armell's Creek

Rosebud Creek

6-23

Sarpy Creek

6-22

Yellowstone River

6-24

Tullock's Fork

Greenleaf Creek

6-23

Rosebud Creek

6-25

Lame Deer Creek

Big Horn River

Little Big Horn River

6-26

Muddy Creek

6-25-27

6-24

6-27

Reno Creek

Davis Ck

Tongue River

Otter Creek

Rosebud Creek

Rotten Grass Creek

Lodge Grass Creek

MONTANA
TERRITORY

WYOMING
TERRITORY

Tongue River

© R. Nichols 1998

163

valley. First came a band of buglers sounding a march, and as they came opposite to General Terry they wheeled out of the column as at review, continuing to play as the command passed along.... General Custer appeared to be in good spirits, chatted freely with us, and was evidently proud of the appearance of his command. The pack-mules, in a compact body, followed the regiment, and behind them came a rear-guard, and as that approached Custer shook hands with us and bade us good-by. As he turned to leave us I made some pleasant remark, warning him against being greedy, and with a gay wave of his hand he called back, "No, I will not," and rode off after his command. Little did we think we had seen him for the last time, or imagine under what circumstances we should next see that command, now mounting the bluffs in the distance with its little guidons gayly fluttering in the breeze.[45]

Each soldier carried the .45 caliber 1873 Springfield Carbine that had been approved by the board chaired by Terry and staffed by Reno just three years before — it would receive its baptism of fire in three days. Each trooper was also equipped with a .45 caliber 1873 Colt revolver, 100 rounds of .45 caliber carbine ammunition and 24 rounds of .45 caliber revolver ammunition. The only confirmed saber being carried by any member of the 7th Cavalry was that of Lieutenant Mathey — to kill snakes.

After marching 12 miles, the regiment went into bivouac in a small valley on the Rosebud. In the evening Custer issued an officer's call to tell his officers how he expected them to conduct themselves in the upcoming campaign. Wallace's official itinerary states, "Orders were given...that trumpet signals would be discontinued, that the stable guards would wake their respective companies at 3 a.m. and the command would march at 5 a.m. General Custer stated that short marches would be made for the first few days, after that they would be increased."[46] In his memoirs Private William O. Taylor states his company was informed that "trumpet calls would be discontinued."[47]

The next day the command continued their march up the Rosebud, advancing 33 miles and passing three abandoned Sioux camps before going into camp at 4:30 p.m. The pack train did not straggle in until sunset. On June 24, the command was on the march at 5 a.m. and proceeded with caution as it was now beyond the route previously explored by Reno on June 17. Crow scouts were sent out at least three times in advance of the command to determine in which direction the Indians were traveling. They returned with information that they had found two large abandoned camps and that the signs were becoming fresher. Custer halted his command at 7:45 p.m. after covering 27 miles. Herendeen later reported: "Toward evening the trail became so fresh that Custer ordered flankers to be left far out and a sharp lookout had for lodges leaving to the right or left. He said he wanted to get the whole village and nothing must leave the trail without his knowing it."[48] Later that evening, Custer was informed as to where the Indians had gone: "Scouts were sent ahead to see which branch of the stream the Indians had followed. About 9 p.m. the scouts returned and reported that the Indians had crossed the divide to the Little Big Horn."[49]

The Crow scouts also informed Custer that from a high observation point on the divide between the Rosebud and Little Big Horn valleys they could see for miles. The

Captain Thomas W. Custer
Lt. Col. Custer's Aide
June 25, 1876

point, called the Crow's Nest, was where the Crows would go when they tried to steal horses from the Sioux. Custer immediately ordered Varnum to take a detail of scouts to the point and determine the location of the Indian village. An officer's call was issued at 9:30 p.m. during which Custer outlined his plan to "cross the divide that night, to conceal the command, the next day find out the locality of the village, and attack the following morning [June 26] at daylight. Orders were given to move at midnight."[50]

The regiment finally got underway at 12:30 a.m. June 25, marching only seven miles before halting on Davis Creek about 3 a.m. Progress had been slow because of the darkness and rough terrain. The men were ordered not to unsaddle their horses but to get some sleep. The regiment would remain at this temporary camp for the next five and a half hours. About the same time, Varnum's scouting party had reached the Crow's Nest and settled down to wait for sufficient light to see into the Little Big Horn Valley. Awakened about 4 o'clock after a short nap, Varnum was told that two of the Crow scouts could see smoke from the Indian village in the valley ahead. Varnum went to see for himself but had trouble seeing any signs of the village:

I crawled up the hill and watched the valley until the sun rose.... The Crows tried to make me see a smoke from the village behind the bluff on the Little Big Horn and gave me a cheap spy-glass, but I could see nothing. They said there was an immense pony herd out grazing and told me to look for worms crawling on the grass and I would make out the herd; but I could not see worms, or ponies either. My eyes were somewhat inflamed from loss of sleep and hard riding in dust and hot sun and were not in the best of condition, but I had excellent eyesight and tried hard to see but failed. About 5 o'clock I sent the Rees back with a note to Custer telling him what the Crows reported, viz a tremendous village on the Little Big Horn.[51]

Custer received Varnum's note about half past 7 o'clock and decided to investigate the situation personally to determine for himself what the terrain was like over which the command would have to march later that night. He then apparently rode around the camp site telling some of the company officers to be ready to ride at 8 o'clock.[52] Custer departed almost immediately for the Crow's Nest. As preparations for the march were being completed, several companies started to move toward the divide about 8:45 a.m. Reno later testified:

On the morning of the 25th the Regiment was lying in some sage brush, I don't know the time exactly, and we had something to eat there, and I remember that Captain Benteen came over to where I was. When he came over there I discovered the column was moving. I was not consulted about any of those things.

The organization into battalions and wings had been annulled before we left the Yellowstone River. I never received any orders direct myself. I exercised the functions of what I imagined to be those of lieutenant colonel.

I was at different positions in the column, sometimes on the flanks and sometimes in the rear. The column moved out and I followed it.[53]

Prior to the command's departure from this halt, Captain Yates learned that a hardtack box had been lost from one of the pack mules during the night march. He sent Sergeant William A. Curtis with a squad back on the trail to recover the missing load. After traveling only a short distance, they found not only the box but several Indians looting it. The troopers fired a few rounds at the Indians to drive them away. Curtis was aware that the regiment's presence had been discovered by the Indians and immediately started back to inform his superiors.[54]

Meanwhile, the command was on the march and moved about four miles before halting at 10 o'clock just short of the divide. Sergeant Curtis caught up with the command during this halt and informed Yates about the Indians looting the hardtack box. Yates then told Captain Keogh and several other officers, including Captain Thomas W. Custer and 1st Lieutenant James T. Calhoun, about the incident. Tom Custer and Calhoun left the camp immediately to report the discovery to Custer, who had not yet returned from the Crow's Nest. When Custer arrived, he issued an officer's call to inform his men that a large Indian village was in the Little Big Horn Valley:

> He [Custer] recounted Captain Keogh's report [about the hard-tack box], and also said that the scouts had seen several Indians moving along the ridge overlooking the valley through which we had marched, as if observing our movements; he thought the Indians must have seen the dust made by the command. At all events our presence had been discovered and further concealment was unnecessary; that we would march at once to attack the village; that he had not intended to make the attack until the next morning, the 26th, but our discovery made it imperative to act at once, as delay would allow the village to scatter and escape.[55]

The command moved out at 11:45 a.m. toward the Rosebud-Little Big Horn divide — the decision had been made to attack the village in broad daylight instead of the morning attack earlier favored by Custer. June 25 would prove to be a momentous day in the history of the 7th Cavalry.

Endnotes

[1] Philip Sheridan, *Outline Descriptions of the Posts in the Military Division of the Missouri, 1876* (Old Army Press, Bellevue, Neb., 1969), p. 38.
[2] Melbourne C. Chandler, *Of Garryowen in Glory*, (Turnpike Press, Annandale, Va., 1960), p. 41.
[3] Post Return from Fort Abraham Lincoln, Dakota Territory, November 1875.
[4] Chandler, p. 45.
[5] Chandler, p. 46.
[6] Edgar I. Stewart, *Custer's Luck* (University of Oklahoma Press, Norman, 1955), p. 77.
[7] Report of the 44th Congress, 1st Session, Senate Executive Document No. 52, pp. 8-9.
[8] Library of Congress, Sheridan Collection, Shelf No. 19.308, Reel 88.
[9] Library of Congress, Sheridan Collection, Shelf No. 19.308, Reel 88.

[10] John S. Gray, *Centennial Campaign* (University of Oklahoma Press, Norman, 1988), p. 86.

[11] Post Returns from Fort Abraham Lincoln, Dakota Territory, March 1876, and Special Orders No. 26, Headquarters, Department of Dakota.

[12] John Upton Terrell and Colonel George Walton, *Faint the Trumpet Sounds* (David McKay Company, Inc., New York, 1966), p. 130.

[13] Record of Events, Post Returns from Fort Abraham Lincoln, Dakota Territory, April 1876.

[14] Charles F. Bates, *Custer's Indian Battles* (Old Army Press, Fort Collins, Colo., N.D.), p. 28.

[15] Bates, p. 28.

[16] Division of the Missouri, Letters Received, April 16, 1876, Record Group 98, NARA.

[17] Library of Congress, Sheridan Collection, Shelf No. 19.308, Reel 58.

[18] Office of the Adjutant General, April 1876, Charges and Specifications, NARA.

[19] Library of Congress, Sheridan Collection, Shelf No. 19.308, Reel 88.

[20] General Orders No. 3, May 6, 1876, Headquarters 7th Cavalry, Fort Abraham Lincoln, D.T.

[21] Stewart, p. 135.

[22] Stewart, p. 136.

[23] Robert Hughes, "The Campaign Against the Sioux," *Journal of the Military Service Institution*, January 1896, p. 13.

[24] General Orders No. 8, May 12, 1876, Headquarters, 7th Cavalry, Fort Abraham Lincoln, D.T.

[25] Special Field Orders No. 11, Department of Dakota, June 10, 1876, NARA.

[26] Gray, p. 128.

[27] Kenneth Hammer (editor), *Custer in '76* (Brigham Young University Press, Provo, Utah, 1976), p. 123. Interview with John McGuire. McGuire stated there were two Gatling guns along but Reno's orders specifically stated one.

[28] Daniel O. Magnussen, *Peter Thompson's Narrative of the Little Bighorn Campaign 1876* (Arthur H. Clark Co., Glendale, Calif., 1974), pp. 67.

[29] Gray, p. 133.

[30] Gray, p. 133.

[31] Magnussen, pp. 74-75.

[32] O. G. Libby, Editor, *The Arikara Narrative of the Campaign Against the Hostile Dakotas June 1876* (Rio Grande Press, Inc., Glorieta, N.M., 1976), pp. 70-71.

[33] J. W. Vaughn, *With Crook at the Rosebud*, (University of Nebraska Press, Lincoln, 1988), p. 50.

[34] Gibbon to Terry, June 18, 1876, Department of Dakota, Letters Received, 1876, Box 19, RG 98, NARA.

[35] Department of Dakota, June 19, 1876, Letters Received, 1876, RG 98, NARA.

[36] Terry, p. 7.

[37] W. A. Graham, *The Story of the Little Big Horn* (The Stackpole Company, Harrisburg, Penna., 1959), Appendix pp. 34-35.

[38] Fred Dustin, *The Custer Tragedy* (Edwards Brothers, Inc., Ann Arbor, Mich., 1939), p.62, footnote 11. Dustin stated: "It is said that when Custer and Reno met at this time, the former made a savage verbal attack on Reno's movements, and that the latter returned the compliment with interest. This is very likely true, as those who knew Custer were well aware of his harsh manner and frequent rudeness to subordinates. Even Godfrey speaks of his 'rasping manner'; letters from officers and men of the regiment, as well as matter in print, are quite convincing that Custer's strictures at this time, as well as his 'Voice from the Tomb,' were not only unwarranted but reprehensible."

[39] *New York Herald*, July 11, 1876, "A Voice From the Tomb."

[40] Elizabeth B. Custer, *Boots and Saddles* (Harper and Brothers, New York, 1885), pp. 311-312.

[41] Bates, pp. 29-30. The original of this letter has never been found. Two interesting and glaring errors are immediately evident from this letter. The original written orders Reno received from Terry concerning the scout did not make any statement admonishing Reno "not to go to the Rosebud," and the orders also specifically stated Reno was to "be supplied with subsistence for twelve days and with forage for the same period at the rate of two pounds of grain the day for each animal," so the statement that Reno "had not the supplies to enable him to go [that] far," was also in error. Why would Terry make these mistakes? Perhaps he had read Custer's dispatch and inadvertently thought he had ordered Reno not to go to the Rosebud.

[42] Annual Reports of the Secretary of War, 1874-1877, Washington, D.C.

[43] Why was Reno not included in these discussions? He was second-in-command of the 7th Cavalry and in the event something happened to Custer during the campaign he would need to know the plan of attack in order to carry it out successfully. Brisbin, Gibbon's second-in-command, was at the meeting. This could be considered a case of gross negligence on Custer's part to exclude Reno from the meeting. Custer, of course, wanted full credit for the success of the operation.

[44] Chandler, p. 50. The entire text of Terry's orders to Custer may be found in Appendix B.

[45] John Gibbon, *Last Summer's Expedition* (The Old Army Press, Bellevue, Neb., 1970), p. 23.

[46] Gray, p. 152. It should be noted that in his official itinerary Wallace does not state that trumpet calls would be used "...in an emergency," as stated by Edward Settle Godfrey ("Custer's Last Battle," *The Century Illustrated Monthly Magazine*, January 1892), p. 365; or as stated by Jim Willert, "...or when nearly in contact with the enemy," *Little Big Horn Diary* (RB Printing Co., Duarte, Calif., 1982), p. 218.

[47] William O. Taylor, *With Custer of the Little Bighorn* (Penquin Books, New York, 1996), p. 27.

[48] John S. Gray, *Custer's Last Campaign* (University of Nebraska Press, Lincoln, 1991), p. 217.

[49] Gray, *Custer's Last Campaign*, p. 218.

[50] Gray, *Centennial Campaign*, p. 165.

[51] Hammer, p. 60.

[52] Gray, *Custer's Last Campaign*, p. 234. It is speculation on Gray's part that "before leaving his sleeping command, he must have left orders for Reno to move the column to

a place of concealment near the divide, for that is precisely what it did at 8:45 a.m."

[53] Ronald H. Nichols (editor), *Proceedings of a Court of Inquiry in the case of Major Marcus A. Reno* (Custer Battlefield Historical and Museum Assn., Inc., Crow Agency, Mont., 1992), pp. 559-560. This statement is counter to what Gray speculates in the previous endnote. It is likely that Captain Tom Custer, who was acting as an aide to his brother, gave the orders for the command to start the movement to the divide. Second Lieutenant Henry M. Harrington was in command of Company in Tom Custer's absence.

[54] The Indians were part of Little Wolf's party of seven lodges of Cheyennes, who had left the Red Cloud agency to join the hostile camp. Gray, *Custer's Last Command*, p. 241.

[55] Edward Settle Godfrey, "Custer's Last Battle" (*The Century Illustrated Monthly Magazine*, January 1892), p. 368

• 10 •

Into the Valley

Shortly after noon June 25, the 7th Cavalry crossed the divide between the Rosebud and Little Big Horn valleys. Custer halted the regiment to make battalion assignments. The regimental organization established at Fort Lincoln into battalions and wings prior to its departure May 17 had been annulled by Custer before the command left camp on the Yellowstone River and proceeded up Rosebud Creek. In reorganizing his command after crossing the divide, Custer assigned a battalion to each of his most senior officers: Reno (Companies A, G and M); Benteen (Companies D, H and K); Keogh (Companies C, I and L); and Yates (Companies E and F). Reno was informed of his assignment by Custer's adjutant, 1st Lieutenant William W. Cooke: "The General directs you to take specific command of Companies M, A and G." Reno replied, "Is that all?" and Cooke responded, "Yes."[1] Custer also ordered the company commanders to assign six enlisted men and one non-commissioned officer from each of their companies to Captain McDougall's Company B to provide protection for the mule-pack train.[2]

Earlier, Custer told his officers the Indian scouts had reported a large Indian village in view from the Crow's Nest, but that he did not believe such himself as he had looked with his glass.[3] Custer had obviously formulated a plan of operations but did not inform any of his battalion commanders of the plan. His strategy was to prevent the Indians from escaping before his troops could capture the non-combatants which would force the Indians to return to their agencies.

Following the division of the regiment, Benteen and his battalion were ordered to move off to the southwest and to proceed out into a line of bluffs about four or five miles away and to pitch into anything they came across. Benteen was to send back word to Custer at once if he came across anything. He had gone only about a mile when the regiment's chief trumpeter, Henry Voss, delivered another message to Benteen that if he "found nothing before reaching the first line of bluffs, to go on to the second line with the same instructions." He had also been instructed to send an officer and six men in advance of his battalion to scout the area. A third message, delivered by Ser-

1st Lieutenant William W. Cooke
Regimential Adjutant

geant Major William H. Sharrow, told him if he saw nothing from the second line of bluffs, to go on into the valley, and if there was nothing in the valley, to go on to the next valley.[4] The remaining three battalions would proceed westward toward the Little Big Horn with the pack train trailing.

Both Keogh's and Yates' battalions, totaling about 215 officers and men, remained with Custer and proceeded westward along the north side of Sundance Creek (later Reno Creek) while Reno and his command moved parallel to Custer along the south side of the stream. About two hours after leaving the divide, Custer signaled Reno to bring his command across the stream to the north bank. Custer and Reno rode together for a short time, approaching a solitary tepee containing the body of a warrior who had died of wounds sustained at a battle between the Indians and General Crook's command June 17 on upper Rosebud Creek. Custer's Arikara scouts set fire to the tepee, which may have alerted every Indian in the valley.

Shortly after arriving in the vicinity of the tepee, scout Fred Girard, riding to the top of a small knoll and pointing toward the Little Big Horn River, called out to Custer, "Here are your Indians, running like devils."[5] Girard stated that Custer then issued orders directly to Reno to "take your battalion and try and overtake and bring them to battle and I will support you."[6] Reno later stated that Custer's orders were issued through Adjutant Cooke who told him, "General Custer directs you to take as rapid a gait as you think prudent and charge the village afterwards, and you will be supported by the whole outfit."[7] Second Lieutenants Benjamin H. Hodgson, Reno's adjutant, and George D. Wallace were with Reno when he received the orders from Cooke. Wallace said the orders came from Cooke: "[T]he Indian are about two mile and a half ahead, on the jump, follow them as fast as you can, and charge them wherever you find them and we will support you."[8]

Custer had neither informed Reno of his battle plans nor of the orders he had issued to Benteen. Reno interpreted his orders to mean that Custer would follow him with Keogh's and Yates' battalions. The orders were direct and positive — no discretion was given or suggested that would allow Reno to retreat before the implied "support from the whole outfit" arrived. Reno did not know if Benteen was ordered to continue his scout to the southwest or return to the trail. Having received his orders, Reno proceeded toward the Little Big Horn, moving his command which was formed in a column-of-twos, at a "fast trot," and covered the two miles from the solitary tepee to the river in about 20 minutes.[9]

Captain Myles Moylan
Company A

Second Lieutenant Charles A. Varnum, commanding Custer's Indian scouts, had traveled along to the left of the Custer-Reno command on their westward march toward the Little Big Horn. As Reno approached the river, Varnum reported to Custer that he had spotted a large number of Indians in the valley. Custer ordered Varnum to take his Indian scouts and go with Reno.

After Cooke gave the orders to Reno, Girard called out to the scouts, "We are ordered to go with this party [Reno] and join them." Reno and his command, on reaching the river, paused momentarily. Girard was alerted by the scouts "to the fact that all the Indians were coming up the valley," and Girard attempted to tell Reno about the Indians: "Major Reno, the Indians are coming up the valley to meet us."[10] Reno did not trust Girard and was hesitate to accept Girard's statement about the Indians.[11] Girard said Reno looked at him, "looked at the valley and gave the order, 'Forward.' "[12] Reno's battalion immediately crossed the river. The crossing was a little difficult and when Reno got on the other side, he halted his battalion for about 10 minutes to reform them into a column-of-fours before proceeding through the fringe of timber along the river. As the command passed onto the open prairie, Reno placed two companies in a line-of-battle formation (Captain Moylan's Company A and Captain French's Company M) with the third company (1st Lieutenant Donald McIntosh's Company G) behind in reserve.[13] Reno was convinced that the Indians were there in overwhelming numbers.[14]

Girard, watching Reno's battalion cross the river, thought it important enough to inform Custer about the Indians. Riding only a short distance toward Custer's command, he met Lieutenant Cooke and told him of the Indians coming up the valley. Cooke said, "All right, I'll go back and report," and then turned and went back to Custer's command.[15] Girard crossed the river and rejoined Reno's command.

As Reno's battalion proceeded cautiously toward the dust cloud farther down the valley, Reno dispatched the first of two messengers, his striker, Private Archibald McIlhargy, to Custer with the message "that Indians were in front of me, and in strong force."[16] Continuing for another mile toward the Indian village, Reno dispatched his second and final message to Custer — Private John Mitchell, a cook, took the same message that McIlhargy had carried a short time before — Indians were in front and were strong. Both messengers reached Custer for the bodies of both McIlhargy and Mitchell were later identified among the dead on the Custer battlefield.

Within half an hour after Reno's departure, Custer, while proceeding toward the Little Big Horn, received three messages about Indians in the valley; one directly from Varnum; one from Girard via Cooke, and a third directly from Reno via Trooper McIlhargy. All the messages possessed a common theme — Indians were in the valley and in front of Reno. Custer turned northward, remaining on the east side of the river instead of crossing the Little Big Horn as Reno expected. Custer may have decided either to launch a flanking attack on the village or approach the village from the north. When he received Reno's second message from Mitchell, he apparently took no action to send a messenger back to Reno indicating that he would move to attack the Indians from a point farther downstream. Custer, at the time he turned north, neither knew the extent of the village nor how he would attack it.

Reno's battalion contained about 165 officers, troopers, civilians and scouts, and he anticipated being supported by the "whole outfit."[17] Of the 124 enlisted personnel of his three companies, about 25 percent were recruits.[18] Reno rode ahead of the line, and the Arikara scouts were on the extreme left. As the command moved downstream toward the Indian village, Reno, seeing the large dust cloud, firmly believed that the Indians were coming up to attack. About a mile from the village, he ordered Hodgson to have Company G move up to the right side of the line in a line-of-battle formation. The line moved forward at a fast trot or gallop.

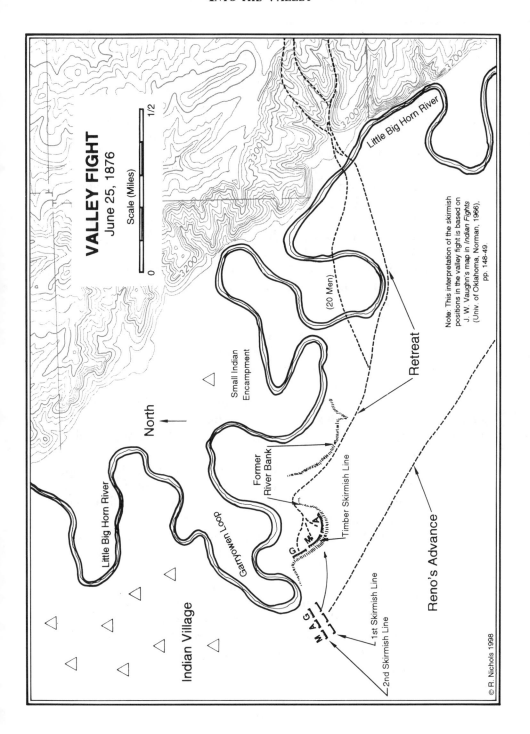

VALLEY FIGHT
June 25, 1876

Scale (Miles)

0   1/2

North

Little Big Horn River

Indian Village

Garryowen Loop

Former
River Bank

Small Indian
Encampment

Timber Skirmish Line

G
M
A

1st Skirmish Line

2nd Skirmish Line

Reno's Advance

Retreat

(20 Men)

Little Big Horn River

Note: This interpretation of the skirmish
positions in the valley fight is based on
J. W. Vaughn's map in *Indian Fights*
(Univ. of Oklahoma, Norman, 1966),
pp. 148-49.

© R. Nichols 1998

175

After moving downstream about two miles, Reno's command was approaching the village. Activity directly ahead of Reno's command had increased significantly. Warriors were coming out from the village to meet the attack while other warriors were creating large clouds of dust to cover their movement. It was obvious to Reno that the Indians were going to stay and fight. Dust forced him to slow his troopers, and aware of a possible Indian ambush, he made the first of several critical decisions — he halted and dismounted his command. Reno gave the order to dismount directly to Moylan and French and instructed Hodgson to inform McIntosh. The battalion formed a skirmish line across the valley floor. The right side of the line was close to, and at right angles to, the timber along the Little Big Horn, while the left side extended well out onto the valley floor. Shortly after Reno halted, Indians poured out of a shallow ravine about 300 or 400 yards to his front.[19] From what he could observe, Reno was certain his command was badly outnumbered by the warriors. He saw "straggling parties of Indians" moving around to his rear, and decided he "could not make an offensive charge" and the large number of Indians forced him into a defensive position.[20]

Aware of his orders to "charge the village," Reno also knew he must use extreme caution. His knowledge of Indian tactics alerted him to the possibility of an ambush if he proceeded head long into the village. He had no desire to be pulled into a trap and have his troops massacred.[21] Second Lieutenant Luther R. Hare, second-in-command of the scouts under Varnum, later testified that "As soon as the skirmish line was dismounted, 400 or 500 [Indians] came out of a coulee which was 400 yards in front of us," and had the command "gone 300 yards farther mounted, I don't think he [Reno] would have got a man out."[22]

First Lieutenant Charles C. DeRudio, second-in-command of Company A, also testified, "I saw that we would have been butchered if we had gone 500 yards further."[23] Moylan indicated "there were about 400 Indians within 500 yards of him at the time."[24]

About this time Varnum saw Custer's command on the bluffs across the river:

> I saw, about the time Major Reno's command dismounted in the bottom, just as I joined it from the left and front, looking on the bluffs across the river to our right, I saw the Gray Horse Company [1st Lieutenant Algernon E. Smith's Company E] of the regiment moving down along those bluffs. As I know now the Gray Horse Company was with his command, I know it was General Custer's column.[25]

Girard also saw part of Custer's command as he left the skirmish line to go into the timber: "I saw Custer's command, or a portion of it, just as I was going down into the timber."[26] While in the timber DeRudio also saw part of Custer's column:

> General Custer, Lieutenant Cooke, and another man I could not recognize came to the highest point of the bluff and waved their hats and made motions like they were cheering, and pretty soon disappeared. I judge by that that probably his column was behind the bluff.[27]

Reno's troopers dismounted in good order and maintained their skirmish line positions. However, every fourth soldier now became a horse-holder, which reduced the number of effective regulars to slightly less than 100. Company G was on the right, closest to the river, Company A in the center, and Company M on the left. The horses were moved into the timber for better protection. The Arikara scouts from the left side of the line broke ranks and proceeded to round up Sioux and Cheyenne ponies.

Dismounted, the skirmish line proceeded slowly forward, the troopers firing their carbines as they moved toward the village. It was reported to Reno that Indians had been seen coming into the timber, thus threatening the horses. He quickly withdrew Company G from the skirmish line and placed it in the woods. He rode into the timber with the troopers to supervise their movements. This left a gap between Moylan's Company A and the timber, so Moylan extended his line to the right to cover the open space. The Indians continued to move out from the village and started around the left side of the valley line. Moylan rode over to the timber and called to Reno "to come up there and look at the situation of affairs.[28] Reno perceived that his skirmish line, which extended well out onto the valley floor, was vulnerable to being surrounded by the warriors. The line had moved about 100 yards in the direction of the village and had remained across the valley floor for about 10 or 15 minutes. Reno ordered Moylan's and French's companies to fall back into the timber.[29] The line wheeled to the right with the end of Company A at the timber line acting as a pivot point.

Over the years the Little Big Horn River had changed its course numerous times — new channels had formed and old loops cut off. Where the right side of Reno's valley skirmish line had been anchored near the timber, just such an old river bend existed. The depression was crescent in shape, 20 to 25 yards in width, and from four to 10 feet below the level of the valley floor. Reno reformed his command into a defensive skirmish line in the timber and along the edge of this depression. This position could be held for an extended

177

period depending on the expenditure of ammunition. Reno realized the soldiers had used considerable ammunition on the valley skirmish line. DeRudio estimated the men, while on the valley line, probably did not fire more than 30 or 40 rounds.[30] Sergeant F. A. Culbertson said that while on the skirmish line, "some of the men were firing very fast. Many were new men, a great many of my own company were new men and were firing fast."[31] Sergeant Edward Davern thought he fired "about 20 rounds," on the skirmish line but that he had fired slower than the other men."[32] Each trooper carried 50 rounds of carbine ammunition and 24 cartridges for his Colt revolver. An additional 50 rounds of carbine ammunition were carried in their saddle packs.

Firing continued along the timber skirmish line for another 20 or 25 minutes. Reno expected support from Custer and his two battalions momentarily. He realized the position in the timber could not be maintained indefinitely. With the continued expenditure of ammunition, the situation would soon become critical. Reno sent Varnum up to the skirmish line and told him to "see how things are going on and come back and report to me." When Varnum moved up to line, he heard Captain Moylan say that his men were out of ammunition and order each alternate man to fall back and get ammunition out of their saddlebags and then return to the line so the other could go and get ammunition from their saddlebags.[33] Hare thought the command could have held the timber position for another 30 minutes by using the ammunition judiciously, although DeRudio later said that with the number of men Reno had, they might have been successful for probably three or four hours "depending on circumstances."[34]

To completely seal off the timber position, Reno knew he would have to both extend his skirmish line along the entire edge of the depression and send other men into the timber to protect the command from the rear. This would force the men on the front skirmish line to be at such long intervals that control of the trooper's fire by the officers and non-coms would be difficult. Few troopers had been killed or wounded at this point. Reno knew "a scout was killed, Sergeant Heyn of A Company was hit, and two or three men in Company M were hit." Wallace thought he saw two men killed and heard about another: "One of them I thought was killed or rather appeared to be dying and the other was shot through the bowels." Company A had "one man killed, and two wounded," according to Moylan, and DeRudio saw "a sergeant killed...two or three others wounded."[35]

Reno and his command continued to defend the timber skirmish line under what he considered "a pretty hot fire." He was on the line near Moylan when he received word that the Indians were seen near the right side of his line. Leaving Hodgson on the line to keep him apprised of the activities there, Reno ordered a number of men of Company G to mount up and ride with him to the river bank. Arriving at the river, he had a good view of the tepees downstream and saw the Indians filtering into the timber, using the woods to shelter themselves while moving toward the soldiers. Reno took his contingent of men back through the timber, had them dismount and establish a rear-guard position. He then rode out onto the valley floor near the skirmish line.[36] Hodgson came over to him and told him the Indians were observed to be passing around the left side of the skirmish line. Hodgson also reported that Indians were also seen crossing the river and moving in behind the command. Reno knew he could "not stay there unless I stayed forever."[37]

Reno still did not know why he had not received either support from Custer "with the whole outfit," or a message from him with new orders. He had to assume the companies from the two battalions with Custer had become scattered and were not capable of providing the promised support. Reno reasoned that without some direction from the regimental commander, and with the Indians continuing to filter into the timber, it was imperative that he take some action before the command was overwhelmed by the Indians. He thought a union with the rest of the regiment was absolutely necessary: "There was no use in my staying in the timber as I could assist no one and could make no diversion."[38]

Indians continued to filter into the woods, endangering both the men and horses. It soon became evident to Reno that his command would shortly be surrounded. The depletion of ammunition was also becoming a serious factor.[39] Without Custer's support, Reno would have to quickly make a decision to move the command and attempt to join up with the rest of the regiment. Although Custer, or part of his command, had been seen earlier across the river by DeRudio, Varnum and Girard, none of them bothered to tell Reno what they saw. When Reno was asked later if anyone had informed him that Custer's column had been seen while his command (Reno's) was in the timber, he replied, "No...never."[40] Reno did not know the location of either Custer's or Benteen's commands.

It was apparent to Reno that remaining in the timber was not an acceptable option. Indians were moving into the timber from different directions. The possibility of some men running out of ammunition would be a disaster for his command. Reno made his decision and gave orders for the command to form up in column-of-fours — they were going to leave the timber and find the rest of the regiment. He personally gave orders to Moylan and McIntosh and sent his adjutant, Hodgson, to inform French.[41] Moylan and McIntosh went to where their companies were positioned on the skirmish line and informed the men to leave the line. They were told to mount up and move to a clearing or glade near the edge of the timber. Since many of the Company G troopers were providing a rear guard action in the timber, they did not hear the orders and only mounted after seeing the other companies doing so. Reno proceeded to the edge of the timber. When Moylan returned, Reno asked him his opinion as to where the command should move. Reno knew the movement would be entirely on the defensive owing to the force of Indians then in sight. Following a short discussion with Moylan, Reno designated a point in the high bluffs across the river where the command would establish itself and await further developments.[42] Wallace said he received word that the command was being surrounded and, "we would have to get on higher ground where we would not be surrounded and where we could defend ourselves better than we could there [in the timber]."[43]

Moylan then left Reno, returned to his company, and moved it out through the timber and onto the open valley floor. He saw Reno sitting on his horse near the edge of the timber watching the formation of the command. Moylan would testify:

> The companies were mounted up and being unable to form in any order in the timber, I gave my men orders to mount up as rapidly as possible individually and move up out of the timber in order that they might be formed out there. When about one half of my company was mounted up, I went out of the timber and formed the men in column-of-fours as they came up. M Company came up very soon after and formed on my left at an interval of 15 or 20 yards. G Company, as I understood, did not mount quite so soon or did not get up quite so soon as the other two companies, but they were in the column before it reached the river. During the time the companies were being formed, Major Reno was there on his horse overlooking the formation of the companies.[44]

Several minutes later, Moylan reported to Reno that Company A was formed and ready to move. About this time, Reno motioned for the scout Bloody Knife to come over to him. Bloody Knife rode over to Reno and started to communicate with him through the use of sign language. Reno wanted to know Bloody Knife's opinion as to what he thought the Indians would do when the command started moving away from the village. Bloody Knife had just started to answer when several Indians suddenly burst through the timber and fired at almost point blank range at the soldiers. Private George Lorentz was hit in the back of the neck with the bullet coming out his mouth.[45] Bloody Knife was hit in the head by a bullet that killed him instantly. Reno, just six or eight feet from Bloody Knife, was sprayed with blood and brain matter. Momentarily distracted, he said to Moylan, "We have got to

Lt. Colonel George Custer & his scouts.
Bloody Knife kneels at left.

get out of here, we have got to charge them."[46] Reno rode to the head of the formation and Private William E. Morris, Company M, heard him say, "Men, we are surrounded, draw your revolvers and follow me."[47] The command had formed in columns-of-fours — Company A in front, followed by Companies M and G.[48]

When the column moved completely out onto the open plain, Reno halted it momentarily to allow the companies time to close up. He left both the

181

wounded and dead behind — he had no way to transport them, and his main concern was to save the command. Some troopers and scouts, including DeRudio, who either didn't get the word that the command was leaving or were unable to get to their horses, were also left behind. Some returned to the command that night and some the following day. Reno was later supported in his decision to leave the timber by Moylan, Wallace, Hare and Sergeant Culberston. Moylan said "I think the most judicious course was to leave the timber, if possible. Had the command stayed there 30 minutes longer, I doubt if it would have gotten out with as many men as it did."[49] When Wallace was later asked about the likely casualties if the command had remained in the timber, he responded, "Major Reno and every man with him would have been killed."[50] Lieutenant Hare said, "If we stayed there much longer we would be shut in so that we could not get out,"[51] and Sergeant Culbertson thought if Reno remained in the timber that he "could have held it but a very few minutes."[52] Varnum stated the timber "was not a very safe place.... I might say that at the time that movement was made a great many bullets had commenced to drop into the woods from the rear. I did not see any Indians there and whether the bullets were from the bluffs above or from below, I don't know."[53]

When the soldiers exited the timber and temporarily paused to reform, the Indians momentarily became confused. The unexpected appearance of Reno's command on the valley floor constituted a significant danger to their village. They did not immediately attack the soldiers but gave way as the soldiers moved out onto the open plain. However, once it became apparent that the soldiers were moving away from the village, the Indians then pressed the attack.

Leading the soldiers was Reno — determined to lead them to safety. "I thought my duty was there, to see about the direction of the column, and have facilities for observing the ford and hill on the other side, and I would be on the top of the hill to rally and reform the men."[54]

The command started from the timber in reasonably good order. Wallace said, "When I got out what I had of my company [G] I saw the other two companies moving at a gallop. It looked like they were moving in column-of-fours in a gallop." Varnum thought that the column-of-fours was a good formation for the limited number of men Reno had with him and it "would give the men an opportunity to use their revolvers, they could not use their carbines."[55] The head of the column was able to maintain some reasonable semblance of order but the rear quickly became strung out. Dr. Henry R. Porter said there was "no order at all, every man seemed to be running on his own hook."[56]

Varnum described the tactics of the Indians:

> The men were moving in column-of-fours and as they would come up to the Indians the Indians would give way and let them pass through and then fire on them. After the men passed through if they [the Indians] saw that a man was not using his pistol they would ride close to him and fire.[57]

Although the total time the column took to reach the river was only six to 10 minutes, with the Indians riding alongside firing into the soldiers, and the soldiers suffering heavy losses, panic was evident. No orders had been given to establish even a rudimentary rear guard, or pause long enough to assure that all the men had joined the formation. Moylan attempted to check his company to provide some coverage for the soldiers in the rear of the formation, but without success. The soldiers were riding for their lives and were not going to stop. As occurred repeatedly during the Civil War, once soldiers broke and ran before the enemy, little could be done to stop them. With about one-fourth of Reno's command being recruits, the chance of establishing any kind of rear guard action was virtually non-existent.

The recrossing of the Little Big Horn was chaotic. The river bank on the western side was about five feet high and the eastern bank eight feet. The soldiers were forced to jump their horses off the western bank, forge the three- to four-foot deep, 40-foot wide stream, and then climb the sharp "cut-bank" on the eastern side. No covering fire was established on the east side of the river by the soldiers after they had crossed. Hare saw "considerable disturbance and confusion" at the crossing and "no troops [were] covering the crossing."[58] Porter said that when he reached the crossing, "everybody was rushing in, trying to get across as fast as they could; the Indians were firing into them. Every man seemed to be looking out for himself, trying to get across as soon as possible."[59] Troopers from the three companies intermingled as they emerged from the river. After Reno crossed, he gave consideration to the immediate reorganization of his command. Varnum said, "The command stopped there and I am pretty certain it was Major Reno said that place on the side hill was no place to form at, we had better go to the top of the hill."[60] Any attempt by Reno to reorganize the command on the move would have been difficult. Soldiers were not willing to stop, dismount and provide protective fire, even under direct orders. For a soldier to remain in the vicinity of the crossing for any length of time meant almost certain death.

Sergeant Culbertson said, after crossing the river, he saw Captain French and Sergeant Lloyd and Lloyd said to Culbertson, "We had better stop and protect the wounded in coming across." Culbertson told him to speak to Captain French about it and Lloyd did. French told Lloyd, "I'll try, I'll try," but then turned and rode up the hill.[61]

After the soldiers crossed the river, they "seemed to be retreating in as good order as could be expected," Sergeant Davern stated.[62] Reno continued to the top of the bluffs. For Reno and his men, the horror of what had already become a long, unpleasant afternoon would only continue.

Endnotes

[1] Ronald H. Nichols, (Ed.), *Reno Court of Inquiry: Proceedings of a Court of Inquiry in the Case of Major Marcus A. Reno Concerning His Conduct at the Battle of the Little Big Horn River on June 25-26, 1876,* (Custer Battlefield Historical and Museum Association, Inc., Crow Agency, Mont., 1992), Reno's testimony, p. 560. This is the "official" version of the inquiry and was taken directly from the National Archives microfilm of the original text. Hereinafter Reno Court.

[2] Reno Court, McDougall's testimony, p. 528. McDougall indicated that his "company was composed of about 45 men and there were about 80 men belonging to the pack train." If each of the other 11 companies provided six men and one non-com, that would total 77 men assigned to the pack train — close to the number estimated by McDougall.

[3] Reno Court, Reno's testimony, p. 560.

[4] Reno Court, Benteen's testimony, p. 403.

[5] Reno Court, Girard's testimony, pp. 84, 112.

[6] Reno Court, Girard's testimony, pp. 86, 112; Girard said Custer gave the message directly to Reno.

[7] Reno Court, Reno's testimony, p. 561. There is a question as to whether Custer (through Cooke) told Reno to charge the "village" or the "Indians." Custer, at the time he issued his orders, did not know the location of the village.

[8] Reno Court, Wallace's testimony, p. 21.

[9] Marcus Reno, *Americana History Magazine,* January-June, 1912, Volume 7, story written by Marcus Reno in 1886; material submitted by Ittie Reno, the wife of Reno's son Robert, p. 260; and Reno Court, Reno's official report, p. 641; Reno Court, Wallace's testimony, p. 46.

[10] Reno Court, Girard's testimony, p. 114.

[11] Reno Court, Reno's testimony, p. 588.

[12] Reno Court, Girard's testimony, p. 114.

[13] Reno Court, Varnum's testimony, p. 169.

[14] Reno Court, Reno's testimony, p. 561; Wallace's testimony, p. 46; Culbertson's testimony, pp. 366-367.

[15] Reno Court, Girard's testimony, p. 87.

[16] Reno Court, Reno's testimony, p. 561.

[17] Reno indicated at the Court of Inquiry that he had 112 men plus the scouts when he crossed the Little Big Horn river. An extensive study by Joe Sills Jr., Baltimore, Md., concerned the actual strength of Reno's battalion as it first crossed the Little Big Horn. Sills believes the entire strength of Reno's battalion was 165 including officers, enlisted men, civilians, and scouts. The breakdown is as follows:

11 officers, who included five regular officers, Reno, Moylan, McIntosh, French and DeRudio; four detached officers, Varnum, Hare, Wallace and Hodgson; and two surgeons, Porter and DeWolf.

124 regular enlisted men, six attached enlisted men, four civilians, two Crows, 13 Arikara, three Sioux and the two Jackson brothers.

The original figure of 124 enlisted men was arrived at by a careful review of the rosters of Companies A, G and M, and deducting those men who were known to be on detached service. The total number was 145 enlisted men, and deducting the 21 men assigned to the pack train would leave a total of 124 enlisted men. Included in the six attached enlisted men crossing the river are McIlhargy and Mitchell who were sent back as messengers. Therefore of the total of 130 enlisted men (regular and attached), 128 reached Reno's first skirmish line in the valley. However, the four attached enlisted men cannot be counted in terms of forming the line—only those on company duty would do so. Therefore a total of 124 enlisted men would be on the line, and since one-fourth of them would be horseholders, a total of 93 enlisted men would remain on the skirmish line to move toward the Indian village. The attached enlisted men would most probably go with the officers/surgeons to whom they were attached. A plausible explanation for why Reno indicated he only had 112 men plus scouts when he crossed the Little Big Horn cannot be given.

[18] Joe Sills, Jr., "The Recruits Controversy: Another Look," *Greasy Grass*, (Custer Battlefield Historical & Museum Association, Inc., Volume V, 1989), p. 5. The total number of recruits with Reno's battalion was 40. If all the enlisted men sent to the pack train were recruits, then 22 recruits would have still remained with Reno. Assuming only half the enlisted men sent to guard the pack train were recruits, then about 31 men, or 25 percent of Reno's command that crossed the river were recruits.

[19] Reno Court, Reno's testimony, p. 590.

[20] Reno Court, Reno's testimony, p. 562.

[21] Reno had military experience fighting Indians when he served with the First Dragoons in Washington Territory (1858-1861), and with the Seventh Cavalry in Kansas (1870-1871). He was also aware of the massacre that occurred on Dec. 21, 1866, of Captain William J. Fetterman's command by Indians outside of Fort Phil Kearny, Wyoming Territory.

[22] Reno Court, Hare's testimony, pp. 277, 302.

[23] Reno Court, DeRudio's testimony, p. 328.

[24] Reno Court, Moylan's testimony, p. 222.

[25] Reno Court, Varnum's testimony, pp. 157-58.

[26] Reno Court, Girard's testimony, pp. 101-02.

[27] Reno Court, DeRudio's testimony, p. 337.

[28] Reno Court, Moylan's testimony, p. 217.

[29] Reno Court, Moylan's testimony, pp. 216-17.

[30] Reno Court, DeRudio's testimony, p. 317.

[31] Reno Court, Culbertson's testimony, p. 367.

[32] Reno Court, Davern's testimony, pp. 354, 358.

[33] Reno Court, Varnum's testimony, p. 142.

[34] Reno Court, Hare's testimony, p. 282; DeRudio's testimony, p. 339.

[35] The exact count of men killed or wounded before Reno left the timber will probably never be known. Reno Court, Reno's testimony, p. 586; Wallace's testimony, p. 28;

Moylan's testimony, p. 229; DeRudio's testimony, p. 317.

[36] This probably was the "mount" command Herendeen heard which he later reported as the quick "mount," "dismount," "mount," sequence of commands issued by Reno at about the time Bloody Knife was killed. Herendeen remembered the commands but was confused on the timing. The "dismount" was likely the order by Reno to the contingent of Company G men as they returned with Reno from the river. The final "mount" command by Reno was issued when the soldiers were in the clearing or glade and getting ready to ride out of the timber. None of the other men or officers reported the quick sequence of commands indicated by Herendeen, or the "dismount," "mount" commands after the killing of Bloody Knife. Fred Dustin in his pamphlet, *The Custer Fight* (Privately printed, Hollywood, Calif., 1936), pages 14-16, covers this sequence of events well.

[37] Reno Court, Reno's testimony, pp. 562-563.

[38] Reno Court, Reno's testimony, p. 563.

[39] E. A. Brininstool, *Major Reno Vindicated*, (from a letter written in 1925 by Colonel W. A. Graham with comments by E. A. Brininstool), (Privately published, Hollywood, Calif., 1935), p.13. Varnum stated that "we did not average five cartridges to the man [remaining]."

[40] Reno Court, Reno's testimony, p. 593.

[41] Reno Court, Reno's testimony, p. 563.

[42] Reno Court, Moylan's testimony, p. 217.

[43] Reno Court, Wallace's testimony, p. 23.

[44] Reno Court, Moylan's testimony, p. 217.

[45] John Ryan in *The Billings Gazette*, June 25, 1923.

[46] Reno Court, Porter's testimony, p. 204.

[47] Fred Dustin, *The Custer Fight*, p. 16.

[48] Reno Court, pp. 27-28, 565. Wallace, Hare, Moylan and Varnum all describe what was done; how the word was passed to get to the horses, how the companies were formed, how the Indians who had gotten into the timber fired into them point-blank, killing Bloody Knife at Reno's side, and mortally wounding another soldier, and how they broke from the timber and formed on the plain in column-of-fours, and with pistols drawn, cut their way to the river.

[49] Reno Court, Moylan's testimony, p. 231.

[50] Reno Court, Wallace's testimony, p. 52.

[51] Reno Court, Hare's testimony, p. 295.

[52] Reno Court, Culbertson's testimony, p. 376.

[53] Reno Court, Varnum's testimony, pp. 149-150.

[54] Reno Court, Reno's testimony, p. 565.

[55] Reno Court, Moylan's testimony, p. 151.

[56] Reno Court, Porter's testimony, p. 197.

[57] Reno Court, Wallace's testimony, p. 28.

[58] Reno Court, Hare's testimony, pp. 280-281.

[59] Reno Court, Porter's testimony, p. 198.

[60] Reno Court, Varnum's testimony, p. 156.

[61] Reno Court, Culbertson's testimony, p. 369.

[62] Reno Court, Davern's testimony, p. 350.

• 11 •

Hilltop Fight

After the division of the regiment at the Rosebud-Little Big Horn divide, Captain Benteen and his three-company battalion moved off to the southwest in what Benteen later described as "valley hunting ad infinitum." He advanced about five miles before deciding to return to the main trail —no Indians were to be found in the hills.[1] About 2:30 p.m., Benteen's command reached the trail left by the rest of the regiment. He stated that his command "struck the trail about a mile ahead of the pack train. I saw it coming on the trail."[2] It was at this point Lieutenant Edgerly later recalled:

> About this time, Mr. Boston Custer, the general's youngest brother, rode by on his pony. He had stayed back with the packtrain and was now hurrying up to join the general's immediate command. He gave me a cheery salutation as he passed, and then with a smile on his face, rode to his death.[3]

Turning westward, Benteen followed the trail toward the Little Big Horn, stopping to water his horses at a morass about a mile from where he had rejoined the trail. Remaining there about 25 minutes, he continued his march down Reno Creek toward the burning tepee that had been set alight by the Arikara scouts.

Meanwhile Custer, with his two battalions, had turned north before reaching the Little Big Horn River.[4] He moved his command up onto the bluffs on the east side of the river, and marched to the west of Sharpshooter's Ridge. Going to the edge of the bluffs, Custer could see much of the Indian village for the first time. He then had Tom Custer tell Sergeant Daniel Kanipe of Company C to "go back to McDougall and bring him and the pack train straight across the country. Tell McDougall to hurry the pack train to Custer and if any of the packs get loose cut them and let them go; do not stop to tighten them."[5] Custer then advanced down Cedar Coulee to the junction with Medicine Tail Coulee where he sent his final message via Trumpeter John Martin: "Benteen, come on, big village, be quick, bring packs. W. W. Cooke, p.s. bring packs."

Captain Frederick W.
Benteen

Boston Custer

Sergeant Daniel Kanipe

Trumpeter John Martin

It was about this time Reno made the decision to recross the river and rejoin the regiment. Reno had not been supported by "the whole outfit" as expected, ammunition was starting to run low, and the Indians had almost completely surrounded his command in the timber.

When Benteen arrived in the area of the tepee where earlier Reno had received his orders to attack the Indians, Kanipe approached with the message to McDougall. Stating the message was not addressed to him, Benteen directed Kanipe back to McDougall and the pack train. The next message he received, carried by Martin, was addressed to him to "be quick." Although the message indicated a certain sense of speed by Custer, Martin, when asked by Benteen about the Indian village, suggested the Indians were "skedaddling." Benteen later stated that if the Indians "were all skedaddling, therefore there was less necessity for me going back for the packs."[6]

Continuing toward the Little Big Horn, Benteen, Weir and Edgerly approached the river at the point where Reno's command had crossed to attack the village. Looking downstream, Edgerly saw "fighting going on in the valley, and very shortly we saw a body of men — upwards of a hundred — make a break for the bluffs on the east side of [the] Little Big Horn River."[7] Benteen said he saw just the remnants of Reno's troopers near the river:

> There were 12 or 13 men in skirmish line that appeared to have been beaten back. The line was then parallel with the river and the Indians were charging and recharging through those men.[8]

Off to his right Benteen saw soldiers on the bluff's summit. He turned his battalion northward to join the soldiers on top of the bluffs.

The retreat from timber and the river crossing had been costly to Reno's command. When he finally succeeded in reaching the top of the bluffs, he had lost three officers, 29 enlisted men killed and seven enlisted men wounded.[9] Lieutenants McIntosh and Hodgson and Acting Assistant Surgeon James M. DeWolf had been killed during the retreat from the timber. McIntosh was killed shortly after leaving the timber and both Hodgson and DeWolf were killed after crossing the river. When Reno reached the top of the bluffs, he "immediately put the command in skirmish line dismounted, a movement that was accomplished through the company commanders."[10]

About 10 minutes after reaching the bluffs, Reno saw Benteen's command approaching and rode out to meet Benteen. He told Benteen what he had done and that he was glad to see him.[11] Trumpeter Martin later said Reno told Benteen, "For God's sake, Benteen, halt your command and help me! I've lost half my men!"[12] Benteen commented about Reno's condition when he first met him on the hill: "He was about as cool as he is now [at the Reno

Court of Inquiry]. He had lost his hat in the run down below." He thought Reno's men "were in pretty good order and well shaken up."[13] When Edgerly first saw Reno on the hilltop, Reno had lost his hat, had a white handkerchief on his head, and was in an "excited condition." After meeting Benteen, Edgerly said Reno turned and fired his pistol at the Indians who were more than a thousand yards away.[14] Reno stated he didn't fire his pistol after meeting Benteen: "I fired my revolver several times coming across the bottom. I don't think when I got on the hill I had a charge in it."[15]

Following the arrival of Benteen's three companies on the hilltop, Reno said to his men, "We have assistance now, and we will go and avenge the loss of our comrades."[16]

The Indians did not pursue Reno's men across the river but continued to linger in the area of the ford. Benteen reported that he "saw about 900 Indians when I arrived circling around in the bottom."[17] Benteen dismounted his troops, formed them into skirmishers, and had them share their ammunition with Reno's men. He then showed Reno the "be quick" message he had received from Custer and asked him where Custer had gone. Reno replied he did not know but thought that with 225 men Custer "could hold off quite a number of Indians," if they were properly disposed.[18] Reno thought Custer's order was directed more at bringing the packs within easier reach and putting them into more defensible positions than bringing the packs into the fight itself. He said the note "did not make any great impression on me at the time because I was absorbed in getting those packs together, and did not intend to move until I had done so."[19] Benteen agreed and saw no need to immediately go in the direction Custer had apparently taken as he thought "General Custer was able to take care of himself."[20] Benteen also said later that they could have made an immediate movement down the stream in the direction it was supposed Custer had gone "but we would all have been there yet."[21]

Shortly after Benteen's command arrived on the hilltop, Reno sent for Lieutenant Hare. Designating Hare as his adjutant, he told him to find out where the pack train was and get it up as soon as possible. Hare borrowed Lieutenant Godfrey's horse and rode back along the trail about a mile and a half and met the pack train. He told them to hurry up as soon as possible and cut out the ammunition packs and send them ahead.[22]

After Hare rode away, the sound of firing was heard downstream. The intensity of the firing was described differently by various members of the joined commands. Doctor Porter said he heard "sharp" firing and Varnum, Godfrey, Hare, Edgerly and Culbertson all reported they heard some firing in the direction where they thought Custer might have gone. Moylan said he heard faint firing and Reno, Benteen and Wallace stated they heard no firing at all. The sound of the firing lasted only a few minutes.[23]

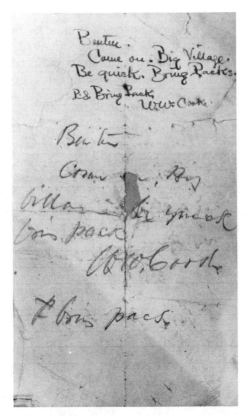

**Last message from Custer -- carried by
Trumpeter John Martin**

Shortly after reading the "be quick" note, Reno told Benteen that Hodgson had been shot while crossing the Little Big Horn. Reno said that because Hodgson was "a great favorite and friend of mine," he would try to find him. He thought perhaps Hodgson had only been wounded and he might be able to do something for him. Only a few Indians remained near the retreat crossing and Reno decided they were not a serious threat to his command. Reno took a number of troopers with him, including Culbertson and Porter, and went to the ford. Reno said, "I suppose I was gone a half an hour. Captain Benteen was the senior officer in command when I went down, and he was a man in whom I had the greatest confidence." Reno found Hodgson's body and removed his West Point ring from his finger and a bunch of keys from his pocket but someone had "rifled" his watch.[24] While Reno was at the ford, the Indians had withdrawn almost completely from the area and Reno's group received only "scattering fire." Returning from the crossing, Reno found that the pack train had not yet arrived.

Captain Weir thought some movement should be made in the direction of Custer's advance to provide the assistance requested. Edgerly agreed and Weir went to Reno to request permission to move his company downstream on reconnaissance. Reno denied the request and an angry exchange of words occurred between the two. Reno told Weir that none of the command would move until the packs came up.[25] Weir, a strong Custer partisan, decided to make his own reconnaissance. When Edgerly saw Weir return, call his orderly, mount his horse and ride off, he assumed Weir had received permission to go. Edgerly then "mounted the men and started out without orders."[26]

Shortly after Edgerly and Company D started downstream, Hare returned and reported to Reno that he had informed McDougall to bring up several mules loaded with ammunition. Reno, obviously displeased with Weir's actions, decided to take advantage of the situation:

> When Lieutenant Hare returned from the pack train, I told him to go to Captain Weir who, on his own hook, had moved out his company, and tell him to communicate with General Custer if he could and tell him where we were. I knew in what direction to send him because General Custer's trail had been found. It was back of the position I took when I went on the hill.[27]

Weir reached a high point about a mile downstream — now known as Weir Point — and could see a great deal of smoke and dust, and presumably the Indians, about three miles to the north. Edgerly rode ahead of his company and up onto to the point where he could also see the smoke and dust. He then returned to his company and started it down Cedar Coulee. He later stated:

> After going a few hundred yards I swung off to the right with the troop and went into a little valley which must have been the one followed by Custer and his men, or nearly parallel to it, and moved right towards the great body of the Indians, whom we had already seen from the highest point. After we had gone a short distance down the valley, Col. Weir, who had remained to our left, on the bluff, saw a large number of Indians coming toward us, and motioned with his hand for me to swing around with the troop to where he was, which I did.[28]

7th CAVALRY MOVEMENTS - JUNE 25, 1876

© R. Nichols 1998

Sharpshooter's Ridge

Reno-Benteen
Defense Area

Reno's Advance

Cedar Coulee

Reno's Retreat

Medicine Tail Coulee

Weir Point

Reno's 2nd Position

Reno's 1st Position

Nye-Cartwright Ridge

Little Big Horn River

Deep Coulee

Indian Encampment

Custer's Ridge

Deep Ravine

Miles

0   1   2

Advance/Retreat to/from Weir Point
Reno's Command
Benteen's Command
Custer's Command
Yates' Command
Keogh's Command

193

During Weir's and Company D's sojourn to Weir Point and beyond, the ammunition mules arrived at the hilltop site, followed shortly by McDougall and the head of the pack train. The pack train had stretched out considerably and it took the better part of an hour until all of the packs were up. McDougall immediately reported to Reno, and having heard firing to the north, told Reno about it. Reno appeared unconcerned about the firing and told McDougall, "Captain, I lost your lieutenant [Hodgson], he is lying down there."[29] Reno directed McDougall to have his men deploy along the skirmish line.

With the arrival of the ammunition mules, the men from Reno's original battalion supplemented the ammunition they had received from Benteen's men. As the rest of the pack train arrived, Reno decided to follow the movement started by Weir's Company D in the direction presumably taken by Custer. After giving Weir the message to open communications with Custer if he had the opportunity to do so, Hare returned and informed Reno that Indians had started to appear in the vicinity of Weir's company. Reno ordered the command to form in column-of-twos with French's Company M in front, followed by Godfrey's Company K, Benteen's Company H and Wallace's Company G. The pack train was positioned next, followed by McDougall's Company B and Moylan's Company A. Moylan had the responsibility for moving the wounded. Numbering about eight, the wounded could be moved only by using the blankets from the pack train and having at least four men carry each wounded man. It took considerable time for Company A to prepare to move. Reno finally gave the order to mount up and started the command toward Weir Point. Benteen had left a few minutes before to see for himself "what was going on around the whole country that could be seen."[30] Reno lead the formation northward.[31] The pack train was quickly strung out along the bluffs and movement was slow. Moylan's Company A, carrying the wounded, was straggling behind. Moylan rode forward and told McDougall that he could not keep up, and McDougall sent half of his company to assist him. Moylan then rode ahead to inform Reno what had taken place. Moylan later said,

> He [Reno] was with the head of the column and he informed me it would hardly be necessary for me to move any farther in that direction as he thought the whole command would have to go back, as from appearances he was under the impression that the whole force of Indians was in front of Captain Weir's command (which was then dismounted) and firing at us.[32]

Reno reached Weir Point about the same time Benteen did. Benteen planted a guidon on the top of Weir Point "to present an object to attract the attention of General Custer's command, if it was in sight."[33] Reno and Benteen remained on the that high point only two or three minutes before the "gorge was filled with Indians rushing towards us." Three companies, H, K and M, had reached Weir Point, and along with Company D, remained there only a short time. As the Indians approached, Weir's company, now considered by Reno as the "advance guard," had already been informed by Hare to return from his advanced position. Benteen was for halting the command "so as to check the Indians and to select a better place when we had ample time, and not be rushed over by them. Major Reno thought, which was better, that we should go to

1st Lieutenant Edward S. Godfrey
Company K

the place where he first got on the hill."[34] Reno left Weir Point and "remained at the rear; the column was put about by fours. I thought as the Indians were coming there, I would be there so as to get the first information. I remained there, the column moving back at a walk, and after a few minutes I galloped to the head to make dispositions of the troops on their arrival."[35]

When Reno rode to the head of the return column, he sent French and Godfrey to get orders from Benteen.[36] Reno wanted to set up his defense in the same location his command had reached after crossing the river:

> I had been impressed with the position I first reached on the hill. I had looked at it a little, it was nearer the water than where I was; and if the companies who were thrown to the rear could hold the Indians in check, we could get there all right.[37]

When Reno reached the hilltop site, he told Benteen to establish the troop dispositions on one side of the area and he would take the other. Reno placed Company D, the strongest company available, into the position where he thought the main Indian attack would occur. It was about 6 o'clock when the last of the command returned to the defense site. Godfrey had dismounted his company to provide a rear guard action, thus allowing the troops to reach the defense site safely. The site consisted of two roughly parallel ridges running east and west with a swale between them. The horses and mules were placed in the swale to protect the wounded.

The last of the command had barely dismounted when the Indians began firing, forcing the men to lie down to present a small target — the soldiers had no protection, except for the sage brush, which was "no protection whatever." The troops had been placed in a horseshoe-shaped defensive position along the ridges with the closed end of the horseshoe in the swale. Moylan's Company A was assigned the swale position. The open end of the horseshoe was on the bluffs facing the river with McDougall's Company B and French's Company M on the north end of the line while Benteen's Company H occupied the other end. Reno walked the whole line to satisfy himself that they were as well placed as possible. He told McDougall, "Captain, be sure to hold that point at all hazards."[38] He also went to the pack train where he "found a good many men and packers who were skulking, and I drove them out."[39] He returned to Company D's position and remained there until about 9 o'clock. The lack of protection would prove costly — seven men were killed and 21 wounded before Indian fire finally slackened about 9 o'clock.[40]

When the firing ended, Reno walked along the line and repositioned some of the companies. He told the company commanders to protect themselves "all they could and give themselves all the shelter they could, that they had to stay there," for they "could not leave those wounded...until some relief came."[41] Reno had the men dig rifle pits and drag dead horses and mules to barricade the lower part of the swale area. He ordered Lieutenant Mathey "to put boxes out to cover the front" where Moylan's company was positioned.[42] Saddles, packsaddles, hardtack boxes and bacon packages were also used as barricades. The number of spades was limited (two or three) and the men used cups and knives to scrape out pits. Benteen decided that the men of his Company H and he were too tired to build any kind of defensive protection:

> On the night of the 25th, Major Reno was upon the hill where my company was stationed after the firing ceased. It was about dark and he instructed me to build breastworks. I was pretty tired and did not think there was much necessity for building them as I had an idea the Indians would leave us, but I sent for spades to carry out his instruction, but could get none.[43]

Between 9 and 10 o'clock, Reno again walked along the defense line. As Reno was making his rounds, Edgerly, having noticed space between several companies, asked him if he should have the gaps closed and Reno agreed.

Edgerly "then went and gave Major Reno's orders to close the gaps."[44] Reno continued his inspection and, as he had previously done, went to the pack train where he found two of the packers skulking. His orders had been that every man, except the wounded, was to be on the line. When he found packers John Frett and B.F. Churchill there, he became annoyed and asked one of the men what he was doing there. The packer's reply angered him more. Thinking that was not exactly the time for moral persuasion, he hit Frett and told him that if he found him there again, he would shoot him.[45] Frett would testify later that Reno "had a bottle of whiskey in his hand and as he slapped me the whiskey flew over me and he staggered. If any other man was in the condition he was, I should call him drunk."[46] Reno was carrying a flask in the inner breast pocket of his uniform sacque on the evening of the 25th but did not take a drink from it until about midnight. Edgerly, who saw Reno at 9 o'clock and again at 2 the next morning, said he had never "the faintest" suspicion that Reno was drunk. He said if Reno had been intoxicated, the officers would not have permitted him to exercise command of the regiment.[47] Benteen was with Reno most of the night:

> I was with him every 15 or 20 minutes nearly all night. I laid down on his bed for 15 or 20 minutes and then went back and kept my walk up all night. Perhaps I did not see him within 15 minutes after I left him the last time, but there was not whiskey enough in the whole command to make him drunk.... I did not know he had any whiskey or I would have been after some.[48]

Mathey, McDougall and Wallace would all later testify that Reno was not intoxicated. Godfrey, who later became a severe critic of Reno's conduct at the Little Big Horn, also indicated Reno was not drunk on the night of June 25: "I don't think Reno was drunk, for I don't believe there was enough whiskey in the command to make a 'drunk.'"[49]

The men worked to build breastworks and rifle pits and then tried to catch a little sleep. Reno made the rounds of the command to assure himself that his orders were being carried out. He had ammunition boxes taken from the pack train and opened and placed along the lines of the different companies so the men would have whatever they needed. At the completion of his rounds he held an impromptu meeting with Benteen and possibly Weir and Moylan. He suggested that with the "great force of Indians against them," they might be driven from their defensive position and be forced to abandon the wounded. Benteen was vehement in his response about the possibility of the wounded being abandoned: "No, by God, we'll never do that!"[50] Private

John McGuire related an incident that occurred on the night after the first day's fight:

> An improvised council of officers took place in my hearing, General Reno being the only one whose name I now recall. The subject being discussed was the propriety of breaking camp and attempting to escape under cover of the darkness. To which council General Reno replied I have here a number of wounded men unfit to be moved and I will stay by them until the last man falls.[51]

Reno had no intention of abandoning the wounded. Reno had previously been informed by one of Terry's staff officers "that there had been a plan agreed upon between himself [Terry] and General Custer to meet in the vicinity of the Little Big Horn."[52] He knew that both Terry and Custer were somewhere in the area, and if he could continue to hold his defensive position on the bluffs, he could expect to be relieved shortly by either one or the other.

The Indians returned to their camp as the night of the 25th fell, leaving only a few warriors to watch the soldiers. While it appeared to the soldiers that an immense victory or scalp dance was being performed by the Indians, in fact the sounds being heard were from the wailing of mourners. They had suffered a number of casualties and, in the Indian custom, it was not time for celebrating. The huge fires witnessed by the soldiers from time to time were from some mourning family burning their lodge. Women gashed themselves in a token of grief and added to the wailing.[53]

As quiet returned to the hilltop position, both the officers and enlisted men wondered what happened to Custer. After the firing heard earlier in the afternoon had stopped, Reno expected to see Custer's command come to his relief. Reno discussed the situation with Benteen: "That evening the whereabouts of the commanding officer of the regiment was the subject of conversation between Captain Benteen and myself while he was lying on my blankets." Reno thought Custer "could take care of himself as well as we could. He had nearly as many men as I had, more than when I opened the fight."[54] Benteen later suggested: "It was the belief of the officers on the hill that General Custer had gone to General Terry and we were abandoned to our fate."[55] None of the officers considered the possibility that Custer's command had been destroyed but many shared a general impression that Custer had wounded men and was unable to come to Reno's relief immediately, just as they were unable to go to him.[56]

Reno wanted Custer to know where his command was and his need for support. Varnum thought Reno would send him on this dangerous mission

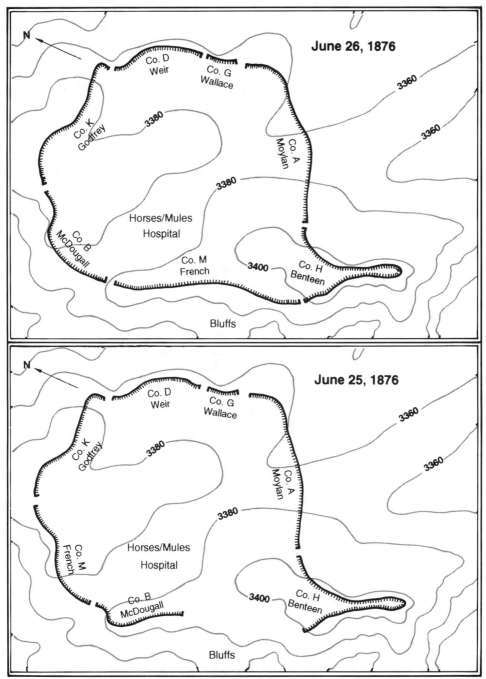

Reno-Benteen Hilltop Defense Positions

© R. Nichols 1998

and asked Sergeant George M. McDermott to volunteer to go with him. McDermott said he did not want to volunteer but if he was detailed he would go.[57] Reno decided not to order any of his men to undertake the task of carrying a message to Custer for he thought "sending a man out on a mission of that kind would be sending him to his death." Several Crow scouts had remained with the command, including Half Yellow Face and White Swan, who had been wounded. Reno thought that perhaps one of them, knowing the country, might be able to get through because of their peculiar abilities "to skulk along and get through the country without being seen, where a white man would be seen."[58] Soon after dark, he sent the scouts out "to look for signs of Custer's command, but they returned after a short absence, saying the country was full of Sioux."[59]

Reno continued to walk the line and about midnight sent an order to Trumpeter Martin to sound reveille at 2 o'clock in the morning. About this time several of the men left in the timber returned to the hilltop position and were immediately placed along the skirmish line. Reno felt confident that his command could hold its own and was ready, to the best degree possible, for the expected Indian attack the following morning. The attack came earlier than anticipated. About 2:30 a.m., with the first faint light of dawn, two rifle shots broke the silence and the Indians opened a massive barrage of fire on the entrenched troops. Reno later stated the fire was as severe as he had ever experienced. The Indians had completely surrounded Reno's position and their firing became so heavy that many troopers were hit on the opposite side of the line from where the shots were fired. Reno estimated his command faced "at least 2,500 warriors."[60]

The men of Benteen's Company H would pay heavily for their recalcitrant company commander's decision not to follow Reno's orders to dig in or provide some protection for themselves. On June 26, Benteen's Company H alone suffered one-third of the men killed and almost one-third of the men wounded that day.[61] Benteen had trouble keeping his men on the line and had to go down to the pack train several times and run them out. He had to take them back to the line and finally had them take sacks of bacon, boxes of hard tack and pack saddles to build a redoubt. Having suffered heavy casualties before a redoubt could be built, Benteen was forced to go to Reno and state "that he was being hard pressed on his line and that it was necessary for him to have more troops over there: that he must have another company."[62] Reno directed French to take Company M over to Benteen's side of the line.

The Indians kept up a steady stream of fire on the troopers from positions that ranged from 100 to 500 yards away. The soldiers could do little except remain behind their makeshift breastworks or in shallow rifle pits. Firing from soldiers was limited due to the shortage of targets. This lack of fire from the soldiers would occasionally embolden the Indians to move forward more openly only to be driven back by substantial fire from the troopers. Reno moved about, spending most of the time with D Company but also checking on Benteen's and Moylan's lines.

Small groups of Indians would use the ravines and coulees for protection as they approached the defensive site. After building the redoubt and turning it over to Lieutenant Gibson, Benteen, along with some of his H Company troopers, successfully mounted a charge to drive four Indians out of a ravine directly to his front. Private James J. Tanner (Jacob Gebhart) was badly wounded on the retreat back to the defense line. A Sioux Indian, Long Road, attempted to count coup on the wounded trooper and was killed in the attempt. First Sergeant John Ryan described the rescue of Tanner:

> Private James Tanner…was badly wounded in this charge, and his body lay on the side of the bluffs in an exposed position. There was a call for volunteers to bring him down, and I grabbed a blanket with three other men, rushed to his assistance, rolled him into the blanket, and made quick tracks in getting him from the side of the bluffs to where our wounded lay. Fortunately none of the rescue party received anything more that a few balls through their clothing. After placing Tanner with the rest of the wounded, he died in a few minutes.[63]

No order or permission had been received from Reno for this movement. Benteen could see Indians close to Reno's side of the line and was concerned that their fire was hitting the rear of his line and, if not driven back, they could mount a charge into the line. He walked behind the line to where the bulk of the companies were massed and said to Reno: "We have charged the Indians from our side and driven them out. They are coming to your left and you ought to drive them out." Asked if he could see the Indians, Benteen replied, "Yes," and Reno said, "If you can see them, give the command to charge." Benteen shouted, "All right, ready boys, now charge and give them hell!" The charge advanced about 40 to 50 yards, flushed a number of Indians from their hiding spots, and returned to the line without losses. The charge was accompanied by Reno while Benteen remained on the line.[64]

Another serious problem confronted Reno — the lack of water for the wounded and the men: "Our throats were parched, the smoke stung our nostrils, it seemed as if our tongues had swollen so we couldn't close our mouths, and the heat of the sun seemed fairly to cook the blood in our veins."[65] Any attempt to secure water was highly risky because the soldiers, after traveling down a ravine that afforded some protection, had to cover about 30 feet of open ground to reach the river. Indians on the west side of the Little Big Horn were controlling the approach with intense fire. A group of volunteers finally agreed to make the attempt and gathered every available cooking pot, kettle, canteen or vessel that would hold water. They first tried to dash across the open space, scoop up the water and return to the safety of the ravine. This approach resulted in the wounding of several troopers, including Saddler Michael Madden who was shot through the ankle and had to be dragged back up the bluffs to the hospital area. Benteen then detailed four sharpshooters to provide covering fire as the troopers made their dash to the water. Although this improved the odds of making the trip successful, six or seven troopers were wounded and one killed. Sufficient water was obtained to provide some relief for the wounded and the remainder of the command. Eighteen of the enlisted men would be awarded the Medal of Honor for their bravery in either bringing water to the wounded or providing cover fire for the water party.

Doctor Porter determined that Madden's leg would have to be amputated — gangrene had set in as a result of the wound. Private William Slaper related the following story:

> Before amputating the member, the surgeon gave Mike a stiff horn of brandy to brace him up. Mike went through the ordeal without a whimper, and was then given another drink. Smacking his lips in appreciation, he whispered to the surgeon, "Docthor, cut off me other leg!"[66]

About 10 o'clock, the heavy Indian fire, which had been almost continuous, slackened noticeably, and Indians could be seen leaving their firing positions and moving away from the command. A number of Indians remained and would fire at any movement of the soldiers. Reno saw the Indians moving down in the valley toward their village, and he thought they were going for ammunition or to get relief and would come back again. The Indians were apparently raising a great deal of dust and smoke rose from where they had set the prairie on fire so Reno had difficulty distinguishing exactly what they were doing. Reno continued to check on his defenses as he was convinced the Indians would continue their attack. Walking across the defense area with Godfrey, the pair drew considerable Indian fire. When an angry-bee buzz of a bullet passed close to him, Reno dodged, Godfrey told how Reno laughed: "Damned if he wanted to be killed by an Indian, he had gone through too many fights."[67]

The sporadic fire continued until about 4 o'clock in the afternoon, and then only Indian sharpshooters remained to harass the soldiers. Varnum went to Reno suggesting that he would endeavor "to get some scouts to try and get outside of the lines with a dispatch."[68] After Varnum finally persuaded two or three Crows to say they would go if the Rees would go, he had Reno write four copies of a note to Terry to send out with the scouts. In the note, Reno described his position on the hill, the attack by the Indians, and the need for medical aid and assistance. The note also said he was holding the Indians in check and did not know the whereabouts of General Custer.[69] The scouts decided either not to leave the line or, if they left, only went a short distance before returning and handing the notes back to Varnum.

After 4 o'clock, the Indian fire stopped almost completely and activity in their camp increased noticeably. The Indians now knew other army units (Terry and Gibbon) were approaching from the north and they did not have sufficient ammunition to engage in another serious battle. The Indian women struck their tepees and by 6 o'clock, the whole village had started moving south. Reno described the length of the Indian column as being "fully equal to that of a large division of the cavalry corps of the Army of the Potomac."[70]

Benteen also described the size of the Indian village as it moved away from their camp:

> They commenced moving about sunset and they were in sight till darkness came.... It was a straight line about three miles and I think it was at least three miles long and a half a mile wide, as densely packed as animals could be. They had an advance guard and platoons formed and were in a regular military order, as any corps or division.... It was the entire village.[71]

Lieutenant DeRudio, who had remained in the timber when Reno retreated to the bluffs, had moved farther south through the woods on June 26 to the original Reno crossing. Accompanied by Private Thomas O'Neill of G Company, he watched the village pass their location of the 26th, only 500 or 600 yards from them. The two men could hear the noise of the travois and the dogs and children. They would return to Reno's command at 3 o'clock the next morning.

After the last of the Indian sharpshooters left and dusk approached, Reno and his command were free to move around the defense area unmolested. The wounded were cared for with what medicine Porter had on hand — further treatment would have to wait until the command was rescued by either Custer or Terry. The horses and mules had also suffered greatly during the siege as they had had little grain and no water since the previous afternoon. Many were wounded and some had to be destroyed. Reno ordered that small groups of horses and mules be led down to the river to drink and then returned to the hilltop to graze. He had the camp moved slightly to the south to secure an unlimited supply of water and to get away from the smell of dead horses and mules. The dead troopers were buried in the rifle pits dug during the 25th and 26th. Because of their numbers, Reno remain cautious about whether the Indians would return and kept sentries posted throughout the night.

Later that evening, Captain McDougall, along with Private Stephen L. Ryan and Farrier James F. Moore of B Company, went down to the retreat crossing and retrieved Lieutenant Hodgson's body and carried it to the hilltop. There they sewed him into a blanket and poncho and buried him the next morning.

When dawn broke on the morning of the 27th, the command was in good spirits. The men had had an opportunity to get some sleep and no Indians were in sight. Reno saw dust down the valley and decided that it was possibly being created by the approach of either Custer's or Terry's command.[72] He had already written a message to Terry:

> Camp on Little Big Horn
> 20 miles from its mouth,
> June 27

General Terry:

I have had a most terrific engagement with the hostile Indians. They left their camp last evening at sundown moving due south in the direction of Big Horn Mountains. I am very much crippled and can not possibly pursue. Lieutenants McIntosh and Hodgson and Dr. DeWolf are among the killed. I have many wounded and many horses and mules shot. I have lost both my own horses. I have not seen or heard from Custer since he ordered me to charge with my battalion (three companies) promising to support me.

I charged about 2 p.m. but meeting no support was forced back to the hills. At this point I was joined by Benteen and three companies and the pack train rear guard (one Co.). I have fought thousands and can still hold my own, but can not leave here on account of the wounded. Send me medical aid at once and rations.

M. A. Reno
Maj. 7th Cavalry

As near as I can say now I have over 100 men killed and wounded.[73]

Reno sent two Arikara scouts, Young Hawk and Forked Horn, out with the message and told them to go as near the approaching column as was safe to determine whether they were white men or Indians. If they were soldiers, the scouts were told to return at once and, if they were Indians, attempt to go around them and push on to General Terry. The messengers returned in a short time accompanied by one of Terry's scouts, Muggins Taylor, who had a note from Terry to Custer, dated June 26, saying Crow scouts had come to camp saying he had been whipped, but that it was not believed. Reno then sent Varnum, Hare and several

Major Marcus Reno
(circa 1876)
(Denver Public Library)

soldiers to Terry to show him where to cross the river and how to ascend the steep bluffs to Reno's command. Terry, Gibbon and Lieutenant Bradley rode into Reno's camp about 10:30 a.m. and informed him of the fate of Custer and his men.

Benteen received permission from Reno to take his company to the field where Custer and five companies had been found. Returning two hours later, Benteen provided a briefing to the officers of what he found:

> He had followed Custer's trail to the scene of the battle opposite the main body of the Indian camp, and amid the rolling hills which borders the river-bank on the north. As he approached the ground scattered bodies of men and horses were found, growing more numerous as he advanced. In the midst of the field a long back-bone ran out obliquely from the river, rising very gradually until it terminated in a little knoll which commanded a view of all the surrounding ground, and of the Indian campground beyond the river. On each side of this back-bone, and sometimes on top of it, dead men and horses were scattered along. These be-

205

came more numerous as the terminating knoll was reached; and on the southwestern slope of that lay the brave Custer surrounded by the bodies of several of his officers and 40 or 50 of his men, whilst horses were scattered about in every direction. All were stripped, and most of the bodies were scalped and mutilated.[74]

Terry and Gibbon established their camp on the west side of the river in the vicinity of Reno's first position in the valley. Starting in the late afternoon or early evening, 54 wounded men were brought down from the defense area using blanket litters, each carried by four or six men. An improvised field hospital had been established and the wounded were made as comfortable as possible. The last of the wounded arrived at the hospital at dusk. Reno moved his command to a new camp site on a small mesa closer to the river just southwest of Company H's hilltop defensive line position. When the encampment was complete, Reno sent his men back to the top of the bluffs to bury the remainder of the dead from the hilltop fight.

At 5 a.m. June 28, Reno proceeded with the remainder of the regiment to the Custer battlefield. What Reno and his men saw was grim. Godfrey described the scene:

> The marble-white bodies, the somber brown of the dead horses and dead ponies scattered all over the field, but thickest near Custer Hill, and the scattering tufts of reddish brown grass and almost ashy-white soil depicts a scene of loneliness and desolation, that "blows down the heart in sorrow." I can never forget the sight; the early morning was bright, as we ascended to the top of the point whence the whole field came into view, with the sun to our backs. "What are those?" exclaimed several as they looked at what appeared to be white boulders. Nervously I took the field glasses and glanced at the objects; then, almost dropped them, and laconically said: "The dead!" Colonel Weir who was sitting near on his horse, exclaimed: "Oh, how white they look! How white!"... Occasionally there was a body with a bloody undershirt or trousers or socks, but the name was invariably cut out. The naked, mutilated bodies, with their bloody, fatal wounds, were nearly unrecognizable, and presented a scene of sickening, ghastly horror![75]

Reno ordered McDougall to take his company to the village to get implements to bury the dead. When McDougall returned, he was ordered to bury Company E, the company which McDougall had formerly commanded for five years, and to identify the men as far as possible. McDougall found about half of the men of his former company in a deep ravine several hundred yards from Custer hill. The other half of his men were found on a line outside the ravine. Reno assigned each of the other companies a certain part of the field to find and bury the bodies and sent orders to Varnum to go to some high bluffs well away from the river with the Indian scouts to act as lookouts.

With the exception of the officers, burials were superficial — tools were scarce, the ground was hard and dry, and time did not permit a decent burial. The graves consisted of a shallow excavation generally only five or six inches with the dirt removed thrown on top of the body. A little more time was spent on the officers' graves with excavations of 12 to 18 inches deep. Identification of the troopers was difficult — the bodies had been exposed to the sun for more than two days and were swollen and discolored, and many had been further mutilated. The wounded had been dispatched by crushing blows to their skulls from the Indian women with axes, making identification even more difficult. John Ryan described the burial of the Custers:

> We dug a shallow grave about 15 to 18 inches deep at the foot of the hillock. We laid the General in as tenderly as a soldier could, with his brother Captain along side of him, covering the bodies with pieces of blankets and tents and spreading earth on top, spreading it as well as we could, making it look as near a mound as possible. We then took a basket off an Indian "travoix" placing it upside down over the grave and pinning it to the ground with stakes, placing large stones around it to keep the wolves from digging it up, and this simple sad mode of burial was the best of all these heroes on that terrible field of Little Big Horn, and I helped to bury 45 enlisted men and commissioned officers.[76]

Wooden stakes were driven in the ground by each grave but only the officers' graves were identified. A piece of paper with the officer's name was inserted into an empty cartridge shell, which was then driven into the stake. Reno reported he buried 204 bodies, including citizens Boston Custer, Autie Reed and Mark Kellogg. During the burials Captain French came over to Reno and asked him, "Have you got any whiskey?" Reno said he had a little and French responded, "Give me a drink for I am sick at the stomach," and Reno gave him what was left in the flask.[77] The burials consumed most of the day and that evening the men of Reno's command returned to their camp, both mentally and physically drained.

Meanwhile Gibbon's command had spent the day improvising litters to carry the wounded to the *Far West* thought to be docked near the mouth of the Little Big Horn. Eight men were required to carry each litter and the procession started in late afternoon. The unevenness of the ground caused the litters to be jostled, much to the anguish of the wounded soldiers. The detail proceeded only four miles before the men carrying the litters became exhausted — it became obvious that a better means of transporting the wounded was required.

The dead had been buried and the wounded were being taken care of — the battle of the Little Big Horn was over.

Endnotes

[1] Reno Court, Benteen's testimony, p. 421.

[2] Reno Court, Benteen's testimony, p. 404.

[3] Gray, *Custer's Last Campaign*, p. 264.

[4] The question here is why did Custer turn north and move downstream on the east side of the Little Big Horn when he had apparently assured Reno, through Cooke, that he would support him "with the whole outfit." Custer's decision to move north on the east side of the river was probably based on two factors: 1) the information he received from Varnum who had seen a large number of Indians in the valley, and 2) as Martin later testified, the location of an Indian trail made by tepee poles that turned to the north on the east side of the river (Reno Court, Martin's testimony, p. 397).

[5] Hammer, *Custer in '76*, pp. 94-95.

[6] Reno Court, Benteen's testimony, p. 404. Custer was concerned about the pack train and wanted it moved forward quickly to prevent it from being attacked by the Indians. He had almost lost his pack train at the Washita in November 1868, and did not want a similar occurrence at the Little Big Horn.

[7] Edgerly's statement from *The Leavenworth Times*, Aug. 18, 1881.

[8] Reno Court, Benteen's testimony, p. 405.

[9] Reno's official report, Camp on Yellowstone River, July 5, 1876. Exhibit No. 4, Reno Court, p. 641. This count is quite accurate — a detailed analysis shows that three officers were killed (McIntosh, DeWolf, Hodgson) and 29 enlisted men killed — eight enlisted men were wounded and reached the bluffs. Also killed in the valley fight were two Indian scouts (Bob Tailed Bull and Little Brave), one interpreter (Bloody Knife), one guide (Charley Reynolds), and one quartermaster interpreter (Isaiah Dorman). See Appendix C for analysis.

[10] Reno Court, Reno's testimony, p. 565.

[11] Reno Court, Reno's testimony, p. 565.

[12] John Martin, "Custer's Last Battle," *Cavalry Journal*, July 1923.

[13] Reno Court, Benteen's testimony, p. 406, 408.

[14] Reno Court, Edgerly's testimony, p. 443.

[15] Reno Court, Reno's testimony, p. 573. Benteen concurred with Reno's statement about not firing his pistol at the Indians when they first met on the hilltop (Benteen's testimony, p. 463).

[16] Reno Court, Hare's testimony, p. 298.

[17] Reno Court, Benteen's testimony, p. 406.

[18] Reno Court, Reno's testimony, p. 582.

[19] Reno Court, Reno's testimony, p. 581. An error appears in this edition of the Reno Court. The question asked just prior to the question to which Reno responded should read: Would you, as an officer, regard that as a direction that he would bring *the packs on into the fight or bring* them within easier reach to put them in a defensible position? The words in italics were inadvertently left out. Reno's response to this question was: "I think the latter supposition would be correct."

[20] Reno Court, Benteen's testimony, p. 407.

[21] Reno Court. Benteen's testimony, p. 408.

[22] Reno Court, Hare's testimony, p. 289.

[23] Why did some of the soldiers hear the firing and others did not? The explanation may be relatively simple. In Reno's official July 5 report he stated, "We had heard firing in that direction and knew it could only be Custer." It should be noted he said "we" and not "I." By the time he wrote his report Reno knew that a number of his men had heard firing downstream in the direction Custer had advanced. Now considering the ages of those who didn't hear the firing at all (both Reno and Benteen were 41) or heard it very faintly (Moylan was 38), those who participated through most if not all of the Civil War (Reno, Benteen and Moylan), and the extremely high noise levels these men were repeatedly exposed to during the war, it is not surprising that they may have sustained considerable hearing loss. The majority of those who heard the firing were considerably younger — Hare, 24; Varnum, 27; Porter, 28; Edgerly, 30; Godfrey, 32; Culbertson, 31 — and none had any lengthy Civil War service.

[24] Reno Court, Reno's testimony, p. 566.

[25] Fred Dustin, *The Custer Fight* (Privately printed, Hollywood, Calif., 1936), pp. 21-22. Dustin states he had some correspondence with a soldier who was in the fight (but doesn't identify the soldier) and the soldier told him, "I heard some loud talking, but what it was I cannot say, all I know is that just as I came up, Weir separated himself from a group, evidently laboring under considerable excitement.... I was told later by Lieut. Wallace that Weir and Reno had some hot words because Reno refused to advance until the packs came up, and that Weir's action in mounting his troop and moving out was really an act of insubordination, and that it was suggested to Reno that he place Weir under arrest, but Reno did not seem disposed to do it." In a letter written by Edgerly on December 5, 1928, to Colonel William Graham, Edgerly said Weir had indicated he "would ask permission of Reno," but later told Edgerly "that he concluded he had better take a look ahead before asking Reno. So he mounted and started to the front with only an orderly." A copy of this letter is in the author's collection; the original is in the Glen Swanson collection.

[26] Reno Court, Edgerly's testimony, p. 444.

[27] Reno Court, Reno's testimony, p. 567.

[28] *The Leavenworth Times*, Aug. 18, 1881.

[29] Reno Court, McDougall's testimony, p. 529.

[30] Reno Court, Benteen's testimony, p. 409.

[31] Reno Court, Wallace's testimony, pp. 59, 79-80; Moylan's testimony, pp. 218-219; Sergeant Davern's testimony, p. 354.

[32] Reno Court, Moylan's testimony, pp. 218-219.

[33] Reno Court, Benteen's testimony, p. 423.

[34] Reno Court, Benteen's testimony, p. 409.

[35] Reno Court, Reno's testimony, p. 567.

[36] Reno Court, Reno's testimony, p. 567.

[37] Reno Court, Reno's testimony, p. 567.

[38] Reno Court, McDougall's testimony, p. 530.

[39] Reno Court, Reno's testimony, p. 576.

[40] See Appendix A.

[41] Reno Court, Reno's testimony, p. 569.

[42] Reno Court, Mathey's testimony, p. 516.

[43] Reno Court, Benteen's testimony, p. 412.

[44] Reno Court, Edgerly's testimony, p. 447.

[45] Reno Court, Reno's testimony, p. 576.

[46] Reno Court, Frett's testimony, p. 505.

[47] Reno Court, Edgerly's testimony, p. 476.

[48] Reno Court, Benteen's testimony, p. 478.

[49] Cyrus Townsend Brady, *Indian Fights and Fighters* (University of Nebraska Press, Lincoln, 1971), Appendix A, p. 376. This statement was from a "memoranda" written by Godfrey to Brady in 1903.

[50] Dustin, p. 25.

[51] Camp Papers, Letter to Camp from John B. McGuire, dated December 4, 1908. Copy in author's collection.

[52] Reno Court, Reno's testimony, p. 569.

[53] Stanley Vestal, *Sitting Bull* (University of Oklahoma Press, Norman, 1957), p. 174; Thomas B. Marquis, *Wooden Leg* (University of Nebraska Press, Lincoln, 1962), pp. 256-257.

[54] Reno Court, Reno's testimony, p. 569.

[55] Reno Court, Benteen's testimony, p. 426.

[56] Reno Court, Culbertson's testimony, p. 379.

[57] Reno Court, Culbertson' testimony, p. 379.

[58] Reno Court, Reno's testimony, p. 589.

[59] *The Century Illustrated Monthly Magazine*, January 1892, "Custer's Last Battle," by One of His Troop Commanders (Lieutenant Godfrey), p. 377.

[60] Reno's official report, Reno Court, p. 642.

[61] See Appendix A.

[62] Reno Court, Godfrey's testimony, p. 491.

[63] Hammer, *Men With* Custer, p. 122.

[64] Reno Court, Edgerly's testimony, p. 450; Godfrey also testified that Reno accompanied the charge, Reno Court, Godfrey's testimony, p. 497.

[65] *The Portland Journal*, "Account of Edwin Pickard," July 31-Aug. 4, 1923: *Winners of the West*, June 24, 1926; *Montana Magazine*, "I Rode With Custer," edited by Edgar I. Stewart, Summer 1954.

[66] E. A. Brininstool, *Troopers With Custer* (The Stackpole Company, Harrisburg, Penna., 1952), p. 59.

[67] Reno Court, Godfrey's testimony, p. 492.

[68] Reno Court, Varnum's testimony, p. 165.

[69] Reno Court, Varnum's testimony, p. 182.

[70] Reno's official report, Reno Court, p. 643.

[71] Reno Court, Benteen's testimony, p. 420.

[72] Reno's official report, Reno Court, p. 643.

[73] Reno Court, Exhibit No. 3, p. 646.

[74] John Gibbon, *American Catholic Quarterly Review*, "Last Summer's Expedition Against the Sioux," Volume II, April and October, 1877.

[75] Letter from E. S. Godfrey to E. S. Paxson, Butte, Mont., Jan. 16, 1896, in *The Custer Myth*, p. 365.

[76] Dustin, p. 185.

[77] Reno Court, Reno's testimony, p. 575. It is interesting to note that although Reno had been accused of being drunk on the night of the 25th, he still had whiskey in his flask on the morning of the 28th.

• 12 •

Return to Fort Lincoln

On the morning of June 29, Reno moved his camp from just below the high bluffs on the east side of the river to the valley floor west of the Little Big Horn. He ordered a detail to burn the equipment that could not be carried — saddles, ammunition and hardtack boxes, mule pack frames, and other miscellaneous military and civilian equipment.[1] Other details were ordered to search the Indian camp grounds and gather material left behind by the Indians and also burn it.

Two messengers, Henry Bostwick, a scout for Gibbon, and Private James A. Goodwin, Company A, 2nd Cavalry, had been dispatched on the morning of June 28 down the Little Big Horn to locate the *Far West*. They finally located the steamboat at the junction of the Little and Big Horn rivers about 3 p.m. June 29 and delivered Terry's message. Aboard the steamboat Captain Stephen Baker, 6th Infantry, hastily penned a note in response: "General Terry's note just received. The couriers are now feeding their horses, and will return to your command in half an hour.... Captain Marsh has been busy all day arranging the boat for the reception of the wounded. We have not seen a hostile Indian up to this time."[2]

Baker and Marsh had their men cut huge amounts of tall grass from the nearby river shore and spread it over the boat's decks. Tarpaulins were thrown over the grass to make bedding for the expected wounded soldiers.

Gibbon's men spent the afternoon of June 29 building mule-litters to carry the wounded. Trying to manhandle the wounded in litters carried by eight men had proved to be extremely exhausting for the carriers and equally painful for the wounded. A number of dead horses were skinned and lodgepoles found in the Indian village were used to make the required number of litters. Although Bostwick and Goodwin had not yet returned, Terry decided to move his command with the mule-litters and wounded, downstream toward the expected location of the *Far West*. Breaking camp about 6 o'clock in the evening, Reno ordered his men to accompany the mule-litters and provide whatever help was required. Terry thought the command would be able to march only a few miles before camping for the night. However, the mule-litters proved successful and Terry decided to continue the march. The column had ad-

213

vanced only four miles when the couriers Bostwick and Goodwin were seen on the bluffs overlooking the river. Reporting to Terry and Gibbon, the scouts provided both the location and direction to the steamboat. The command pushed on and arrived at the *Far West* at 3 o'clock on the morning of June 30. The wounded were quickly loaded aboard and given additional medical attention.

The lone survivor under Custer's immediate command who had been found on the battlefield following the fight was also loaded aboard the *Far West* — Comanche, Captain Keogh's horse. He had been found June 28, badly wounded and emaciated, but it was determined that he would probably survive his wounds.[3]

Terry and his staff, Major Brisbin, and Lieutenant William H. Low, Jr. with his Gatling gun battery and crew also boarded the steamboat. Gibbon would remain in charge of the command, including Reno's 7th Cavalry, for its overland march to the base camp at the confluence of the Big Horn and Yellowstone. About the time the *Far West* was to leave its mooring on the Big Horn, Terry briefed Captain Grant Marsh:

> Captain, you are about to start on a trip with fifty-two wounded men on your boat. This is a bad river to navigate and accidents are liable to happen. I wish to ask of you that you use all the skill you possess, all the caution you can command, to make the journey safely. Captain, you have on board the most precious cargo a boat ever carried. Every soldier here who is suffering from wounds is the victim of a terrible blunder: a sad and terrible blunder.[4]

The *Far West* cast off at 1:40 p.m. to make the trip down to the Yellowstone. About 4 o'clock, Gibbon moved his command across the Little Big Horn and went into camp on the north side of the river "in an attractive spot among large cottonwoods."[5] Reno had a muster taken to establish the casualties suffered by the 7th Cavalry — it was a difficult task as the rosters of the five companies with Custer had been with the first sergeants, all of whom had been killed. Reno was able to determine that at least 260 men had been killed and 52 wounded.[6]

The morning of July 1, 1876, dawned bright and clear, and the entire command would be on the march northward by 5 a.m., covering 20 miles before bivouacking for the night. The *Far West* had already arrived at the north bank of the Yellowstone, mooring near Fort Pease. The wounded were taken off while the boat's supplies were unloaded. Gibbon's column was on the march by 4:30 a.m., remained on the east side of the Big Horn and traveled 28 miles before arriving at the Yellowstone about six o'clock in the evening. The column was then ferried across the river and went into camp at 10 o'clock, about two miles above Fort Pease. Terry wrote two telegrams to Sheridan, the first involved the movement of the wounded, and the second, marked confidential, covered his plan for Custer and Gibbon to trap the Indians in the Little Big Horn Valley and why the plan was not successful:

> In the action itself, so far as I can make out, Custer acted under a misapprehension. He thought, I am confident, that the Indians were running. For fear they might get away, he attacked without getting all his men up, and divided his command so that they were beaten in detail.[7]

Terry also asked for instructions and told Sheridan he would refit as rapidly as possible to be in a position to continue the campaign.

At 4 o'clock July 3, the *Far West*, loaded with the wounded and a large quantity of wood "followed by the cheers and fervent good wishes of the assembled troops, backed away from the bank and started her paddles for Bismarck and Fort Lincoln, 700 miles away."[8] Still on board were 38 wounded — 14 had recovered sufficiently to remain with the command. Terry's adjutant, Major Edward W. Smith, remained on board to deliver the dispatches to Sheridan requesting replacement soldiers, horses and supplies.

July 4 was to be a day of rest and relaxation for the troops. At the Big Horn camp Major Brisbin delivered a short speech to the assembled troops in a patriotic celebration of Independence Day. It had only been a week before that Reno's troops had watched Terry and Gibbon coming up the valley to inform them of Custer's fate. It had also been a week of activity among the enlisted men. A petition had been prepared by the non-commissioned officers of the 7th Cavalry to promote Reno to lieutenant colonel and Benteen to major in appreciation for their leadership in saving their lives at the Little Big Horn:

Camp near Big Horn on
Yellowstone River,
July 4th, 1876

To his Excellency the President
 and the Honorable Representatives
of the United States.

Gentlemen:

We the enlisted men the survivors of the battle on the Height of Little Horn River, on the 25th and 26th of June 1876, of the 7th Regiment of Cavalry who subscribe our names to this petition, most earnestly solicit the President and Representatives of our Country, that the vacancies among the Commissioned Officers of our Regiment, made by the slaughter of our brave, heroic, now lamented Lieutenant Colonel George A. Custer, and the other noble dead Commissioned Officers of our Regiment who fell close by him on the bloody field, daring the savage demons to the last, be filled by the Officers of the Regiment only. That Major M. A. Reno, be our Lieutenant Colonel vice Custer, killed; Captain F. W. Benteen our Major vice Reno, promoted. The other vacancies to be filled by officers of the Regiment by seniority. Your petitioners know this to be contrary to the established rule of promotion, but prayerfully solicit a deviation from the usual rule in this case, as it will be conferring a bravely fought for and a justly merited promotion on officers who by their bravery, coolness and decision on the 25th and 26th of June 1876, saved the lives of every man now living of the 7th Cavalry who participated in the battle, one of the most bloody on record and one that would have ended with the loss of life of every officer and enlisted man on the field only for the position taken by Major Reno, which we held with bitter tenacity against fearful odds to the last.

To support this assertion — had our position been taken 100 yards back from the brink of the heights overlooking the river we would have been entirely cut off from water; and from behind those heights the Indian demons would have swarmed in hundreds picking off our men by detail, and before midday June 26th not an officer or enlisted man of our Regiment would have been left to tell of our dreadful fate as we then would have been completely surrounded.

With prayerful hope that our petitions be granted, we have the honor to forward it through our Commanding Officer.

Very Respectfully,
(236 signatures)[9]

The petition missed the *Far West*, which had left the day before, and eventually was forwarded via the steamboat *Josephine*, which departed July 16. The petition was not received in Washington until after promotions of 7th Cavalry officers had already been announced. On Aug. 5, Sherman disapproved the petition:

> The judicious and skillful conduct of Major Reno and Captain Benteen is appreciated, but the promotions caused by General Custer's death have been made by the President and confirmed by the Senate; therefore this petition cannot be granted. When the Sioux campaign is over I shall be most happy to recognize the valuable services of both officers by granting favors or recommending actual promotions.[10]

On July 3, Godfrey had submitted an application to Reno requesting a transfer from Company K to Company L, the company commanded by the late Lieutenant James Calhoun's at the Little Big Horn. The regular commander of Company L, Captain Michael V. Sheridan, was on detached service. Godfrey expected Sheridan to be permanently transferred and the company's first lieutenant, Charles Braden, to retire, thus giving him command of the company. Reno declined to approve the change but finally said he would move Godfrey when Sheridan, who was not in the fight, was transferred. Godfrey withdrew his application.[11]

Reno was obviously pleased to see the enlisted men's petition requesting a promotion for Benteen and himself. Although he had not completed his official report, he had given some serious thought about the battle — why the command had suffered such serious casualties, and why the Indians were allowed to escape. He wrote directly to General Sheridan July 4, expressing his views:

> Dear Gen'l.
> I know you sympathize with the Regt. [Regiment] and that you will see we did wonders in getting away with anyone belonging to it, the trouble has been that no one out here is at all experienced and the forces have been and are worked to bad advantage. I think Custer was deceived as to the number of Indians and that he did not give that consideration to the plan of campaign that the subject demands. He went in hastily and with one of his usual harrahs first splitting the Regt. into three different parts. There never were men and officers fought better than did the 7th Cavy. that were with me and there is every evidence they did the same thing with Custer, but were simply overwhelmed — but after all, the expedition would not have been a failure had Gibbon used then the cavalry force at his disposal. I know, and have

stated it fully in my report and which you will see later on, that he has been doubting and hesitating from the start. When he heard from the Crow scouts that Custer was killed with his command and others were still fighting he would not believe and on the day of the 26 June would not let Ball [Captain Edward Ball, 2nd Cavalry] go ahead to determine whether it was so or not. Had he done so the destruction of them was certain and the expedition would not have been a failure. But the truth is he was scared and when he came into my lines on the morning of the 27th he constantly insisted upon Gen. Terry moving my command to his camp at once as it was of the first importance. I said I would not move a step without my wounded. I write this letter to you for it is truth and I feel that the failure of the expedition was due to a stampede in Gibbon's command when the Crow scouts reached him with the news of Custer's defeat and not that the 7th Cavy. did not do its whole duty. Why even his own Crow scouts left his command and went home, saying too much Sioux, and this with 180 Cavy, 150 Infy, and a battery of three Gatling guns. The distance he was from the Indians on the evening of June 26 is fixed. They camped 9 measured miles from my entrenchments. I was 4 1/2 miles from the village — he must have been the same distance. At 7 p.m. I saw the village moving and it was so reported to him. And he went into camp saying it was too late and his officers and men went to bed squabbling as to whether they were Indians or cavalry. I have said this in my official report but I tell you it is true that he was stampeded beyond any thing you ever heard of. When we commenced to fall back to the boat at the mouth of "Big Horn" I thought that all right but we did not stop until we put the Yellowstone between us and Custer's battleground. We could have stayed as long as there was anything to eat, not to take the offensive perhaps but could have remained in their country in spite of them and not have come skulking back here like a whipped dog with his tail between his legs. I think Custer was whipped because he was rash. He was under a cloud, he wanted to get a coign of advantage from which to strike back at those he fancied had injured him and a big victory over the Sioux was that coign — to get in before anybody else could. He runs his command down and attacked with tired and exhausted horses and men, a very large and strong village of Indians and did it by detachment and at a time when they were all ready and fixed. For however strong as they were, I believe the 7th Cavalry would have whipped them properly handled — if I could stand them off with half the Regt. should not the whole whip them.[12]

The following day Terry dispatched two groups of five Arikara scouts to ride eastward to the mouths of the Rosebud and Tongue to look for any recent Indian signs. Captain Ball was ordered to take Company H, 2nd Cavalry, west on a reconnaissance patrol for the same purpose. Reno completed his official report of the recent campaign and sent it to Captain Edward Smith, 18th Infantry, Acting Assistant Adjutant General for General Terry. Reno indicated in the report that as the "senior surviving officer from the battle of the 25th and 26th of June, between the Seventh Cavalry and Sitting Bull's band of hostile Sioux, on the Little Big Horn River," it was his duty to report the 7th Cavalry's "operations from the time of leaving the main column until the command was united in the vicinity of the Indian village."[13]

The *Far West* steamed through the night of July 3, stopping near the mouth of the Powder River during the early morning hours of July 4 to bury Private William George of Company H who had died during the night. At the same time the private property of the officers killed at the Little Big Horn that had been left with the wagons was taken on board. Continuing on, Captain Marsh pushed the steamboat to its limits, stopping at Fort Buford to take on wood and put off the wounded Arikara scout Goose. The next stop was Fort Stevenson on the afternoon of the 5th to again take on wood. Shortly after leaving Stevenson, the boat's derrick and jack-staff were draped with black and the flag lowered to half-staff to honor the dead and wounded. The *Far West* arrived at Bismarck at 11 o'clock that night, after covering 710 miles in just 54 hours. Two of the first people aroused after the boat docked were Clement A. Lounsberry, editor of the *Bismarck Tribune*, and John M. Carnahan, the telegraph operator. Their first message to the *New York Herald* read:

> Bismarck, D.T., July 5, 1876: — General Custer attacked the Indians June 25, and he, with every officer and man in five companies, were killed. Reno with seven companies fought in intrenched (sic) position three days. The *Bismarck Tribune's* special correspondent was with the expedition and was killed.[14]

The *Far West* remained at the dock in Bismarck for only a few hours before slipping its mooring and heading down river with the wounded and Captain Smith's message to the families of those killed at the Little Big Horn. Early on the morning of July 6, the *Far West* arrived at Fort Lincoln. Lieutenant C. L. Gurley, 6th Infantry, related what followed:

The news came to me about 2 am. William S. McCaskey, 20th Infantry, summoned all the officers to his quarters at once, and there read to them the communication he had just received — per steamer *Far West*, from Capt. Ed. W. Smith, General Terry's adjutant general. After we had recovered from the shock Captain McCaskey requested us to assist him in breaking the news to the widows. It fell to my lot to accompany Captain McCaskey and Dr. J. V. D. Middleton, our post surgeon, to the quarters of Mrs. Custer, immediately east of those occupied by myself. We started on our sad errand a little before seven o'clock on the 6th of July morning. I went to the rear of the Custer house, woke up Maria, Mrs. Custer's housemaid, and requested her to rap on Mrs. Custer's door, and say to her that she and Mrs. Calhoun and Miss Reed were wanted in the parlor. On my way through the hall to open the front door, I heard the opening of the door of Mrs. Custer's room. She had been awakened by the footsteps in the hall. She called me by name and asked me the cause of my early visit. I made no reply, but followed Captain McCaskey and Doctor Middletown into the parlor. There we were almost immediately followed by the ladies of the Custer household, and there we told to them their first intimation of the awful result of the battle on the Little Big Horn.

Imagine the grief of those stricken women, their sobs, their flood of tears, the grief that knew no consolation.[15]

That same day at Terry's camp near Fort Pease, Reno's 7th Cavalry continued their leisure pace — until replacement men and horses arrived there was little to do but wait. The steamboat *Josephine* arrived with rations and forage for the command. It was about this time Benteen and the other officers of the 7th had an opportunity to read Reno's official report to Terry. Benteen was later to state that all the officers except Wallace were "well rabidly incensed at Reno at not mentioning them by name in his official report of the battle, and they, in some measure, seemed to hold me responsible for such action on his part, when however, the fact is known that I was scarcely on good terms with Reno, and knew no more of what he intended reporting than you [Goldin] did, and cared as little, too!"[16]

Although as of yet unseen by Reno, a letter from Thomas Rosser to the editor of the *St. Paul and Minneapolis Pioneer-Press and Tribune* was printed July 8 and reprinted in the *New York Herald* July 11, 1876. Rosser, a friend of George Custer from his West Point days and former major general in the

Confederate army, took issue with the *Pioneer-Press and Tribune* about a previously published editorial:

> I am surprised and deeply mortified to see that our neighbor the *Pioneer-Press and Tribune*, in its morning issue, has seen fit to adjudge the true, brave and heroic Custer so harshly as to attribute his late terrible disaster with the Sioux Indians to reckless indiscretion.... [F]rom my standpoint, I fail to see anything very rash in the planning of it, or reckless in its attempted execution. On the contrary, I feel that Custer would have succeeded had Reno, with all the reserve of seven companies, passed through and joined Custer after the first repulse. It is not safe at this distance, and in the absence of full details, to criticise too closely the conduct of any officer of his command, but I think it quite certain that Gen. Custer had agreed with Reno upon a place of junction in case of the repulse of either or both of the detachments, and instead of any effort being made by Reno for such a junction, as soon as he encountered heavy resistance he took refuge in the hills, and abandoned Custer and his gallant comrades to their fate.[17]

On the afternoon of July 11, Reno issued orders to move the 7th Cavalry to a new campsite a half mile down the river for better grass. The move was not appreciated by the men. Godfrey said, "After we got here everybody was in an ill humor about the camp. The bottom is broken up into a dust-heap. We've not had any rain for several weeks and the ground is very dry."[18] Reno also took the opportunity to write a letter to General Stephen Vincent Benet, chief of ordnance, concerning the operation of the 1873 Springfield Carbine and the expenditure of ammunition at the Little Big Horn battle:

> [O]ut of 380 carbines in my command, six were rendered unserviceable...by the failure of the breech block to close...and when the piece was discharged and the block thrown open, the head of the cartridge was pulled off, and the cylinder remained in the chamber, whence with the means at hand it was impossible to extract it. I believe this is a radical defect, and in the hands of hastily organized troops would lead to the most disastrous results.... [A]n Indian scout, who was with that portion of the regiment which Custer took into battle, in relating what he saw in that part of the battle, says that from his hiding place he could see the men sitting down under fire, and working at their guns — a

story that finds confirmation in the fact that officers, who afterwards examined the battlefields as they were burying the dead, found knives with broken blades lying near the dead bodies.[19]

The next few days were relatively quiet in the Reno camp and the men spent their leisure time fishing, swimming and writing letters. Several severe rain storms hit the area, accompanied by heavy thunder and spectacular displays of lightning — a tree just 20 feet from Gibbon's tent was struck but no one was injured.[20] Most of the camp sites were flooded and many men were forced to move their tents to higher ground. To add to the men's misery an invasion of grasshoppers made their appearance and got into everything.

The steamboat *Josephine* departed at 12:30 p.m. July 16 for Bismarck with Terry and his staff on board. Terry wanted to meet the *Far West*, loaded with horses and supplies, and establish a supply depot on the Yellowstone across from the mouth of the Powder River. Captain Moylan's Company A accompanied as escort and Captain Benteen went along with about 20 men of the 7th Cavalry whose enlistments expired before Aug. 15. Lieutenant Godfrey asked Reno if he objected to his going on board the *Josephine* for the trip down to Lincoln to see his family: "Yes! if we find where Crook is we'll go to him."[21]

Just after midnight July 19, Indians attempted to steal 7th Cavalry horses. Gibbon reported, "Although no Indians had been seen since leaving Custer's battleground, we had reason to suspect we were watched, and on the night of the 19th two were fired upon whilst approaching our pickets, evidently with the design of spying out our camp, and attempting to steal our stock."[22]

On July 22, Reno ordered the 7th Cavalry to again relocate its bivouac about three miles downstream to provide fresh grass for the horses. Godfrey noted, "Ordered to move today to change camp to about 1 mile below Fort Pease — moved at 3:30 pm about 3 miles towards home to a much safer & comfortable camp."[23] Later that evening a number of apparent "hostile" Indians were seen on the bluffs overlooking the camp. Several Crows immediately took up the chase. When they returned several hours later, the "hostiles" turned out to be friendly Arkiara scouts who had had a difficult time convincing the Crows they were not Sioux.[24] However, Gibbon was concerned about the possibility that Sioux or Cheyenne warriors could be watching the camp and ordered Reno, over his protests, to send some of his scouts from his regiment as videttes. Gibbon later decided that Reno's protests amounted to insubordination and on the morning of July 24 had him placed under arrest. The next day Reno received the charges against him and Godfrey noted: "I presume however Col. Reno's manner has as much to do with the results, as his manner

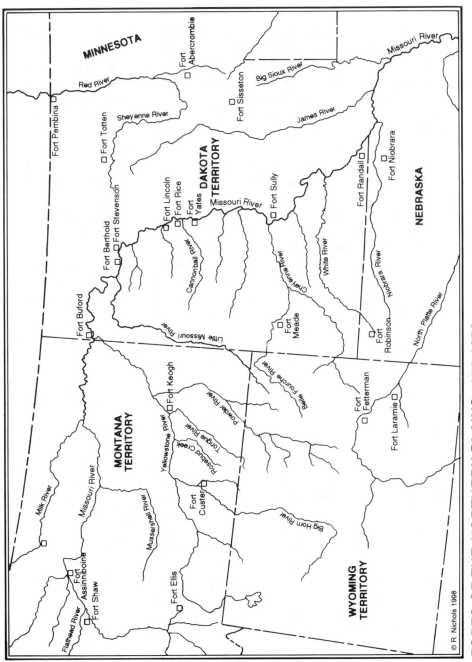

FORTS OF THE NORTHERN PLAINS 1876-1878

© R. Nichols 1998

is rather aggressive & he protested against the scouts being taken from the Reg't."[25]

Terry had met the *Far West* July 17, and completed the supply depot by the 19th. Traveling up the Yellowstone, the *Far West* reached the Fort Pease area on the 26th and Terry immediately ordered the entire command to move downstream and establish a new base camp of operations opposite the mouth of Rosebud Creek. He also reviewed Gibbon's charges against Reno and dismissed them.[26] Reno relayed the order to his officers (Benteen had returned with Terry and rejoined the regiment) and told them to be ready to move by 11 o'clock the next morning. The 7th Cavalry broke camp at 10:30 a.m. on the 27th and had traveled only three miles when it was forced to stop and construct a bridge over a wide and deep ravine — the operation took about an hour. The command moved barely a mile before a second ravine was encountered that required bridging. Reno had his troopers start the construction but decided it would be completed too late to continue that day. The area had good grass for the horses so the decision was made to camp there for the night. Reveille was at daybreak and the 7th Cavalry with the supply wagons was again on the move by 7:30 a.m. Godfrey reported: "The train had to take to the table land and experienced some difficulty getting up the hill. Our progress was very slow on account of the Diamond R teams which moved like a water wagon train.... We got to the Little Porcupine at 12 [noon] where we lunched and after marching about 4 or 5 miles went into camp on the bank of the Yellowstone...good camp."[27] The command had marched a total of 21 miles before going into camp at about 3 o'clock.

On July 29, the 7th Cavalry broke camp at 5:30 a.m., marched 17 miles, crossed the Great Porcupine and went into camp after having covered more than 22 miles. That same day farther downstream, the steamboat *Carroll*, loaded with soldiers of Colonel Elwell S. Otis' 22nd Infantry and almost 150 7th Cavalry recruits, encountered Indians removing grain from the supply depot established by Terry at the Powder River. Several companies were put ashore and briefly skirmished with the Indians. Casualties were light with only one soldier suffering a minor wound. The *Carroll* continued up the Yellowstone with its reinforcements.

Reno had the 7th Cavalry on the march by 5:15 the next morning on what would be the final march to the Rosebud encampment, arriving there shortly after noon. On Aug. 1, the steamboat *Carroll* arrived with the six companies of the 22nd Infantry and the 7th Cavalry recruits bringing the strength of Reno's command up to approximately 390. Also onboard the *Carroll* was correspondent James J. O'Kelly of the *New York Herald* who interviewed Terry and asked him about his plans for a new campaign against the Indians. Terry stated:

The plan of the new campaign is that we will move along the valley of the Rosebud, as far as the nature of the ground will permit, then cross over to the valley of the Little Big Horn, and endeavor to form a junction with General Crook, if that General will permit us, and Mr. Sitting Bull throws no insurmountable obstacles in the way. The main reliance of General Terry's command will be the infantry, though the cavalry puts up quite a respectable force since arrival of recruits for the Seventh [Cavalry]; but these men are wholly inexperienced in Indian fighting, and have not yet got their horses. Some of the infantry recruits...scarcely know the goose step, but in their case, it does not make so much difference.[28]

Reno had obtained a copy of the July 8 issue of the *St. Paul and Minneapolis Pioneer-Press and Tribune* which contained Rosser's criticism of him and the 7th Cavalry. When O'Kelly spoke to Reno on the morning of Aug. 2, it was evident that Reno was considerably annoyed about the Rosser article. O'Kelly wrote:

Considerable annoyance is felt by the officers who participated in Custer's fight on account of the incorrect or garbled accounts published in some papers. They claim that a good many who know nothing of it, and that they have perhaps unwittingly done their comrades serious injustice.

Under the circumstances I thought it well to interview both Colonel Reno and Colonel Benteen, who, by general consent, were the persons who could give the fullest account of the whole affair.

Colonel Reno is of middle stature, very strongly built, has a swarthy complexion and dark eyes, combined with a certain rapid action and frankness of manner which makes a favorable impression. He looks every inch a soldier, and judging from his appearance and temperament would be the last man to leave a comrade in a tight place without making an effort to save him. He is very much annoyed at the unfair criticism passed on the surviving officers of the Seventh by the people who knew nothing of the battle. General Rosser's letter he thinks wholly unwarranted. Colonel Reno said: "I don't usually pay attention to what is written about me, but in this case I felt compelled to reply, as much on behalf of the other officers of the Seventh as in my own."[29]

225

Reno had written a letter July 30 responding to Rosser's criticism and gave permission for O'Kelly to publish it in the *Herald*. O'Kelly inserted the letter into his dispatch which then went aboard the *Carroll* which was leaving for Fort Lincoln that same day. Reno's letter, published in the *Herald* Aug. 8 and the *Army and Navy Journal* Aug. 12, took Rosser to task for his lack of knowledge about the Little Big Horn battle and his criticism of the 7th Cavalry and its officers:

Headquarters, Seventh Regiment of Cavalry
Camp on the Yellowstone, July 30, 1876

Mr. T. L. Rosser:

Sir: When I read the first part of your letter...my thought was that your motive had only the object of a defense of a personal friend — a gallant soldier against whom you fought; but after reading all of it I could no longer look upon it as the tribute of a generous enemy, since, through me, you have attacked as brave officers as ever served the government, and with the same recklessness and ignorance of circumstances as Custer is charged with in his attack upon the hostile Indians. Both charges — the one made against him and the one made by you against us — are equally untrue. You say: — "I feel Custer would have succeeded had Reno, with all the reserve of seven companies, passed through and joined Custer after the first repulse"; and after confessing that you are firing at long range say further: — "I think it quite certain that Custer had agreed with Reno upon a place of junction in case of a repulse of either or both detachments, and instead of an effort being made by Reno for such a junction, as soon as he encountered heavy resistance he took refuge in the hills, and abandoned Custer and his gallant comrades to their fate."

As I shall show, both the premises are false, and consequently all the conclusions of your letter fall to the ground.... [There was] no mention of any plan, no thought of junction, only the usual orders to the advance guard to attack at a charge.... I was the advance and the first to be engaged and draw fire, and was consequently the command to be supported, and not the one from which support could be expected. All I know of Custer from the time he ordered me to attack till I saw him buried is that he did not follow my trail, but kept on his side of the river and along the crest of the bluff on the opposite side from the village and from my command; that he heard and saw my action I believe... My getting the command of the seven companies was not the result of any order or prearranged plan.... They [Benteen and McDougall] attempted to go down the trail of General Custer but the advanced companies soon sent back word that they were being surrounded. Crowds of reds were seen on all sides of us, and Custer's fate had evidently been determined. I knew the position I had first taken on the bluff was near and a strong one. I at once moved there, dismounted and herded the pack train, and had but just time to do so when they came upon me by thousands. Had we been twenty minutes later effecting the junction not a man of that regiment would be living today to tell the tale.

As you have the reputation of a soldier, and, if it is not undeserved, there is in you a spirit that will give you no rest until you have righted, as in you lies, the wrong that was perpetrated upon gallant men by your defense of Custer, and I request you will publish this letter with such comments as that spirit will dictate.

Respectfully, Marcus Reno, Major, Seventh Cavalry[30]

O'Kelly had also interviewed Captain Benteen, whose statement appeared in the Aug. 8 issue of the *Herald* and the Aug. 12 issue of the *Army and Navy Journal.* Benteen summarized his role in the battle and concluded:

While the command was awaiting the arrival of the pack mules a company was sent forward in the direction supposed to have been taken by Custer. After proceeding about a mile they were attacked and driven back. During this time I heard no heavy firing, and there was nothing to indicate that a heavy fight was going on, and I believe that at this time Custer's command had been annihilated.

The rest of the story you must get from Colonel Reno, as he took command and knows more than anyone else.

Also arriving at the Yellowstone camp on the afternoon of Aug. 2 were the steamboats *E. H. Durfee* and *Josephine* carrying Colonel Nelson A. Miles, six companies of the 5th Infantry, another 150 recruits and three officers for the 7th Cavalry, 60 horses and tons of supplies. The additional recruits and officers would bring the strength of Reno's 7th Cavalry up to 16 officers and 543 enlisted men.[31]

During the next several days when Miles, Terry and their staff officers had an opportunity to discuss the Little Big Horn battle, some thought Reno was to blame for not attacking through the Indian village to support Custer. Rumors of this conversation found its way into the camp and were not well received by the men of the 7th Cavalry. Scout William Jackson was later to write:

> Around the evening campfires, the one subject of conversation was now the terrible defeat of the Seventh Cavalry, the pride regiment of the United States Army. One night it came to the ears of us scouts, that all of the officers, with the exception of those who had been with Reno's troops on June 25th, were blaming Reno for General Custer's defeat, they maintaining that he, Reno, had made a cowardly retreat, and that, if he had held the position where he was first attacked, he could then have rejoined Custer, and, together, they would have won the battle. We were all of us pretty angry when we heard this. Said Girard: "If those officers had been with us, they would not now be talking this way!"… It was and is the firm belief of us scouts and soldiers who were with Reno that 25th day of June, 1876, that the day was lost by General Custer himself.[32]

The next several days the steamboats *E. H. Durfee, Josephine* and *Far West* ferried Terry's entire command across the Yellowstone to new camp sites on the south bank and up Rosebud Creek. Reno's 7th Cavalry was described by an unidentified correspondent who saw the soldiers:

> [T]heir [faces] bronzed and hardened by exposure, their clothes worn and dust begrimed, and with every non-descript style of felt or straw hat. But a minute inspection of their arms and ammunition will reveal neither rust nor dirt. The officers do not present that brilliant and gilt-edged appearance of the local officer of the young ladies of the east, for this camp sign means hard work for all, high and low. The entire command are in fine health and spirits.[33]

The last of the 7th Cavalry was ferried across the Yellowstone at 11 o'clock Aug. 6 and moved about one mile up the Rosebud to establish a camp site. The lack of horses prevented the entire regiment from being mounted and many of the new 7th Cavalry recruits were assigned to either guard duty aboard the three steamboats or duty constructing breastworks at "Fort Beans." On Aug. 7, Reno issued General Order No. 18, reorganizing the regiment into two battalions and providing replacement mounts only for Company C.

First Battalion was commanded by Captain Benteen and consisted of Companies C, G, H and M; 2nd Battalion was commanded by Captain Weir and consisted of Companies A, B, D and K. Reno assigned Lieutenant Wallace as his adjutant and Lieutenant Edgerly as the regimental quartermaster. Reno inspected the entire regiment on the morning of Aug. 8. Correspondent O'Kelly wrote:

> This morning the gallant Seventh had a muster and was inspected by Major Reno. The regiment has been reorganized. As a good many of the vacant files have been filled up by recruits, it presents a fine, soldierly appearance. Some of the companies are very strong, while those that suffered most severely in the Custer fight are merely the skeletons of their former selves, and it was not considered advisable to fill them up immediately with new recruits...two officers, Captains [Henry] Jackson and [James M.] Bell...have not joined this command. General Sheridan's order commanding them to immediately report to their regiment was issued on the 12th of July.... [F]ailure of the...officers named...to put in an appearance has given rise to a good deal of unfavorable comment, and the fighting men of the command speak of them as "coffee coolers," which is the frontier term of contempt for stay-at-home soldiers.[34]

At 5 a.m. Aug. 8, what was now known as the Yellowstone Column under General Terry, headed south up Rosebud Creek. The command consisted of elements of the 5th, 6th, 7th and 22nd Infantry, the 2nd and 7th Cavalry, a battery of three Rodman guns, and more than 200 six-mule wagons loaded with 35 days rations and forage. Four companies of the 2nd Cavalry under Major Brisbin took the lead position, the wagon caravan came next with the infantry along the flanks, and finally followed by Reno's eight companies of the 7th Cavalry. Progress was limited because of the wagons, and distances covered ranged between eight and 10 miles. High temperatures and occasional heavy rain added to the soldiers discomfort.

For the next two days, the column moved southward and about 11 o'clock Aug. 10, "those of our Indian scouts who are in advance come rushing back shouting 'Sioux', and calling our attention to a large cloud of dust seen rising from behind a hill a few miles up the valley."[35] The command was immediately formed in battle line and Reno ordered Weir's battalion to form into a mounted skirmish line "at full gallop." Four companies of the 2nd Cavalry moved into columns on the flanks. The wagons were closed up and the infantry positioned along its flanks. Reno ordered Benteen's battalion, which was acting as rear guard, to move up to the front. Terry gave orders to send out a reconnaissance and Reno gave French's Company M the assignment. As French started out, a lone horseman was observed coming toward the command. Correspondent O'Kelly wrote: "As we strained our ears for the report of the first gun, the horseman advanced toward the skirmishers, making signs of friendship, and was allowed to approach. It proved to be [William F.] Cody, the scout, better known as 'Buffalo Bill,' dressed in the magnificence of border fashion."[36] Cody was the lead scout for Crook's Wyoming Column — the dust cloud reported by the Indians and their shouts of "Sioux" had turned out to be Crook's command of cavalry and infantry troops. Weir rode out to meet Cody and escort him back to Terry.

Terry's command then continued south and a bivouac was established with Crook's command. Terry assumed command of the combined forces. He dispatched Miles with four companies of the 5th Infantry back to the mouth of the Rosebud to board the *Far West* and patrol the Yellowstone between the Tongue and Powder to prevent the Indians from escaping to the north. Terry also ordered a pack train to be made up with 15 days rations and ammunition to continue his plan of pursuing the Indians.

When Terry's column joined Crook's, correspondent John F. Finerty noted:

> The principal thing that attracted my attention, and that of all our force, was the remnant of the 7th Cavalry. It came in, formed into seven [eight] small companies, led by Major Reno — a short, stout man, about fifty years old [41], with a determined visage, his face showing intimate acquaintance with the sun and wind.[37]

Crook's column had been in the field for a number of weeks while Terry's was only three days out from an almost civilized environment created by the arrival of the steamboats. Officers of Crook's command visited with Terry's officers and Captain Charles King noted:

> Their tents were brightly lighted and comfortably furnished. Even the Seventh Cavalry were housed like Sybarites to our unaccustomed eyes. "Great guns!" said our new major, almost exploding at a revelation so preposterous. "Look at Reno's tent — he's got a Brussels carpet!" But they made us cordially welcome, and were civilly unconscious of our motley attire.[38]

The morning of Aug. 11 saw Terry's combined command ready to continue its pursuit of the Indians. The march started about 9 o'clock. The wagons were sent back to the Yellowstone and more than 200 pack mules were loaded with the necessary supplies to support the column for 15 days. The column turned east, crossed the Tongue River and arrived at the Powder River Aug. 15. Godfrey noted in his diary for that day:

> [Lieutenant Henry P.] Walker says he has been detailed as personal Aide-de-camp on the staff of Gen'l. Terry, apparently for the purpose of carrying orders to the Commdg. off. of 7th Cav. Maj. Reno has been playing "*ass*" right along and is so taken up with his own importance that he thinks he can "snip" everybody and comment on the orders he receives from Genl. Terry's Hdqrs. and insult his staff, so there is not any one [of] the personal staff on speaking terms.[39]

Terry would continue to follow the Indian trail north on the Powder for the next two days but would encounter no hostiles, reaching the confluence of the Powder and Yellowstone on the afternoon of Aug. 17. The combined forces would remain at the Powder River confluence awaiting supplies for the next week, with Terry's Yellowstone column occupying the east bank of the Powder and Crook's Wyoming column the west bank. With the arrival of several steamboats over the next few days, Crook refurbished his supplies and on Aug. 24, he took his Wyoming Column south on the Powder to follow the abandoned Indian trails. On Aug. 26, Reno's 7th Cavalry, along with ele- ments of the 5th, 7th and 22nd Infantry and 2nd Cavalry, under the com- mand of Colonel Gibbon, was ordered down the south bank of the Yellow- stone to O'Fallon's Creek. There they would be met by one or more steam- boats and ferried to the north bank to join the balance of Terry's command which would be moving along the north bank.

On Aug. 22, Rosser's reply to Reno's Aug. 8 letter appeared in the *New York Herald*. Rosser had read Terry's official report of the Little Big Horn battle and "now writes with a fuller information of the details of General Reno's position."[40]

> Major:
> A letter appeared in the *New York Herald* of 8th inst., ad- dressed to me and signed by yourself, complaining of injustice having been done you in a letter of mine written to the *Minne- apolis Evening Tribune* upon the receipt here of Custer's tragic death. My letter...was written in advance of the receipt of the details of this engagement...and before I had seen the official report of General Terry.... Having once been a soldier myself I

fully appreciate your sensitiveness to criticisms which involved the vital elements of a soldier's honor and reputation. Your patriotism and courage I have never questioned...but now, Major, as to the manner in which you, as detachment commander, performed your duty.... The errors which I believe you committed in that engagement were attributed to what I believed to have been a lack of judgment and a want of experience in Indian warfare.... I have heard that someone has advanced the theory that Custer was met...by overwhelming numbers, and so beaten that his line from that point on was one of retreat. This is simply ridiculous.... He did that which in ninety-nine cases out of a hundred will succeed, but this by chance was the fatal exception, yet the result does not impair the value of the rule.... You know that even in civilized warfare the bolder movements are generally successful, and the general who plans for the enemy and is counseled by his fears is sure to fail.[41]

Reno would not see Rosser's latest article for several more weeks but when he finally had the opportunity to read it he must have decided a response was not warranted. No record of a published response has been found.

The steamers *Carroll* and *Yellowstone* arrived early on the morning of Aug. 27 and spent most of the day ferrying Gibbon's troops across to the north bank of the Yellowstone. Terry arrived at the same point that afternoon and ordered a march to the northeast — the command finally went into camp at 9 o'clock. For the next four days, the command continued its march toward the northeast but finally turned back toward the Yellowstone, camping Aug. 30 about 45 miles southwest of Fort Buford. Terry directed Reno "with the whole of the 7th Cavalry, and a detachment of scouts...to make a reconnaissance from our camp to the mouth of the Yellowstone.... [Reno] was instructed to proceed with his regiment to a point on the river 40 or 50 miles below Glendive [near Fox Creek], and to send his scouts thence to the Missouri."[42]

The 7th Cavalry broke camp at 8:15 a.m. Aug. 31 and moved over rough terrain. For several days the 7th Cavalry scouted the lower Yellowstone looking for Indians who had been reported in the area a few days before. Scouting as far as the confluence of the Yellowstone and Missouri, Reno was unable to find any fresh sign of Indian activity. The 7th Cavalry broke camp Sept. 2 and moved southwest along the Yellowstone to rejoin Terry's command. During the bivouac later that day the steamboats *Josephine* and *Benton* passed the camp site on their way to Fort Buford. Captain Benteen, having received orders of a reassignment to recruiting service, boarded one of the boats for the trip to Buford. Benteen's battalion would now be commanded directly by Reno. Breaking camp early the next morning, Reno's command joined up with Terry later that afternoon.

With no signs of recent Indian activity, Terry decided the summer campaign against the Indians was virtually at an end, and on Sept. 5, ordered Colonel Gibbon's 7th Infantry and 2nd Cavalry to return to their posts at Fort Ellis, Fort Shaw and Camp Baker. The 5th Infantry would accompany Gibbon's column to the newly established cantonment at the Tongue River and the 22nd Infantry was assigned to guard supplies at Glendive. Reno was ordered to take the 7th Cavalry to Fort Buford, accompanied by three companies of the 6th Infantry. Reno was to continue scouting along the north bank of the Yellowstone "to prevent any considerable body of Indians from crossing."[43] Terry and his staff boarded the *Josephine* for the trip downstream to Fort Buford.

The 7th Cavalry broke camp at 7 a.m. Sept. 7 and for the next two days marched along the Yellowstone. Terry had arrived at Fort Buford on the 8th and received a dispatch on the 9th that a large force of Sioux had appeared at Wolf's Point, along the upper Missouri, 85 miles from Buford. He sent a courier to Reno to move his command to Wolf's Point to determine if the Indians were crossing the Missouri.[44]

The courier with Terry's message arrived at Reno's camp site on the morning of Sept. 10. Correspondent O'Kelly wrote: "Our sudden expedition to Wolf's Point was caused by a report that Long Dog, with some 150 followers, had crossed the Missouri, and that the river bank for a mile was covered with Indians."[45] Reno immediately had a problem with the message — no one in his command knew the country between their location on the Yellowstone and Wolf's Point. Reno sent a message back with the courier:

> Your…dispatch received. I will start today for Wolf's Pt. I find there is no one here that knows the country, but I dare say I will get thru' all right. My course will be W 25 [degrees] N & should any further information in regard to Indians be received, please forward to me.… I keep one of the scouts who has been to Wolf's Pt.[46]

Reno's command, including the three companies of 6th Infantry and a number of mule-drawn ambulances, left their bivouac at 11 a.m. and marched 22 miles before stopping for the night. The march was resumed at 6:30 a.m. the following day and the command crossed the divide between the Missouri and the Yellowstone about 9:30 a.m. The column finally halted at 5 o'clock after covering more than 25 miles. Reno issued orders to reduce the daily ration since he did not know how much longer the command would be in the field without resupply. Godfrey noted: "We were ordered to make the rations last to include the 17th two days addition, so it gave us about 2/3 rations — this is done in anticipation of 'no boat' when we reach the [Missouri] river and have to march down to Buford."[47] Reno also ordered the troops not to hunt as the noise might be heard by the Indians.

Sept. 12 was a rough day for Reno's detachment — rain and "rugged, steep, slippery" terrain slowed the march considerably.[48] Reaching the Missouri in the early afternoon, the command stopped to prepare dinner before proceeding upstream, finally camping about three miles from the Assinoboine Agency at Wolf's Point. That same day Terry and his staff boarded the steamboat *John M. Chambers* at Buford for the trip up the Missouri to the Assinoboine Agency.

The next morning, after marching the command to Wolf's Point, Reno, Hare and Wallace, with a small escort, crossed the river to the north bank to talk to Indian Agent, Thomas J. Mitchell, who indicated that Lone Dog and a small number of followers had crossed the river several days before and had probably gone into Canada.[49]

Reno moved his column to a better camp site and awaited further orders. The steamboat *John M. Chambers* arrived with Terry and his staff about noon Sept. 15. Learning from Reno that the Indians were already a number of days ahead of the scouting party and well on their way to Canada, Terry decided to cease all further operations. Reno's command was transferred to the north bank with orders to proceed overland to Fort Buford. The 6th Infantry companies would be transported by steamboat to Fort Buford.

Reno planned to start for Buford immediately but decided to delay the march until the next day. Godfrey noted: "It was intended to move a few miles down the river but a few drinks put that out of mind and we concluded to have a 'sing'.... Got some commissary stores and a sack of potatoes from the Agency."[50]

The 7th Cavalry marched 30 miles eastward along the Missouri on Sept. 16. Long marches on the next two days brought the command to Fort Buford and established a camp about a half mile away. Reno received orders from Terry to return to Fort Lincoln on reaching Fort Buford. On Sept. 19, Reno boarded a steamboat for Fort Lincoln and turned the eight companies of the 7th Cavalry over to Captain Weir. The command reached Fort Lincoln Sept. 26. Reno, who had arrived at Lincoln on the 22nd, was there to greet the 7th Cavalry when it arrived at the fort. A correspondent described the scene:

> The 7th Cavalry arrived this Tuesday morning. As they rode over the hill north of Bismarck, the view presented was magnifi-

cent — but tears came unbidden to many an eye, for Custer, the brave Custer, his noble brothers and fellows, were not there. Col. Weir was in command of the regiment, though Major Reno, the superior officer, who came down from Buford on the boat with headquarters, rode out to meet them. The stock was in fine condition, in the main, but the men were sunburnt, worn and dusty. A few familiar faces were recognized, but those with whom Bismarck people were best acquainted lie in the trenches on the Little Horn: the Custers, Keogh, Yates, Smith, Hodgson, McIntosh, Harrington, Curtis [Sturgis], Porter and Crittenden, not to speak of Kellogg, Reynolds and many enlisted men [who] were our friends, neighbors and associates, and we mourn their loss as we should mourn the loss of a like number of the best and most prominent of citizens.... Fred Girard and a few of his Indian scouts came on Monday.... The troops that left Lincoln in the spring are now all in except Major [Louis] Sanger's battalion [17th Infantry] and those who sleep the long sleep.[51]

The summer campaign was over — but the turbulent times for Marcus Reno were just beginning.

Endnotes

[1] Douglas D. Scott (editor), *Papers on Little Bighorn Battlefield Archeology: The Equipment Dump, Marker 7, and the Reno Crossing*, (J & L Reprint Co., Lincoln, Neb., 1991). It covers the results of the archaeology survey conducted at the Custer Battlefield National Monument in 1989.

[2] Letter from Captain Stephen Baker to John Gibbon, dated June 29, 1876. Department of Dakota, Letters Received, 1876, Record Group 98, NARA.

[3] In fact Comanche did recover and under the care of Blacksmith Gustave Korn and John Burkman survived to the age of 30 when he died on Nov. 6, 1891 at Fort Riley, Kan. Comanche is now displayed at the Dyche Museum at the University of Kansas in Lawrence.

[4] Joseph Mills Hanson, *The Conquest of the Missouri*, (Murray Hill Books, Inc., New York, 1946), p. 298.

[5] James Willert, *March of the Columns*, (Upton & Sons, El Segundo, Calif., 1994), p. 43.

[6] The most accurate accounting of the casualties suffered by the 7th Cavalry can be found in Ken Hammer's *Men With Custer: Biographies of the 7th Cavalry*, (Custer Battlefield Historical & Museum Association Inc., Hardin, Mont., 1995), p. xvii, pp. 392-409.

[7] Fred Dustin, *The Custer Tragedy*, (Edward Brothers, Inc., Ann Arbor, Mich., 1939), p. 197.

[8] Hanson, p. 303.

[9] W. A. Graham, *The Story of the Little Big Horn*, (The Stackpole Co., Harrisburg, Penna., 1959), pp. 159-161.

[10] John S. Gray, "The Reno Petition," *The Westerners Brand Book* (Volume XXIV, Chicago, August 1967, Number Six), pp. 41-42. The question of the authenticity of the petition has been debated for a number of years. In his article concerning the petition Gray notes, "It is certain, however, that the names were not simply transcribed from company rosters by non-commissioned officers, for they are not in order by companies, nor in order by rank, or by alphabet, within company runs. It is significant that considerable care was taken to exclude the names of some hundreds of men who were detached from the regiment at the time of the battle." However, Gray also states, "It is possible, though not certain, that pressure, either overt or simply inherent in the military context, was brought to bear on the enlisted men" to sign the petition.

[11] Edgar & Jane Stewart (editors), *The Field Diary of Lt. Edward Settle Godfrey* (The Champoeg Press, Portland, Ore., 1957), p. 21.

[12] Letter from M. A. Reno to General Philip H. Sheridan, date July 4, 1876, Library of Congress, Sheridan Collection. Reno's letter directly to Sheridan was a serious breach of military protocol — the letter should have been sent to Terry. Perhaps Reno thought that because Terry's decisions may have had a significant bearing on Gibbon's actions, a letter to Terry would not be well received and Sheridan would not have the benefit of Reno's opinion as to why the battle went so poorly.

[13] The entire text of Reno's July 5 report may be found in Appendix D.

[14] Hanson, p. 307.

[15] Hanson, pp. 312-313.

[16] John M. Carroll (editor), *The Benteen-Goldin Letters on Custer and His Last Battle* (Liveright, N.Y., 1974), p. 219. This was in Benteen's letter to Theodore W. Goldin, dated March 19, 1892.

[17] William A. Graham, *The Custer Myth* (Stackpole Company, Harrisburg, Penna., 1953), p. 225.

[18] Stewart, *Field* Diary, p. 22.

[19] July 11, 1876, report from 7th Cavalry Headquarters, Camp on Yellowstone River, to General S. V. Benet, chief of ordnance, from Major Marcus A. Reno. Reprinted in the *Army and Navy Journal*, Aug. 19, 1876. The Indian scout mentioned in this report was probably the Crow Scout Curley. It is doubtful that Curley was close enough to see Custer's men "sitting down under fire, and working at their guns." He probably heard some of Reno's men talking about the hilltop fight and the problems they had with their weapons, and incorporated it into his own story to enhance it. Much of jamming was due to the use of copper cartridge cases which, when left in contact with leather and subjected to the type of weather encountered during the campaign, developed a greenish/blue deposit of verdigris. These deposits, if not removed prior to use and when combined with a hot chamber, caused the cartridge case to jam in the chamber and when the extractor attempted to remove it, simply tore through the case. The Ordnance Department changed from copper cartridge cases to brass in late 1877.

[20] George A. Schneider (editor), *The Freeman Journal* (Presidio Press, San Rafael, Calif., 1977), p. 68. This is Captain Henry B. Freeman's journal.

[21] Stewart, *Field Diary*, p. 24. It is interesting that Godfrey would even make the request. The 7th Cavalry was short of officers and allowing Godfrey to leave would have made the situation worse.

[22] John Gibbon, *Gibbon on the Sioux Campaign of 1876* (Old Army Press, Bellevue, Neb., 1970), p. 48. Reprinted from *The American Catholic Quarterly Review*, April 1877.

[23] Stewart, *Field Diary*, p. 26.

[24] Gibbon, p. 48.

[25] Stewart, *Field Diary*, p. 27.

[26] There is no record of the charges going higher than Terry so it is assumed that he thought there was insufficient evidence to warrant a court-martial.

[27] Stewart, *Field Diary*, pp. 28-29.

[28] *New York Herald*, Aug. 7, 1876, interview of General Terry by James J. O'Kelly.

[29] *New York Herald*, Aug. 7, 1876, interview of Reno by O'Kelly.

[30] *Army and Navy Journal*, Volume 14, Aug. 12, 1876.

[31] James Willert, *After Little Big Horn: 1876 Campaign Rosters* (Private Printing, La Mirada, Calif., 1985), page following Introduction, entitled "Dakota-Montana Column." Willert indicates there were 17 officers but a careful count agrees with Terry's count of 7th Cavalry officers, 16.

[32] James Willard Schultz, *William Jackson Indian Scout* (William K. Cavanagh, Springfield, Ill., 1976), pp. 157-158.

[33] *New York Times*, Aug. 18, 1876, p. 2.

[34] *New York Herald*, Aug. 15, 1876, p. 10., Also Sheridan's letter to Brig. Gen. E. E. Townsend, dated Chicago, July 11, 1876. Library of Congress, Sheridan Records, Shelf No. 19,308, Reel 58.

[35] Edward J. McClernand, *Narrative and Journal*, 1876.

[36] *New York Herald*, Aug. 24, 1876, p. 3.

[37] John F. Finerty, *War-Path and Bivouac* (Donohue & Henneberry, Chicago, Ill., 1890), p. 224.

[38] Charles King, *Campaigning With Crook and Stories of Army Life* (Harper & Brothers, New York, 1890), p. 82.

[39] Stewart, *Field Diary*, p. 36.

[40] *New York Herald*, Aug. 22, 1876.

[41] *New York Herald*, Aug. 22, 1876.

[42] Charles E. Deland, "The Sioux Wars," *South Dakota Historical Collections*, Volume XVII (Pierre, S. D., 1934), p. 182.

[43] Deland, p. 184.

[44] Information from telegram sent from Terry to Sheridan, dated Sept. 18, 1876. NARA Record Group 393, Item #6869.

[45] *New York Herald*, Sept. 21, 1876, p.10.

[46] Department of Dakota, NARA Record Group 393, pp. 1414-1415.

[47] Stewart, *Field Diary*, p. 50.

[48] Journal of Private Wilmot P. Sanford, Company D, 6th Infantry. Western Americana Collection, Yale University.

[49] *New York Herald*, Sept. 21, 1876, p. 10.

[50] Stewart, *Field Diary*, p. 52.

[51] *Bismarck Tribune*, Little Bighorn Battlefield National Monument, Microfilm roll #18 — scrapbook of Nettie Bowen Smith, no date.

Turbulent Times

When Major Reno returned to Fort Abraham Lincoln Sept. 22, he was the ranking officer and immediately assumed command of the post. The return of the 7th Cavalry Sept. 26, 1876, was a sad affair — no band greeted them when they arrived that Tuesday morning. The facings and trimmings of the doorways and windows of the officers quarters had been painted black as a symbol of mourning for the men who had lost their lives at the Little Big Horn three months earlier.[1]

Headquarters, Band and Companies A, C, D, E, F and L occupied quarters at Fort Lincoln while the remaining six companies went into camp just south of the post.

The officers and men would finally have an opportunity to bathe and put on fresh clothing — something they had been unable to do for many weeks. In the early evening, many of the cavalry and infantry officers gathered at the Officers' Club Room on the post to enjoy a good meal and have a few drinks. Attendees on the evening of the 26th included Reno; Captain Thomas Weir; 1st Lieutenants Charles Varnum, Luther Hare, W. W. Robinson, William Craycroft and Edwin Eckerson, 7th Cavalry; 1st Lieutenant John A. Manley, 20th Infantry; 2nd Lieutenants Alexander Ogle and Charles Finley, 6th Infantry; wagon master Frederick Snow; and Post Trader William Harmon.

As the evening wore on and most of the participants had consumed a number of drinks, the talk became loud and boisterous. A chance remark by Manley, apparently in support of Rosser's criticism of Reno, but overheard by Reno, led first to verbal discussion, then to a physical altercation between the two. The scene was described: "[Reno]…did, by his malicious and insulting remarks to a brother officer, provoke a personal encounter and did engage in a fisticuffs and rough-and-tumble fight…in which he [Reno]…did roll on the floor of the Officers' Club Room…in the slops and filth caused by spittle and the spilling of liquor upon…[the] floor." Reno then attempted to throw Manley out of the club, using "arbitrary and abusive language."

Varnum stepped in to mediate the situation and stop Reno from expelling Manley. A shouting match between those two ensued and Reno told Varnum in no uncertain terms, "If you intervene, Mr. Varnum, I will make it a personal matter with you." At this point Varnum backed off and Weir endeavored to persuade Reno to shake hands with Varnum. When Varnum held out his, Reno responded, "Don't you touch my hand." He was furious with Varnum for interfering to the point of challenging him to a duel. Reno threatened to send for pistols, and when Lieutenant Robinson threatened to place Reno under arrest if he allowed pistols to be brought into the club for dueling, Reno replied, "Who the hell are you?" The situation finally quieted down and the participants found their way back to their respective quarters without further incident.[2]

The next morning the previous night's fracas apparently had been forgotten but would come back to haunt Reno in the future. During the next three weeks, more than 500 recruits and 500 horses arrived at Fort Lincoln, increasing the strength of the regiment to more than 1,200. Little time remained to train the new men and horses sufficiently for the field work soon to be undertaken. Sixteen officers were absent from the regiment and five new, inexperienced officers had only recently joined the command. Reno worked hard during this period to shape up the regiment, and with long hours of training the regiment was at least partially ready by mid-October for its new assignment of field service.

It was not all work — a number of social gatherings took place to which the post's commanding officer usually had a standing invitation. Reno enjoyed socializing with the new officers and their wives. The widows and families of those killed at the Little Big Horn had left the post and a number of newly assigned officers and their families had moved into the vacated quarters. One of the officers who arrived before Reno's return to the post was Captain James M. Bell and his wife, Emily. Reno had first met the Bells at Fort Snelling, Minn., in the spring of 1873. Emily, 26, was 13 years younger than her husband and was described by the contemporary press as "of more than ordinary beauty and…of a vivacious disposition…a general favorite with the officers and their wives."[3] Rumors and "disparaging remarks" about her character, suggesting her past was somewhat tarnished, circulated in the regiment. When the Bells were stationed at Shreveport, La., from the fall of 1874 to the spring of 1876, an incident occurred about which George Wallace was later to state "that she was not a true wife."[4] Reno would socialize with the Bells several times in the next few weeks. During this period, Reno described an event that occurred concerning several photographs: "I was asked by her [Emily Bell] & Mrs. [Mary] Godfrey to give them a picture of myself. I declined, as I had none to spare, they asked me if I had pictures, where they were, I told them & during my absence they went to my house & took each a copy."[5] While Reno was in the field during late October and early November, Bell was reassigned to Fort Abercrombie, and his wife and he left for their new post.

At this time, Reno, a veteran of more than 19 years of active military service, was a 41-year-old widower with a 12-year-old son in Harrisburg. He was described as "not, in the estimate of officers who served under him, a particularly pleasant person.... He was sleek but with a thin mustache, thin-lipped mouth and tired sunken eyes."[6] His drinking habits had previously been portrayed by Edgerly: "He was, in those days when almost everybody drank, what was called a moderate drinker and I never saw him drunk."[7] He was a smoker, played poker, shot billiards and mixed socially with the other officers. Criticism of his actions at the Little Big Horn, already started by Rosser, would only get worse.

Colonel Samuel D. Sturgis returned to Fort Lincoln Oct. 18, 1876, and relieved Reno as post and regimental commander. Prior to his return, Sturgis had ordered eight companies of the 7th Cavalry (B, E, F, H, I, K, L and M), two companies of the 17th Infantry (A and H), one company of the 20th Infantry (D), a section of Parrott guns and 28 scouts to cross the Missouri near Fort Lincoln and be prepared to march on the 20th to disarm and dismount the Indians at the Standing Rock and Cheyenne agencies. Reno was assigned the remaining four 7th Cavalry companies (A, C, D and G) and ordered to the Standing Rock Agency Oct. 21.

Early on the 20th, Sturgis moved his column down the east bank of the Missouri and arrived at the Standing Rock Agency on the 22nd. Reno's column left Fort Lincoln Oct. 21, reached Fort Rice later that day, and traveled down the west bank of the Missouri the following day to the Standing Rock Agency. The combined commands spent the next four days disarming and dismounting the Indians. Sturgis left the Standing Rock Agency Oct. 26 and marched his column to the Cheyenne Agency, arriving there Oct. 30. Reno remained at the Standing Rock Agency for a few more days before returning to Fort Lincoln Nov. 3 with several wagons loaded with weapons and about 900 Indian ponies.[8] Reno assumed command of the post until Sturgis returned Nov. 11 to reassume command of the regiment and garrison.[9]

With the Indians disarmed and demobilized, the local threat from Indian attack was minimized and the regiment could be placed in its winter quarters. Companies of the 7th Cavalry were stationed at Forts Abercrombie (F), Rice (A, D, H and M), Totten (C) and Lincoln (B, E, G, I, K and L). When Sturgis returned to the post, Reno received permission to take a 20-day leave of absence beginning Nov. 17.[10] He left the post on the 17th and there is no record where he spent his leave — probably Bismarck or Minneapolis-St. Paul — a trip to Harrisburg and back would have taken almost the entire 20 days. Reno returned to his post and regiment Dec. 6. Orders were issued from the Department of Dakota for him to take station at Fort Abercrombie and he left Fort Lincoln Dec. 15, arriving at Abercrombie on the 17th.[11]

Fort Abercrombie, about 220 rail miles from Fort Lincoln, was established in 1857 on the Red River of the North in a broad valley described as a "perfectly flat prairie, broken only by many streams." Timber was found only along the river bank and was scarce. In the spring, the river could rise rapidly, sometimes 40 feet above its usual level. The climate, for four to five months of the year, was cold, frequently 40 degrees below zero, and in the summer hot, rising to 100 degrees in the shade. A telegraph and railroad station was found at Breckenridge, 12 miles distant, and Moorhead and Fargo were each about 30 miles to the north. Quarters existed for three companies of infantry or cavalry and the post's officers. There were a number of other buildings constructed of wood except for the brick magazines.[12]

The garrison at the time of Reno's arrival consisted of Company A, 17th Infantry, under the command of Captain William M. Van Horne, and Company F, 7th Cavalry, under the command of Captain James Bell. Other officers stationed at the post included 1st Lieutenant Thomas G. Troxel, 17th Infantry regimental quartermaster; 1st Lieutenant William W. Robinson, Jr., 7th Cavalry, post adjutant; and 2nd Lieutenant Herbert J. Slocum, Company F, 7th Cavalry. These five officers were married and, with the exception of Slocum, had their wives with them.

About the time Reno was transferring to Fort Abercrombie, an event occurred that would significantly impact Reno's life and military career — the publication of Frederick Whittaker's *A Complete Life of General George A. Custer.* The book was extremely critical of both Reno's and Benteen's role at the Little Big Horn battle and essentially blamed both for Custer's defeat. Some of the prose used by Whittaker provides the reader with the theme of the book:

> This book aims to give to the world the life of a great man, one of the few really great men that America has produced.... Much of Custer's success has been attributed to good fortune, while it was really the result of a wonderful capacity for hard and energetic work, and a rapidity of intuition which is seldom found apart from military genius of the highest order...to paint in sober earnest colors the truthful portrait of such a knight of romance as has not honored the world with his presence since the days of Bayard.[13]

The reasons for Custer's defeat were simple according to Whittaker's book: "Reno's incapacity and Benteen's disobedience."[14] To Whittaker, the conclusions were obvious:

242

1. Had Reno fought as Custer fought, and had Benteen obeyed Custer's orders, the battle of the Little [Big] Horn might have proved Custer's last and greatest Indian victory.

2. Had not President Grant, moved by private revenge, displaced Custer from command of the Fort Lincoln column, Custer would be alive today and the Indian war settled.[15]

Reno would not have an opportunity to read it for several months but the book was reviewed in the Dec. 23, 1876, issue of the *Army and Navy Journal*:

The really great successes of the fiery leader of the third Cavalry Division seems to intoxicate the author, and with reckless pen he thrusts right and left, careless of reputations, regardless of facts, darkening the lives of other men in the vain hope that one name may shine more brightly on the page of history.... Later on Capt. Whittaker seems to have forgotten his prudent counsel, and ere yet the smoke of the battle of the Little Big Horn has settled down, and before the official reports of the General and the Lieutenant General of the Army have been made, this rash writer furiously arraigns, tries, convicts, and sentences the President, Major Reno, and Captain Benteen for indirectly causing the death of General Custer. Since the book appeared in print Gen. Sherman and Lieut. General Sheridan — to whose personal regard for the gallant Custer, his biographer bears frequent testimony — have, in their report to the War Department, after months of careful consideration of all the facts and of much evidence, not made public, unequivocally commended Reno as a brave and discreet man, who had performed his whole duty and plainly ascribed the disastrous termination of Custer's fight to the unfortunate division of his command.[16]

The *Army and Navy Journal* responded in their Jan. 6, 1877, issue following a letter from Whittaker, critical of the *Journal's* review of his book:

In our review of Capt. Whittaker's "Life of Gen. Custer," we were compelled to criticize with some severity certain portions of that work. We fail, however, to see the "patient research" of a few months, or a conscientious desire on the author's part, to "tell the truth as he sees it," any good reason for making charges affecting the reputation of officers who do not deserve to be publicly branded without an opportunity for public defense. The reports of anonymous newspaper correspondents, and an ex parte statement of the conclusions drawn from letters, of which we have not so much as the names of the writers, is not proof on which to base criticism affecting character and reputation.[17]

Benteen, who had been temporarily assigned to recruiting duty in Philadelphia in September, returned to Fort Rice after being relieved by Captain Weir. Benteen did have the opportunity to read both Whittaker's book and the review published in the Dec. 23 issue of the *Army and Navy Journal*. He wasted little time in responding:

> Sir: In the issue of your paper of December 23 I see that you reviewed "The Complete Life of General G. A. Custer," by Brevet Captain Frederick Whittaker, 6th New York Cavalry.
>
> I desire to thank you for the sensible remarks therein contained. "1st. Had Reno fought as Custer fought, and Benteen obeyed Custer's orders, the battle of the Little Big Horn <u>might</u> have proved Custer's last and greatest victory." I put right here, without fear of contradiction: Yes, and his <u>first</u> Indian victory too!
>
> "The battle of the Washita" is comprised in this grand total. (I do not mean to include Custer's war record in this assertion.) I have been with General Custer since the organization of the 7th Cavalry, and claim to know whereof I speak; nor do I desire to get into a controversy about his merits — or otherwise — as seen from my standpoint, as now I cannot, or would not, say what I would, and did, when General Custer was alive. I say here, that Colonel Reno and I thought during the siege of June 25th and 26th, at the Little Big Horn, that he Reno, was the abandoned party, and spoke of it as another "Major Elliott affair;" thinking that General Custer had retreated to the mouth of the river, where the steamboat was supposed to be, and that Reno's command was left to <u>its</u> fate. I am accused of disobeying Custer's orders. Nothing is further from the truth in point of fact, and I do not think the matter of sufficient importance to attempt to vindicate myself, but can rest contentedly under the ban when I have the consoling belief that the contrary is so well known by all my military superiors and comrades.
>
> You spoke justly when you denominated Whittaker as a "rash writer" for, in a letter to me, he acknowledges his information has been obtained from what I can demonstrate to be most question-

able authority. I have not attempted to defend myself on such insinuations, because the game is not worth the candle.... There was a slight undercurrent in the 7th Cavalry which you, as a public organ, might know, and which knowledge may throw some light on matters on which Mr. O'Kelly, the *Herald* reporter, wrote, and from which Whittaker obtained his cue, viz.: Colonel Reno's official report of the battle of Little Big Horn brought not with it the need of satisfaction which I believe the writer wished, but his mentioning me specially was as invidiousness of which he thought not. Most certainly Colonel Reno asked me not for counsel in preparing his report. However, the report when received by the regiment drew from one officer the exclamation in public, "But he doesn't mention me!" (Calling out his own name). From that moment can be said, the Society for Mutual Admiration was organized in the regiment and assiduously did they work — Colonel Reno being the chief objective point, I the second, from being unfortunate enough to have been specially mentioned by Colonel Reno in his official report. The meetings of the society have been held in secret; no 1st class men were contributing members; none of them can bear the test of light and truth; but still they don't want their light hidden under a bushel, and they have succeeded in getting vile slanders into public print, through the greatest organ in this country, and yet they are not happy! Now through Whittaker, the story goes into history?[18]

Reno arrived at Fort Abercrombie on the afternoon of Sunday, Dec. 17, 1876, and was invited to the home of Captain and Mrs. Van Horne for dinner. That evening Reno called on Captain and Mrs. Bell and found the Van Hornes also there. Earlier that day Bell had received a telegram that his father was seriously ill in Altoona, Penna., and he was preparing to leave for the east immediately. Bell left the gathering before the evening was out to ride to the railroad station at Breckenridge, some 12 miles distant.

Prior to Reno's arrival, Bell and his wife had temporarily moved into the vacant commanding officer's quarters. With Bell's departure and Reno now the senior officer on the post, the commanding officer's quarters would be his. The next morning Mrs. Bell moved their possessions out of the house they had occupied for six weeks and moved into one side of a set of duplex quarters. The Van Hornes lived in the other side, and the two were joined by a common "storm screen" room at the front.

Reno visited Mrs. Bell at her quarters on Monday morning with a number of other people but stayed only about 15 or 20 minutes. Calling on Mrs.

Bell Tuesday morning, Reno extended, but Mrs. Bell declined, an invitation "to drive" with him.[19] It was a visit to Mrs. Bell's residence later that day that would get Reno into serious trouble. When he arrived at her house in the early evening, he was somewhat startled to find Lieutenant Slocum there — he had been "reading" to her. Slocum left after a "few moments" and Reno was to be alone with her for "probably two hours." Emily was later to testify:

> When Colonel Reno got up to go that evening he stood up. I rose when he rose to go, and he took both my hands in his and attempted to pull me towards him. I took both my hands away. He then said good night Mrs. Bell, and took my hand and slipped his fingers up towards my arm. I said, "Col. Reno, is that the Masonic grip?" He said, "Yes, I have a book at home that tells all about it: would you like to read it?" I said, "Yes, if it is about masonry I should like to read it."… He then left the house and said goodnight.[20]

The Van Hornes visited Mrs. Bell after Reno had left and Emily told them it was her intention never "to invite him in my house again."[21]

On Wednesday, Dec. 20, Reno officially assumed the position of post commander. The following day a second incident occurred between Reno and Mrs. Bell that would put their relationship on a much colder and more formal basis. In the late afternoon, Reno called on Mrs. Bell to escort her to Lieutenant Robinson's quarters to say good bye to Robinson's sister, who was returning home later that day. The visit took only about 20 minutes and Reno escorted Mrs. Bell back to her quarters. He followed her into her house uninvited but stayed only a couple of minutes. Reno said, "good evening," went out and closed the door behind him. Mrs. Bell then decided to go next door to the Van Hornes and opened the door while Reno was still in the "storm screen" room that connected the two houses. Mrs. Bell said:

> I pulled my skirt away from being caught in the door. As I was pulling the door to, I felt Colonel Reno's arms about my waist. I twisted myself out of his embrace and got in front of Mrs. Van Horne's door — the storm house enclosed both doors; I turned to him and said, "Colonel Reno, don't you do that again." He laughed and said, "That is not any harm." I said, "Don't you do that again!"[22]

She later told Mrs. Van Horne about the incident and told her she was angry with Reno. Mrs. Bell did not demand an apology from Reno for either incident — apparently she would wait for her husband to return. She later said, "I don't think I ever exchanged a half dozen words with Colonel Reno ever since that Thursday evening."[23] Reno did not think the incident at Mrs. Bell's house Thursday evening was significant and on Friday asked Mrs. Bell if he might be her escort to the enlisted men's Christmas party that evening. Her response was, "Colonel, I can't promise." Not receiving a negative reply, Reno assumed she would accompany him to the party. When he went to her quarters in the evening, he knocked but received no reply. After he left, Slocum entered the storm house and knocked but he also received no reply. Later at the party an verbal exchange took place between Reno and Slocum, the latter thinking Mrs. Bell had been insulted in some way.

Reno finally decided the situation was getting out of control and that he would keep the relationship between Mrs. Bell and himself on a strictly formal basis. He sent her a note asking for the return of the photograph that she had taken from his quarters at Fort Lincoln — it was, he wrote, "the only copy he had, and he wished to retain it." She admitted later that the note was in "very gentlemanly terms," but she was not pleased with the request and told her friends, "You see here again what that man has done."[24]

On Christmas day, Mrs. Bell extended verbal invitations to the post officers and their wives, the post doctor and trader for a Christmas party at her home — she deliberately excluded Reno. She stated later that "I did not intend to invite Colonel Reno," and her friends told her that she should not "after what he had done to you." Reno went to the Officers' Club Room to have a few drinks. He sent a note to the post trader, John Hazelhurst, who came to the club room about midnight. Reno was obviously angry at being excluded from the party — the post commander, according to protocol, was invited to every social function at his post. Reno told the trader, "This certainly meant war.... I'll make it hot for her since she has thrown down the gauntlet."[25]

Peace was maintained on the post for the next three days until the arrival of the Rev. Richard Wainwright from Fargo. He was 46, married, with three daughters, and was the minister of the Episcopal Church in Fargo. Wainwright had been invited by former post commander Van Horne to perform services at Fort Abercrombie, and had a standing invitation to stay with the Bells while he was at the post. When Reno was enroute to Abercrombie Dec. 16, he had met Wainwright in Fargo and also suggested he come down to the post during the holidays. In a letter to the Bells, Wainwright indicated he would be at the post on the 29th. With Captain Bell on leave, the letter was referred to Reno who met Wainwright and escorted him to the commanding officer's quarters. Reno informed him that Captain Bell was away and invited him to stay at his house to which Wainwright replied, "That did not make much difference, I will go and see if Mrs. Bell is not expecting to entertain me, I shall be very glad to accept your invitation." Wainwright then went over to the Bell residence and she indicated she would be pleased to act as his host and he could stay there.[26] When informed by Wainwright that he would be staying at Mrs. Bell's house, Reno did not like the arrangement — even though Wainwright was a preacher, he was a married man staying in the home of a married women whose husband was absent. Reno apparently said nothing to either Wainwright or Mrs. Bell at the time.

Later in the day, in a discussion with Hazelhurst at the post club room, Reno thought the post trader was opposed to Wainwright holding services at the post. The following morning, Dec. 30, Reno met with Wainwright to discuss the services and tentatively agreed to the arrangements. That afternoon, in a discussion with Robinson, the post adjutant, Reno remarked, "I do not see why Mrs. Bell would make this fight with me, her character was too vulnerable." Robinson let the remark pass without comment.[27] Reno obviously continued to think about the situation and came to a decision — he sent a note to Wainwright:

> My attention having been again called to the subject of your holding service, I am convinced that it is in the interests of peace and harmony in the garrison that you should not do so. I need scarcely assure you of the deep regret with which I make you acquainted with this decision.[28]

When confronted by Wainwright, Reno told him, "In the club room the other day…there were several lewd and licentious or obscene remarks about you, [and] I said, 'indeed sir? to what effect?' 'to what purpose?' said he, 'oh, general[ly]; amongst others there is this expression: The minister, Mr. Wainwright, will have his goose as well as another man, and he can have it with Mrs. Bell.' "[29] At a meeting among Hazelhurst, Wainwright and Reno later in the day, Hazelhurst said he "had no objection to him [Wainwright] preaching there." Reno then reinstated the services to be performed by Wainwright and he announced his decision to the garrison later that evening at retreat.[30]

Reno was still concerned about the appearance of Wainwright staying overnight in Mrs. Bell's house while the captain was away. He requested an audience with Wainwright and told him, "I hear you have made up your mind to remain with Mrs. Bell."

Wainwright replied, "I have, sir."

Reno said, "It has caused very many unpleasant remarks in the garrison."

Wainwright responded, "I don't see why it should, it is an event which occurs very frequently. It is no unusual thing for me to stay at the house of a friend, when the husband was away.... [I]f my remaining with Mrs. Bell while here, will cast any imputation I will be advised upon the matter."

Wainwright later said Reno replied that it was not Mrs. Bell's reputation he was concerned about because "that is like a spoiled egg, you cannot hurt that; your own good name, the welfare of the church, and the good of the service, all demand that you should leave Mrs. Bell's.... [L]et me advise you to leave Mrs. Bell's for she is a notorious character in the regiment, and several officers of the garrison have repeatedly asked me to...have her expelled [from] the regiment." Then Reno supposedly gave Wainwright the names of Benteen, Wallace and Hodgson as those officers who had asked him to expel Mrs. Bell from the regiment.[31]

When asked again if he would leave Mrs. Bell's residence, Wainwright said he would think the matter over and let Reno know later that day.[32] Reno recalled the conversation differently:

> I felt it my duty to tell him that he should leave Mrs. Bell's & I remember distinctly telling him on Bell's account as well as other reasons & repeated to him what is common talk in the Regiment regarding the reputation of Mrs. Bell. I never said, "I had been requested to put her out of the Regiment," an expression prima facie absurd. I thought this a confidential conversation though I did not say so.[33]

Wainwright met at the club room with some of the officers, including Van Horne, Troxel and Hatch, to discuss the situation. They thought Captain Bell should be informed. Wainwright then penned a note to Reno:

> Having just been to your quarters and found you were not there, I (in accordance with my promise) communicate my decision on the subject of staying at Captain Bell's quarters whilst I am [here at] Abercrombie. After advising, I have decided not to change, as I find I cannot remove without offering a slight to Captain Bell in the person of his wife.[34]

New Year's Eve would create another problem for Reno. Not pleased with Wainwright's decision, Reno told his adjutant, Lieutenant Robinson, to inform Mrs. Bell she would not be allowed to play the organ at the services that evening. He threatened to stop the services if she attempted to play but she was still anxious to perform until Robinson spoke to her: "You must not play the organ; Col. Reno has said that the services would be stopped if you attempted to play."[35] The services were held without music and Reno did not attend.

After the services, several officers and their wives met with Mrs. Bell and advised her to send for the captain. Mrs. Van Horne also thought it advisable for Wainwright to move into their quarters for the remainder of his stay, which he did on the morning of Jan. 2. When he informed Reno of the move, the major indicated he could stay as long as he pleased provided it was not with Mrs. Bell. Reno also told Wainwright that if he had not moved, he would have had him removed from the post.[36]

On Jan. 5, Captain Bell returned to the post and met with Van Horne and Wainwright. A meeting of the three men with Reno later that morning resulted in a heated exchange with Reno stating to Bell, "I deny everything that this holy, Christian man, this meddler, has said, and I have never said anything derogatory to (sic) Mrs. Bell to anybody."[37] After this meeting Bell had Troxel prepare a set of charges and specifications against Reno and left the post Jan. 6 for department headquarters in St. Paul to ask Terry, the department commander, to convene a court-martial. Terry requested a meeting with Bell, Reno and Wainwright at his office to attempt some kind of reconciliation. Bell remained in St. Paul until Reno arrived there Jan. 9. At the meeting the next day with Terry, Reno again denied the allegations that he had been asked to expel Mrs. Bell out of the regiment. The meeting failed to resolve the conflict and Bell requested permission to go to Fort Lincoln to talk to Benteen and Wallace.

On Jan. 14, Reno went to Fort Lincoln and the next day wrote a letter to Bell again denying he had said that several 7th Cavalry officers had asked him to expel Mrs. Bell from the regiment. Bell talked to Benteen and Wallace and decided to continue his effort to press charges against Reno. Returning to Fort Abercrombie, Bell sent his request, with the charges and specifications to Terry, formally requesting a court-martial. On Feb. 20, the headquarters of the Department of Dakota issued Special Order No. 20, convening a general court-martial at St. Paul on March 8, 1877, to try Reno on two charges of "Conduct unbecoming an officer and a gentleman." Reno was relieved of his command at Fort Abercrombie Feb. 28 and placed under house arrest.

The trial began as scheduled March 8 with Colonel William B. Hazen, 6th Infantry, appointed president. Officers detailed to the court were Colonel George Sykes, 20th Infantry; Lieutenant Colonel George P. Buell, 11th Infantry; Lieutenant Colonel Pinkney Lugenbeel, 1st Infantry; Lieutenant Colonel Lewis C. Hunt, 20th Infantry; Lieutenant Colonel Daniel Huston, 6th Infantry; Lieutenant Colonel William P. Carlin, 17th Infantry; Major Robert E. A. Crofton, 17th Infantry; and Major Charles G. Bartlett, 11th Infantry.

Six of the nine officers were West Point graduates and all had served in the Civil War.

For the Army, Major Thomas F. Barr, judge advocate of the Department of Dakota, conducted the prosecution while Reno hired two capable attorneys to defend him, Cushman K. Davis and Stanford Newell. The summarized specifications on the first charge were:

> 1st. Major Reno…did, during the temporary absence from the post of the said Captain Bell, in disregard of his honor and duty as commanding officer, visit the quarters of the said Captain Bell, and then and there take improper and insulting liberties with the wife of the said Captain Bell, by taking both her hands in his own, and attempting to draw her person close up to his own….
>
> 2nd. Major Reno…did visit the quarters of the said Captain Bell and while the wife of said Captain Bell was passing through the storm screen connecting said quarters with adjoining set of quarters, take improper and insulting liberties with her, by placing his arm around her waist….
>
> 3rd. Major Reno…alone, of all the officers of the garrison, failed to receive an invitation to a social gathering held by invitation of the wife of Captain James M. Bell…did say to Mr. John Hazelhurst,…"This means war! Mrs. Bell has thrown down the gauntlet, and I will take it up,"…and did further say: "I will make it hot for her (meaning Mrs. Bell); I will drive her out of the regiment,"…thereby dishonorably and maliciously threatening to use his power as commanding officer…to revenge himself upon the said Mrs. Bell for her failure to invite him to the social gathering as aforesaid.
>
> 4th. Major Reno…did write…and sign and send to the Rev. R. Wainwright…a communication [canceling the services]…and did…say to him…that his action in declining to permit religious service was taken because a member of the garrison (meaning the post trader, Mr. John Hazelhurst) had objected to Mr. Wainwright's preaching…and that the names of Mr. Wainwright and Mrs. Bell had been mentioned by an officer of the garrison in the clubroom at Fort Arbercrombie, in the presence of several other officers, connected together in an obscene and licentious expression, to wit: "That Mr. Wainwright would have his goose as well as another man, and he could have it with Mrs. Bell," which statements of reasons were willfully and maliciously false,

and given for the dishonorable purpose of injuring the good name and repute of the said Mrs. Bell....

5th. Major Reno...did, in an interview with the Rev. R. Wainwright, urge him to leave the quarters of Captain Bell when he was a guest, and did say to the said Wainwright, "Mrs. Bell's reputation is like a spoiled egg — you can't hurt it. She is notorious in the regiment as a loose character," and did further say that Captain Benteen and Lieutenant Wallace...had repeatedly asked him to expel her from the regime; which last statement was maliciously false, no such request ever having been by them; and all of which statements were made for the dishonorable purpose of injuring the good name and repute of the said Mrs. Bell....

6th. Major Reno...did state to Lieutenant W. W. Robinson, "Mrs. Bell ought to know better than to make a fight with me; her character is too vulnerable,"...meaning thereby to express an intention to assail the reputation of the wife of Captain Bell, and to assert that her character was bad....

7th. Major Reno...did, dishonorably, willfully, and maliciously attempt and endeavor to annoy and humiliate the wife of Captain James M. Bell...[in] that Mrs. Bell would not be permitted to play the organ at the services....

Each specification was followed by "This to the scandal and disgrace of the military service, at Fort Abercrombie, Dak., on or about the [date of incident]."

A second charge of "Conduct unbecoming an officer and a gentleman" was also added with a specification indicating Reno had attempted to bribe a colored servant, Eliza Galloway, into providing false testimony favorable to his case. This supposedly occurred Feb. 15 at Abercrombie.

Reno pleaded not guilty to all charges and specifications. The trial's first day was spent reading the charges and specifications and Reno then requested an adjournment. The following day, March 9, Mrs. Bell was the first witness to appear and she recounted her story of the two incidents with Reno at her house and his preventing her from playing the organ at the religious services. Wainwright was the next witness and was pounded hard by Reno's lawyers as to why he didn't move from Mrs. Bell's residence when requested to do so by Major Reno — would it not have better protected Wainwright and Mrs. Bell from any scandal arising from the arrangement? To which Wainwright responded, "There was no protection needed."[38]

Wainwright completed his testimony the next day and was followed by John Hazelhurst taking the stand. Hazelhurst testified about the "making it hot" statement by Reno and his withdrawal of the objection to Wainwright's preaching at the holiday services. On the fourth day of trial Robinson related the story of how Reno prevented Mrs. Bell from playing the organ on New Year's Eve. Cross examination by Reno's lawyers focused on the "goose" remark as to whom and where it was said. The next two witnesses for the prosecution were Wallace and Benteen, who both denied ever asking Reno to have Mrs. Bell expelled from the regiment. Final witnesses for the prosecution were Slocum, who was questioned only about the "goose" remark; Van Horne, who offered only vague testimony; and Troxel, who, during cross-examination, was questioned about his role in the preparation of the charges for Bell. The prosecution rested its case and the court adjourned for the day.

When court opened March 14, Wainwright again found himself in the witness chair and was examined by the defense concerning Reno's denial that he had ever told Wainwright about requests to have Mrs. Bell expelled from the regiment. Benteen was the next witness and after stating Reno's character was "first rate," testified that he had discussed Mrs. Bell's character with Reno and that her reputation was indeed bad.[39] The following day Wallace confirmed that Reno's character "has been very good" and provided additional testimony about Mrs. Bell's character. The final witness for the day was Captain Bell, who was questioned about the Jan. 15 letter to him from Reno which again denied the "expelling" requests — the letter was not accepted in evidence.

Friday, March 16, produced testimony from only one witness — Major Lewis Merrill. He testified about Mrs. Bell's reputation and indicated her character had received "rather unfavorable criticism."[40] When court reconvened Monday, Reno's attorney Davis read two statements for the defense — the first a seven-page narrative by Reno and the second a complicated legal brief. Concerning the first incident with Mrs. Bell, Reno's statement indicated he had never attempted to draw her toward him and had only taken her hand gently while they were seated and had then said good night. In the second incident, he said that when she stepped through the door, he extended his hand and she apparently missed the step and was thrown into his arms.[41] Davis stated that since Mrs. Bell had not asked for an apology for the two alleged liberties against her, it appeared that she condoned Reno's actions. He also pointed out that she purposely did not invite him to her Christmas party, which was attended by all the other officers and their wives, thus embarrassing the post commander and starting a social vendetta against Reno. He said Reno had the right to maintain good order in the garrison, and while he may have shown bad taste and poor judgment, his actions were justified in the line of duty. At the conclusion of Davis' brief, Barr requested a recess until the next day to prepare his response.

Barr took most of the morning of March 20 to review the evidence presented to the court. He defended Mrs. Bell's honor and her "exposed" position at the post while her husband was on leave. Barr concluded with a rhetorical question: "If she was a person void of character, a person whose reputation could not be further injured, what was he, the post commander, doing at her quarters so constantly."[42] At noon, the court was cleared and closed so the members of the court could review the evidence presented and render a decision.

The court found Reno guilty on the first charge of "conduct unbecoming an officer and gentleman," and all specifications (with minor exceptions) except the 6th (Emily's reputation). On the second charge and specification of bribing the colored servant, Reno was found not guilty. The sentence was mandatory under the 61st Article of War: "And the Court does therefore sentence him, Major Marcus A. Reno, Seventh Regiment of Cavalry, 'To be dismissed the service'."[43]

The decision reached by the court would not be announced until the reviewing authority had completed and approved the findings — the accused would not be notified until the review was complete and the process usually took a number of weeks. A sentence of dismissal had to be approved by the president. Terry had to first review and approve or disapprove the proceedings, findings and sentence and, if he approved, then the record was forwarded to the War Department. Finding no irregularities, Terry sent the records, without comment, to the War Department on March 26, 1877.

The case findings were reviewed April 4 by the judge advocate general, Brigadier General William McK. Dunn. His critique of the findings produced a lengthy list of comments and recommendations, the last being potentially damaging to Reno's case:

> His [Reno's] course I cannot thus but regard as having been highly discreditable to himself, and as having most seriously compromised the respectability and honor of the military service. In the recent similar, but much less grave, case of Lieutenant O'Connor, the sentence of dismissal was approved without hesitation by the President; and in the present instance I can have no alternative but to recommend the same action.[44]

On April 11, the case was referred to the General of the Army Sherman, who wrote a short review and, although he included a note of recognition for Reno, "who has borne the reputation of a brave officer," confirmed the sentence. Sherman's position was stated in his final comment: "Personally the blow is a terrible one, but the President of the United States should demand and Enforce against the 'Commanding officers of Posts,' the highest morality and purest Honor."[45] The final step of the process was a decision by Rutherford B. Hayes, who had been elected president in November 1876 and inaugurated March 5, 1877. Hayes had been a volunteer officer during the Civil War and understood the trials and tribulations of an army officer. When the record reached his office, he endorsed it on May 1:

> The foregoing proceedings, findings and sentence are approved. The sentence is commuted to suspension from rank and pay for two years from May 1st, 1877.[46]

The case was then returned to the George W. McCrary, secretary of war, who added his comments May 8:

> The proceedings of this case, having been forwarded under the One Hundred and Sixth Article of War, to the Secretary of War, have been most carefully considered, and have been submitted to the President, who approves the proceedings, findings, and sentence but is pleased to mitigate the latter.... Major Reno's conduct towards the wife of an absent officer, and in using the whole force of his power as commanding officer of the post to gratify his resentment against her was despicable and cannot be too strongly condemned; but after long deliberation upon all the circumstances of the case, as shown in the record of the trial, it is thought that his offenses, grave as they are, do not warrant the sentence of dismissal, and all its consequences, upon one who for twenty years borne the reputation of a brave and honorable officer, and had maintained that reputation upon the battlefields of the Rebellion and in combats with Indians.
>
> The President has therefore modified the sentence, and it is hoped that Major Reno will appreciate the clemency thus shown him, as well as the very reprehensible character of the acts of which he was found guilty.[47]

Reno knew that conviction on the charge of "conduct unbecoming an officer and gentleman" would mean an end to his army career. The announcement of the court-martial verdict May 8, 1877, was received by Reno with mixed emotion — grateful for President Hayes' commutation of the dismissal verdict, but now facing a two-year suspension from rank and pay. Still considered an army officer, he would be forced to serve the suspension within the Department of Dakota boundaries unless permission was granted for him to leave the limits of the department. On May 28, while still in St. Paul, Reno requested this authorization:

> Sir: I have the honor to request authority to leave the limits of this Dep't. during the time of my suspension from rank & also the limits of the United States. A reply to this would reach me at the post office in Harrisburg, Penna.[48]

Reno had already received permission to take a 30-day leave of absence and decided not to wait in St. Paul for a response to his request. He left St. Paul May 30 for Harrisburg but first stopped in Pittsburgh to see his now teenage son. It was the first opportunity he had to visit with Ross whom he had not seen since October 1875. Ross was living in Pittsburgh with Mary Hannah's younger sister and brother-in-law, Bertie E. and J. Wilson Orth, who were paying for his education, clothing and boarding. Income from his mother's estate was being sent to his guardian, John Bigler, who in turn provided the funds to the Orths.[49]

Reno arrived in Pittsburgh June 1 but would spend only a few days visiting with his son. The relationship between Reno and the Orths had been strained since his failure to come to Harrisburg immediately following Mary Hannah's funeral in July 1874. Also contributing to the strained relationship was Reno's appointment of John Bigler as Robert's guardian instead of the Orths. Reno left Pittsburgh about June 6, arrived in Harrisburg the same day, and obtained lodging at the Lochiel Hotel. He received a reply from General Terry, dated June 9, concerning his May 28 request:

> Sir: You are respectfully informed that your request of the 28th ultimo, for authority to leave the limits of the Department of Dakota and of the United States during the period of your suspension from rank, has been submitted to the General of the Army and the Secretary of War, who approve of your being absent from your post during your suspension but do not approve your request for permission to go abroad.[50]

On June 6, Sherman, in his endorsement of the request, commented about Reno's petition to leave the limits of the United States: "I cannot approve of his being abroad — that would seem to alleviate the punishment, if not to strip it of all effect."[51] Reno would remain at the Lochiel Hotel for most of the next two years awaiting the completion of his suspension. Funds from Mary

Hannah's estate would provide him a comfortable stay at one of the best hotels in the Pennsylvania capital.

The receipt of the news that Reno's dismissal from the service had been modified to a suspension of rank and pay for two years was greeted by Captain Bell and Lieutenants Robinson and Slocum with less than great enthusiasm. Their attempt to have Reno cashiered from the army had not been successful but they were not willing to give up. Bell wanted Reno out of the regiment and sent a request to the Adjutant General, May 22, that either Reno "be transferred to another regiment, or else he, Captain Bell, may be transferred." Included in this request was a request by "certain officers of the regiment expressing the desire for the retention of Captain Bell in preference to Major Reno." The request was forwarded by Terry to the Adjutant General Aug. 17, but no action was taken.[52]

Captain Bell and Company F were transferred from Fort Abercrombie to Fort Lincoln in early April 1877, for the assembly of the entire regiment for a summer campaign against hostile Indians. Taking to the field in mid-May, the regiment moved up the Yellowstone Valley and went into camp May 28 a few miles from Cedar Creek. It was here that a new set of charges and specifications were drawn up by Lieutenant Robinson against Reno, almost all dating back to the 7th Cavalry's arrive at Fort Lincoln in September of the previous year.

The first charge was "Drunkeness on duty, in violation of the 38th Article of War," and included two specifications:

> 1st. Major Marcus A. Reno...being in command of the military post of Fort Abraham Lincoln...at a time when said post was exposed and liable to attacks from hostile Sioux Indians, did become drunk...on or about the 26th day of September 1876.
> 2nd. Major Marcus A. Reno...did become drunk. This at Fort Abercrombie...on or about the 31st day of December 1876.

The second charge was "Conduct unbecoming an officer and a gentleman," and included only one specification:

> 1st. Major Marcus A. Reno did by his malicious and insulting remarks to a brother officer, provoke a personal encounter...and engage in a fisticuff and rough-and-tumble fight with...1st Lieut. John A. Manly...this to the disgrace of the military service in presence of civilians and junior officers...on or about the 26th day of September 1876.

The third charge was "Conduct prejudicial to good order and military discipline," and included two specifications:

> 1st. Major Marcus A. Reno...did...provoke a personal encounter with 1st. Lieut. John A. Manly...and...[in] an ungentlemanly and unofficer like manner attempted to expell the said Manley from the Officers' Club Room.... [He] did further provoke a personal encounter with 1st Lieut. Charles A. Varnum...inferring that he would challenge the said Varnum to fight a duel...on or about the 26th day of September 1876.
> 2nd. Major Marcus A. Reno...did allow pistols to be sent-for for the purpose of engaging in such duel with the said Varnum...on or about the 26th day of September 1876.[53]

The petition included as witnesses every officer and civilian who was present at the Fort Lincoln Officers' Club Room the night of Sept. 26. Lieutenant Slocum and Dr. George W. Hatch were the only two witnesses to the 2nd specification of the first charge. Also included was an endorsement by a number of the 7th Cavalry officers:

> We the undersigned officers of the 7th U. S. Cavalry, earnestly desire in justice towards our regiment and the military Service of the United States, that Major M. A. Reno, 7th Cavalry, be brought to trial on the foregoing charges and specifications.

Officers signing the endorsement included Captains Bell, McDougall and Moylan; 1st Lieutenants Robinson, DeRudio, and Edwin P. Eckerson; 2nd Lieutenants Herbert J. Slocum, E. B. Fuller, J. C. Gresham, Lloyd S. McCormick and A. Russell; and Dr. John W. Williams.[54] Bell, Robinson and Slocum were obviously able to talk some of the other officers into signing the petition, some of whom had only joined the 7th Cavalry after its return to Fort Lincoln in September, and therefore would have had little contact with Reno. On May 28, 1877, Robinson submitted the charges and specifications to Sturgis for his endorsement. Sturgis was not willing to agree to the charade, and on June 1 forwarded his comments to General Terry:

> These charges and specifications are respectfully forwarded, disapproved. If Major Reno was guilty of the conduct herein alleged, charges should have been preferred against him at the time — they appear now with a bad grace, and do not carry with them the idea that they proceed from conscientious motives. I was not

at Ft. Lincoln at the time of the alleged occurrences; but am credibly informed that the occasion was the return of the Regt. from the field and the "opening" of the Club room at Lincoln — and that the debauchery was pretty general — and in my opinion it would be difficult to get at the real state of the facts, notwithstanding the large array of witnesses.[55]

When Terry received the charges and Stugis' recommendation, he forwarded the charges July 5 to Lieutenant General R. C. Drum with his comments:

> As Major Reno is not now in this Department, these charges are respectfully forwarded to Headquarters Military Division of the Missouri. In forwarding them, however, I desire to say that I concur in the opinion of Colonel Sturgis and recommend that they be not tried.[56]

When the petition finally reached the Adjutant General's Office, Assistant Adjutant General Thomas M. Vincent, noted on July 16, 1877: "Views of the C.O. 7th Cavalry and the Comd'g. Gen'l., Department of Dakota concurred in by the Secretary of War."[57] Reno's adversaries had once again failed to have him dismissed from the service.

Endnotes

[1] *Army and Navy Journal*, Nov. 7, 1885. They remained black until October 1885 when they were repainted.

[2] The details of this evening of debauchery are covered in the Charges and Specifications preferred against Major Marcus A. Reno, by a group of officers in 1877 following the commuting of the court-martial sentence by President Hayes from dismissal from the service to two years suspension from rank and pay for two years. The charges and specification are discussed later in this chapter and can be found in detail in the Reno file R314 CB 1865, ACP 1877, Record Group 94, NARA.

[3] The *Chicago Times*, as quoted in *The Fargo Forum*, Dec. 23, 1956.

[4] Court-martial of Marcus A. Reno, 1877, QQ87, Records of the Judge Advocate General, Record Group 153, NARA, pp. 269, 271-278, 287.

[5] Court-martial, 1877, Exhibit "F," p. 1.

[6] Frederick F. Van de Water, *Glory Hunter* (Bobbs-Merrill Co., Indianapolis, Ind., 1934), p. 236.

[7] William A. Graham, *The Custer Myth* (The Stackpole Company, Harrisburg, Penna., 1953), p. 323.

[8] Melbourne C. Chandler, *Of Garryowen in Glory: The History of the 7th U.S. Cavalry* (The Turnpike Press, Annadale, Va, 1960), p. 73.

[9] Post Returns from Fort Abraham Lincoln, November, 1876.

[10] Special Order No. 142, Headquarters, Department of Dakota, 1876.

[11] Post Returns from Fort Abraham Lincoln, December, 1876.

[12] P. H. Sheridan, *Outline Descriptions of the Posts in the Military Division of the Missouri* (Old Army Press, Fort Collins, Colo., 1972), pp. 13-16.

[13] Frederick Whittaker, *A Popular Life of Gen'l. Geo. A. Custer* (Sheldon & Co., New York, 1876), pp. 1-2.

[14] Whittaker, p. 591.

[15] Whittaker, pp. 606-607.

[16] Review of Whittaker's Book, *Army and Navy Journal*, Dec. 23, 1876.

[17] *Army and Navy Journal*, Jan. 6, 1877.

[18] *Army and Navy Journal*, Jan. 20, 1877.

[19] Court-martial, 1877, pp. 28-29.

[20] Court-martial, 1877, p. 15.

[21] Court-martial, 1877, p. 52.

[22] Court-martial, 1877, p. 17.

[23] Court-martial, 1877, p. 74.

[24] Court-martial, 1877, p. 60, 69-70.

[25] Court-martial, 1877, pp. 66-72; Exhibit "F," p. 4.

[26] Court-martial, 1877, pp. 87-106.

[27] Court-martial, 1877, pp. 185-86, 201-02, Exhibit "F," p. 4-5.

[28] Court-martial, 1877, p. 108 and Exhibit "A."

[29] Court-martial, 1877, pp. 84-85.

[30] Court-martial, 1877, pp. 85-86, 124-30, 165-69.

[31] Benteen was stationed at Fort Rice and Wallace at Fort Lincoln. Lieutenant Hodgson had been killed at the Little Big Horn June 25, 1876.

[32] Court-martial, 1877, pp. 88-90.

[33] Court-martial, 1877, Exhibit "F," pp. 5-6.

[34] Court-martial, 1877, pp. 116-32.

[35] Court-martial, 1877, pp. 193-94.

[36] Court-martial, 1877, pp. 134-36.

[37] This conversation was reported by Wainwright at the court-martial, pp. 135-36, 241-48.

[38] Court-martial, 1877, pp. 115-16.

[39] Court-martial, 1877, pp. 250-69.

[40] Court-martial, 1877, pp. 286-88.

[41] Court-martial, 1877, Exhibit "F."

[42] Court-martial, 1877, Exhibit "G."

[43] Court-martial, 1877, pp. 191-94.

[44] Report of the Judge Advocate General in the case of M. A. Reno, QQ87, Record Group 153, NARA.

[45] Sherman's Endorsement, April 11, 1877, attached to the Report of the Judge Advocate General.

46 Court-martial, 1877, p. 296.

47 Adjutant General's Office, Washington, D.C, May 8, 1877, General Court-Martial Orders, No. 41, signed by George W. McCrary, Secretary of War, and by the command of General Sherman, E. D. Townsend, Adjutant General.

48 Letter dated May 28, 1877, Reno's Military File, R314 CB 1865, File 2505 ACP 1877, NARA, Record Group 94.

49 Dauphin County, Penna., Orphans Court, Accounts Drawer #53, filed December 30, 1878.

50 June 9, 1877, letter from Terry to Reno, File 2505 ACP 1877.

51 June 6, 1877, Sherman's Endorsement, File 2224 ACP 1877.

52 May 22, 1877, File 3581 ACP 1877 — this does not include the names of the "certain officers."

53 File 3151 ACP 1877.

54 File 3151 ACP 1877.

55 File 3151 ACP 1877.

56 File 3151 ACP 1877.

57 File 3151 ACP 1877.

• 14 •

Accusations & the Court of Inquiry

In July 1876, the nation had been shocked when it learned of the June 25, 1876, defeat of Lieutenant Colonel George A. Custer's 7th U.S. Cavalry at the Little Big Horn River. The spring campaign to return the Indians to their reservations had proved a disaster. The defeat of General George Crook's forces on Rosebud Creek June 17 and the loss of five entire companies of the 7th Cavalry June 25 amounted to a tragedy that would not soon be forgotten.

Before the 7th Cavalry returned to Fort Lincoln Sept. 26, the task of establishing blame for the disaster first fell on Brigadier General Alfred H. Terry, commander of the Dakota column. Prior to Custer's march up the Rosebud in pursuit of the Indians, Terry had prepared a set of detailed written orders for Custer's conduct on the march. These orders, dated June 22, 1876, appeared to give Custer a free hand; "[Y]ou [Custer] should conform to them unless you shall see sufficient reason for departing from them."[1] This had the appearance of allowing Custer to do as he decided was necessary and consequently got Terry off the hook.

Attention next focused on Reno and Benteen and both men were accused of failure to assist Custer at the Little Big Horn, even though both were engaged in a desperate struggle just three and one-half miles to the south of Custer's position. They remained in their defensive positions until relieved the morning of June 27 by the arrival of Terry's command.

In December 1876, Frederick Whittaker published *The Complete Life of Major General George Armstrong Custer.*[2] The book charged both Reno and Benteen of cowardly conduct which, according to Whittaker's interpretation, resulted directly in Custer's death. Well-known historian William A. Graham noted about Whittaker's book: "After a careful study, only one conclusion can be arrived at; namely, that so far as relates to the last battle it is a tissue of violently prejudiced misstatements."[3]

The Custer battle controversy appeared to be subsiding and the next year proved to be quiet, if lonely, for Reno. On May 15, 1878, while he was in Washington, D.C., Reno wrote to the president requesting forgiveness of the remainder of his court-martial sentence:

To His Excellency, The President

I have the honor to apply for the remission of the unexecuted portion of the sentence imposed upon me by General Court Martial order No. 41 sines of 1877.

In justice to myself, I desire to say, I have never sought to injure the character of the woman concerned in any improper way, and have never talked <u>publicly</u> in regard to her, — what it is charged I said, was said to <u>one</u> person, and which the seal of confidence was not put upon this conversation, it was intended as confidential, and its betrayal was something I never could have anticipated, as I repeated what had been told me as Commanding Officer, and to the person who betrayed it, solely for his benefit, and the good of the service, and not to injure the woman.

I claim that my punishment has been, <u>even now</u>, incommensurate with the offense as charged as there was nothing criminal in it; the anguish and humiliation which I underwent at the promulgation of the sentence, and the publication in the newspapers spreading it over this country was, to me, an extreme punishment, although its poignancy has been much blunted by the sympathy of true and warm hearted friends who have known me as main Army for a quarter of a century.

So far then as my punishment goes, I have undergone all that I can but the stoppage of pay, a matter of no amount to the Government, works seriously against the interests of my boy to whom I am bound to give a support and education and to do which, I depended upon the money I received for my professional services. I feel myself competent in business but the remaining time is too short to make it possible for me to enter any pursuit, while long enough to bring upon me pressing necessities, it is besides too late for me to abandon a career in which the best part of my life has been spent, and, as I believe testimonials in the War office will show, not unprofitably to the Government.

It seems now that by going on duty with the Regiment, an opportunity may offer active service and to participate in which would be my greatest desire.

Trusting that my application may receive the favorable consideration of your Excellency.[4]

The response to Reno's request for remission of his sentence was acted upon quickly by the Secretary of War George McCrary. In a letter, dated May 18, 1878, McCrary wrote to Reno:

Major Marcus Reno
(U.S. Military Academy - West Point)

> Sir: I am directed by the President to inform you that the question of a further modification of your sentence has been considered by him and he feels constrained to decline to reopen the case, or change his order therein. I am obliged to inform you that the President's decision in this matter is final.[5]

With this final admonishment about his court-martial sentence, Reno was now faced with the fact it would be another year before he could put on his uniform and return to his regiment — or so he thought. Sales of Whittaker's book had apparently slowed considerably and Whittaker was upset that nothing was being done about the two men whom he thought were the direct cause of Custer's death. On May 18, 1878, he wrote to W. W. Corlett, the delegate to Congress from Wyoming Territory, reiterating his charges against the two senior 7th Cavalry officers:

> Having been called upon to prepare the biography of the late Brevet Major General George A. Custer, U.S.A., a great amount of evidence, oral and written, came into my hands tending to prove that the sacrifice of his life and the lives of his immediate command at the battle of the Little Big Horn was useless, and owing to the cowardice of his subordinates. I desire, therefore, to call your attention, and that of Congress, through you, to the necessity of ordering an official investigation by a committee of your honorable body into the conduct of the United States troops engaged in the battle of the Little Big Horn, fought June 25, 1876, otherwise known as the Custer Massacre, in which Lieut. Col. Custer, Seventh United States Cavalry, perished, with five companies of the Seventh Cavalry, at the hands of the Indians. The reasons on which I found my request are as follows:
> First: Information...that gross cowardice was displayed therein by Major Marcus A. Reno...second-in-command that day; and that owing to such cowardice, the orders of Lieut. Col. Custer, commanding officer, to said Reno, to execute a certain attack, were not made. That the failure of this movement, owing to his cowardice and disobedience, caused the defeat of the United States forces...and that had Custer's orders been obeyed, the troops would probably have defeated the Indians. That after Major Reno's cowardly flight, he was joined by Captain F. W. Benteen...and that he remained idle with this force while his superior officer was fighting against the whole force of the Indians, the battle

being within his knowledge, the sound of firing audible from his position, and his forces out of immediate danger from the enemy. That the consequences of this second exhibition of cowardice and incompetency was the massacre of Lieut. Col. Custer and five companies of the Seventh United States Cavalry.

Second: The proof of these facts lies in the evidence of persons in the service...and no power short of Congress can compel their attendance and protect them from annoyance and persecution if they openly testify to the cowardice exhibited on the above occasion.

Third: The only official record of the battle now extant is the report written by Major Reno...and is, in the main, false and libelous to the memory of the late Lieut. Col. Custer, in that it represents the defeat of the United States forces on that occasion as owing to the division by Custer of his forces into three detachments, to overmanning his forces, and to ignorance of the enemy's force, all serious charges against the capacity of said Custer as an officer; whereas the defeat was really owing to the cowardice and disobedience of said Reno and to the willful neglect of said Reno and Capt. Benteen to join battle with the Indians in support of their commanding officer when they might have done it, and it was their plain duty to do so.

Fourth: The welfare of the United States Army demands that in case of a massacre of a large party of troops, under circumstances covered with suspicion, it should be officially established where the blame belongs, to the end that the service may not deteriorate by the retention of cowards.

Fifth: Justice to an officer of the previously unstained record of Lieut. Col. Custer, demands that the accusation under which his memory now rests, in the only official account of the battle...now extant, should be proved or disproved.

I have thus given you, as briefly as I can, my reasons for asking this investigation, and the facts I am confident of being able to prove. My witnesses will be all the living officers of the Seventh United States Cavalry who were present at the battle of June 25, including Major Reno and Captain Benteen; myself to prove statements of an officer since deceased, made to me a few days before his death; F. T. Girard...; Dr. Porter...; Lieut. Carland..., and other whose names I can find in time for the committee's session, should the same be ordered.

Trusting, dear Sir, that this letter may result in an investigation which shall decide the whole truth about the battle of the 25 June 1876, and the purgation of the Service.[6]

Whittaker's letter to Corlett was referred to the House Committee on Military Affairs on June 12 for its consideration and action. The committee's decision was reported in the newspapers the following day:

The House Committee on Military Affairs decided today [June 12] to report favorable to the House a resolution directing an investigation into the Custer Massacre. Mr. Bragg will present a resolution for a subcommittee to sit in recess and send for persons and papers. The basis of this action is embraced in a letter addressed by Frederick Whittaker of Mount Vernon, N.Y., to Mr. Corlett, representing Wyoming Territory, and by him turned over to the Committee on Military Affairs, on whom it seems to have made a very decided impression. Whittaker's letter...[followed].[7]

Reno probably read Whittaker's accusations and the action recommended by the House Committee that same day in one of the Harrisburg newspapers. He was certainly not pleased with Whittaker's statements but did welcome the possibility of an opportunity to clear his name. Reno traveled to Washington, D.C., and on June 17 wrote to Military Committee Chairman H. B. Banning to urge him to present the resolution to the full House for an appointment of a subcommittee before going into the summer recess. Published in the June 21, 1878, issue of *Army and Navy Journal* Reno's request stated:

I beg leave to inform you that I came to Washington to express personally to your committee my earnest desire that the contemplated investigation be ordered as soon as practicable. During the last two years I have been compelled to suffer the circulation of various malignant reports concerning this affair about myself, emanating, it is presumed, from the same irresponsible source. This being the first time that the author, perhaps emboldened by my silence, has ventured to give them definite shape, I respectfully demand that I may have this opportunity to vindicate my character and record which have been thus widely assailed.[8]

In the same issue of the *Army and Navy Journal*, the editors noted: "It is to be hoped that his investigation into the battle of the Little Big Horn will be made. There has been currently altogether too much loose assertion and irresponsible camp gossip about the matter, and it is high time the facts should be known." However, Congress adjourned without taking action on the House Committee's resolution. On June 22, a disappointed Reno wrote directly to President Hayes:

> A letter addressed to Hon. W. W. Corlett, Delegate of Congress from Wyoming Territory, and by him referred to the House Committee of Military Affairs, and thus made semi-official, appeared in the press of the 13th inst. As the object of this letter was to request an investigation of my conduct at the battle of the Little Big Horn River, and was also the first time various reports and rumors had been put into definite shape, I addressed a communication to the same Committee, through its chairman, urging that the investigation be resolved upon. The Congress adjourned without taking any action, and I now respectfully appeal to the Executive for a "Court of Inquiry" to investigate the affair, that the many rumors started by camp gossip may be set at rest and the truth made fully known.
>
> The letter to Mr. Corlett which is referred to, is hereto attached.[9]

Reno's request was endorsed June 25 by General Sherman: "Respectfully referred to the Hon. Secretary of War, 'Approved' — On the application of any officer a Court of Inquiry may be ordered by his Dept. Commander and this investigation if made should be at Fort Abraham Lincoln, where the witnesses are most available." Adjutant General Townsend endorsed the request on the same day: "The Secretary of War approves Genl. Sherman's views and directs that this be referred to the Dept. Commander to order the Court of Inquiry and that Major Reno be ordered to report in person to the Dept. Commander for that purpose." The following day the Headquarters of the Army issued special orders to have Reno report to the commanding general of the Department of Dakota (Terry).[10] Terry was visiting at West Point when he received the order to convene the court of inquiry but the orders did not suggest a schedule for conducting the investigation. He wrote to Army Headquarters July 1 and received a reply dated July 30:

> [A]s soon as the season of active operations is over, when witnesses can be obtained, and the general service will not be inconvenienced, he [Sherman] will order a suitable Court of Inquiry to investigate the conduct of Major M. A. Reno, 7th Cav'y. at the

battle of the Little Big Horn River "on the application of the accused" — this course having received the approval of the Secy. of War.[11]

Reno was to have his day in court. However, even though he had received a letter from Secretary of War McCrary, telling him that the president's decision on remission of his sentence was final, he decided it was worth another attempt. He wrote to McCrary Aug. 18 from the Lochiel Hotel:

> Sir: I submit the following appeal to you and I make it unofficial, knowing that the subject matter is fully understood by you, and requires no endorsement. Under the existing order by which I am suspended, all pay is stopped from me — a sentence I believe unprecedented in the service except accompanied by imprisonment. I am now in receipt of a letter from the A.G.O. stating that at the return of my Regiment from the plains, and when witnesses can be obtained without incommoding the service, a Court of Inquiry will be ordered to investigate my conduct at the battle of Little Big Horn River and for which I asked, it is not possible however that the court will be convened at my home where I can live, but that I will be compelled to go to some strange place and be at greater expense than I can afford. I have therefore to ask that my pay, at least in part, be restored to me, besides have I not been punished far beyond my guilt, even if guilty as charged? The amount of my fine has already reached the sum of $4,600.00, more than any jury would access as damages under the same circumstances. I appeal to you as a lawyer and one acquainted with the character of the woman in the case if this statement is not true. Now does it not strike you that all that justice demands has been fully satisfied in this case? I feel assured if that is your view and is strongly presented by you to the executive that a remission of my sentence would surely follow.
>
> Thanking you for the already many kindnesses you have shown me, and for which I shall always be grateful.[12]

No record indicates Reno received a reply of his letter to McCrary. Reno wrote to the Adjutant General's office Nov. 1 requesting a copy of the petition signed by the enlisted men of the 7th Cavalry immediately following the Little Big Horn battle. He indicated it was for the court of inquiry to provide "the sentiment and feeling of the enlisted men of my command when the incident of the battle of the Little Big Horn River was fresh in their minds."[13]

Colonel Wesley Merritt
5th Cavalry
(Gilbert Family Collection)

Colonel John H. King
9th Infantry
(Gilbert Family Collection)

An extract from Special Orders No. 255 of the Adjutant General's Office, dated Nov. 25, 1878, ordered:

> By direction of the President, and on the application of Major Marcus A. Reno, 7th Cavalry, a Court of Inquiry is hereby appointed to assemble at Chicago, Illinois, on Monday the 13th day of January 1879, or as soon thereafter as practicable for the purpose of inquiring into Major Reno's conduct at the battle of the Little Big Horn River on the 25th and 26th days of June 1876.
>
> The Court will report the facts and its opinion as to whether, from all the circumstances in the case, any further proceedings are necessary.
>
> Detail for the Court:
> Colonel John H. King, 9th Infantry
> Colonel Wesley Merritt, 5th Cavalry
> Lieutenant Colonel W. B. Royall, 3rd Cavalry
> 1st Lieutenant Jesse M. Lee, Adjutant, 9th Infantry, is
>   appointed Recorder of the Court.[14]

Libbie Custer was pleased that Merritt had been selected to serve on the court as she believed his presence would assure justice would be done in her husband's memory.[15]

The *Army and Navy Journal* issue of Nov. 30, 1878, stated its opinion of the court of inquiry: "We trust that its investigations will be complete and decisive. The accusations against Major Reno are so formal and definite as to take them out of the newspaper forum, where they have long been bandied."

Reno was aware that he would have to spend considerable time in Chicago at the inquiry and the cost of staying at the Palmer House (the site of the inquiry) would be significant. He had been without military pay for one and a half years. For living expenses, he had been relying on rental income from the New Cumberland farm and the Harrisburg Front Street House as well as his inheritance from Mary Hannah's estate. Not wanting to draw too much money from his inheritance, Reno decided to borrow $800 from his son's trust fund, and on Dec. 24, 1878, pledged his life insurance policy as collateral with Lyman Gilbert, Ross' financial guardian. Repayment of the loan would be made at some future date.

The Dec. 30 issue of the *Harrisburg Daily Telegraph* published a news item under the title of "Major Reno and the Little Big Horn Battle." Apparently a telegram had been received by the *New York Herald* from Washington, D.C., allegedly from "Colonel [Thomas B.] Weir, who commanded a company under Reno," charging Reno with cowardice at the Little Big Horn battle. Reno replied to the *Herald* editors:

> Do you think it is just or fair to lend the columns of your paper to the publication of what is an evident attempt to manufacture public opinion in regard to the Little Big Horn battle in face of an official investigation, the Court for which is to soon convene? I pronounce every statement published in your issue of today as emanating from Colonel Weir to be absolutely false, and shall so prove to the Court of Inquiry.[16]

Reno left Harrisburg and arrived in Chicago Jan. 9, 1879. He had been given permission by General Terry to wear his uniform during the proceedings. The Chicago newspapers published a number of articles and editorials about the upcoming court and interviewed several Army officers:

> The officers attached to Gen. Sheridan's staff express no opinion regarding the charges of cowardice alleged against Major Reno. They believe, however, that the Court will be able to elicit a vast amount of highly interesting testimony relating to the fight in

272

which Custer and his band met with extermination. Other officers of the army, temporarily sojourning here, are more outspoken in their views of the case. Some of them do not scruple to say that the inquiry will result in tarnishing the luster of General Custer's name and renown as a warrior. They are of opinion that it will be shown that Custer, by a hot headed haste to achieve all the glory for himself, and by a virtual disobedience of orders, brought about the awful disaster which appalled the nation and the world. This, they think, will be one of the results of the inquiry; not that Custer's conduct is under investigation, but because, in showing what Reno did or did not do to avert the calamity, it will also be shown in what degree Custer was alone responsible for his own lamented fate. The testimony of Captain Bentine (sic), of the Seventh cavalry, will, it is claimed in army circles, throw much light on the subject, not only of Major Reno, but of Gen. Custer as well. It is understood that Bentine (sic) and Custer were at feud for many years, but the captain has the credit of being a fair minded, honorable gentleman, and his friends say he will not allow his prejudices to warp his duties as a witness. At least a dozen officers have been summoned to give testimony before the Court of Inquiry.[17]

The court convened Jan. 13, 1879, at the Palmer House in Chicago and King was appointed its president. H. C. Hollister was employed as court stenographer. Reno was to be represented by Lyman D. Gilbert, a graduate of Yale College in 1865, who was admitted to the Pennsylvania bar in 1868. In March 1873, Gilbert had been appointed deputy attorney general of Pennsylvania by the attorney general, S. E. Dimmick, and for a number of months after the death of Dimmick acted as attorney general. He was serving as deputy attorney general when he agreed to represent Reno in Chicago. Gilbert was unable to get to Chicago for the first day's hearing, so no witnesses were called to testify and the court made only two significant decisions: "[I]t will sit with open doors, but further decided that no record or notes of the proceedings shall be taken for publication," and "Mr. Whittaker shall be subpoenaed to appear and invited to suggest the names of witnesses in this case."[18]

A total of 23 witnesses, including all but three officers of the 7th Cavalry who had survived the battle, would be called to provide testimony. Included were: Reno; Captains Benteen, Godfrey, Mathey, McDougall and Moylan; Lieutenants DeRudio, Edgerly, Hare, Varnum and Wallace; and Acting Assistant Surgeon H.R. Porter. The three missing officers were Captain Weir, who had died in December 1876; Captain Thomas H. French, who was being court-martialled at Fort Lincoln; and 1st Lieutenant Frank M. Gibson. Enlisted men to be called to testify included Sergeants F. A. Culbertson and Edward Davern and trumpeter John Martin. Civilians who were to testify included mule packers B.F. Churchill and John Frett; interpreter Frederic F. Girard; and scout George Herendeen. Testimony would also be solicited from non-battle participants: Colonel John Gibbon, 7th Infantry; Lieutenant Colonel Michael V. Sheridan, military secretary to Lieutenant General Sheridan; Captain J. S. Payne, 5th Cavalry; and 1st Lieutenant Edward Maguire, Corps of Engineers.

An article appeared in the Jan. 14, 1879, issue of the *Chicago Times* describing the officers present in the court:

> The Court appointed by President Hayes to inquire into the behavior of Marcus A. Reno at the Battle of the Little Big Horn got into working order at the Palmer House on yesterday. The Members are officers who have seen enough service to enable them to decide whether Major Reno did his duty or was guilty of unsoldier-like conduct.... The officers composing the Board of Inquiry are all men of commanding presence. Col. King, president of the Court, has frequently served in court-martialing trials. They appeared in full military dress on yesterday. Major Reno was also rigged out in full uniform, down to the white gloves. His manner at the opening of the Court was very earnest, and it was evident that he appreciated the investigation in its fullest importance, and that it must result in either removing a great cloud from his record or stamping him as a most unworthy soldier.[19]

> Colonel King...is about five feet eight in height, his corners are well rounded off, and there is a perpetual smile on his face. His hair and whiskers, which he wears in the English fashion, are of a silvery color.... Colonel Merritt's...appearance is entirely different from that of Col. King. Although he has seen his fortieth summer, there is not the slightest tinge of gray in his hair. He wears a dark brown, coarse mustache, with a comfortable Jeff Davis beard of the same color.... Colonel Royall...is a soldier of a scholastic and philosophical type. He does not say much, but thinks a great deal. The cast of his face reminds one of the old models of Lord Bacon or Sir Walter Raleigh.[20]

When the court opened Jan. 14, Gilbert was present and was accepted as Reno's counsel.[21] He was described by the *Chicago Journal* as a "rather young

Captain Frederick W. Benteen & Lyman Gilbert
(Gilbert Family Collection)

man, with a very gentlemanly address, and dressed in very approved style. He is small, both in height and frame, and the most noticeable feature of his face is a clear eye, with a tendency to a humorous twinkle at time, and his very affable address, as well as excellent language and precision in sentence-making."[22]

Sparring between Gilbert and Lee on legal terms and the extent of the inquiry took up most of the morning. It was decided that the principal issue of the inquiry would be to determine Reno's conduct on the two days of the battle and whether his decisions contributed to Custer's defeat and the total loss of five cavalry companies.

The first official witness was 1st Lieutenant Edward Maguire, who had accompanied General Terry as engineer officer. Maguire had arrived June 27 at the battle site and had met Reno on the hilltop. Asked if Reno were cool or otherwise, he stated, "He was cool in my judgment."[23] A map, prepared by Maguire showing the topography around the battlefield, was offered in evidence to the court and provided the locations of the Indian village, Custer's march and final positions, and Reno's movements June 25. Almost without exception, throughout the inquiry, every witness indicated that the map was not accurate, and several witnesses even marked on the map to indicate changes they thought necessary.

1st Lt. George D. Wallace
Company G

Interpreter Frederic F. Girard

The next witness was 1st Lieutenant George D. Wallace, who had been assigned as the engineer officer with Custer's column and whose duty was to keep the trip's itinerary. Wallace supported Reno in his decision to leave the timber. Asked how many casualties would have occurred if the command had remained in the timber, Wallace responded: "Major Reno and every man with him would have been killed."[24] Gilbert then inquired about Reno's judgment and courage in the timber: "All that you could expect from anyone," and "I could not find any fault, I think it was good," Wallace answered.[25] Asked if he saw any indication of fear or timidity on Reno's part, Wallace answered, "None."[26]

At the start of the fourth day of testimony (Jan. 16), Gilbert made a "brief speech in which he referred to the remarkable feats of memory performed by the reporters and suggested that the interests of both sides would be subserved if the order against note-taking were rescinded." The court conferred for a few minutes and decided that the reporters could take notes of the proceedings: "Hereupon there was considerable rustling of paper, pencils were produced, memories were relieved from all distressing strain, and the scribes prepared to do their duty in their customary manner."[27]

Wallace's testimony continued. Gilbert again inquired into Reno's courage and command capability, asking the officer to "recall the events of those two days and state in what point, if any, Major Reno exhibited any lack of courage as an officer and a soldier?" Wallace replied, "None that I can recall, or can find fault with." Gilbert next asked, "Was there any point at which

Major Reno showed any want of military skill in handling his command?" "No, I do not recall any," Wallace responded.[28]

Frederic F. Girard, the civilian interpreter, followed Wallace on the stand on the afternoon of the fifth day of testimony. Girard thought that when Reno's command was in the timber, "they could have held against the whole number of Indians as long as their ammunition and provisions would have lasted.."[29] He also said he saw the Custer command on the bluffs just as he was going into the timber but didn't tell Reno.[30] Girard had been fired as an interpreter by Reno at Fort Lincoln and was later reinstated by Custer. Asked if he had "unkind feelings toward him [Reno] on that account," Girard said, "None at all, sir."[31] Girard's testimony continued until the early afternoon of the eighth day (Jan. 21).

The third witness was 1st Lieutenant Charles A. Varnum, who would testify until the afternoon of the 10th day. He had commanded a detachment of Indian scouts on June 25. When the skirmish line was being formed by Reno on the valley floor, Varnum saw the Gray Horse Company (Company E) on the bluffs across the river. He admitted that at no time while in the timber or during the general engagement had he told Reno about seeing the Gray Horse Company.[32] About Reno's conduct during the battle, he said, "Certainly there was no sign of cowardice or anything of that sort in his conduct and nothing specially the other way."[33] Asked about the command's position in the timber and whether it could have remained there, he stated, "It does not seem to me now that he had men enough to hold that entire piece of timber."[34]

Dr. H. R. Porter was the next to testify but would spend only about one full day on the witness stand. About Reno's conduct in the timber, he said, "I saw nothing in his conduct particularly heroic or particularly the reverse. I think he was some little embarrassed and flurried. The bullets were coming in pretty fast and I think he did not know whether it was best to stay there or leave. That was my impression at the time."[35]

Porter also stated that he knew when the command was going to leave the woods as he heard Reno say, "We have got to get out of here, we have got to charge them." Porter also testified that after the command had reached the bluffs, he asked Reno if the men were pretty well demoralized and Reno replied, "No, that was a charge, sir!"[36]

The commander of Company A, Captain Miles Moylan, then took the stand as a witness on the afternoon of Jan. 24. He thought the command had used "about two-thirds" of its ammunition in the valley fight. While they were in the timber, he had sent several men from the line to retrieve ammunition from saddlebags.[37] Recorder Lee asked Moylan about Reno's courage during the valley fight: "Major Reno...rode at the head of the column.... All

| 1st Lieutenant Charles A. Varnum Regimental Quartermaster | Scout George Herendeen |

his orders which I received…were given as coolly as a man under such circumstances usually can give them and I saw nothing that indicated cowardice about him."[38] Questioned about Reno's conduct in the timber, he replied: "There was a certain amount of excitement, I suppose, visible on his face, as well as that of anybody else, but any traces of cowardice I failed to discover."[39] Moylan also supported Reno's decision to leave the timber: "In my judgment the command, without assistance, would have been annihilated in the timber."[40]

Lee also asked Moylan whether he had seen any evidence of cowardice on Reno's part during that night or on the next day. Moylan responded, "No, sir, I saw no evidences of cowardice."[41] Moylan's testimony was completed on Monday, Jan. 27.

George Herendeen, the civilian scout, was the next to testify. He added little to the testimony that had not already been given by Wallace, Girard, Moylan, Varnum and Porter. Herendeen discussed the meeting with Reno in the timber about the time Bloody Knife was killed: "[T]his volley was fired [by the Indians] and this Indian [Bloody Knife] and a soldier was hit. The soldier hallooed and Major Reno gave the order to dismount, and the soldiers had just struck the ground when he gave the order to mount and then everything left the timber on a run."[42] Herendeen apparently was implying that the killing of Bloody Knife started the run from the timber and that Reno lost control of the situation at that time. But before dismissing Herendeen from

278

the witness stand, Lee did not follow up with any additional questions about Reno's conduct.

The next witness was Captain J. S. Payne, 5th Cavalry, whose basic testimony concerned the terrain surrounding the area where Custer fell. He indicated it offered little cover for a defensive stand. Gilbert asked, "What facility, if any, would a command of 200 men have for making a prolonged defense on that line? Say there were 1,500 Indians."

Payne's answer was to the point: "Well, sir, I should say their case was a hopeless one."[43]

First Lieutenant Luther R. Hare was the next witness called by the recorder. He testified for only a short time before the court recessed for the day.

Whittaker was not pleased with the exchange between Lee and Herendeen and knew, from his own previous discussions with Herendeen, that if he could question him, Herendeen's responses would be damaging to Reno. When court opened Tuesday morning, Jan. 28, Whittaker submitted a list of questions he wanted Herendeen to answer, and requested that "I should be permitted to ask questions, if necessary in my own person, of this or any other witness, subject to the discretion of the Court in the same manner as Major Reno and his counsel."[44]

Recorder Lee objected to Whittaker's request: "I feel that I am, if I may be allowed to say so, competent to go on with the matter as I have done heretofore." Gilbert also objected to allowing Whittaker the role of assistant prosecutor: "I think it is evident to the Court that the Recorder does not require it."

The court was then cleared and closed. When it was reopened, its decision was announced: "The request of Mr. Whittaker to appear before the Court as an accuser or assistant to the Recorder will not be allowed."[45]

Lee then recalled Herendeen to the stand to ask him some of the questions submitted by Whittaker. He was asked what effect the killing of Bloody Knife in the timber had on Reno: "I thought at the time it demoralized him a good deal when Bloody Knife was killed in front of him and that soldier was killed and hollered. The Indians were not over thirty feet from us when they fired."

Lee then asked: "State whether you then thought he [Reno] started under the influence of fear for his own personal safety." Herendeen responded, "I judged the firing of that volley and the killing of that man was cause of his starting."

Gilbert then had the opportunity to question Herendeen: "You formed your judgment of his [Reno's] cowardice by the volley that was fired that killed the Indian and wounded the white man before you left the timber?" to which Herendeen replied, "I am not saying that he is a coward at

1st Lieutenant Luther R. Hare
Company I

all."[46] Herendeen was then dismissed and the examination of Lieutenant Hare was resumed.

Gilbert asked Hare what would have been the effect on the column if Reno had continued to advance in the direction of the village. "I don't think he would have got a man through...[the column would not have lasted] over five minutes," Hare responded.[47]

Reno's decision to leave the timber had been supported by Wallace's and Moylan's testimony, but Gilbert wanted to continue to pursue the point, asking, "What was the opinion of the officers in regard to leaving the timber?" Hare replied, "My own private opinion, at the time, and my subsequent opinion, was that if we stayed there much longer we would be shut in so that we could not get out."[48] Hare thought Reno had the same opinion: "My impression was that Major Reno thought that we would be shut up in there and the best way to get out of there was to charge."[49]

Asked about Reno's coolness, courage and efficiency, Hare answered: "I know of but one instance of gallantry which I saw him do, and I know of no instances of cowardice at any time. When Captain Benteen's command joined on the hill, Major Reno turned around and said in a very inspiriting way to his men, 'We have assistance now, and we will go and avenge the loss of our comrades'."[50]

Gilbert solicited Hare's opinion about Reno's conduct on the hill: "[D]id you see any indications whatever of cowardice?"

"I did not," Hare replied.[51]

When the court opened Wednesday Jan. 29, the first witness called was 1st Lieutenant Charles DeRudio. He had remained in the woods when the command left and did not rejoin the regiment until early on the morning of June 27. Asked about Reno's decision to dismount and establish a skirmish line in the valley, he said, "I thought at the time he halted and said, 'good for you.' I saw that we would have been butchered if we had gone 500 yards further."[52] DeRudio testified that he saw Reno for about 10 minutes on the skirmish line in the timber and "admired his conduct."[53] In later testimony he stated that soon after going into the timber, he saw Custer, Cooke and a third man on the bluffs east of the Little Big Horn. Asked if he told Reno, DeRudio said "Not at that time."[54] He also said he saw no evidence of cowardice on Reno's part [55]

The next two witnesses were enlisted men: Sergeant Edward Davern, who had been a private and Reno's orderly in the valley and hilltop fights, and Sergeant Ferdinand A. Culbertson, who had been serving in Company A under Captain Moylan at the time of the battle. Davern told Gilbert he saw no evidence of cowardice at any time on the part of Reno.[56] Gilbert asked Culbertson the same question and drew a similar answer, "None at all."[57] Culbertson

1st Lieuteant Charles C. DeRudio
Company E

also testified about how long Reno could have held his position in the timber: "I don't think he could have held it but a very few minutes."[58]

Trumpeter John Martin, the man who carried the last message from Custer, was next up on the stand. His testimony concentrated on what he saw and heard as he rode along with Custer as his orderly trumpeter, and when and where he received the "Benteen, come on, be quick" message.

On Saturday Feb. 1, Captain Frederick W. Benteen was called as a witness. Benteen described the route he took off to the left per Custer's orders, his return to the trail taken by the regiment, his receipt of Custer's message via Martin, and the joining with Reno's command on the hilltop. Asked about Reno's condition when he arrived at the hilltop, Benteen replied: "He was about as cool as he is now. He had lost his hat in the run down below."[59] Questioned about Reno's "courage, coolness, and confidence" during the defensive stand, Benteen indicated that he thought "it was all right, sir."[60] Asked if he saw any evidence of cowardice on Reno's part, he replied, "None whatever." He also said he had to caution Reno while the troops were digging rifle pits because "he was standing around there in front of that point as there were volleys coming there constantly."[61] When Lee asked if his opinion that Reno's conduct had been "all right" had changed since the battle, Benteen said, "Not at all."[62]

Captain Frederick W. Benteen
Company H
(Gilbert Family Collection)

First Lieutenant Winfield S. Edgerly took the stand late on the afternoon of Monday, Feb. 3, and testified to Reno's conduct on June 25 and 26: "When I first got up there [on the hill] he was excited but not enough to impair his efficiency or have a bad effect on the troops. He did everything that was necessary to be done.... I saw Major Reno walk across the line as I saw other officers and he seemed very cool and I think the position we had was the best possible with a radius of a great many miles."[63] Gilbert inquired if Edgerly saw at any time any evidence of cowardice on the part of Reno: "I did not" was Edgerly's reply.[64]

The court began its 20th day in session and heard its first testimony suggesting Reno had been drunk on the night of June 25. Civilian mule packer B.F. Churchill testified that when John Frett and he had gone into the pack train to get blankets and food between 9 and 10 o'clock on the night of June 25, Reno found them there and demanded to know why they were not on the line. An argument apparently broke out between Reno and Frett and "Reno made a pass to strike Frett and some whiskey flew over myself and Frett and that Major Reno stepped back and picked up a carbine, but whether he intended to strike Frett with it, I don't know....My impression at the time was that he was a little under the influence of whiskey or liquor."[65]

Edgerly was recalled to the stand and asked about Reno's sobriety when he saw him on the night of June 25. Edgerly said he saw Reno "about 9 o'clock...and [he] was perfectly sober" When he saw him again about 2 a.m. June 26, "he was perfectly sober."[66] Asked by Gilbert if at any time the men or officers suspected Reno of not being sober, Edgerly answered, "Not the faintest. I never heard of it till I came to Chicago this time," and if Reno had been stammering and staggering and acting like a drunken man, the officers would not have permitted him to exercise command.[67] Gilbert recalled Benteen and queried him about Reno's sobriety on the night of the 25th. "He was sober as he is now.... I think he is entirely sober now and he was then," Benteen replied.

"Could he have been staggering and stammering during that time?" Gilbert asked. "Not without my knowing it," Benteen answered.[68]

If Reno had been drunk between 9 and 10 o'clock, "I would have known something about it. I did not know he had any whiskey or I would have been after some," Benteen added.[69]

The next witness was Captain Edward S. Godfrey, who did not have a high opinion of Reno's leadership role in the hilltop defensive stand. Asked by Lee about Reno's courage, coolness and efficiency as commanding officer at that time, Godfrey responded: "I was not particularly impressed with any of the qualifications.... It was my opinion then that Captain Benteen was exercising the functions principally of commanding officer."[70] Godfrey thought Reno's remark about dodging bullets and not wanting to be killed by Indians was a sign of "nervous timidity." He refused to give Reno credit for exposing himself to Indian fire while establishing the skirmish line on the hill and encouraging the men to hold their positions.[71]

The second civilian mule packer, John Frett, was the next witness. In response to Gilbert's questions, he said on the evening of June 25, Churchill and he went into the mule herd to get blankets and food. He encountered Reno, who asked him "Are the mules tight?" Frett asked "Tight? What do you mean by tight?" Reno replied "Tight, God damn you!" and slapped him in the face. He said Reno had a bottle of whiskey in his hand and when he slapped him, "the whiskey flew over me and he staggered. If any other man was in the condition he was, I should call him drunk."[72] Frett said, "His language was not very plain," and he had to brace himself against a pack because he was almost incapable of walking.[73]

Captain E. G. Mathey, who had been in charge of the pack train from June 22 to June 28, then took the witness stand. Lee questioned him about Reno's conduct on June 25-26: "When Major Reno first came up he was, as any man would naturally be under the circumstances, somewhat excited. I suppose it was not long since he had come out of the fight and that would be the natural condition for a man to be in. I did not see much of his conduct.... I did not think to question his courage. I saw no action on his part to indicate want of courage or indicating cowardice."[74]

Gilbert asked whether Mathey had seen or heard about Reno being drunk during the battle. Mathey saw no indication of Reno being drunk and mentioned that the subject had not even come up for discussion until the spring of 1878 when Girard talked to him about it.[75] Concerning Reno's courage, Mathey stated he had no "charge of cowardice to make against Major Reno."[76]

The next witness was Captain Thomas M. McDougall who commanded the rear guard with the pack train. McDougall testified that when he arrived on the hilltop, he found Reno to be "perfectly cool [and]...was as brave as any

Newspaper cut of the Reno Court of Inquiry.
Major Reno at center window, Lt. DeRudio testifying.

man there in my opinion." Lee asked him if he "saw enough of Major Reno during those days to have conclusive opinion in your own mind as to his conduct." McDougall said, "I thought after he came the next afternoon and asked me to take a walk with him, he had plenty of nerve. The balls were flying around, and the men were in their entrenchments firing away. We took it easily and slowly."[77] Gilbert inquired about Reno's sobriety. McDougall said he saw no whiskey in the command, and if Reno had been stammering and staggering on the night of June 25, someone would have found out.[78]

Gilbert recalled Wallace and asked him if he saw any evidence of insobriety on Reno's part during any of those engagements. Wallace said he saw none and "never heard it till the second day of this month...in Chicago."[79] Did he observe "at any time any failure on the part of Major Reno to do the duty that was expected and required of a commanding officer?" Gilbert inquired. Wallace responded, "No, sir, I did not."[80]

Lieutenant Colonel Michael V. Sheridan, military secretary to his brother General Philip Sheridan, was called as the last witness to testify on the 22nd day (Feb. 6) of the proceedings. Sheridan discussed the topography of the battlefield and the positions of the bodies that he found when he visited the battlefield in early summer 1877.

Mathey was then recalled to the witness stand by Lee and asked what the officers with Reno on June 25-26 had said about his conduct in the timber. Mathey said he heard some officers discuss the battle and "some seemed to think it would have been better to have remained down below." One officer in particular, Mathey said, expressed an opinion that made such an impression on his mind that he remembered it ever since: "If we had not been commanded by a coward we would have been killed." He identified DeRudio as that officer.[81]

The final scheduled witness of the proceedings was Colonel John Gibbon, 7th Infantry. He had reached the battlefield after the battle was over and could only express his opinion about the defensibility of the timber and hilltop positions. Gibbon thought the hilltop was exceedingly weak for a prolonged defense but offered no opinion as to where a better defensive position might have been found.

Reno requested to appear before the court as a witness but the court decided he could not unless he made a formal written request to do so. He submitted the required request and was called to the stand by his counsel, Lyman Gilbert. He testified in his own behalf for the next two days and provided details of the events of June 25-26. The salient points he made were: The timber position was not tenable and cowardice did not prompt him to leave there; he did carry a flask but was strictly sober on the afternoon and night of the 25th and still had some in the flask on the morning of the 28th; he found several packers skulking in the pack train, did strike one of them, and told him he would shoot him if he found him there again; and finally, he indicated he had done everything he could to support Custer, short of sacrificing his own command.[82]

On Monday, Feb. 10, Reno presented, through his counsel, his written statement which was read to the court, and the following morning Recorder Lee read his written reply to the statement. The court was then cleared and closed for deliberation, and "after maturely considering the evidence adduced," the members issued their findings, which concluded with the statement:

> The conduct of the officers throughout was excellent, and while subordinates in some instances did more for the safety of the command by brilliant displays of courage than did Major Reno, there was nothing in his conduct which required the animadversion [adverse criticism] from this Court.[83]

The court was then adjourned by Colonel King. The findings were forwarded to the Bureau of Military Justice, War Department, for its approval or disapproval.

285

Reno remained in Chicago for several days following the inquiry before returning to Harrisburg. On Feb. 18, he stopped in Rushville, Ill., to visit his sister, Mrs. John Knowles. The local newspaper noted that he "has just passed through a long trial at Chicago on the charge of not doing his duty in the memorable fight with the Indians at the time Gen. Custer and his troops were slaughtered, the trial having terminated last week and the evidence forwarded to the War Department. It is generally conceded that he will be honorably acquitted."[84] Reno left Rushville Feb. 24, stopped in Pittsburgh to pick up Ross, and arrived at the Lochiel Hotel in Harrisburg later that week.

On Feb. 21, after reviewing the proceedings of the court, Judge Advocate General, W. M. Dunn, recommended to the secretary of war that the conclusions of the court be approved. He stated: "I concur with the Court in its exoneration of Major Reno from the charges of cowardice which have been brought against him, and in its conclusion that no further action is required."[85] General Sherman approved the findings March 5 and forwarded them to Secretary of War George W. McCrary, who approved the proceedings and findings, "by order of the President," on the same day. Reno was notified of the results of his court of inquiry and was pleased with the findings. This was reflected in a Harrisburg newspaper article published shortly after Reno returned from visiting his sister in Illinois:

> Major M. A. Reno, U.S.A., is here, and is kept busy receiving the congratulations of his friends on his vindication. Major Reno, like all army officers, is very punctilious as to what he says about a matter in which he is personally involved, and which concerns his brother officers, and refuses to be interviewed. He said to the Telegraph correspondent last evening that he is very well satisfied with the verdict of the Court of Inquiry, as well satisfied, in fact, as if he had written it himself. It confirms his report of the battle of the Little Big Horn made to his superior officer after it was fought — something he was very desirous of having done. Major Reno has received congratulatory letters from all parts of the country on the result of the finding of the Court.[86]

Not everyone was pleased with the court's findings. Custer's widow was furious at the verdict. Whittaker claimed the verdict was "a complete and scientific whitewash," and even suggested that "ladies of pleasure" had been used to influence the witnesses in favor of Reno. Merritt thought the decision was fair based on the evidence presented but Elizabeth Custer believed that the old rivalry between her husband and Merritt was the cause for the verdict clearing Reno. Merritt later remarked to his adjutant, Lieutenant Eben Swift

Jr., that he would liked to have heard more adverse testimony about Reno and felt the court had "damned Reno with faint praise."[87]

Whittaker sent a letter to the editor of the *Chicago Times* that was published March 12. His animosity for the court was obvious: "Owing to the precautions of Maj. Reno's counsel, and the orders under which the Court was acting, I was barred out from my rightful position of accuser or prosecutor in the inquiry, on the narrowest technical grounds." Whittaker then went into a long dissertation about how he had come to Chicago "to vindicate Custer as a soldier and myself as a man of truth." He continued:

> [T]he evidence adduced before this Court show all that I could desire. Before the date of this Inquiry Custer stood charged before the country with two military crimes — rashness and disobedience. Grant, Reno, Benteen and a host of others charged him with the first; Gen. Terry and Ex-President Grant with the last. This trial has established facts which prove Custer to have been, not rash, but prudent; not defeated by the enemy, but abandoned by the treachery or timidity of his subordinates.[88]

Reno's suspension from rank and pay would be coming to an end in another six weeks — he would be able to return to his regiment. At age 44, he still had a long and promising military career before him.

Endnotes

[1] Alfred H. Terry, *The Field Diary of General Alfred H. Terry, The Yellowstone Expedition - 1876* (The Old Army Press, Bellevue, Neb.), pp. 26-27.

[2] Frederick Whittaker, *A Popular Life of Major Gen'l. Geo. A. Custer* (Sheldon & Co., New York, 1876).

[3] Colonel W. A. Graham, *The Custer Myth, A Source Book of Custeriana* (Stackpole Press, Harrisburg, Pa., 1953), p. 392.

[4] File 2324 ACP 1878.

[5] File 2324 ACP 1878.

[6] Ronald H. Nichols, (editor), *Reno Court of Inquiry* (Custer Battlefield Historical & Museum Assn., Inc., Crow Agency, Mont., 1992), pp. 634-35. Hereinafter Reno Court.

[7] Reno Court, Exhibit No. 1, p. 633.

[8] *Army and Navy Journal*, issue of June 21, 1878.

[9] Reno Court, Exhibit No. 1, p. 633. Often considerable confusion arises over what constitutes a military court-martial and a court of inquiry. Possibly the simplest explanation is covered in a letter, dated Dec. 9, 1932, from Colonel W. A. Graham, chief, Military Affairs Section, Judge Advocates Office, to Donald M. Frost of Boston. The letter states, in part:

"Court-martial - the officer concerned is known as the accused, and is formally charged as in an indictment with specific offenses against military law. He is required to plead to such charges, which are then formally tried under rules of evidence, the prosecutor being represented by an officer known as the trial judge-advocate, which functions similarly to a states or district attorney, while the accused is represented by an officer known as the defense counsel, or by a civilian counsel of his own choice. The court-martial is, in short, a military criminal prosecution.

"A court of inquiry, on the other hand, is purely an investigatory body, convened by a competent authority at the request of an officer whose conduct has been made the subject of criticism, official or otherwise, and its purpose is to inquire into and establish the facts. Sometimes a court of inquiry is required to express an opinion, and to make recommendations as to the necessity for further proceedings, by way of court-martial or otherwise, but this is not invariable."

[10] Records of the War Department, File 4448, Adjutant General's Office (AGO) 1878 (filed with 3770 AGO 1876).

[11] File 4647 AGO 1878 (filed with 3770 AGO 1876, and 4448 AGO 1878).

[12] File 3770 AGO 1876.

[13] File 5164 ACP 1878.

[14] Reno Court, Extract, p. 1.

[15] Don E. Alberts, *Brandy Station to Manila Bay: A Biography of General Wesley Merritt* (Presidial Press, Austin, Texas, 1980), p. 250.

[16] Harrisburg *Daily Telegraph*, Dec. 30, 1878. The interesting thing about this item is that Captain Thomas Weir had died in New York Dec. 9, 1876 — more than two years before. Perhaps it was sent by Whittaker indicating it was the testimony that Weir would have given if he was still alive.

[17] Harrisburg *Daily Telegraph*, Jan. 10, 1879. Repeated from one of the Chicago newspapers.

[18] Reno Court, p. 3.

[19] *Chicago Times*, Tuesday, Jan. 14, 1879.

[20] *Chicago Times*, date unknown but probably about Jan. 20, 1879.

[21] Luther Reily Kelker, *History of Dauphin County, Pennsylvania* (The Lewis Publishing Company, New York & Chicago, 1907), pp. 39-40. John W. Leonard, *Who's Who in Pennsylvania* (L. R. Hamersly & Co., Harrisburg, Pa., 1908), p. 296.

[22] Harrisburg *Daily Telegraph*, Jan. 20, 1879.

[23] Reno Court, Maguire's testimony, p. 16.

[24] Reno Court, Wallace's testimony, p. 52.

[25] Reno Court, Wallace's testimony, pp. 50, 53.

[26] Reno Court, Wallace's testimony, p. 55.

[27] *Chicago Times*, Jan. 17, 1879.

[28] Reno Court, Wallace's testimony, p. 71.

[29] Reno Court, Girard's testimony, p. 104.

[30] Reno Court, Girard's testimony, p. 122.

[31] Reno Court, Girard's testimony, p. 129. Girard was being less than honest with this testimony. On Feb. 22, 1879, the *Bismarck Tribune* published a scathing letter from Girard about Reno.

[32] Reno Court, Varnum's testimony, p. 175.

[33] Reno Court, Varnum's testimony, p. 169.

[34] Reno Court, Varnum's testimony, p. 156.

[35] Reno Court, Porter's testimony, p. 198.

[36] Reno Court, Porter's testimony, p. 191.

[37] Reno Court, Moylan's testimony, p. 230.

[38] Reno Court, Moylan's testimony, p. 238.

[39] Reno Court, Moylan's testimony, p. 241.

[40] Reno Court, Moylan's testimony, p. 241.

[41] Reno Court, Moylan's testimony, p. 244.

[42] Reno Court, Herendeen's testimony, p. 255. Herendeen is the only witness who thought there was a quick sequence of "mount" "dismount" "mount" commands as previously discussed in Chapter 10.

[43] Reno Court, Payne's testimony, p. 273.

[44] Reno Court, Exhibit No. 3, p. 639.

[45] Reno Court, p. 283

[46] Reno Court, Herendeen's testimony, p. 284-86.

[47] Reno Court, Hare's testimony, p. 301.

[48] Reno Court, Hare's testimony, p. 295.

[49] Reno Court, Hare's testimony, p. 296.

[50] Reno Court, Hare's testimony, p. 298.

[51] Reno Court, Hare's testimony, p. 304.

[52] Reno Court, DeRudio's testimony, p. 328.

[53] Reno Court, DeRudio's testimony, p. 323.

[54] Reno Court, DeRudio's testimony, p. 340. Three witnesses (Varnum, DeRudio and Girard) testified that they saw Custer or part of his command on the bluffs on the east side of the Little Big Horn, and none of them informed Reno.

[55] Reno Court, DeRudio's testimony, p. 328.

[56] Reno Court, Davern's testimony, p. 366.

[57] Reno Court, Culbertson's testimony, p. 381.

[58] Reno Court, Culbertson's testimony, p. 376.

[59] Reno Court, Benteen's testimony, p. 408.

[60] Reno Court, Benteen's testimony, p. 413.

[61] Reno Court, Benteen's testimony, p. 420.

[62] Reno Court, Benteen's testimony, p. 435.

[63] Reno Court, Edgerly's testimony, p. 450.

[64] Reno Court, Edgerly's testimony, p. 456.

[65] Reno Court, Churchill's testimony, p. 470.

[66] Reno Court, Edgerly's testimony, p. 475.

[67] Reno Court, Edgerly's testimony, p. 476.

[68] Reno Court, Benteen's testimony, p. 477.

[69] Reno Court, Benteen's testimony, p. 478.

[70] Reno Court, Godfrey's testimony, pp. 492-93.

[71] Reno Court, Godfrey's testimony, p. 499.

[72] Reno Court, Frett's testimony, p. 505.

[73] Reno Court, Frett's testimony, pp. 508-09.

[74] Reno Court, Mathey's testimony, p. 519.

[75] Reno Court, Mathey's testimony, pp. 520-21, 527.

[76] Reno Court, Mathey's testimony, p. 523.

[77] Reno Court, McDougall's testimony, p. 533-34.

[78] Reno Court, McDougall's testimony, pp. 538-39.

[79] Reno Court, Wallace's testimony, p. 543.

[80] Reno Court, Wallace's testimony, p. 544.

[81] Reno Court, Mathey's testimony, pp. 551-52.

[82] Reno Court, Reno's testimony, pp. 573, 575, 576, 592.

[83] Reno Court, p. 629. While some Custer supporters would later claim the Court of Inquiry testimony was not accurate and purposely skewed to protect Reno and the other survivors of the 7th Cavalry, there is no direct evidence to support this claim. The official testimony shows quite clearly that the others who were there with Reno on that fateful and unfortunate day believed he acted reasonably and may well have saved their lives.

[84] *The Rushville Times*, Rushville, Ill., issue of Friday, Feb. 21, 1879.

[85] Reno Court, p. 631.

[86] "Major Reno's Arrival," *Harrisburg Daily Telegraph*, clipping undated but obviously written within several weeks after he received the results of the proceedings.

[87] Alberts, p. 250.

[88] *Chicago Times*, March 12, 1879.

• 15 •

Fort Meade

Marcus Reno would spend the last few weeks of his suspension traveling with his son and preparing for his return to the military. He took Ross to Philadelphia March 8, 1879, to buy him some clothes, and they traveled back to Pittsburgh March 12. Although Ross' aunt, Bertie Orth, had died Aug. 21, 1878, he was still under the care of his uncle, J. Wilson Orth, in Pittsburgh. Reno returned to the Lochiel Hotel in Harrisburg and talked to Lyman Gilbert about filing a libel suit against Sheldon and Company, the publisher of Whittaker's book. He considered the statements made in the book and the circulars issued concerning it libelous because of the court's finding that "there was nothing in his conduct which required the animadversion from this Court."[1]

As his suspension drew to an end, Reno realized he had not received orders directing him to either Fort Abercrombie or another duty station. Deciding to go directly to the War Department in Washington for instructions, he registered April 9 at the Ebbitt House in Washington. The War Department told him to report his residence by letter to the Adjutant General's office and he would be informed of his new orders. Returning to Harrisburg, he sent a letter April 29 to General Townsend informing him that "I have the honor to report that I am at the 'Lochiel Hotel' in this city, awaiting orders."[2] The letter was received at the Adjutant General's office May 3 and Townsend commented:

> Major Reno was suspended from rank and command for two years from <u>May 1, 1877</u>. By letter June 9, 1877, he was authorized to leave the limits of the Department of Dakota. His station was Fort Abercrombie when he left the Department of Dakota. Telegraph him that he should have rejoined his station by the 1st of May.

A telegram was sent to Reno at the Lochiel Hotel May 5 indicating he should have already rejoined his regiment. Reno believed it was necessary to

291

explain why he had not done so and on May 5 sent a letter back to General R. C. Drum, assistant adjutant general:

> I have the honor to acknowledge receipt of your telegram of this date, and in reply think to state as explanation of my awaiting orders at this point that when in Washington I went to consult at the War Department as to the proper thing for me to do at the expiration of my sentence of suspension from rank and pay. I received a reply that a report by letter was what was right. This agreed with my own opinion, as I was relieved from duty by the authority of the War Department and no lesser authority could assign me duty, and no officer can put himself on duty by virtue of his commission alone.
>
> I submit this reply in justification of my action in this matter. I shall be enroute to my Regiment before this will reach the Headquarters of the Army.[3]

Reno was ready to leave but was still not clear on where he should report. On May 6, he sent a telegram to the Adjutant General: "Was informed by you I should report by letter. Did so. Where is my station? Will start at once." The Adjutant General's Office replied by telegram May 7 that he was to report to Fort Meade, Dakota Territory.[4] The Harrisburg *Daily Telegraph* reported in its May 8, 1879, edition: "Major M. A. Reno, U.S.A., left this city last night to join the Seventh regiment at Fort Custer, Montana Territory (sic)."[5]

In July 1878, Colonel Sturgis marched eight companies of the 7th Cavalry from Fort Lincoln to an area on the northeastern edge of the Black Hills near Bear Butte. Here he established a cavalry camp which he named "Camp J. G. Sturgis" in honor of his son Jack, killed at the Little Big Horn. On July 20, General Sheridan and his party, including his secretary and younger brother, Lieutenant Colonel Michael V. Sheridan, arrived at Camp Sturgis to select a site for a new fort. General Sheridan decided on a location just a half-mile south of Bear Butte Creek, about 5 miles from the 7th Cavalry's camp, and 15 miles east of Deadwood. Construction was started Aug. 27 by two companies of the 7th Cavalry (E and M), and two companies of the 1st Infantry (F and K) under the direction of Major Henry M. Lazelle. The new site was temporarily known as Camp Ruhlen for its builder, 1st Lieutenant George Ruhlen, 17th Infantry. Building progressed slowly, hampered by cold weather in November, and the first building, the guardhouse, was completed and first used Nov. 8. Nevertheless, construction continued through November and December, and on Dec. 31, the post was renamed Fort Meade in honor of Gen-

Fort Meade, Dakato Territory, 1882

eral George C. Meade. Most of the buildings were completed in early spring 1879.

Reno arrived at the almost completed Fort Meade May 21 and assumed command from Major Lazelle the following day. In June, the 7th Cavalry field staff, band, and Companies A, C, G and H were transferred from Fort Lincoln to Fort Meade. Also arriving with the troops was "Comanche," Captain Myles Keogh's horse at the Little Big Horn, who would be used only in ceremonial regimental formations. With most of the post construction complete and the weather pleasant, Reno took a few days off and rode into Deadwood June 19 to have a little "fun." On July 4, he took the regimental band to Deadwood to help its citizens celebrate the holiday — he was "commended for being present" with the band by the local newspaper.[6]

Sturgis arrived with his family July 16 and took command of the post the following day. Included in the Sturgis family was his wife, daughter Ella, 21, son Sam Jr., 18, and daughter Mary, 14. Ella was described as "a very handsome girl, tall, slender, with large expressive gray eyes, dark skin and hair and marked eye brows, with color enough to make her brunet beauty effective."[7] With the lieutenant colonel of the regiment, Elmer Otis, and the two more senior majors, Joseph C. Tilford and Lewis Merrill, on detached service, Reno, as the next most senior officer present, was Sturgis' second-in-command at the post. First Lieutenant Ernest A. Garlington was the regimental adjutant, 1st Lieutenant Charles A. Varnum was the regimental quartermaster, and two medical officers were present: Assistant Surgeon Louis Brechemin, and contract Surgeon Ralph Bell.

Early on the morning of Sunday, Aug. 3, the post trader's store and the commissary were destroyed by fire. Post trader William D. Fanshawe had gone to Rapid City and was not expected to return until later in the day. Fanshawe's wife was extremely nervous while she awaited her husband's return, and Reno came to see her several times "asking if there was anything he could do for" her.[8] By early evening, when Fanshawe had still not arrived, Reno suggested that Mrs. Fanshawe and he use his buggy and drive down the road in the direction of Rapid City with the anticipation of meeting her husband on his way back. Mrs. Fanshawe agreed and they went seven or eight miles toward Rapid City without encountering her husband. Returning to the post, Reno and Mrs. Fanshawe spent the evening on the porch of the Fanshawe residence in the company of 2nd Lieutenant William J. Nicholson, 7th Cavalry, Doctor Bell, and Edward W. Johnson, who had a part interest in the trading post.

Mr. Fanshawe finally arrived home between midnight and 1 a.m., and Reno suggested that Bell, Nicholson and Johnson go to his quarters to have a drink so Fanshawe could have a few moments alone with his wife. As they were leaving, Fanshawe invited them to return in a few minutes for supper. At Reno's quarters they each had a drink and then returned to the Fanshawe residence a little after 1 o'clock. Whiskey was served with the supper and Reno had two drinks. Johnson later recalled that Reno was quiet during the meal.[9] After 20 or 30 minutes, Mrs. Fanshawe noticed that Reno was swaying in his chair, his speech appeared garbled and he had the hiccups. She thought he was very much under the influence of liquor and asked Johnson not to give him anything else to drink as he was "drunk enough."[10] When they left the Fanshawe residence, Johnson offered to help Reno down a high step from the porch to the ground. Reno declined the offer saying, "I am able to take care of myself."[11] Reno, Johnson, Bell and Nicholson then returned to their own quarters.

Four days later, on the evening of Aug. 7, shortly before taps, Reno went to the Officers' Club Room (billiard saloon) on the post for a game of billiards.[12] Present when Reno arrived were Captain Benteen, Doctors Bell and Brechemin, Lieutenant Scott, the bartender Joseph Smythe and several other officers. About 10 o'clock, after a few drinks by everyone, a four-handed game of billiards was organized with Reno and Bell playing against Benteen and Brechemin. As play progressed, Reno missed an easy shot and as he turned from the table struck a chair and, angry at missing the shot, picked up the chair by its back and tossed it toward a window. It broke one of the two bottom panes of glass (the other already being broken). About midnight, Reno decided to settle his bill with the bartender and handed Scott either a $5 or $10 bill. He wanted to be certain that Scott was aware the bill was settled. Scott gave the bartender the money to pay Reno's bill, which included the cost of replacing the broken window. When Smythe returned with Reno's change, he started to hand it to Scott. Reno wanted to know why Smythe was giving his change to Scott, and Smythe said that since Scott had paid the bill, he thought it was his place to return the change to him. Smythe then offered the change to Reno who struck Smythe's hand, scattering the change over the floor. After retrieving the change, Smythe again attempted to hand the money to Reno and again Reno hit Smythe's hand and scattered the change. Smythe picked up part of the money and placed in on the wainscoting ledge. Scott and Reno left the club room about 1:30 a.m. and went to Reno's quarters where Scott finally left him, sitting on the stoop, about 2 o'clock and returned to his own quarters.[13]

Since the return of Sturgis and his family in mid-July, the widowed 44-year-old Reno had been taken by Ella Sturgis' beauty. He went out of his way to show attention to the young woman but she showed little interest in the major. His 1877 court-martial conviction, which had included his unwanted attention to another officer's wife while her husband was on leave, was general

Major Marcus Reno, circa 1880
(Americana Magazine, March 1912)
(Richard Metcalfe Collection)

knowledge among the 7th Cavalry officers and especially Colonel Sturgis. An earlier romance between Ella and 2nd Lieutenant Charles M. Carrow had turned to tragedy when the young lieutenant killed himself in May, apparently over the broken romance.[14] Her parents were protective of the young woman and, with the loss of their son Jack at the Little Big Horn where Reno's command had not gone to Custer's aid, they had little fondness for the major.

On Friday, Sept. 26, Reno rode into Deadwood and registered at the Welch Hotel. Deadwood was described as consisting of "one business street which ran right down along the west side of Deadwood Creek. Buildings on one side of the street backed up to the creek, and on the other side the rear end of the buildings were against the mountain. It was a flourishing town because the placer mines here were not yet worked out."[15] Reno had found the bar and by midnight was intoxicated to the point of staggering and in a fighting mood. Future Congressman R. F. Pettigrew was also staying at the Welch Hotel when about 1 o'clock he heard "a great commotion" in the hallway, When he opened his door, he saw three men fighting at the end of the hall:

> General Reno of Custer's Battlefield fame, was one of the three, and he was fighting drunk, and the other two men were trying to get him out of the hotel which was all on fire. They finally knocked Reno down and took him out the back door.... In fact, the whole town of Deadwood burned that night, all of it that was in the Deadwood Gulch.[16]

As the second-in-command, Reno was invited to all general entertainment that occurred at the post including those at the home of Colonel Sturgis. On Oct. 1, Reno made a social visit to the Sturgis home while the colonel was out riding in the country. He did not send his name in first as was the social custom, but simply knocked at the door and when it was opened went into the house. He stayed for at least two hours and was still there when Sturgis returned from his ride. Sturgis was later to comment that if he had been at home, Reno would not have been received in his home for a social visit.[17]

During the next several weeks Reno made frequent visits to the Officers' Club Room and often played billiards and pool. Apparently heavy betting was placed on the outcome of these games and by Oct. 25, Reno owed Lieutenant Nicholson $380. That morning Nicholson met Reno in front of his quarters and Reno said to him, "Mr. Nicholson about that money." Nicholson replied, "Colonel...it was all right," and nothing more was said about the debt.

When Reno went to the club room that evening, Doctor Bell, Captain James T. Peale, 2nd Cavalry, Lieutenants Pettit and Nicholson, and bartender Smythe were there. As the evening wore on, Reno challenged Nicholson to a game of pool, betting $100 on the game. Reno won and Nicholson remarked that it "leaves us now $280 on pool," to which Reno immediately objected. He said Nicholson had told him early that day "the pool [debt] was square." Nicholson said Reno still owed the money and Reno said he did not owe him "any such damned thing." Nicholson wanted to call in the bartender Smythe to settle the argument but Reno refused, saying, "No, I don't want him to settle it, he is not the proper person to settle it." The dispute continued to elevate to the point that Nicholson told Reno that he "could lick him in two minutes in any way he wanted." Reno considered the remark to be made "in a grossly insulting manner" but remained silent and stood at the end of the pool table with a pool cue, knocking the balls about the table. Reno later said, "My silence seemed to encourage him to insult me more grossly." Nicholson then loudly repeated the threat and slammed his fist down on the pool table, attracting the attention of everybody in the club room. Nicholson again proclaimed loudly that he could whip Reno in short order. This last action finally provoked Reno "beyond the limits of patience and in a fit of passion, with the cue in my hand, I walked towards him and struck him."[18] Nicholson deflected the blow with his left arm, breaking the cue, then jumped Reno, grabbed him by the throat, put him on the floor, and was preparing to hit him when Bell said, "Nicholson, for God['s] sake don't hit him." Captain Peale and Lieutenant Pettit threatened to put them under arrest unless they stopped. Both men obeyed and two minutes later, Reno put on his overcoat, left the club room with Bell and returned to his quarters.[19]

When Sturgis was informed of the brawl, he questioned the different officers present at the club that night and decided to bring charges against Reno. Sturgis placed Reno under arrest Oct. 28, confined him to the post, and had the charges and specifications drawn up. He had the Aug. 3 drinking incident at the Fanshawe residence and the Aug. 7 window-breaking occurrence included in the specifications. Lodged against Reno was a single charge, "Conduct unbecoming an officer and gentleman," and three specifications:

1st. Reno...did create and engage in a disreputable disturbance or brawl in a public billiard saloon, and did violently assault and strike 2nd Lieutenant Wm. J. Nicholson, 7th Cavalry, with a billiard cue, with the manifest intent of inflicting severe bodily injury...and did persist in continuing said disturbance until threatened with arrest by 2nd Lieut. Jas. S. Pettit...on or about 25th of October, 1879.

2nd. Reno...was drunk and disorderly in a public billiard saloon, and did several times, wantonly and in a riotous manner, knock money out of the hands of the saloon keeper (or tender), Mr. Joseph Smythe, scattering said money over the floor, and did, in a wanton and riotous manner, smash in with chairs the glass of one or more of the windows of said billiard saloon...on or about the 8th of August, 1879.

3rd. Reno...was in a disgusting condition of intoxication at the residence of Mr. W. D. Fanshawe, post trader...on or about the 3rd of August, 1879.

Each of the specifications concluded with "to the scandal and disgrace of the military service."[20]

Sturgis, of course, approved the charge and specifications when he forwarded them to General Terry, commander of the Department of Dakota. Terry approved Sturgis' recommendation and issued Special Orders No. 123, dated Nov. 5, 1879, ordering a general court-martial to be convened at Fort Meade Nov. 28, with Colonel W. H. Wood, 11th Infantry, as president.[21]

Reno was not particularly concerned about the charge with its three specifications. The second specification he considered to be the result of a "frolic," that he was sober when the chair was tossed, and that knocking the change out of Smythe's hand was not done in a "wanton and riotous manner." On the third specification he admitted to being "drowsy" after the supper but saw nothing improper in his conduct at the Fanshawe home. While the first specification was more serious, he believed he had been provoked by Nicholson and his "grossly insulting" remarks, that no serious injury had occurred to Nicholson, and the scuffle had stopped at once when Peale and Pettit ordered it to halt. Reno felt so confident about being acquitted of the charge he decided it was unnecessary to either hire an attorney or ask one of this fellow officers to represent him during the trial — he would act as his own counsel.

At Fort Meade, the commanding officer's two-story house, occupied by the Sturgis family, was located in the middle of officer's row on the south side of the parade ground with houses on either side. The Sturgis house was set back about 60 feet from the pathway, Captain Moylan's house was more than 100 feet to the west, and Lieutenant Garlington's quarters were to the east. Confined to the post while under arrest, Reno usually took a late evening walk around the post for exercise, weather permitting. The evening of Nov. 10 was dark and cool, and about 10:30 p.m., just as Reno was walking past the Sturgis residence, Garlington emerged from the front door. Reno stopped for about two minutes, looked at the house, and as Garlington came up the walkway from the house, turned and proceeded along the pathway in an easterly direction. Garlington also turned east when he reached the walkway and turned into his quarters just as he caught up with Reno. Reno continued eastward, came to the end of the pathway, turned around and walked west. He passed two officers on the walkway near the Sturgis house: 2nd Lieutenants B. D. Spilman, 7th Cavalry, and B. G. Starr, 1st Infantry.

In front of the Sturgis house Reno again stopped. He could see through one of the two front windows of the fully lighted sitting room (the other window had the shade drawn). In the sitting room, located in the northwest corner of the house, he saw the beautiful, fully dressed Ella Sturgis. Since he was under post arrest, regulations prevented him from going to the commanding officer's quarters for any reason without being invited, so he obviously could not simply walk up and knock on the front door. Continuing westward along the walkway, he turned and saw that the sitting room's side window shade was not drawn. He was so infatuated with the young Ella that the temptation to see her was just too great to resist. Without regard to the possible consequences of his action, he crossed the front lawn and went to the side window of the sitting room. The window ledge was high and Reno was forced to stand on his tiptoes to see into the room. He saw Ella sitting there but did not see Mrs. Sturgis who was also in the room. What occurred next was like a comic opera.

Ella was seated about four feet from the side window and in front of the fireplace while her mother sat by the front window that had the drawn shade. Ella heard a noise at the side window but ignored it until Reno tapped on the window to get her attention. She saw someone at the window jump back, told her mother that someone was at the window, and when she sat forward in her chair to look out the window, she saw a face gradually appear. Her eyes met Reno's and she said she was so frightened, she could not move. She finally said in a whisper, "Mama, it is Major Reno; it is Major Reno; it is Major Reno." After several seconds, and after her mother hurriedly left the room, she moved to the corner of the room where she couldn't be seen from either the side or front windows.[22]

The colonel had retired about 9 o'clock but was still awake at 11 when Mrs. Sturgis called for him to come downstairs quickly. Stopping to put on a garment, he heard his wife call again "come quickly, Major Reno." He ran down the stairs, saw his daughter in the corner of the sitting room, and asked her where she saw Reno. She pointed at the side window and Sturgis picked up a cane, went out the front door, around the side of the house, but found no one there. He wanted to go and find Reno but his wife and daughter did not want him to leave the house, fearing Reno might still be somewhere around the house.

Sturgis quickly went next door and asked Garlington to come over to the Sturgis house. When Garlington arrived, he found the family in an excited state. He described Ella as being "very nervous, intensely nervous, very pale, as though she had been laboring under some excitement of intense character, and her own statement of how much she had been frightened."[23] Sturgis then sent him to Reno's quarters to see if he could get some explanation of the evening's events. Reno had returned to his quarters and realized he was in serious trouble with his commanding officer. When Garlington questioned him about his motives in what had happened, Reno would not tell him why he did it. Garlington returned to the Sturgis house and informed the colonel that Reno would give him no explanation for his conduct.[24]

The next morning, Sturgis placed Reno under house arrest and sent a telegram to Terry requesting an additional charge and specification be added to the pending court-martial proceedings against Reno — the additional charge being the same as the previous charge, "Conduct unbecoming and officer and gentleman." The specification read:

> 1st. Reno...did in the darkness and at a late hour in the evening, surreptitiously enter the side grounds adjoining the private residence or quarters of his commanding officer...and did peer into a side (and retired) window of the family sitting-room of said private residence or quarters, approaching so near and so stealthily as to very seriously affright and alarm that portion of the family of said...Sturgis...which had not yet retired for the night, and were still below stairs and occupants of said family

sitting-room. All this at Fort Meade, D.T., between the hours of 9 and 11 o'clock on or about the 10th of November, 1879.[25]

On Nov. 11, after receiving a copy of the additional charge and specification to be filed against him, Reno wrote an apology to Mrs. Sturgis and Ella. He was in close house arrest so it was not until noon of the 12th that it was sent:

> Whatever others may say or think I do not wish to be misunderstood by you, and I write this that you may appreciate what motives actuated me when I stopped to look through your window. It has been my habit since in arrest to walk on favorable nights on the pathway in front of officers quarters two or three times for exercise. On the evening in question I saw your daughter in complete toilet through the window, and it was such a picture that I said to myself, can there be any harm in looking upon it, no one will know it and in my loneliness and thoughts of the past, I felt myself impatient to resist the temptation. When you started in alarm without reflecting I went to my quarters instead of into your house as I should have done, and when the Adjutant came to my quarters that evening, I could not tell him all as I can you. It would be a matter of deep regret to my dying day should you and she think me capable of an untruth of being a spy or doing anything with a mean motive. This is the truth as I expect to answer for it before my God, and I sincerely ask your pardon for all that does not seem to you as innocent, for I do assure you if not guiltless the fault was in the judgment and not heart. Of course I would like you to show this to "E," in addition I desire to say that the relation between Colonel Sturgis' family in one member and myself were very friendly in the time passed, and I have the greatest respect and admiration for her. I had been in arrest for several days, and in seeing her, as Lieutenant Spilman and several others did, I turned from the pathway and stopped in front of the side window to look at her. I did not approach the window stealthily or surreptitiously but walked there as I would walk [on parade], from out of the shadow of the house into the full glare of the light of the window, if my face expressed any other sentiment than admiration it greatly belied my feelings. I had no intention to alarm her and would rather suffer my right hand severed from my arm than harm one hair of her head.[26]

The Department of Dakota issued Special Orders No. 123, on Nov. 5, 1879, which appointed a general court-martial to meet at Fort Meade, Dakota Territory, at 10 o'clock Monday, Nov. 24, 1879. Officers detailed for the court were:

Colonel William H. Wood, 11th Infantry
Colonel William R. Shafter, 1st Infantry
Colonel John W. Davidson, 2nd Cavalry
Lieutenant Colonel Elmer Otis, 7th Cavalry
Lieutenant Colonel A. J. Alexander, 2nd Cavalry
Lieutenant Colonel Edwin F. Townsend, 11th Infantry
Major Bernard J. D. Irwin, Medical Department
Major Lewis Merrill, 7th Cavalry
Major Joseph S. Conrad, 17th Infantry
Captain W. W. Sanders, 6th Infantry, Judge Advocate

When Reno read Special Orders No. 123, he immediately protested to Department Headquarters about the appointment of Major Lewis Merrill, 7th Cavalry, to the court-martial panel. Reno had had a conflict with Merrill in Kansas in the early 1870s and believed that Merrill would not provide a fair and impartial decision. Headquarters issued Special Order No. 128, dated Nov. 13, 1879, replacing Merrill with Major Orlando H. Moore, 6th Infantry.[27]

The court's president, Colonel Wood, was the same officer who caught Reno as a cadet at West Point singing on guard duty in the cadet's barracks. When challenged by then 1st Lieutenant Wood, Reno said he had a right to sing on post. Wood disagreed and brought Reno up on a charge of "conduct to the prejudice of good order and military discipline" that resulted in Reno's suspension from the academy for one class year. More than 23 years had passed since that incident and Reno did not protest Wood's appointment to the panel.

The court convened as ordered Nov. 24, but of the nine field officers appointed to the court, only four were present: Wood, Shafter, Alexander and Irwin. Lacking a quorum, the members present adjourned to meet the following day at 10 o'clock. For the next two days, Nov. 25 and 26, only the same four officers were present, and without a quorum the trial could not start. The panel decided not to meet until at least one additional appointed officer arrived at Fort Meade. Wood finally called the court to order on the 28th with the original four officers and Otis, Moore, Conrad and Judge Advocate Sanders present.

The charges and specifications were read and Reno pleaded "not guilty" to both charges and all specifications, except the 3rd specification of the first charge to which he pleaded "bar of trial." He indicated the offense alleged in that specification (the incident at the Fanshawe residence) was not a military offense and therefore should not have been within the jurisdiction of the court. The court considered Reno's argument but his objection was not sustained. Sanders requested an adjournment until the following day so he could examine his witnesses.

When the court opened Nov. 29 with a quorum present, Judge Advocate Sanders called Nicholson as his first witness. Nicholson told his version of the Oct. 25 episode in the officer's club room: how Reno won the $100 pool game but denied owing Nicholson $280; how he told Reno he could "lick him in two minutes in any way he wanted" and repeated it two or three times; how he was struck by the pool cue and wrestled Reno to the floor; and finally how he was threatened with arrest if he didn't stop fighting. Sanders asked him about Reno's drinking at the Fanshawe home Aug. 3, and Nicholson thought Reno's appearance that night was "of a man who had taken too much liquor." Under cross examination by Reno, Nicholson said the difficulty with Reno in the club room was a private affair and did not have an official relation.[28]

The next witness was Lieutenant Pettit, who related the events of Oct. 25 as he saw them. Under cross examination, he indicated his threat to arrest the two men as they struggled on the floor "was more particularly directed towards Lieutenant Nicholson" than toward Reno.[29]

Bartender Smythe next took the witness stand and in his version of the Oct. 25 event said, "There was a little altercation between a couple of officers," and he did "not see anything unusual happen" on the evening of Aug. 7 when the window was broken in the club room. Smythe testified that he did not see Reno toss the chair, that Reno had knocked the change from his hand twice, and that he finally picked up part of it and placed in on the wainscoting ledge. He said Reno had been drinking and "he showed it slightly. He walked all right and was playing a game of billiards."[30] Smythe's testimony ended the first full day of court activity and the court adjourned for the weekend.

On Monday, Nov. 1, the first witness to testify was Lieutenant Scott, who provided the court with what he saw on the evening of Aug. 7 in the officers' club room: "Major Reno came to the billiard room about tattoo, played billiards, took a good many drinks of whiskey, he picked up a chair. . .and threw it against the partition between the billiard room and barroom, after it fell to the floor, he picked it up and punched it against the window near the barroom [and] broke out one pane of glass." Asked about Reno's condition when the window was broken, Scott testified Reno "could walk straight, and had full possession of his mental faculties," but after leaving the club at 1:30 in the morning "the liquor had taken such effect upon him that he fell down three times." Under cross examination, Scott agreed that if the chair had been "violently and wantonly thrown" against the window, the entire sash "would have been broken to pieces," but also thought the window had been broken intentionally.[31]

Doctor Bell was the next witness for the prosecution and testified he heard Nicholson tell Reno "that he could whip [him] any day, or any way that he wanted to fight," and Reno paid no attention to the remark until it had been repeated several more times and then Reno hit Nicholson with the pool cue. After the fight was broken up, Bell said, the threat of arrest made by Lieutenant Pettit was addressed to Nicholson and not to Reno. Concerning the evening of Aug. 7 and the broken window, Bell testified that Reno "was not drunk while I was there" and had full possession of his mental faculties. He also thought Reno "was slightly under the influence of liquor" at the Fanshawe residence on the night of Aug. 3.[32] Doctor Brechemin, who was also at the club room on the evening of Aug. 7, followed Bell on the stand. He testified Reno "was sitting on the top of a chair, pretending it was a horse, a piece of fun, [and] shortly afterwards he picked up the same chair and giving it a toss broke two panes of glass in the window of the club room. He expressed no malice towards anyone during the evening and these acts were done seemingly more in a spirit of fun than anything else. I regarded him simply good humorously drunk."[33]

Post trader Fanshawe was the next to testify. On the evening of Aug. 3 at his home, he "thought he [Reno] was a little under the influence of liquor…he was a little drowsy and his utterance a little thick," but Reno did not insult him or his wife in any way that evening.[34] Edward Johnson, the next witness, stated he "observed no signs of intoxication of Colonel Reno or others at the table" during that same evening and noticed Reno was quiet during the meal. He also testified that when Fanshawe and he had gone into an adjoining room, Mrs. Fanshawe came in and handed him a cigar and said, "For heavens sake don't offer Colonel Reno any more to drink." Johnson's testimony ended the 6th day of the trial.

Johnson, a witness for the prosecution, was recalled when the court convened the following morning. He thought Reno had "three drinks, probably four. One at his house, and two or three at the table of Mr. Fanshawe's house," but some whiskey remained in the glass when Reno left the table. Asked why he had offered Reno help getting down off the porch, he replied, "The step was high, he was a stout man and Mrs. Fanshawe's remark caused me to think possibly he might need it."[35]

Garlington was called as the next witness and testified he saw Reno standing on the walk in front of Colonel Sturgis' house about half past 10 on the evening of Nov. 10. When summoned to the Sturgis residence by the colonel himself, he indicated that when he arrived, the women were "very much excited," especially Miss Sturgis.[36]

Lieutenant Spilman took the stand and stated he had seen Reno on the pathway walking away from the Sturgis house at between half past 10 and 11 o'clock. He said he saw Ella Sturgis in the sitting room twice that evening, once just before passing the major on the walk, and again about 30 to 45 minutes later. The second time, he testified, "Her features were considerably distorted," and he considered going to the house "but taking a step or two towards the house I saw General Sturgis smoking in the sitting room and thought nothing could be the matter."[37] Following Spilman was Lieutenant Starr who confirmed that he had seen Reno on the walkway in front of the officers quarters between 10 and 11 o'clock on the evening in question.[38]

The final witness for the day was Colonel Sturgis, who went into particulars about that evening's events, almost to the point of being melodramatic. His description of Ella's condition demonstrated this clearly:

> She seemed in great state of excitement and alarm and very pale after this was all over, and I returned, and we were talking it over. She was in such a nervous and shaky condition that we were fearful that she might be taken by something like Saint Vitus dance and so expressed it at the time, and all tried to quiet her on that account.[39]

Sturgis returned to the stand the following morning with a floor plan of his house showing the location of the sitting room and its side window. He was asked if Reno was "on social visiting relations with your family at the time of the alleged offense." Reno objected to the question but was overruled by the court and Sturgis was required to respond: "This is a very difficult question to answer. Social covers a large ground. So far as my family are concerned, he certainly was not on cordial visiting relations." Sturgis then related the story about how Reno came to his house Oct. 1 when he was away, spent two hours there, and would not have even been received if the colonel had been at home.[40]

Ella Sturgis was the next witness and her testimony would end the session for the day. She provided a detailed account of what occurred in the sitting room on the night of Oct. 25 after hearing a noise and saw something at the side window:

Some little time elapsed when I heard a noise and saw the same thing, but even then I could not suppose anyone could come to a side window so thought nothing of it until a moment afterwards. I heard someone *tap on the window* and looked just in time to see a figure jump back. Just then I said "Mother, there is someone at that window." When I sat forward and looked out into the darkness and saw a face gradually appear. I sat paralyzed, my eyes met Major Reno's. He evidently saw no one in the room but myself…his eyes were fixed on mine. I was so frightened I could not move and was only able to say above a whisper, "Mama, it is Major Reno," several times I repeated his name…. When I first said it Mama replied no it is not, as if it could not be possible, but when she saw the state that I was in and when I repeated his name, she said, "Ella run," but I could not move, and it was only when I heard mother run [and] leave the room, and call for father who was upstairs, I had strength enough to get out of the chair and over into the corner which was between the fireplace and front window. I should have said some time ago that the face was immediately against the pane, and that I saw Major Reno for at least six seconds. My impression at first was that I would be shot if I moved for I knew that he must have feelings against father, and as his face was very pale, and he looked as if he was about to do something desperate, very excited, and his expression was that of anger, and as if to threaten…[and] if he had waited five minutes…he would have probably found me alone…. [Y]ou can imagine what a state I was in that night, twitching and nervous as I could be, almost Saint Vitus Dance, when papa found me.[41]

Following Ella's testimony Reno chose not to cross-examine her.

When the trial continued Thursday, Dec. 4, the first witness of the day, Mrs. Fanshawe, would also be the last witness to testify for the prosecution. She said that the impression Reno made on her the night he had supper at the Fanshawe house was "that of being disgustingly drunk," and "the disgusting part in my estimation was when Major Reno had the hiccups. I did not know at what moment he might be ill." She also testified that when Reno arrived at her home that night, she "did not notice that he was under the influence of liquor in the slightest." At this point the judge advocate rested his case and Reno, acting as his own defense counsel, recalled Mrs. Fanshawe as his first defense witness. She indicated Reno had been helpful during the day after the trading post fire, and that he had not insulted her in either speech or action in any way.[42]

Miss Ella Sturgis
(Robert Lee Collection)

Reno then called Major Irwin, Medical Department, from his place on the board to testify for the defense. He tried to make the case that his acting drowsy at the Fanshawe residence resulted from moving from the cold porch to a small and close dining room. Irwin stated, "It possibly might, in some cases in going from a cold atmosphere to a warm room, the heat or change of temperature produce considerable effect upon some people."[43] The witness was excused and Lieutenant Scott was called to the stand. Asked if the chair tossing occurrence at the club room Aug. 7 was not unusual, as Scott had previously testified, what were some of the worst things Scott had witnessed at the club room. A series of objections were raised to this question that were finally sustained by the court and Scott was dismissed without answering any further questions.[44]

Reno then recalled Colonel Sturgis as a defense witness. Reno inquired: "Have you not a note of apology written by me to your wife and daughter jointly?" The judge advocate objected on the grounds that the note was not referred to in any of the charges and specifications. Reno indicated it was an explanation of his motive for why he stopped and looked into the sitting room window. The court sustained the objection by the judge advocate and Sturgis, like Scott, was dismissed without providing a response.[45]

Reno then had himself sworn as a witness for the defense and proceeded to both ask and answer the questions. He first described the Nicholson incident of Oct. 25 and why he finally ended up striking him with the pool cue. Moving on to the incident at the Sturgis home, Reno said in response to his own question of where he was on the night of Nov. 10, "in answer to that question, I want to submit to the court the original draught of a note of apology which I sent to the ladies of the house." When he had completed the reading of the apology note, the court was adjourned for the day.[46]

Reno resumed his testimony the following day, continuing with the episode at the Sturgis house, and referring to Ella's comment about the possibility of being shot, stated: "I never carry a pistol, except on a scout, and my first inquiring after hearing the testimony of Miss Sturgis was on going to my quarters as to where my pistol was. For I did not know myself." Concerning the incident at the Fanshawe residence, he said he "took two drinks, not consuming all of the second one, as I felt a sensation which I could not account for. I was not in a state of intoxication, as I know that I can stand more whiskey than I drank, and when I got in the open air, I went to my quarters and bed without any assistance."

Reno described the evening of Aug. 7 at the club room and how knocking the change from the bartender's hand created some amusement among those present. When Smythe offered him the change a second time, "I did likewise.

It was in the purest spirit of pleasantry and without any other thought than that of fun." Reno then stated he had no further evidence for the defense.[47]

Captain Sanders, who had originally objected to Reno's apology being introduced into the record, now, after hearing the contents of the apology, thought "that it would have been ungenerous of [Sturgis'] part not to have accepted Major Reno's apology…if he had believed them to have been his real motives." Sanders wanted to be allowed to produce witnesses in rebuttal to show that Reno was not actuated by the motive set forth in the apology. Reno objected "on the ground that my motive cannot be legally controverted after the testimony of myself." The court did not sustain Reno's objection and Sanders called Mrs. Fanshawe back to the stand. Asked about a conversation she had with Reno on Nov. 9, she stated Reno threatened to bring Ella Sturgis to the stand during his court-martial. She said he didn't tell her how he would do it and she "wondered what he could possibly do to force her upon the stand." She had been at the Sturgis residence Nov. 12 when Reno's apology arrived, and it had been read to her. Asked if she expressed any opinion at that time as to its truth she replied, "to me the explanation did not seem true."[48]

Reno was extremely displeased with Mrs. Fanshawe's testimony, which implied that the only motive he had to look into Ella's window was just to force her to testify at his court-martial. He called Garlington back to the stand and asked him about a conversation the two had at Reno's quarters Nov. 11 about placing a certain witness on the stand. Garlington stated the conversation referred to Miss Sturgis and that Reno had told him emphatically, "He made no such threats and that the person or persons who said so told a goddamn lie." Garlington also related that someone else had told him Reno had threatened to bring Miss Sturgis before the court but he could not remember who told him. The court finally realized the testimony of Mrs. Fanshawe and Lieutenant Garlington on the subject of bringing a specific witness to testify was irrelevant and wanted no more such testimony.[49]

Reno wanted to call one more witness to testify about his motives in writing the letter of apology. The court agreed and Captain Frederick Benteen was called to the stand. Benteen said he was at Reno's quarters Nov. 11 and Reno had read him the letter of apology, but Reno had not expressed his true motives. Just as he was asked to explain what he meant by the true motive, the court was closed for deliberation by the panel — the subject of the discussion was not stated in the court records. When the court reopened, but before Benteen could continue his testimony, Colonel Sturgis asked the court to allow him to appear before the court as "assisting prosecutor." He thought the judge advocate had "not taken cognizance of one or two important points in the ruling of evidence." Sturgis claimed there were rulings "on the books of law which if followed would absolutely rule the present witness out of the chair and all similar witnesses." Reno told the court "that the remarks of Colonel Sturgis were not admissible," and the court agreed, refusing to allow Sturgis to act as an "assisting prosecutor."[50] The court then adjourned to meet the following day.

Benteen was the first witness to take the stand when the court convened Saturday, Dec. 6. The court informed Benteen to "strictly confine himself to an answer of this question" concerning Reno's real motive for writing the apology to Mrs. Sturgis and Ella. Benteen replied, "He [Reno] did not express all that he meant and felt. That he was dead in love with the young lady, was my belief." Benteen was then asked, "Do you know or believe, whether or not this letter was written in good faith with honorable motives fully up to its expression." Sanders objected to the question on the grounds "that the witness could only give his opinion of the accused's good faith and honorable motive, and that only facts or acts could be given to rebut the evidence." The court overruled the judge advocate and Benteen answered, "I believe it was, but I believe that it was not fully up to what he meant or felt."[51]

Reno then took the stand and in response to a question about threats to Ella Sturgis responded: "When I was first arraigned I asked the judge advocate if the party in question was coming on the stand, but at the time of making my plea he could not tell me. Later on when he was informed that the daughter of Colonel Sturgis would be called as a witness I went to him and said I would change my pleas in regard to this specification by permission of the court if, by it, it would prevent her appearing. This was my action which I think would show my motive. I never made such threats."

This concluded Reno's presentation of witnesses and evidence for his defense and he requested an adjournment of the court under Monday, Dec. 8, to prepare his defense statement. The court agreed and was adjourned.[52]

The only proceeding on the trial's final day was Reno reading his 11-page defense statement. He stepped carefully through each of the specifications, conceding most of the facts as presented during the trial with the major exception of being drunk at the Fanshawe residence. Concerning the incident with Ella, Reno asserted he had not entered the grounds in stealth or surreptitiously, but boldly, and did not peer into the window but looked in boldly. He brought out that even the judge advocate thought Colonel Sturgis was "ungenerous" in not accepting his apology.

Reno knew he was the target of those who had admired Custer and still considered him to be the cause of Custer's death: "It has been my misfortune to have attained a wide spread notoriety through the country by means of the press, open to my enemies 'who know not why they are so, but like the village cur, bark when their fellows do' and a greater degree of attention will be called to what I do than other officers not so widely advertised."

He cited his 22 years of service to his country and, using O'Brien's "Treatise on Military Law," made a strong point of the differences between acts which are such that the accused forfeits "all claim to the character of a gentleman," and those which are "youthful follies or trivial deviations from rectitude [virtue] such as the best of men may fall into in an unguarded or excited moment." Reno stated his offenses fall into the second category and not the first. He thanked the court "for the patience and kindness shown me through this somewhat protracted trial and I conveniently rely upon the wisdom, justice and impartiality of its findings."[53]

The court was then cleared and met to decide on the verdict. Records do not indicate how long the panel met or when the court was finally adjourned. Their findings were:

> On the first specification (the Nicholson incident) Reno was found guilty, except the words "create and," "disreputable," and "and did persist in continuing said disturbance until threatened with arrest by 2nd Lieutenant James S. Pettit, 1st U.S. Infantry," and "to the scandal and disgrace of the military service," where he was found not guilty.
>
> On the second specification (the chair tossing incident) Reno was found guilty, except the words "wantonly and in a riotous manner," "in a wanton and riotous manner," and "to the scandal and disgrace of the military service," where he was found not guilty.
>
> On the third specification (at the Fanshawe residence), Reno was found guilty, except the words "disgusting," and "to the scandal and disgrace of the military service," where he was found not guilty.
>
> On the charge "conduct unbecoming an officer and gentleman," associated with these three specifications, Reno was found not guilty, but was found guilty of "conduct to the prejudice of good order and military discipline."

The change in wording of the three specifications made them considerably less serious and with the finding of guilty on the charge of "conduct to the prejudice of good order and military discipline," instead of "conduct unbecoming an officer and gentleman," Reno would not lose his commission but would be sentenced to a lengthy suspension. However, the findings on the additional charge and specification could provide the coup de grace:

On the specification (at the Sturgis residence) Reno was found guilty, except the words "surreptitiously," "and so stealthily," and "very seriously," where he was found not guilty.

On the charge "conduct unbecoming an officer and gentleman," associated with this specification, Reno was found guilty.

The sentence for being found guilty on the additional charge was automatic as stated in the 61st Article of War: "To be dismissed from the military service of the United States."[54] Five members of the court — Wood, Alexander, Irwin, Moore and Conrad — found the punishment of dismissal to be too severe for the incurred infractions and signed a recommendation:

> The court having thus performed the painful duty of awarding punishment in strict conformity to an article of war which deprived it of all discretionary power, begs leave to recommend the case of Major Marcus A. Reno, 7th Cavalry, to the merciful consideration of the confirming authority.[55]

Otis and Shafter did not sign the recommendation but records do not indicate why.

Reno, of course, would not know the findings of the court until it was endorsed by the authorities up to and including President Hayes. However, the defense statement Reno provided to the court on the final day of the trial had convinced the local newspapers to predict his acquittal:

> *Black Hills Journal*: Major Reno will not be convicted. We think the Major ought to be transferred to another regiment. The good of the service demands it, as well as justice to himself. He will always be an element of discord in the Seventh Cavalry.[56]
>
> *Black Hills Times*: Newspapers throughout the length and breadth of our country, which attacked Major Reno in a very savage, thoughtless and inhumane manner upon the first publication of the charges against him, have since been set right on the subject by the *Times*, and are now doing him the simple justice he deserves, by giving the facts in his case. If the members of the court-martial render an unbiased verdict, which in all probability they will, Major Reno will not suffer to the extent that his accusers are bound to, by the late Fort Meade farce, and we have no hesitancy, in view of the evidence, to predict his acquittal on the charges preferred. That Reno has been as much sinned against as sinning there is no room for doubt, according to the evidence of

his accusers. The only offenses remaining against him — if they can be termed offenses — are the facts of the major's conviviality, and of looking into Col. Sturgis' library room window.[57]

On Dec. 16, 1879, Major Thomas Barr, judge advocate, prepared an eight-page review of the case for the department commander. He carefully studied the evidence presented in the case and stated: "[I] find myself unable to agree with the Court, in their judgment that the sentence of dismissal, which is adjudged, is warranted by the proved conduct of Major Reno." Barr thought "the court would have been justified in acquitting him of the additional charge and its specification," at the Sturgis residence as it had found him "not guilty of the most serious parts of the specification, those which characterized the circumstances of his entry to the yard and approach to the window — those eliminated, there is but little left." The looking in the window, which Reno admitted, was not, in Barr's mind, an act "which came within the purview of the 61st Article of War." Concerning Mrs. Fanshawe's testimony about Reno stating to her that he would bring Ella Sturgis to the stand in his court-martial, then going to the Sturgis residence and looking into the sitting room to attract Ella's attention just to bring her to the stand, Barr wrote, "It is difficult to believe that any sane man would be guilty of adopting such a measure." He commented on the fact that five of seven members of the court recommended clemency and had only adjudged the penalty of dismissal "because it was mandatory under the additional charge." He agreed with the findings of the court on the first charge and specifications, and thought while the fight between Reno and Nicholson was "highly discreditable to both those officers, there was some excuse for the assault made by the former." Barr then signed the report and forwarded it to Terry.[58]

More than two weeks had passed since the completion of the trial and while Reno had heard no official findings of the court, rumors reached him that the court had passed the sentence of dismissal. He sent a telegram to Secretary of War Alexander Ramsey Dec. 26: "Do not let me be dismissed. Rather resign if such conclusion be reached."[59] Terry had not yet completed his review of the case therefore Washington could do nothing about Reno's request.

Another two weeks would pass before Terry completed his review and forwarded it to Washington. He approved the findings of the court on the first charge and the three specifications. On the second charge and its specification he agreed with the recommendation of the five officers for clemency and wrote:

313

Such being the view taken of the case by these members of the Court, the finding upon this charge should not have been guilty, with a recommendation to mercy, but it should have been not guilty to the charge. Therefore the finding upon the specification to the additional charge is approved, but the finding upon the additional charge itself, is disapproved.

The sentence is manifestly excessive as a punishment for the acts of which Major Reno was found guilty, under the first charge and its specifications, but as I have no power to modify it, and so my disapproval of it would put an end to the case, leaving Major Reno without any punishment whatever, I formally approve it.

I join, however, in the recommendation of a majority of the members of the Court, that it be modified.[60]

When Terry's report, with Major Barr's review attached, reached Washington, it was reviewed by the Bureau of Military Justice before being presented to the secretary of war and the president. Two officers of the bureau, Judge Advocate General W. M. Dunn and Major Henry Goodfellow, wrote reviews of the case. Dunn's 31-page report, written Jan. 21, 1880, provided a detailed review of almost every aspect of the case. He stated, "I have found myself unable to concur in all respects in the opinions expressed by them [Barr and Terry], which seem to me in some degree too lenient...and that punishment of considerable severity would seem to be forcibly demanded." He took the court to task for finding Reno not guilty of the word "disreputable" in the specification concerning the striking of Nicholson with the pool cue, of the word "wanton" in the chair-tossing specification, and of the word "disgusting" in the incident at the Fanshawe house specification. Dunn also objected to the finding of not guilty on the statement "to the scandal and disgrace of the military service," in each of three specifications to the first charge. He also disagreed with the court's finding that the fright of the ladies of the Sturgis house was "not serious; the testimony showing that one of them at least was temporarily almost paralyzed with terror, and of both the nervous shock and agitation were not only excessive at the time but in some degree dangerous." He paraphrased Barr's words when he wrote:

I am quite of the opinion that it is difficult to believe that any sane man could be guilty of the breach of decorum committed by Major Reno, with the object testified to by Mrs. Fanshawe; and no doubt his statement that he would call Miss Sturgis as a witness (assuming that Mrs. Fanshawe states the truth), may admit of some other explanation. It is possible too that his own explana-

314

tion is true, that he was led to do as he did by admiration and by no improper motive. But whatever his motive, it seems to me that his act, even if not done stealthily and surreptitiously, was, in view of his condition of arrest at the time and his relations with his commanding officer and his family, one of the gravest violations of the obligation of a gentleman he could have committed…nor in my opinion can such an outrageous offense as his was, be claimed to have been condoned and wiped out by a letter of apology, no matter how profuse.

Dunn now had to make his final recommendation as to approving or disapproving the findings and sentence of the court:

> I have with some difficulty brought myself to believe that even dismissal from the service, severe as such a punishment is, is [not] too severe for the succession of excesses of which Major Reno has been found guilty. My opinion is clear that if commutation be deemed expedient and just, Major Reno's present (and past) offenses against the rules which should govern the conduct of officers and gentlemen cannot claim any great extent of lenity.[61]

On Jan. 29, General Sherman reviewed the proceedings of the court and made his recommendation about the sentence of dismissal:

> In view of the recommendation of members of the General Court Martial in the case of Major Reno, and of the concurring recommendation of the Department Commander, it is respectfully recommended, that the sentence of the Court be modified to a suspension from command for the space of one year with a loss of half pay, and that during the time of such suspension Major Reno be confined to the limits of the Post where the Headquarters of his Regiment may be, and that he be reduced five files in the list of Majors of Cavalry.[62]

The final review of the case was conducted by Major Goodfellow, who again went over every aspect of the evidence and the conclusions of the court. He acknowledged that Terry disapproved the finding of the additional charge but did approve the finding of the first charge and specifications. He cited the opinion of the judge advocate general if "lenity is to be again shown Major Reno…it should not be any great extent of lenity," and noted Sherman's recommendation of suspension for one year and the reduction of five files in rank. Goodfellow suggested that if Sherman's recommendation were accepted, Reno's confinement should be somewhere besides the 7th Cavalry's headquarters "because in view of the gross indecorum shown by Major Reno towards Colonel Sturgis and his family, it is probable that the colonel would prefer that the prisoner should be at some other post than his own." Goodfellow's conclusion appeared to dismiss the recommendations of Barr, Terry and Sherman:

> The case however may be regarded as presenting the serious question whether Major Reno's recent history in the light of this and a former trial does not demonstrate him as unfit to retain his commission.
>
> Whether he is not shown to be deficient in that respect to the female sex which is so essential a motive to every man's self respect, and whether he is not a pernicious example to younger men who should look up to an officer of his years as an example of decency and respectability rather than as a leader in vice and immorality!
>
> While the Government is dismissing lieutenants and young captains, and sending wayward cadets home to their distressed mothers should it show undue mercy to an officer of mature years who has once already disregarded most impressive admonitions. [63]

Goodfellow forwarded his report to the secretary of war, who would make the final recommendation to President Hayes. Meanwhile, Reno was still under post arrest at Fort Meade awaiting the final decision. The same rumors he had heard in December indicating the sentence of the court was dismissal, and to which he responded by sending the "do not let me be dismissed" telegram, now suggested that recommendations had been made to modify it. With this information Reno decided he stood a good chance at keeping his commission, and at 4:30 p.m., March 16, sent a telegram to Secretary of War Ramsey: "I withdraw request to resign."[64] Ironically on the same day, March 16, Hayes wrote his endorsement: "The sentence in the foregoing case of Major Marcus A. Reno 7th Cavalry is confirmed."[65]

On March 17, 1880, the Adjutant General's Office issued General Court-Martial Orders No. 20:

> III. By direction of the Secretary of War, the sentence in the case of Major Marcus A. Reno, 7th Cavalry, will take effect April

1, 1880, from which date he will cease to be an officer of the Army.[66]

The following day at Fort Meade, Reno was stunned when informed of the decision of the secretary of war and the president. A career that spanned more than 28 years as a cadet and soldier was over, but he was not willing to give up without a fight. On the same day he wrote to the Secretary of War's Office requesting a copy of the proceeding of his general court-martial, and that he would like it completed by the time he reached Washington.[67] It would be a battle that would last for the rest of his life.

Endnotes

[1] *Army and Navy Journal*, issue of April 12, 1879. There is no record the suit was ever filed.

[2] Record & Pension Office, War Department, Item 2259 ACP 1879, letter from Reno to E. D. Townsend, Adjutant General, Record Group 94, NARA.

[3] Item 2336 ACP 1879, also in Reno's personal file R314 CB 1865, Record Group 94, NARA.

[4] Item 2314 ACP 1879.

[5] *Harrisburg Daily Telegraph*, May 8, 1879.

[6] *Black Hills Times*, June 19 and July 4 issues.

[7] *Bismarck Tribune*, Dec. 16, 1879.

[8] Proceedings of a General Court-Martial, QQ1554, Records of the Judge Advocate General, Record Group 153, NARA, p. 83.

[9] Court-martial, 1879, p. 48.

[10] Court-martial, 1879, p. 81.

[11] Court-martial, 1879, p. 52.

[12] There appears to be some confusion about the date. The bartender Smythe says the 8th; Scott says the 7th but later does not object when questioned when he is asked if he was in the club room on the 8th; Brechemin says the 7th; and Reno says the 7th. It is irrelevant as to whether it was the 7th or 8th.

[13] Court-martial, 1879, pp. 34-35.

[14] Robert Lee, *Fort Meade and the Black Hills* (University of Nebraska Press, Lincoln, 1991), p. 255, and the *Bismarck Tribune*, issue of May 24, 1879.

[15] "Pettigrew Visits the Black Hills," *The Sunshine State, South Dakota's Own Magazine*, March 1926, p. 39.

[16] "Pettigrew Visits the Black Hills," p. 39.

[17] Court-martial, 1879, pp. 72-73.

[18] Court-martial, 1879, pp. 87-88.

[19] Court-martial, 1879, pp. 13-14.

[20] General Court-Martial Orders No. 20, Headquarters of the Army, Adjutant General's Office, Washington, March 17, 1880.

[21] Court-martial Orders No. 20.

[22] Court-martial, 1879, pp. 75-77.

[23] Court-martial, 1879, p. 56.

[24] Court-martial, 1879, p. 90.

[25] Court-Martial Orders No. 20.

[26] Court-martial, 1879, pp. 89-90. This was read into the record by Reno during the court-martial and the original note sent to the Sturgis family was not included in the records. In his original note to Mrs. Sturgis Reno used the phrase "as I would walk on parade." The note read into the court records said, "as I would walk into this Court room." In his defense statement he used the phrase, "as I would walk on parade."

[27] Special Orders No. 128, Nov. 13, 1879.

[28] Court-martial, 1879, pp. 12-18.

[29] Court-martial, 1879, p. 23.

[30] Court-martial, 1879, pp. 28-31.

[31] Court-martial, 1879, pp. 34-38.

[32] Court-martial, 1879, pp. 39-43.

[33] Court-martial, 1879, pp. 44-45.

[34] Court-martial, 1879, pp. 46-47.

[35] Court-martial, 1879, pp. 50-53.

[36] Court-martial, 1879, pp. 54-55.

[37] Court-martial, 1879, p. 60.

[38] Court-martial, 1879, p. 62.

[39] Court-martial, 1879, p. 64.

[40] Court-martial, 1879, p. 72.

[41] Court-martial, 1879, pp. 76-78. The italics are the author's — the definition of a "peeping Tom" is "one who derives pleasure from prudently and secretly spying on others." Tapping on the window could scarcely be considered "secretly" and remaining there for the six seconds Ella testified to, certainly indicates he wanted to be seen.

[42] Court-martial, 1879, pp. 81-83.

[43] Court-martial, 1879, p. 84.

[44] Court-martial, 1879, p. 85.

[45] Court-martial, 1879, p. 86.

[46] Court-martial, 1879, pp. 87-91.

[47] Court-martial, 1879, pp. 93-97.

[48] Court-martial, 1879, pp. 98-99.

[49] Court-martial, 1879, pp. 100-01.

[50] Court-martial, 1879, pp. 102-03.

[51] Court-martial, 1879, pp. 105-06.

[52] Court-martial, 1879, pp. 106-07.

[53] Court-martial, 1879, p. 109, and Exhibit "E."

[54] Court-martial, 1879, pp. 109-10.

[55] Court-martial, 1879, p. 114.

[56] *Black Hills* (Dakota Territory) *Journal*, Rapid City, Dec. 6, 1879.

[57] *Black Hills* (Dakota Territory) *Times*, Deadwood, Dec. 13, 1879.

[58] Report of Major Thomas Barr, Dec. 16, 1879, attached to the court-martial, 1879.

[59] Telegram, Reno to Ramsey, Fort Meade, Dakota Territory, Dec. 26, 1879, attached to the court-martial, 1879.

[60] Headquarters Department of Dakota, Saint Paul, Minn., Jan. 10, 1880, Terry's report to Ramsey, attached to the court-martial, 1879.

[61] War Department, Bureau of Military Justice, Jan. 21, 1880, attached to the court-martial, 1879. It is apparent from the tone of the review that the word "not" was left out due to a clerical error.

[62] Headquarters of the Army, Washington, D.C., Jan. 29, 1880, attached to the court-martial, 1879. The reduction of five files in the list of majors would cost Reno several years for an opportunity for promotion to lieutenant colonel.

[63] War Department, Bureau of Military Justice, Jan. 30, 1880, attached to the court-martial, 1879.

[64] Telegram from Reno to Ramsey, March 16, 1880, attached to the court-martial, 1879.

[65] Executive Mansion, Washington, D.C., March 16, 1880, attached to the court-martial, 1879.

[66] Headquarters of the Army, Adjutant General's Office, General Court Martial Order No. 20, March 17, 1880, Washington, D.C.

[67] Reno to Dunn, March 18, 1880, Fort Mead, D.T., attached to the court-martial, 1879.

• 16 •

Quest for Reinstatement

Even before Marcus Reno left Fort Meade, criticism arose in the military of the harsh sentence confirmed by President Hayes. The *Army and Navy Journal*, widely circulated in the military community, commented:

> The punishment would appear to be a severe one in the case of an officer of twenty-nine (sic) years service, for the offenses proven, but it is evident that Major Reno's previous escapade had left him no reserve of leniency upon which to draw for favorable judgment in this case.[1]

Reno departed Fort Meade April 1, traveling by rail to Chicago and on to Harrisburg, where he arrived about April 5. He remained in Harrisburg for only a day before traveling to Washington, D.C., to pick up the requested copy of the court-martial transcript. He received a copy at the War Department April 7, but noted it was missing the report to General Terry from Major Barr, judge advocate, Department of Dakota. Reno requested a copy of Barr's report that same day and the War Department provided it April 8. For the first time Reno was able to read the recommendation of five members of the court that they found the punishment of dismissal too severe, and Barr's finding that dismissal was not warranted by the evidence presented. Reno now believed he had a strong case for reinstatement and wasted little time before talking to two elected officials from Illinois, Senator David Davis and Representative James W. Singleton, about the introduction of a bill to reinstate him as a major of cavalry.

Reno still had considerable assets from the estate of his late wife Mary Hannah, plus the income from the lease of the Front Street property in Harrisburg and the farm in New Cumberland County, all of which would at least provide a modest means of support. He borrowed $1,000 from Ross' estate, with the permission of both Ross and his financial guardian, Lyman Gilbert, to hire the necessary legal counsel needed to continue to pursue his case in Congress.[2] Reno's objective was to return to the Army as quickly as possible — it was his career and the only occupation he had known for almost 30 years. While a major's income was only $300 a month, when combined with government-furnished housing, it provided him with a comfortable living and he enjoyed the military social life.

On Reno's departure from the Army April 1, Captain Edward Ball, 2nd Cavalry, senior captain of cavalry, was nominated for promotion to the open position of major, 7th Cavalry. Ball received the confirmation of the Senate and on April 23, 1880, acknowledged the receipt of his new commission.[3]

On April 23, less than two weeks after Reno had talked to Senator Davis, a bill, S. 1657, was introduced into the Senate and referred to the Committee on Military Affairs. The previous day the committee chairman, Senator Theodore F. Randolph of New Jersey, sent a letter to the secretary of war:

> Please furnish his [Reno's] military record and copies of reports, letters and orders relating to his service in the U.S. Army, for the consideration of the case by the Committee on Military Affairs.[4]

Five days later a similar bill, H.R. 5977, was introduced by Congressman Singleton into the House of Representatives:

A BILL
For the relief of Marcus A. Reno

> Be it enacted by the Senate and House of Representatives of the United States of America in Congress assembled, that the President be, and he is hereby, authorized to nominate and, by and with the advice and consent of the Senate, appoint Marcus A. Reno, late a major of the Seventh Cavalry, a major of cavalry in the Army of the United States, with his former rank and date of commission, and that he shall be assigned to the first vacancy occurring in such grade in the cavalry arm of the service: Provided, however, that he shall only receive pay from the date of appointment under this act.[5]

The information requested by Senator Randolph included Terry's report on the 1876 campaign, the enlisted men's petition, the 1877 court-martial transcript, and a summary of the court of inquiry. Reno had a copy made of his 1879 court-martial and its endorsements and furnished it directly to

Randolph's committee.[6] Reno left Washington about April 20 and returned to Harrisburg to consult with his friend and counsel Lyman Gilbert. Reno asked Gilbert to represent him in the pursuit of his case for reinstatement. Gilbert declined because of his duties as assistant attorney general for Pennsylvania, but suggested a prestigious law firm in New York, Lord, Van Dyke & Lord, that could provide the legal and political advice Reno needed to gain back his commission. Reno traveled to New York and discussed the case with Scott Lord, a partner of the law firm, who accepted the case. Lord immediately requested full copies of Reno's 1877 and 1879 courts-martial from the Adjutant General's office. Its reply indicated that Reno had a full copy of the 1879 court-martial that he could provide to his counsel, and it would furnish Lord with a summary of the 1877 court-martial but thought it unnecessary to provide full copies of each trial.[7]

The Bureau of Military Justice sent the documents requested by Senator Randolph to the Adjutant General's Office May 20, and they were forwarded to the Committee on Military Affairs. The committee did not have sufficient time to study the large volume of provided information before Congress adjourned June 16, 1880. Reno would have to wait for any further action on the Senate bill until Congress was called back into the "lame duck" session scheduled to begin Dec. 16, 1880.

Reno spent the next six months at either the Lochiel Hotel in Harrisburg or in New York awaiting Congress to return to session. He went to Washington in late September and stayed at the home of an old friend, General James McBride. Reno used the occasion to write to the adjutant general Oct. 2, requesting copies of letters "as may contain commendatous reports of my character as an officer and are in file in the War Department."[8] The reply, dated Oct. 4, stated:

> [I]t is the rule of the Department to furnish copies of official records only to Congress or the committees thereof.... [I]n May last the Senate Military Committee, in response to its request for your military records, copies of papers, etc., was provided with copies of all letters and reports of a commendatory character which are of record, in connection with your conduct in the battle with Indians June 25 and 26, 1876, together with copies of proceedings of the courts-martial in your case in 1877 and 1879, and of transcripts of your military records.[9]

Reno decided he still wanted copies of the letters that were "commendatory of my conduct during the war" and wrote from the National Hotel in

Washington directly to the secretary of war Nov. 8 with his request. The records indicate a number of items were sent to Reno Nov. 11, 1880.[10]

While in New York, Reno met and started courting an attractive widow, Isabella Ray McGunnegle, 48. She had been married to Navy Lieutenant Commander Wilson McGunnegle, who had died a few years earlier. Isabella had three grown children: 25-year-old 1st Lieutenant George K. McGunnegle, 15th Infantry; 23-year-old Catherine; and 21-year-old Ray. She was living alone when she met Reno and seemed pleased to have an escort to visit the sights of the big city. At the time, she was working as a $75 a month government clerk and receiving a government pension of $30 a month from the military service rendered by her late husband.

Congress reconvened Dec. 6, 1880, but it would be another two months before Reno's bill for reinstatement would be reported out of committee. On Feb. 7, 1881, Senator Ambrose E. Burnside, Rhode Island, submitted the committee's findings:

> The Committee on Military Affairs, to whom was referred the bill (S. 1657) for the relief of Marcus A. Reno, having duly considered the same, beg leave to submit the following report:
> Upon examining the voluminous papers filed in connection with this bill, and from their personal knowledge of the circumstances attending the dismissal of Major Reno, your committee do not feel justified in recommending the passage of the bill. They therefore report the bill back adversely, and recommend its indefinite postponement.[11]

The House of Representatives bill appeared to have died in committee without being reported — apparently the adverse report of the Senate made the reporting of the House bill a moot point. The next regularly scheduled session of Congress, now the 47th, was Dec. 5, 1881, and although there was two special sessions of the Senate before that time, no new bill for "the relief of Marcus A. Reno" was introduced.

Reno had rented a flat at 320 Indiana Ave. in Washington which provided him with close access to the Capital's facilities. He was able to obtain copies of the information provided to the Senate committee and, for the first time, read Terry's disapproval of the guilty finding on the second charge and his recommendation that the sentence be modified, Sherman's endorsement of suspension instead of dismissal, and the reports from the Bureau of Military Justice written by Judge Advocate General W. M. Dunn and Major Henry Goodfellow. The wide disparity between the recommendations of Barr and Terry, and those of Dunn and Goodfellow, lead Reno to believe that a gross injustice had occurred in his dismissal. On March 10, 1882, he wrote to the new Secretary of War Robert Todd Lincoln:

> Among the copies of papers submitted upon the request of the Senate Military Committee was the revision of the Court Martial proceedings in my case by the late Judge Advocate General: so great and striking was the disparity between that and the reviews by General A. H. Terry, Commanding Department of Dakota, and Colonel T. F. Barr, Judge Advocate, of same department, I am convinced that injustice was attempted to be done me, because of the prejudice entertained against me and that in the composition of his endorsement, personal spite and malice actuated the late Judge Advocate General; In view of this fact and that such a record may not stand against me, I respectfully request, that a re-review of the proceedings may be made by the present incumbent of that office.[12]

Robert Todd Lincoln, son of the assassinated president, had succeeded Ramsey as secretary of war March 3 when the administration of James A. Garfield took office. Holding his first public office, Lincoln referred Reno's letter to the new Judge Advocate General David G. Swaim, who had replaced Dunn Feb. 18. Swaim had been in the Bureau of Military Justice for 11 years prior to his promotion so it would be expected he would defend the decisions made by his predecessor. On March 11, he wrote a private response to the secretary of war:

> I have carefully examined the extended report of the Judge Advocate General, of Jan. 21, 1880, in the case of Major M. A. Reno, 7th Infantry (sic), in connection with a review of the testimony contained in the record of his trail, and I am unable to perceive that any substantial injustice has been done him in that report or in the final action of the President upon his case.... The offenses for which the accused was last tried, as exhibited by the evidence, appear to me to have been, on the whole, scarcely less discreditable to a member of the military profession than were those on account of which he was originally dismissed. The fact of a repetition by the officer of most unmilitary and ungentleman like acts so soon after the exercise in his case of the exceptional clemency extended to him after the first trial, would of itself go far to deter me from recommending a favorable consideration of the present application. But, upon the testimony alone, as set

forth in the record of the last trial, I am of opinion that the conclusion thereon of the court martial did no real injustice to this officer, but were rather indulgent to him than otherwise, and that, in the absence of any new evidence now produced by the applicant, he must be deemed to have been rightfully dismissed from the military service.

In declining to pass favorably upon the matter of Mr. Reno's within communication to the Secretary of War, I may remark that his charge that "personal spite and malice actuated the late Judge Advocate General," in the making of his report, is quite in keeping with the general tone of his speech and conduct as illustrated on both his trials, while being — as I need hardly add — wholly without foundation.[13]

This was not the entry Swaim placed in the summary files of the Judge Advocate General's office — the entry for March 15 read:

Respectfully returned to the Secretary of War. The case referred to in this application, so far as executive action is concerned, is legally concluded. The executive jurisdiction was exhausted in its final action. If wrong has been done or error committed, redress or correction must now be sought through congressional action.[14]

The letter addressed to Reno from Secretary of War Lincoln, dated March 18, 1881, referred to Reno's letter of March 10 and informed him that his request for a re-review had been referred to the judge advocate general. Lincoln quoted Swaim's response as stated in the summary files of the Judge Advocate General's office.[15]

Reno returned to Harrisburg in late June to sign the transfer of deeds to his brother-in-law Andrew Ross for a number of land parcels that Reno owned. He sold Ross a large lot situated in Lower Allen Township, 13 acres located at Front Street and Locust Alley, Harrisburg, and five lots on the town plan of New Cumberland, Penna. Reno received only a "token" fee of $100 for all of these land parcels, but obviously received other benefits from the sale which were not recorded.[16] Reno also found that while he was in Washington attempting to get a favorable review and a reduction of his dismissal sentence, his son Ross had run up considerable debt while living at the Lochiel Hotel. Ross had purchased, on credit, clothing, jewelry, cigars, confections, shoes, hats, plus a number of other items, "very little of which" was necessary. Lyman Gilbert had to petition the Orphans' Court of Dauphin County to get the money from Ross' trust fund to pay the debts. Marcus had to sign a statement that "as the father and guardian by nature of the said Robert Ross Reno, he concurs in the said petition and requests the court to grant the order prayed for, believing that his son has suffered great mental anxiety and trouble because of said debts and that, if he were relieved from their burden and annoyance, he would be benefited in mind and disposition and would refrain from like conduct in the future."[17] The court approved the payment of the debt. Marcus would remain with his son in the Lochiel Hotel in Harrisburg for the next several months.

In Washington July 2, just as President James Garfield was about to leave to attend his 25th reunion at Williams College, he was shot and wounded in an attempted assassination. He suffered two bullet wounds, one in the hand and the other in the back. Garfield lingered for 80 days before dying Sept. 19, 1881. Vice President Chester A. Arthur assumed the presidency at 2 a.m. Sept. 20. Arthur had not served in the Civil War, unlike his three predecessors, Grant, Hayes and Garfield, and therefore had little knowledge of Army personnel or military affairs. Reno thought Arthur might be more sympathetic than Garfield to a direct request for reinstatement. He contacted his counsel, Scott Lord, in New York City and suggested the law firm prepare a direct appeal to the new president, presenting Reno's military accomplishments during 23 years of service and a legal brief indicating why the sentence of dismissal was not valid.

On Nov. 10, 1881, Lord sent Arthur "the application of Major Marcus A. Reno and Addenda sustaining it; and a printed case based upon records in the Department of War." Lord continued:

> What induced the then President, Mr. Hayes, to confirm so extreme a sentence, which the Court under a mistaken finding was compelled to make...need not now be stated, sufficient to say that when the reviewing officer [Terry] disapproved the principal finding the proceedings fell, and by the statute the sentence could not be executed.[18]

The 14-page printed pamphlet submitted by Lord with his letter to the president included a copy of a bill "Intended to be introduced on the first legislative day of the Forty-Seventh Congress U.S." — the bill's wording was identical to the two which had failed in the previous session of Congress. Also contained in the pamphlet was Reno's military history and the findings of the 1879 court-martial with Barr's and Terry's reviews.[19]

The "application" noted by Scott requested Arthur:

[T]hat you direct his [Reno's] recognition as a "Major in the cavalry arm of the service of the United States Army,"…because the "direction" of the Secretary of War…that after April 1st, 1880 he should "cease to be an officer of the army," was without authority of law. Major Reno was tried upon two charges for "conduct unbecoming an officer and a gentleman." Of the first he was found "not guilty." Of the second he was found "guilty," and of the specifications, modified…and was sentenced to dismissal from the service, as required by the 61st Article of War. The finding requiring this was "disapproved,"…by the reviewing officer [Terry], and under Article 104 the proceedings fell, and also because he, in fact, disapproved of the sentence.[20]

The 104th Article of War stated: "No sentence of a court-martial shall be carried into execution until the whole proceedings shall have been approved by the officer ordering the court, or by the officer commanding for the time being." Terry had not approved the "whole proceedings," Lord argued, and "It follows that the execution of the sentence, after the disapproval by the reviewing officer, was illegal and all orders subsequent to such disapproval void and as void as though no court martial had been held."[21] Lord continued, "It was assumed that the then president would modify the sentence. How much wiser the law than such a lottery?"[22]

Lord concluded in his statement to Arthur:

If wrong upon the law then you are requested to take such action as will reinstate Major Reno as a major of cavalry;

First: Under his record found [in the military section of the pamphlet].

Second: Under the statements and recommendations…of five members of the court martial, of the Judge Advocate, the reviewing officer and of General Sherman.

The extent of the disorderly conduct of which he was found guilty is well stated by the Judge Advocate in his report to the commanding officer, and such officer should have said "better that such conduct go unpunished than that an officer should suffer a punishment manifestly excessive."

Major Reno has now been suspended from the service six months longer than the extremist limit…suggested by General Sherman. Has not his punishment been more than enough?[23]

The president forwarded Lord's letter and the enclosures to Secretary of War Lincoln Nov. 19 to prepare a response. Lincoln wrote a six-page memorandum beginning with an acknowledgment that Lord had made several good legal arguments:

> It is plain from the recommendation of the court, and the remarks of the reviewing officer, that if Major Reno had been tried only on the one charge, the finding on which was concurred in by the court and the Commanding General, the sentence would have been less severe than dismissal. The sentence as submitted to the President, was therefore the artificial result of a rigid form of proceeding, and presented the actual views as to punishment, of neither the court nor the reviewing officer.[24]

Lincoln then proceeded through a lengthy review of Lord's position that the sentence of dismissal was "illegal" because Terry had not approved the "whole proceedings" and therefore all orders after that event were void. One of the arguments stated by Lincoln was that with Captain Ball's appointment to major because of Reno's dismissal, no majority openings existed in the cavalry. Lincoln concluded his memorandum:

> Admitting all the argument of counsel, we reach nothing but error in the proceedings, not nullity. The court was lawful and pronounced a sentence which was not legally excessive, the sentence was formally approved by the reviewing officer, and confirmed by the President.
>
> Therefore, whether we consider the court martial or not, Major Reno, the officer dismissed, is out of the army. If the President afterwards finds that injustice has been done, he cannot undo it by annulling the order of dismissal — that is beyond his recall, but he may make amends, if it seems to him proper, by appointing the dismissed officer, by and with the advice and consent of the Senate, to any office in the Army to which he could appoint any other civilian.
>
> Section 1228, Revised Statutes, U.S.
>
> Under existing laws, the President could not appoint a civilian to be a Major of Cavalry. Such a position is filled by promotion only.
>
> Section 1204, Revised Statutes, U.S.
>
> The application therefore of Major Reno, could only be granted under legislative authority, general or special, hereafter to

be given. If special authority should be hereafter given by Congress for that purpose, the propriety of his appointment to the rank authorized, would be the subject of a discussion which would include matters not now under consideration.[25]

On Dec. 2, Lincoln sent a letter to Lord quoting almost verbatim from his memorandum. Reno had rented a room at 37 West 32nd Street in New York and had the opportunity to read Lincoln's letter when it was received by Lord. Lincoln indicated that even if trial errors had occurred, the sentence of dismissal was not nullified, and since Captain Ball was already "appointed to the office held by Major Reno...and if there had been no court martial, sentence, confirmation, or order of dismissal, this appointment would have, of itself, operated in law to supersede Major Reno, and he would thereby in virtue of the appointment of Captain Ball, have ceased to be an officer of the Army from and after, at least, the date at which the appointment took effect." Reno directed Lord to respond to Lincoln, and this Lord did in a letter to the secretary of war dated Dec. 10:

> I thank you on behalf of my client Major Reno, as well as for myself, for your courteous and considerate letter of the 2nd inst. I thought I had exhausted all the Military Law bearing on the question but I did not look in the direction enunciated in Blake v. U.S. It certainly was to me a startling proposition that the President, by and with the advice and consent of the Senate, can remove any officer in the Army, but such seems to be the law, as judicially determined, so that, a President and Senate in harmony, the officers of the army cannot be very independent, perhaps they ought not to be.
>
> In regard to the question presented by me to the President I regarded all action after the disapproval of the findings and sentence as absolutely void. I see the force of your reasoning and authorities but as a decision of the Supreme Court puts us out of the army by virtue of the nomination and confirmation of another, and would have done so if there had been "no court martial, sentence, confirmation or order of dismissal," I need not further examine the question.[26]

While in New York Reno continued to court Isabella McGunnegle and apparently they enjoyed each other's company and the varied social life the city had to offer. However, aside from enjoying the casual life, Reno was not about to concede defeat in his quest for reinstatement and contacted Colonel

Rufus Ingalls, assistant quartermaster general, and asked him to write a letter to the president on his behalf. Ingalls wrote to the president Dec. 14 and stated he would:

> [C]heerfully subscribe to the fact that his [Reno's] reinstatement to a commission in the Army would be an act of justice to a deserving officer. I have known Major Reno for almost a quarter of a century, both on the frontier and during the late civil war, and can testify to his zeal and energy and faithful discharge of duty.... After a review and consideration of the proceedings, I think, with an experience of many years in the Army, that the Executive action was harsh almost to the verge of cruelty in depriving Major Reno of a profession for which he had been educated, to which he had devoted the best years of his life, and in pursuit of which, in the defense of his country, he had often been exposed to great danger.[27]

Reno also contacted former President Grant and asked him to review the court-martial proceedings and write to President Arthur with his comments. Grant wrote Dec. 15:

> I would suggest that the President examine for himself, or through his Secretary of War or Attorney General, the proceeding in the case of Major Reno, and then take such action as in his judgment is due to the Major. It seems to me, in view of the recommendation of the Court which tried Major Reno; of the fact that he was found "not guilty" of the most serious parts of the specifications; and that the reviewing officers — the Department Commander, the Judge Advocate and the General of the Army — concur in the opinion that the Court should have found the accused "not guilty" of the charge under which alone he could have been dismissed from the Army, is a full justification for reviewing his case at this late date.[28]

Scott Lord wrote to former Secretary of War McCrary and requested his comments on the modification of Reno's 1877 court-martial sentence from dismissal to suspension for two years without pay. McCrary replied Feb. 13, 1882, "I can only say that the evidence before me at the time satisfied me that his action was not malicious, and led me to recommend a mitigation of his sentence, which was concurred in by the President."[29]

A six-page, undated letter written by Lord was sent to President Arthur with copies of the three letters from Ingalls, Grant and McCrary. Lord again requested that the president reappoint Reno a "Major in the Cavalry arm of the service of the United States Army." He cited Reno's military history, including the citations he had received when awarded the brevet ranks of major, lieutenant colonel and colonel in the regular army, and brigadier general of volunteers, and Sherman's comment about "the judicious and skillful conduct" by Reno at the Little Big Horn. Lord continued, "In regard to his general character and fitness, Major Reno has the honor to refer your excellency to [three U.S. Senators, seven members of the House of Representatives], and Major Thomas Barr of the War Department."[30] On April 11 Lord wrote to Secretary of War Lincoln, enclosing a copy of his six-page letter to President Arthur, and challenged Lincoln's interpretation of Revised Statutes 1204 and 1228:

> [I]f I am correctly informed, this construction was adopted rather than made by you, and the present Attorney General has expressed serious doubts as to its correctness. I certainly fail to see how the restoration of an officer to the identical rank from which he had been unjustly or illegally dismissed interferes with the promotions, the subject of Section 1204. I am confident that the President will respond favorably if he has the power. If he has not, is it too much to ask of you [to prepare] such a letter [that] will aid Major Reno in securing the aid of the Congress.[31]

A second letter from Lord to Lincoln, dated April 17, asked, "Cannot Major Reno, by and with the advice and consent of the Senate, be appointed to the office of Major from which he was dismissed through a mistake of the Court-Martial, and after the proceedings against him fell, without removing a Major from the service?"[32]

On April 19, Lincoln responded: "I am not aware that Section 1228 has been directly construed by the Attorney General, but to myself, its language is very clear. It gives no authority to the President." Concerning Section 1204, Lincoln wrote, "The views of the Attorney General were approved by the President [in another case], who directs me to advise you that they are considered by him to cover also the case of Marcus A. Reno, and to prevent favorable action upon your present application." In response to Lord's April 17 letter, Lincoln rejoined, "In answer to your second inquiry, I have to reply that, as the number of Majors of Cavalry is limited by law, and the list is full, Major Reno could not be appointed to that grade without removing a Major from the service, and that, if there were a vacancy in that grade, the senior Captain of Cavalry would be entitled, under the law, to the place."[33]

It was now apparent to both Reno and Lord that Lincoln and the War Department were not going to respond positively to their request for Reno's reinstatement — not even a letter from the department to Congress to "aid" Reno. The only remaining hope now was to pursue the issue through Congress. They decided to wait until the 47th Congress met for its second session Dec. 5, 1882, to submit a new bill for Reno's reinstatement.

Reno remained in New York for another two and half months before returning to Harrisburg where he registered at the Lochiel Hotel in early July. The following month Reno went to the resort area of Cape May, N.J., about 45 miles southwest of Atlantic City. His reputation appeared to follow him even there. In an article that appeared in the *Harrisburg Daily Telegraph* issue of Sept. 11, 1882, it was reported thus:

Major Reno Denies It
An Alleged Cape May Sensation Spoiled

The *Philadelphia Press* issue of today says Cape May furnishes a little sensation in the shape of a jealous lover, a discarded suitor, a challenge to mortal combat and a general effort at secrecy. The particulars are that Major M. A. Reno, of this city, while at Cape May was introduced to Mrs. Waterman, of Philadelphia, who is said to be engaged to Mr. Howell, of Howell & Bros., the bankers of Third street. The Major was often her escort and was regarded by her with favor. It is alleged that Mr. Howell, hearing of this, informed Mrs. Waterman of certain rumors derogatory to Major Reno's character, which the lady repeated to the Major. The latter, it is intimated, was very angry and at once sent the broker a demand for the satisfaction due a gentleman and an officer. Mr. Howell was seen by a reporter and denied all knowledge of the affair, and that he had received a challenge. It was intimated, also, that Mr. Howell would not accept the challenge if received.

Major Reno was seen this morning by a *Telegraph* reporter who questioned him regarding the truth of the *Press* article.

"It is a lie from beginning to end," said Major Reno. "It is true that I was at Cape May, and I met Mrs. Waterman there, but I was not introduced to her, because I had known her for years. She was my wife's most intimate friend before her death, years ago, and at our marriage was her bridesmaid. It was no more than common courtesy that our acquaintance and friendship should be continued. I regret the publication of her name, because it makes prominent in a light manner a pure and noble lady. As to her relations to Mr. Howell I do not know, but I am certain he never told her anything derogatory about me. The charge that I sent him a challenge is a lie out of the whole-cloth — a most odious lie. Mr. Howell is a gentleman, and in his interview with the reporter shows an appreciation of the truth. I consider that I have been basely libeled by the *Press* and will probably enter suit against the publishers."[34]

No record indicates Reno ever filed a suit against the *Philadelphia Press*. He returned to New York in early October and decided to again try his hand at marriage. On Oct. 20, 1882, Isabella Ray McGunnegle and he were married in New York City by Dr. John R. Paxton in the West Presbyterian Church. Reno and his new wife returned to Harrisburg on the evening of Oct. 23, and Isabella had her first opportunity to met her new stepson. It would only be a few days before friction arose between the two — Isabella did not care for Ross' life style, and Ross, at 18, didn't want daily supervision from his stepmother. Ross was later to state that she had caused an estrangement between his father and him.[35]

On Dec. 5, Senator J. Donald Cameron of Pennsylvania, an old friend of Reno, introduced a bill, S. 2190, into the Senate. The bill was identical to the previous bills that called for the appointment of Reno to the rank of major in the cavalry. It was read twice in the Senate and then referred to the Committee on Military Affairs, chaired by John A. Logan of Illinois. Committee member Benjamin Harrison, senator from Indiana, was given the assignment by Logan to gather the necessary information pertaining to the bill. Harrison wrote to Secretary of War Lincoln Dec. 27 and requested "the military record of this officer, and such other information concerning the case, as will be of value in reporting upon it. I should also be pleased to hear any suggestions you are willing to make."[36] Lincoln replied to Harrison Jan. 9, 1883, supplying the requested information but made no suggestions. Harrison reviewed the file and reported to the committee several days later, indicating that Reno had "performed valuable and even distinguished services in the war of the rebellion, and also in the Indian Wars since." However, also included in the file were the final dispositions and sentences of Reno's 1877 and 1879 courtsmartial. The committee discussed the issues and Harrison's report concluded: "The committee are unanimously of the opinion that this officer ought not to be reinstated in the Army, and therefore recommend that the bill be indefinitely postponed."[37] The adverse reporting of this bill eliminated any chance Reno had for possible reinstatement by the 47th Congress.

On March 15, Reno responded to a letter from his old West Point friend William W. Averell, and wanted to invite him for a visit: "I will be too glad when I can offer you a visit in my house, but it will be some time before I get my farm as I had leased it, and the man will not give it up until the lease expires some time hence." Reno's letter continued in a more sober tone which reflected some of the disappointment he felt after almost three years of futile attempts for reinstatement. He wrote:

> It is melancholy that the efforts of so many brave devoted men should be gradually ignored as they are by the rising genera-tion and it seems to me that ending, if the sentiment continues growing, that it will be a reproach to have been in the army, as to have seceded, as I told a member of Congress the other day "I was beginning to think I had been on the wrong side." Well good-bye, let us hope that brighter days are coming for a faithful dis-charge of duty to our country will meet its reward in the next world if not in this.[38]

Marcus, Isabella and Ross would remain at the Lochiel Hotel for the re-mainder of 1883. But before the year ended, an incident would put additional strain on the relationship between Ross and his stepmother. The *Army and Navy Journal* issue of Jan. 5, 1884, reported:

> Miss Carrie Swain, the actress, staying at the Lochiel Hotel, was awakened Christmas night by three or four gentle raps on the window. Soon the window was raised, and a young man sprang into the room. Miss Swain cried for help. Her maid, who slept in an adjoining room, at once responded, as did a number of hotel employees, and the intruder proved to be Ross Reno, a son of Marcus A. Reno, late Major U.S.A. Miss Swain declined to pros-ecute the young man, but the proprietor of the Lochiel told him that he must seek other quarters.[39]

The Jan. 5 issue of the *Journal* also reported that on Jan. 1, Mr. and Mrs. Robert Lincoln had received guests at their home from 2 o'clock until 6 and were assisted by Miss Ella Sturgis.[40] Colonel Sturgis was staying in Washing-ton during this period and was on friendly terms with the secretary of war. This relationship between the Sturgis family and Lincoln certainly did not appear to be beneficial to Reno.

Following Ross' escapade on Christmas day, he was sent to Pittsburgh to live with his uncle, J. Wilson Orth. On Feb. 4, Reno executed a will naming his "beloved wife Isabella Ray Reno" as the executrix and directing $1,000 to be paid to his son for the money he had borrowed when he returned home from Fort Meade in 1880. The remainder of his estate was willed to his Isabella.

On March 4, Reno also assigned Isabella the $6,000 insurance policy he had purchased Dec. 11, 1877, for which he had paid the full premium in a single payment of $2,645. The policy was to be paid on his death to "his executors, administrators or assigns."[41] The policy, physically held by Ross, quickly become a matter of dispute between Isabella and Ross. Isabella sent a letter to Ross in Pittsburgh requesting the return of the policy to her. Ross replied to "Mrs. Reno" May 19, "I would like to do what you desire, but it is impossible, so I must respectfully decline to give up the policy. Trusting you are well." On the reverse of the note, Ross penned, "I shall write to father on Friday, and let him know just what I intend to do."[42] Ross' great-grandmother, Eliza E. Haldeman, died March 17, leaving Ross $500 and a diamond butterfly pin, which were placed in trust with Lyman Gilbert.

The failure of several reinstatement bills in the House and Senate, produced some bitter feelings in Reno towards the whole process. Reno especially blamed former President Hayes for ignoring the recommendations of Barr, Terry and Sherman to modify the dismissal sentence. On July 9, 1884, Reno wrote directly to the former president and his anger was clear:

> R. B. Hayes,
> I do not prefix Hon. to your name because you do not deserve it. For many months I have debated in my own mind as to the propriety of writing this letter. I have the best reason in the world to hate you as <u>bitterly</u> and <u>deeply</u> as ever a man had to hate another. This <u>deep</u> <u>bitter</u> <u>hatred</u>, would suggest some means of revenge but that desire is more than gratified when I reflect that the <u>whole</u> American people hold you in the utmost contempt as a <u>fraud</u>, a <u>hypocrit</u> (sic) and a <u>liar</u>.
>
> M. A. Reno[43]

The Renos would remain at the Lochiel Hotel until mid-November when they moved to Washington and rented a house at 2088 "P" Street. Reno had just celebrated his 50th birthday and still wanted to return to military life. Before the start of the 2nd session of the 48th Congress, scheduled to begin Dec. 1, he made the rounds of Washington, meeting with a number of congressman. He convinced Congressman Philip B. Thompson of Kentucky to introduce another bill for reinstatement into the House of Representatives. On Dec. 8, 1884, the bill, H.R. 7665, was read twice in the House and then referred to the Committee of Military Affairs. There it met the same fate as the previous three bills and died in committee without being reported.

Grover Cleveland's inauguration March 20, 1885, brought an end to Robert Lincoln's term as secretary of war when he was replaced by William C. Endicott. Reno considered appealing to the new administration but Scott Lord was convinced the legal interpretation established by Lincoln in the case would be used by Endicott to deny Reno's application.

In March 1885, Isabella wrote to Secretary of the Interior L. Q. C. Lamar, asking to be considered an applicant for employment in the Interior Department "in any grade in which there may exist a vacancy."[44]

Ross Reno had moved from Pittsburgh to Nashville, Tenn., sometime in 1884, and started working as a salesman for the firm of Kinney, McLaughlin & Company, wholesale liquor dealers. During his employment he met Ittie Kinney, the daughter of one of the firm's partners, George Kinney. Ross began courting Ittie and by the time he reached his majority in April 1885, Ittie and he had decided to marry. A marriage license was issued May 10, 1885, by Davidson County, Tenn., to Robert Ross Reno and Ittie Kinney. Ross sent a telegram to his father in Washington inviting him to the wedding, scheduled for May 20, in Nashville. Because of the poor relations between his stepmother and him, Ross probably asked his father not to bring Isabella to the wedding.

The elaborate wedding ceremony, conducted by Bishop Joseph Rademacher, took place at St. Mary's Church and was attended by more than 200 people — Ross' father and stepmother were not among the attendees. As a wedding present Ross gave Ittie the diamond butterfly pin that he had inherited from his great-grandmother.[45]

Reaching his majority allowed Ross access to the trust being held for him by Lyman Gilbert. George Kinney held a one-half share in Kinney, McLaughlin & Company, James McLaughlin, a one-fourth interest, and Granville P. Lipscomb, the remaining one-fourth. Several months after the wedding, McLaughlin decided to retire and sell his share. Ross purchased the one-fourth interest in the firm for $15,000.

In late summer of 1885, Marcus and Isabella moved from their "P" Street residence to 316 Indiana Ave. in Washington. Boredom was finally beginning to set in with Reno — he had been out of the military for more than five years and had not held any type of employment during that period. He was still receiving money from the leases on the property he owned but the large sum he had inherited from Mary Hannah was rapidly disappearing. Isabella was still unemployed, for she had not received an offer in response to her March request at the Department of the Interior. Reno applied for a position at the Interior Department in early November 1885, and on Nov. 16 was recom-

50TH CONGRESS,
1ST SESSION.

H. R. 1215.

IN THE HOUSE OF REPRESENTATIVES.

JANUARY 5, 1886.

Read twice, referred to the Committee on Military Affairs, and ordered to be printed.

Mr. MAYBURY introduced the following bill:

A BILL

For the relief of Marcus A. Reno.

1   *Be it enacted by the Senate and House of Representa-*
2   *tives of the United States of America in Congress assembled,*
3   That the President be, and he is hereby, authorized to nomi-
4   nate and, by and with the advice and consent of the Senate,
5   appoint Marcus A. Reno, late a major of the Seventh Cavalry, a
6   major of cavalry in the Army of the United States, with his for-
7   mer rank and date of commission, and that he shall be assigned
8   to the first vacancy occurring in such grade in the cavalry arm
9   of the service: *Provided, however,* That he shall only receive
10 . pay from the date of appointment under this act.

mended by Pension Office Commissioner John C. Black for employment: "Mr. Marcus A. Reno of Illinois, having been examined and found qualified, I would respectfully recommend his appointment as Special Examiner in this Office at $1,400, to take effect when he shall file the oath of office and enter on duty."[46] Reno started work with the Pension Office on Nov. 19, 1885, and was almost immediately transferred to New York. The Renos moved from their rented house in Washington to a rented flat at 23 W. 10th Street in New York.

Prior to October 1885, the editor of the *Philadelphia Weekly Press*, I. R. Pennypacker, decided to run a series of stories on high profile Pennsylvania Civil War officers and Pennsylvania Regimental histories. The editor invited contributors to submit material for which they would be compensated if accepted. Reno wrote to the editor early in November and received the circular from Pennypacker with the criteria required for articles to be acceptable for publication. Reno thought an article or two discussing his Civil and Indian War experiences would meet Pennypacker's requirements, and on Nov. 26 wrote that he would "send an article for next week, upon the noted guerrilla Mosby, with whom I had a skirmish with the 12th Pa Cavalry. Later I will send an article on the 'Custer Massacre.'" Apparently Pennypacker was more interested in an article about Custer than one about Mosby, for he wrote to Reno Dec. 5 requesting more details about the Custer battle. Reno responded Dec. 7:

> My article on the "Custer Massacre" will be voluminous, & will probably make two contributions. I have found a diary, kept by myself & written on the battlefield, lying on the grass within scent of the dead horses, which were killed in the fight, & for that reason, of undoubted veracity & accuracy.... I would be obliged to you if you will inform me, what compensation you will give me in case you accept my contribution as I am in need of money.

Reno wrote again on the 24th:

> Your favor of 23d inst. rec'd. I mailed to your address on Monday the completion of the manuscript of the account of the Custer Massacre, & have woven in such pages of my diary as in my opinion would prove interesting. You say nothing about my article on Mosby. I am now completing a history of the Cavalry Corps, A. of P. [Army of the Potomac]. I have only evenings that I can devote to this employment, as I am in a position in the Pension Office that takes all my time in the day — Please send

Marcus Reno, circa 1885
(U.S. Military Academy - West Point)

me a line & tell me if the manuscript already forwarded will be published. The Custer article is complete — & also the Mosby article — How much will they be worth —

When he received Pennypacker's offer, he was not pleased and responded Nov. 29:

Your letter announcing $35, as the amt. you will pay for the two articles I wrote, was today rec'd. I do not think that Am't. a liberal offer & must request you to return the manuscript by express C.O.D. to my address given in the caption of this letter — I am very well posted as to the payment made by the press generally for a readable & interesting article. If this offer is a sample of your liberality I do not think you will have the pleasure of reading my "History of the Cavy. Corps A. of P.," unless you happen to secure a copy of the paper in which it will be published.

In the final letter of this series, dated Jan. 3, 1886, Reno offered the articles to Pennypacker for $100: "Articles like these written from the experience & personal observations of myself, could not well be accounted as ordinary correspondence, & for that reason should not be subjected to the usual rates of pay." He asked Pennypacker to return the articles if the *Press* did not want to publish them. The articles were never published in the *Philadelphia Weekly Press*.[47]

The first session of the 49th Congress started Dec. 7, 1885, and two bills in behalf of Reno were submitted Jan. 5, 1886. Representative William C. Maybury of Michigan (Democrat) submitted bill H.R. 1215, and Representative James Laird (Republican) submitted bill H.R. 1447. Both bills, identical to those that had failed previously in the House, were read twice and referred to the Committee on Military Affairs.[48] On March 15, Committee Chairman Edward S. Bragg of Wisconsin, requested the War Department's "views" of the bills and Reno's military records. The Chief of Ordnance, Stephen V. Benet, acting secretary of war, responded to Bragg March 27, enclosing a statement of Reno's military record and copies of his two courts-martial. Benet added "that similar bills for the restoration of Major Reno have been twice reported adversely by the Senate Military Committee."[49] Neither bill was reported out of committee and died, as had all similar attempts.

Late in the first session of the 49th Congress, Senator Shelby M. Cullom of Illinois, introduced a bill, S. 2655, for Reno's reinstatement into the Senate. As had occurred in the House, the bill was read twice and then referred to the Senate Committee of Military Affairs where it too, was never reported out of committee.

Reno continued his work as special examiner for the Pension Office of the Interior Department in New York. As one of the 14 individuals who had originally been appointed for a probationary period of six months, he needed to be recommended for reappointment to continue his employment with the Interior Department. On May 15, Secretary Lamar approved Reno's reappointment to the Department to June 30, when the terms of all Special Examiners ended. Reno was one of 139 Special Examiners reappointed on July 1, 1886.[50] The Renos would remain in New York all of 1886.

At the beginning of the new year, Reno was notified that he was reassigned from the Pension Office in New York back to Washington. The Renos returned to Washington in late January, renting a flat at 814 Connecticut Ave. Isabella and he had been having marital difficulties for a number of months and on Feb. 15, 1887, she left him, moving to Harrisburg where she rented living accommodations. She later filed a petition with the Common Pleas Court of Dauphin County, Penna., stating:

> That your petitioner was on the twentieth day of October, 1882 lawfully joined in marriage with Marcus A. Reno, her present husband, and from that time until the fifteenth day February 1887 lived and co-habited with him, and hath in all respects demeaned herself as a kind and affectionate wife, and although by the laws of God, as well as by the mutual vows plighted to each other they were bound to that uniform constancy and regard which ought to be inseparable from the marriage state, yet so it is that the parties being at the time domiciled within the Commonwealth of Pennsylvania, the said Marcus A. Reno has offered such indignities to the person of your petitioner, as to render her condition intolerable, and her life burdensome, and thereby forced her to withdraw from his house and family.[51]

Things would not get better for Reno. In the same month Isabella left, the *Army and Navy Journal* reported that a story about Reno being circulated among the daily papers was "without any apparent justification at this time." The story dealt with the bills for Reno's reinstatement that had been submitted more than a year before to the House of Representatives during the first session of the 49th Congress:

Major Reno
His Application for Restoration to the
Army before the House at Washington

There is likely to be a revival of the Custer controversy in a few days, when the adverse report of the Committee on Military Affairs on the application of Major Reno for restoration to the Army is brought before the House of Representatives. Major Reno was tried by a court martial for striking a brother officer in a billiard room quarrel and for gazing into Colonel Sturgis's windows, thereby scaring a young lady, and was dismissed from the service for not rescuing Custer from the trap into which he ran. Major Reno will submit letters of recommendations from General Grant, General Ingalls and ex-Secretary McCrary, all testifying to his worth as a soldier. If there is any debate in the House that body will resolve itself into Custerites and anti-Custerites, and Major Reno's abilities will be a secondary issue; to vindicate or condemn Custer will be the choice the House will open to itself.[52]

The lease on the farm in Cumberland County, equally owned by Marcus and Ross, finally came to end in April 1887, and they agreed to sell the property. They expected the farm to sell for more than $32,000 and each would receive at least $16,000. Reno had the necessary legal papers drawn up by his attorney to place the money in trust and pay "the sum of five hundred dollars annually in two equal installments unto R. Ross Reno...until the sum of two thousand and six hundred dollars with interest from date is fully paid."[53] The farm was not sold and no trust fund for Ross was established.

Reno was reappointed a special examiner for the Pension Office July 1, 1887. Now that he was back in Washington he decided to spend more time on his campaign for reinstatement. On July 18, he submitted his resignation to John Black: "I have the honor to tender my resignation as a Special Examiner of U.S. Pension Bureau." His resignation was accepted by Black July 19, "to take effect Aug. 13, 1887, and that he be granted leave until that date."[54]

The first session of the 50th Congress was scheduled to meet Dec. 5. Representative Daniel Ermentrout of Pennsylvania agreed to introduce the identical bill as previously submitted to the House for Reno's reinstatement. Ermentrout introduced bill H.R. 545, on Dec. 21, and, as before, the bill was read twice in the House and then referred to the House Committee of Military Affairs. On Jan. 4, 1888, Senator Cushman K. Davis of Minnesota, who had defended Reno at his 1877 court-martial, introduced the same bill, S.

1131, in the Senate, where it was read and referred to the Senate Committee of Military Affairs. Reno knew these two bills might be his last opportunity for reinstatement, and he was also aware that the chances either bill would be reported out of committee were slim — the possibility of ever being returned to the army appeared remote.

Reno had resigned his position with the Pension Officer in July but decided perhaps he had acted hastily and submitted a request to the Interior Department for the restoration of his job. On Dec. 28, he was reappointed, not to his old job of Special Examiner that paid $1,400 a year, but to a new job as "Clerk of Class $1000."[55] He returned to work Jan. 9, 1888.

On Jan. 16, Senator Joseph R. Hawley of Connecticut, chairman of the Military Affairs Committee, requested the secretary of war provide Reno's military records for consideration of bill S. 1131 and the "views of the Department." Adjutant General R. C. Drum provided the information to Secretary Endicott Jan. 23, noting that similar bills had been reported adversely by the 46th and 47th Senate committee. Drum also added: "If Major Reno should be restored, with his original date of rank, as proposed in this bill, he would stand at the head of the list of Majors of Cavalry, and be entitled to be promoted to the first vacancy of lieutenant-colonel happening in the Cavalry arm."[56] Endicott replied to Hawley Jan. 25, and enclosed the Adjutant General's report, along with Reno's military records. The bill failed to be reported out of committee.

Representative John H. Gear of Iowa provided the House committee with Reno's military record and a summary of the two courts-martial. In his Feb. 7, 1888, report, Gear noted the recommendation from the Senate Committee on Military Affairs of the 47th Congress: "The committee are unanimously of the opinion that this officer ought not to be reinstated in the Army, and therefore recommend that the bill be indefinitely postponed." This was also Gear's conclusion: "In view of all the facts set forth in the report of the committee of the Forty-seventh Congress, your committee recommend the indefinite postponement of the bill."[57] With the failure of the House bill to be reported out of committee, Reno's last chance for reinstatement by the 50th Congress was gone.

Reno knew the chances of either bill being approved had not been good, but it was difficult for him to accept the fact that perhaps his attempts to return to the military were coming to an end. To add to his disappointment, he received a letter from his former commander, General Terry, which only convinced him that he had been right all along — the punishment was excessive and he should have never been dismissed:

St. Augustine, Fla. March 2, 1888

Dear Colonel:

I have your note asking me for a copy of the letter that I sent you long ago expressing my opinion in regard to the action taken upon the record of your trial by court-martial. I am sorry to say that I preserved no copy of that letter, and that I cannot reproduce it from memory.

I can, however, say that I was never more surprised than I was when the sentence of the court was confirmed. I had in my endorsement on the record expressed the opinion that the sentence was "excessive" and I had only formally approved it. I did not suppose that in the face of such an endorsement the confirming authority would think of ordering the sentence to be carried into execution. Had I supposed that it would be confirmed, I should have exercised my undoubted right & should have given no opportunity for such action. I should have disapproved the finding upon the charge and thus have put an end to the whole case.[58]

The spring of 1888 also brought Reno a continuation of problems with his estranged wife Isabella. He had not been paying her any support and she wrote to the secretary of the interior April 25 "to cause her husband, Marcus A. Reno, a Special Examiner (sic) of the Pension Office, to contribute the sum of $40.00 per month for her support, in accordance with a certain article of agreement entered into between themselves." She enclosed a copy of the agreement with her letter. Receiving no response to her letter, she went to the office of Representative Joseph Wheeler of Alabama and requested that he write to the secretary in her behalf. Wheeler sent a letter to the interior secretary May 8: "Mrs. General Reno (sic), the daughter of a navy officer and formerly the widow of a navy officer, desires to see you upon a personal matter — not an application for office — for a very few minutes, and I hope you will be able to receive her."[59] On May 11, the matter was referred to Commissioner of Pensions John Black, but records do not show that Isabella ever got to see the secretary or received any support from her husband.

Reno received a letter from his son asking him to come to Nashville — Ross had some pressing financial problems he needed to discuss with his father. Reno took a short leave from his job at the Interior Department and went to Nashville in early May. Arriving there, he found out that the firm in which Ross had a one-fourth interest, Kinney & Co. (formerly Kinney, McLaughlin & Co.), was insolvent, and creditors were starting to make demands on Ross' personal assets. On May 24, Ross conveyed some of his personal property to his wife, including $2,600 in cash, and a phaeton and horse. Marcus and Ross agreed to transfer the title of the New Cumberland farm and

Reno Farm, circa 1880
(Public Library, New Cumberland, Penna.)

Reno Farm, circa 1880
(Public Library, New Cumberland, Penna.)

the house at 223 Front Street, Harrisburg, to Ittie to prevent them from being seized by the creditors. Marcus had had a life-estate interest in these properties and it was agreed that he would continue to receive the rental income from both properties. With the transfer of these properties to Ittie, Ross had no personal or real property assets, save his interest in the firm of Kinney & Co.[60] Asked later why he made the conveyances, Ross said: "I did it as a protection to myself, having contracted very convivial habits, and I might have made a sacrifice of them (the lands conveyed) if I had not done so." Ittie confirmed Ross' bad habits: "Mr. Reno had contracted rather rapid habits and I felt that he should protect me against himself. He had been gambling very largely and losing very heavily." When she was asked, "Was it your object to protect him against these habits?," she replied, "It was to protect me against his habits."[61]

While Marcus was in Nashville, he had the opportunity to visit another of his old classmates from West Point, William H. Jackson, class of 1856. Jackson, a former brigadier general in the Confederate army, had prospered following the Civil War and owned, in conjunction with his brother, "Belle Meade," an estate of 6,000 acres near Nashville. The brothers were raising about 350 thoroughbred race horses. Reno stayed at Belle Meade for about a week before returning to his small room at 420 Sixth St. in Washington.

On Aug. 10, Isabella appeared at the office of Alderman D. C. Maurer in Harrisburg and had him issue a warrant for Reno's arrest charging him with refusing and neglecting to support and maintain her for the past year.[62] On Saturday, Sept. 1, when Reno arrived in Harrisburg on the train from Washington, he was arrested and taken to Alderman Maurer's office where bail was set at $4,000. Bertha F. Meyer, the proprietress of the Lancaster House Hotel, 21 N. Sixth St., Harrisburg, where Reno had stayed a number of times, signed as surety for him.[63] He was ordered to appear before the court Oct. 9 to determine the amount of maintenance he owed Isabella.

Reno appeared in the Dauphin County Court on the scheduled date and he was ordered to pay Isabella $50 a month and give bail in the amount of $1,000.[64] That same day Isabella signed a petition similar to the one she had previously filed with the Common Pleas Court stating that on Feb. 15, 1887, Reno had "offered such indignities to the person of your petitioner, as to render her condition intolerable, and her life burdensome, and thereby forced her to withdraw from his house and family." She asked for a subpoena to be issued to direct him to appear during the January 1889 term to answer the complaint and "also that a decree…be made for the divorcing of her, the said Isabella R. Reno from the bonds of matrimony, as if she had never been married."[65]

Apparently despondent over the decision of the court, Reno was subjected to rumors that he had attempted to commit suicide Oct. 11. The Harrisburg *Patriot* reported Oct. 12:

Did Not Commit Suicide

Major M. A. Reno, who has been in the city for some time past, has lately been acting rather queerly. Yesterday it was reported that he had attempted to commit suicide. The report arose from the fact that the major had asserted that he had so much trouble that he would take his own life. The major's actions are entirely due to drink, and his friends think his mind is becoming unbalanced.[66]

Reno was served with the divorce subpoena Oct. 12 and ordered to appear in court Jan. 14, 1889. He also was ordered to appear in court the next day (Oct. 13) for additional decisions in Isabella's support and maintenance case. Although he had signed over the Front Street and New Cumberland property to Ittie Reno, the court determined that the rental fees he was collecting should be used as security to assure payments to Isabella. The court appointed Christian W. Lynch of Harrisburg as trustee and Reno signed the necessary legal documents giving Lynch the authority to collect the rents and make the payments directly to Isabella.[67] Reno remained in Harrisburg until Oct. 18, when he returned to Washington.

Reno had been a heavy smoker all of his adult life, and that, combined with an excessive consumption of liquor over at least the previous decade, was finally taking a toll on his physical health. A sore on his tongue, which he had noticed sometime before, did not seem to want to heal, and smoking continued to aggravate it. Reno had little time to worry about his health — his work at the Interior Department kept him busy just trying to make ends meet. Reno had been notified that his court date in Harrisburg had been changed from Jan. 14 to the 21st, and Reno appeared in court that day as required.[68] Isabella's lawyer, John E. Lord, presented a written statement to the court about her request for a divorce, but the court did not render a judgment at that time.[69]

Reno continued his work at the Department of the Interior while enduring the worsening pain in his mouth. In late February 1889, he decided it was time to settle the divorce issue with Isabella and he filed his own divorce request as reported by the *Army and Navy Journal*:

Marcus A. Reno, formerly of the army, in a bill of equity filed last week in Washington, D.C., asks for a divorce from Isabella R. Reno, to whom he was married in New York in 1882, she being a widow by the name of McGunnigle. Instead, says the *Critic*, "of being grateful to him for rescuing her from that name and substituting the classic appellation, she showed no appreciation whatever, and, according to the allegation of the bill, deserted him in February 1887."[70]

By the middle of March, the pain in Reno's mouth began to affect his speech and eating became difficult. About March 15, he finally consulted his doctor friend, John B. Hamilton, who quickly diagnosed the problem — cancer of the tongue — and recommended an immediate operation to remove the now obvious cancerous growth. Reno was admitted to Providence Hospital in Washington March 19 and Hamilton performed the operation the same day. He was able to remove the cancer from Reno's tongue, but was unable to determine what long-term effects it might have on Reno's speech. Reno remained heavily sedated to relieve the pain. On March 26, Reno developed erysipelas, an acute inflammation of the skin, on his right hand, which caused him even more discomfort. Two days later, pneumonia attacked both lungs and early on the morning of March 30, 1889, he slipped into unconsciousness and death soon followed.[71]

Hamilton sent Ross a telegram notifying him of his father's death and requested he come to Washington to make the necessary arrangements. Reno's remains were taken to the John W. Lee Funeral Home in Washington where he was embalmed and would remain until his son's arrival. Ross sent a telegram to his father's Sixth Avenue landlady stating he was in Cleveland, Tenn., and would arrive in Washington April 1.

The April 1, 1889, issue of the *Harrisburg Patriot*, announced Reno's death: "He Misses the Arrows of the Indians to Become a Victim of Pneumonia," and the April 6, 1889, issue of the *Army and Navy Journal* summed up Reno's epitaph: "Thus ends a life which in the past gave promise of unusual brilliancy."

Even after his death, controversy, which seemed to follow him relentlessly after the Little Big Horn, continued as to where he was to be buried. Reno had planned to be buried with his first wife, Mary Hannah, in the Ross family plot in Harrisburg, but no previous arrangements had been made with the Ross family. Both Ross and Isabella decided to have Reno buried in the Glenwood Cemetery in Washington until further arrangements might be made to move the remains to their final resting place. Reno was buried April 2 in the Glenwood Cemetery in an unmarked grave — no stone was purchased as it was expected the body to be moved shortly to Harrisburg.

Ross, accompanied by Ittie, arrived in Harrisburg April 3 to discuss the final burial arrangements with the Ross family.[72] Ross was informed by Andrew Ross, Mary Hannah's brother, that the Ross Lot in the Harrisburg Cemetery was filled, and Mary Hannah was buried in the middle of a row of graves. Andrew did not want his sister's remains moved to another lot in the cemetery. They appeared to have little choice at this point except, at least temporarily, to leave Reno's remains in the grave at Glenwood Cemetery in Washington. Reno would occupy this "temporary" grave for another 78 years.

Endnotes

[1] *Army and Navy Journal,* March 27, 1880.

[2] Gilbert W. Beckley, *New Cumberland Frontier* (NP, 1873), p. 93 — copy of 1884 Last Will and Testament of Marcus A. Reno.

[3] Edward Ball to the Adjutant General, April 23, 1880, in Ball's A.C.P. File, Record Group 94, NARA.

[4] Judge Advocate General's Files, 1880, letter from Randolph to Secretary of War, item 2184.

[5] Report of the 46th Congress, Second Session, Dec. 1, 1879, to June 16, 1880.

[6] Item 2184 A.C.P. 1880, 2nd Endorsement, April 27, 1880, by G. D. Townsend.

[7] Item 2184 A.C.P. 1880, note dated April 26, 1880.

[8] Letter from Reno to Adjutant General's Officer, Oct. 2, 1880, Washington, D.C., item 5428 A.C.P. 1880.

[9] Item 5428 A.C.P. 1880, Adjutant General's Office.

[10] Item 5932 A.C.P. 1880, Adjutant General's Office.

[11] Senate Report No. 845, 46th Congress, 3rd Session, Feb. 7, 1881.

[12] March 10, 1881, letter from Reno to Secretary of War Robert Todd Lincoln, Reno's personal file.

[13] March 11, 1881, War Department, Bureau of Military Justice, Judge Advocate General to the Secretary of War, Reno's personal file, NARA.

[14] Item 204 BMJ 1881, dated March 15, 1881.

[15] Letter to Reno from Robert Todd Lincoln, dated March 18, 1882, Reno's personal file.

[16] Recorders Office, Cumberland County Courthouse, Carlisle, Penna, Volume 3, Book S, p. 545, Marcus A. Reno to Andrew Ross.

[17] Dauphin County Orphan's Court Records, Dauphin County Courthouse, Harrisburg, Penna, File #70, dated July 9, 1881.

[18] Item 6302 A.C.P. 1881, in Reno's personal file.

[19] *The Case of Marcus A. Reno, Late Major 7th U.S. Cavalry* (Washington, D.C. [1881]).

[20] Item 6302 A.C.P. 1881, Application, pp. 1 and 2, in Reno's personal file.

[21] Item 6302 A.C.P. 1881, Addenda, p. 2, "Third" citation of "Point I," in Reno's personal file.

[22] Item 6302 A.C.P. 1881, Application, p. 2, in Reno's personal file.

[23] Item 6302 A.C.P. 1881, Application, p. 2 and 3, In Reno's personal file.

[24] Item 6302 A.C.P. 1881, Memorandum on the application of M. A. Reno, late Major U.S. Army, for reinstatement, date Nov. 29, 1881, in Reno's personal file.

[25] Item 6302 A.C.P. 1881, Lincoln Memorandum, pp. 5 and 6.

[26] Item 6302 A.C.P. 1881, Letter from Scott Lord to Lincoln, dated Dec. 10, 1881, in Reno's personal file.

[27] Letter from Rufus Ingalls to President Arthur, Dec. 14, 1881, in Reno's personal file.

[28] "In the Congress…In The Matter of Marcus A. Reno, Late a Major in the Seventh Cavalry," privately printed, n.d. [1882], p. 18.

[29] "In the Congress," p. 18.

[30] Item 2552 A.C.P. 1882, Letter to Arthur from Lord, no date, in Reno's personal file.

[31] Letter from Lord to Lincoln, dated April 11, 1882, in Reno's personal file.

[32] Letter from Lord to Lincoln, dated April 17, 1882, in Reno's personal file.

[33] Item 2552 A.C.P. 1882, Letter from Lincoln to Lord, dated April 19, 1882, in Reno's personal file.

[34] *Harrisburg Daily Telegraph*, issue of Sept. 11, 1882.

[35] Tennessee Supreme Court Records, Record Box 899, Tennessee State Library and Archives, Extract of disposition of R. R. Reno in a law suit with the Mutual Life Insurance Company of New York.

[36] Item 7141 A.C.P. 1882, Letter from Harrison to Lincoln, dated Dec. 27, 1882, in Reno's personal file.

[37] Senate Report 926, 47th Congress, 2nd Session, and also noted in Reno's personal file that Bill S. 2190 was "reported adversely."

[38] Letter from Reno to William W. Averell, dated March 15, 1883, in Averell's personal file. Averell had been removed from his command by Sheridan during the Shenandoah Valley campaign for not following the Confederates after their defeat at Fisher's Hill in September 1864. Averell resigned in May 1865, but attempted to regain his rank in 1880 — his request was denied. See Edward K. Eckert & Nicholas J. Amato (editors), *Ten Years in the Saddle* (Presidio Press, San Rafael, Calif., 1978), pp. 396-404. Reno and Averell could commiserate on their respective difficulties.

[39] *Army and Navy Journal*, issue of Jan. 5, 1884.

[40] *Army and Navy Journal*, issue of Jan. 5, 1884.

[41] Extract of Mid-Tennessee Supreme Court record of Mutual Life Insurance Co. of N.Y. vs. Robert R. Reno & Isabella Reno, Tennessee State Library Supreme Court Records, Record Box 899.

[42] Letter from Ross Reno to Isabella Reno, dated May 19, 1885. Copy in author's collection. Note that the letter from Ross was written on the day before his wedding, May 20.

[43] Letter to R. B. Hayes from Reno, dated July 9, 1884, Harrisburg, Penna. In the Rutherford B. Hayes Library, Fremont, Ohio. A note was written on the bottom of the letter, perhaps by Hayes, "Marcus A. Reno dismissed from the Army, 1 April 1880." Thanks to Bill Moody for a copy of this letter now in the author's collection.

[44] Letter from Isabella Reno to Lamar, dated March 25, 1885, Department of the Interior, Appointments, Pension Office, File 2269-85, Record Group 48, NARA.

[45] *Harrisburg Daily Telegraph*, issue of May 26,1885.

[46] Letter from Black to Lamar, Secretary of the Interior, dated Nov. 16, 1885. Record Group 48, Department of the Interior, Appointment Pension Officer, File 3142-85.

[47] Original letters in the collection of James S. Hutchins, Columbus, Ohio. The statement by Reno that he "found a diary, kept by myself & written on the battlefield," is certainly questionable. This diary has never been found, and in all probability, never existed. Reno simply made the statement to Pennypacker to assure him that the article on the "Custer Massacre" was of "undoubted veracity & accuracy."

[48] Copies of both bills are in Reno's personal file.

[49] Item 1572 A.C.P. 1886, Letter from Benet to Bragg, dated March 27, 1886, in Reno's personal file.

[50] File 106-86 and 118-86, Department of the Interior, Pension Office, Appointment Division, dated May 20 and July 1, 1886, respectively, Record Group 48, NARA.

[51] Original papers, dated Oct. 9, 1888, on file Prothonotary's Office, Dauphin County, Penna, Courthouse, Harrisburg, Penna.

[52] *Harrisburg Daily Telegraph*, issue of Feb. 1, 1887.

[53] Note from the Commonwealth Guarantee Trust and Safe Deposit Company, Harrisburg, dated April 1887, signed by M. A. Reno. The $2,600 was the repayment of the $800 borrowed from Ross' trust fund in 1878, and the $1,000 borrowed from the same trust fund in 1880. Interest at the rate of about four and a half percent per year would have increased the amount of principle and interest owed to approximately $2,600 in 1887. Copy in the author's collection.

[54] Department of the Interior, Appointments, Pension Officer, File 513-87, Record Group 48.

[55] Interior Dept., File 513-87.

[56] Letter from Drum to Endicott, dated Jan. 23, 1888, in Reno's personal file.

[57] House of Representatives Report No. 332, 50th Congress, 1st Session.

[58] Letter from Terry to Reno, dated March 2, 1888. Original letter filed with Senate Bill S. 1131.

[59] Department of the Interior, Appointments, Pension Office, File 513-87, Record Group 48. Representative Joseph Wheeler was the former Confederate Cavalry General "Fightin' Joe Wheeler," who would later serve as a U.S. general in the Spanish American War.

[60] Supreme Court of Tennessee, No. 78, Tennessee State Library Archives, Records box 1006, 1894, p. 25.

[61] Supreme Court, p. 45-46.

[62] Dauphin County, Pennsylvania Courthouse, Clerk of Court Officer, Case number 253 1888.

[63] *Harrisburg Patriot*, issue of Sept. 3, 1888.

[64] *Harrisburg Patriot*, issue of Oct. 10, 1888.

[65] Petition signed by Isabella R. Reno, Oct. 9, 1888, In the Court of Common Pleas of Dauphin County, Penna., Record Group 47, Location L-16, Historical & Museum Commission, Pennsylvania State Archives.

66 *Harrisburg Patriot*, Penna.,, issue of Oct. 12, 1888.

67 Dauphin County, Penna., Courthouse, Clerk of Court Officer, Case number 253 1888.

68 *Harrisburg Daily Telegraph*, issue of Jan. 21, 1889.

69 "Libel in Divorce," 1889 Appearance Docket, Prothonotary's Office, Dauphin County Courthouse, Harrisburg, Penna., p. 42.

70 *Army and Navy Journal*, issue of March 2, 1889.

71 *Washington Post*, April 1, 1889; *Harrisburg Daily Telegraph*, April 1, 1889; Letter from Providence Hospital to Eugene D. Hart, dated Sept. 28, 1937, copy in author's collection.

72 *Harrisburg Daily Telegraph*, issue of April 3, 1889.

• 17 •

Honor Restored

In 1961, Kenneth E. Shiflet's book, *The Convenient Coward*, was published and described as "A fictionalized biography based on the life of Marcus A. Reno, who commanded the battalion of the 7th Cavalry that survived the Custer Massacre."[1] That same year, Kenneth M. Hammer's article on Reno's life and military career appeared in the New York Westerners' *Brand Book*. The following year, Lieutenant Colonel Chester Shore, state adjutant of the Montana American Legion, asked members of the Montana Reserve Officers Association "to support a drive to move the bones of Indian fighter Marcus A. Reno from a potter's field to Custer National Cemetery." Shore stated, "The place for his reburial should be in the Custer Cemetery near where he made his successful stand against the Indians."[2]

No immediate action resulted from Shore's request but he determined that for the reburial to take place, authorization would be required from a relative or descendent of the major. He contacted Montana's two U.S. senators, Mike Mansfield and Lee Metcalf, soliciting their help in getting Reno's remains moved to the Custer National Cemetery. Metcalf had read an editorial defending Reno and wrote to the Department of the Interior to find out if Reno's remains could be reburied on the battlefield. Metcalf's letter was referred to Colonel George Walton who was writing a biography of Reno. Walton contacted Shore and they agreed to search for a Reno relative or descendent. Unfortunately, their extensive search for such a person was unsuccessful.

In 1966, additional interest in Reno was generated with the publication of Terrell's and Walton's book *Faint the Trumpet Sounds*: "The full story of Major Marcus A. Reno — man and soldier — his military exploits, his fight to defend himself against his detractors, his lonely death and burial in an unmarked grave — is told here in a compelling narrative that goes far toward rehabilitating his reputation and putting the events of his life in their proper historical perspective."[3] Shore and Walton had continued their search for a Reno descendent or relative but found only what Shore described as "phonies."[4]

Shortly after publication of his book, Walton was staying at the Skyline Motor Inn in New York and went to the cocktail lounge. While waiting at the bar, he heard someone say "Reno," and he turned to a man at the bar who had mentioned the name. Walton said, "Did you say Reno?" The man replied, "Yes, if you get west of the Mississippi just tell them you know Charles Reno."

Walton asked, "Who is Charles Reno" and the man pointed to the bartender.[5] Introducing himself to Charles Reno, Walton asked him if he were a relative of Marcus Reno. Charles replied that he was and that his sister in Billings, Mrs. Leora Skates, had the records to prove it. Walton hurriedly called Shore in Billings who stated he had known Mrs. Skates for 10 years but did not know she was related to Marcus Reno. After conversing with Shore, Walton returned to the bar with a copy of his book and introduced his wife to Charles. Looking at the picture in the book, she commented, "My goodness, there is even a likeness."[6] After three years of searching, Shore and Walton had finally found their Reno descendent.

Walton urged Charles to file an application for the correction of Marcus Reno's military records to set aside the 1879 less than honorable dismissal verdict of the general court-martial. On Oct. 29, 1966, Charles completed Form DD 149, and in support of the application submitted as evidence the statement: "If justice is ever to prevail in this most deserving case then by all means this case should have its Day in Court and be formally heard. Col. George Walton the author of book entitled 'Faint the Trumpet Sounds' relates the story of Major Marcus A. Reno. He is most willing to appear before the board and make known the research etc. that should be of material aid in producing a clear picture for your consideration." Where the form asked for the name and address of counsel, Charles wrote "The American Legion."

On Nov. 1, John J. Corcoran, director, The American Legion, National Rehabilitation Commission, submitted Form DD 149, completed by Charles Reno, to the Army Board for Correction of Military Records on behalf of Marcus Reno.[7] The board had been established by the Legislative Reorganization Act of 1946, which gave the authority for the correction of military or naval records to civilian officers or employees of the Department of the Army. Private bills or resolutions to correct military or naval records could no longer be considered by either the Senate or the House of Representatives. The Correction Board, with three members constituting a quorum, was to be appointed by the secretary of the army and would provide recommendations to the secretary, who would take final action on the application. The applicant, or his relative or heir, had to have "exhausted all effective administrative remedies afforded him by existing law or regulations," before the Correction Board would consider reviewing the case. Charles Reno, in his application to the board, asked them to waive the three-year limitation for filing an application:

"I request the board to waive a failure to timely file on grounds of injustice as a glaring injustice does exists in the case concerned."[8]

The Correction Board received Charles Reno's application but wondered who was asking for the review and what was his relationship to Marcus Reno. A letter from Charles, received at the Army Correction Board Nov. 18, indicated he was the "great-grandson" of Marcus and stated: "I do hereby request that you review this application for the correction of record of Marcus A. Reno."[9] On Dec. 5, 1966, Charles sent another letter to the Correction Board asking for an amendment to his previous request: "As a great-nephew, and next of kin, I do hereby request that you review this application for the correction of record of Marcus A. Reno."[10]

On Jan. 20, 1967, the mayor of Billings, Mont., Willard E. Fraser, wrote to the Correction Board requesting the status of Charles Reno's application for the reinstatement of Major Reno. Fraser indicated the city of Billings was interested in conducting reinterment services for the major if the board's recommendation were favorable. Raymond J. Williams, executive secretary, Army Board for Correction of Military Records, responded Jan. 31: "The application for correction of Major Reno's records is currently undergoing preliminary processing in the Examining Branch of the staff of this board. The records in question are largely in the custody of the Archivist of the United States, are quite voluminous and will require considerable research and extraction prior to presentation to the board.... Your interest in Major Reno's case is appreciated and you will be advised of the final decision in the case."[11]

In a letter also dated Jan. 31, Williams wrote to the superintendent of the U.S. Military Academy at West Point: "In order to assist this board in resolution of an application for recharacterization of Major Reno's separation, it is requested that a transcript or summary of Major Reno's records while a cadet at the Military Academy be furnished." To obtain Reno's military records, Williams wrote to the National Archives requesting "copies of the pertinent [Reno] records" be furnished to the board.[12]

The membership of the Army Board for Correction of Military Records was reconstituted by the secretary of the army Feb. 7 and included 15 names of Department of the Army personnel eligible to serve. The board would convene at the call of the executive secretary (Williams) for "consideration and determination of applications in accordance with the regulations and procedures prescribed by AR 15-185. Three members present will constitute a quorum."[13] Williams reviewed the information furnished by the Military Academy and the National Archives and Records Administration and determined that a formal hearing should be held. On April 13, he sent a "Notice of Case Hearing" to Charles Reno indicating the hearing would convene May 3 and asked him to indicate if he would be present and represented by counsel.

Charles replied April 18 that he would be present on the date scheduled and would be represented by counsel.[14]

The board convened in Room 2D731 at the Pentagon May 3, 1967, at the call of the Board Chairman Albert J. Esgain and consisted of board members Chelsea L. Henson, Sherry B. Myers, Roswell M. Yingling, and Harold F. Hufendick, all civilian employees of the Department of the Army. Williams was executive secretary and the examiner was Francis X. Foley. Charles Reno was present and was represented by Samuel C. Borzilleri, legal consultant for the American Legion, and Gene L. Fattig, supervisor of the Review and Corrections Board for The American Legion. Listed as "Co-Counsels" were George Walton and Chester K. Shore. Several newspaper reporters were also present to cover the proceedings.

The first to testify was Gene Fattig, who stated the case: "The American Legion, in behalf of Charles Reno and Marcus Reno, are petitioning the board for a correction of military records for the purpose of restoring Marcus Reno to his military rank and to be buried with honors along with the other heroes who contributed to the history of our great nation."[15] Fattig then called on Borzilleri to introduce the witnesses who were to be asked to provide information to the board.

Borzilleri indicated to the board that testimony would be provided in four phases: He would give a brief background of the events leading to Major Reno's dismissal from the service; Fattig would detail the historical background of Reno's life and military career; Shore would relate the facts about Reno he found in 15 years of research; and Walton, with Shore, would "bring out from the graves of the dead what they found." Borzilleri's opening statement would set the tone of the proceedings by his picturesque description of the relationship between George Custer and Marcus Reno:

> Marcus Reno's downfall began at the Battle of Little Big Horn, with General Custer. History will tell that General Custer and Marcus Reno had mutual admiration for each other. They were both very fine officers, and they both respected each other. I am certain that if General Custer had been alive when Marcus Reno was having his difficulties, he would have had a champion.... The important fact here is that General Custer depended on Marcus Reno; that Marcus Reno was considered a competent and a cautious officer.

Borzilleri continued with his dramatized description of the Little Big Horn battle and why Custer lost:

> They [7th Cavalry] were decoyed, they were out-maneuvered and outplayed by Sitting Bull and Crazy Horse, as Chief of Staff; and they managed to divide them by leading Reno into the trap and obviously leading General Custer into a trap; and Captain Benteen was out so far on the left flank that he did not know what the other two were doing. To make a long story short, they both were confined to battle and before you knew it Custer was surrounded and Reno was not able to go to his assistance.

Borzilleri briefly described the findings of the 1879 Court of Inquiry, and the results of the 1877 court-martial. He stated President Grant had mitigated the 1877 court-martial sentence, but no one on the board corrected him that it was not Grant but President Hayes. His summary of the 1879 court-martial was somewhat more accurate, although he tended to overstate Reno's military ability: "He [Reno] was the Patton of General George Custer, of the 1880s. He was not a garrison soldier. He was out in the field." Borzilleri reviewed each of the incidents that led to the court-martial and thought the court had "emasculated" each of the specifications relating to the first charge of "conduct unbecoming an officer and a gentleman," and had, in fact, found Reno not guilty of this charge but guilty of "conduct to the prejudice of good order and military discipline."

Concerning the second charge of "conduct unbecoming an officer and a gentleman" and the specification dealing with the looking into the side window of Colonel Sturgis' house, Borzilleri said, "At this point someone had gotten fed up with Marcus Reno and was going to do more than give him a short lesson." He noted that "not only was Colonel Sturgis the accuser, but he desired to be the prosecutor." He also pointed out that Colonel Sturgis had a son killed at the Little Big Horn battle and "knowing the attitude against Custer [by Sturgis] and the doubt that there had been against Reno, it is highly significant that all that took place on that particular date could have been permeated with what took place at Custer's Last Stand." Borzilleri told the board about the recommendation of clemency by five of the seven court members, the various recommendations of the reviewing officials before the court's findings were presented to the president, the dismissal decision made by President Hayes, and the efforts attempted by Reno in Congress to be reinstated.

Borzilleri continued, "It is significant, Gentlemen, that this officer, after 22 years and a great fighter and one of the men who had contributed emphatically to the opening of the West, who contributed emphatically to the unification of the Nation at the time of the Rebellion, found himself no longer an officer on such flimsy specifications as conduct unbecoming an officer."

He then discussed the Articles of War in effect at the time of the court-martial and how he thought the reviewing authorities had improperly interpreted the articles and had decided "mistakenly" that it was "mandatory that Marcus Reno be disbarred from the service." Borzilleri concluded his testimony: "I am sold that Marcus Reno deserves a place in history and he should be honored and given the privilege of burial in our National Cemetery."[16]

Counsel Gene Fattig was then asked to give a brief background on Reno's early life as a cadet at West Point. Fattig informed the board that Reno had wanted to become a soldier from his earliest teenage years and "his adjustment at West Point reflects his determination to achieve this goal and does firmly establish great strength of character as well as outstanding integrity." He told them about Reno being charged with "destroying" a tree; being dismissed with six other cadets because he exceeded the allowable number of demerits, but returning to the academy the following academic year; and in the final incident, singing on guard duty and being dismissed for a second time only to return again to complete his education. "How many fellows who were not destined to be a great soldier would have again returned? Our man, Marcus, returned. He graduated in 1857."

Fattig continued his testimony with a long summary of Reno's Civil War career and, like Borzilleri, somewhat embellished the facts:

> Before Reno was 30 years of age he became General Torbett's Chief of Staff. Even though he was burdened with heavy responsibilities as a Staff Officer, he took every possible opportunity to ride at the head of the troops, exposing himself recklessly to the enemy fire and led charges and was relentless in his pursuit of Confederate troops. His action, gallant in nature, as well as outstanding leadership, I am sure, was responsible for his climbing the ladder. He was climbing that ladder on his own. He had no father that was a close friend of the Secretary of War, or something of that nature.

He reviewed Reno's career following the Civil War and presented a garbled description of the Little Big Horn battle. Fattig told the board he thought Mrs. Custer was at least partially to blame for Reno's problems:

> But the very fine soldier named Custer, and he was quite a soldier, left a widow who, by the way, didn't get around to dying until 1933. This widow was obsessed, I think, and some historians I know think, about this bit of Custer's Last Stand and was not about to let well enough alone. We believe that as a result of

her persistent efforts to place the blame on someone besides her own husband, General George Custer, the victim ended up being a man named Marcus Reno.

Fattig continued his narrative by reviewing the results of the 1879 Court of Inquiry, and then, following questions from the board chairman, proceeded to a more detailed discussion on the relationship between Ella Sturgis and Reno. He stated, "From my review I felt that Marcus certainly thought he was courting this young lady. Whether or not she felt the same, I don't know." Fattig concluded his testimony: "So it was just one thing after another that seemed to relate it all back entirely to a wrong feeling about Reno's relationship to the Custer event."[17]

Next on the agenda was Shore, who provided the board with his background and his interest in Reno which dated to 1948: "I thought it was a disgrace that here was Marcus Reno buried in an unmarked grave...and there were all kinds of tombstones, even a big stone on Reno's Point [Custer Hill] there to all the men of the 7th Cavalry but Reno was an unknown." Shore continued: "I wanted to find out if Reno's remains could be reburied on the Battlefield." Shore suggested to the board that unless Reno was cleared of the less than honorable discharge, he could not be buried in the Custer Battlefield National Cemetery.

Chairman Esgain interrupted Shore, asking, "Are you saying that unless he is cleared, he won't be eligible for reburial at this place?" Shore replied, "That has been my prime objective, to get his remains reburied in the Battlefield, where he should be." As the proceedings continued, Esgain asked Shore, "But you are convinced in your own mind that there has been a great injustice based upon your research?" Shore completed his testimony with his response, "Yes, sir, and I have always been for the underdog. In my newspaper work I would take up the fight for the underdog."[18]

Walton was the next witness and reviewed his efforts in writing *Faint the Trumpet Sounds*:

> I spent about five years researching on the life of Marcus Reno. It took me all over the United States. I spent literally weeks and weeks in the National Archives, going over the records there; and I finally wrote a manuscript of some 1200 pages. As a matter of fact, my co-author was brought into the picture just to cut down the length of my manuscript. I think I know quite a little about the life of Marcus Reno.... I arrived at some definite conclusions, and one of them was that he had been quite unfairly dismissed from the Army.

Continuing his testimony, Walton covered some of the legal aspects of Reno's dismissal, concluding:

> Secretary [of War] Lincoln in his reply [to Scott Lord] admitted that the proceedings which had resulted in Major Reno's dismissal were defective.... I think that is a very, very strong point, that the Secretary of War himself admitted that the entire proceedings that had resulted in the dismissal were defective.

Walton was asked by Esgain why he thought President Hayes disregarded the recommendations of the military court and most of the reviewing authorities. Walton replied, "There is nothing conclusive...there is no indication why he refused to accept the recommendations of the entire chain of command, including five members of the Court that had convicted Major Reno."[19]

The final witness to appear before the board was Charles Reno, great-nephew of Marcus Reno, and Esgain asked him, "Why was it that you yourself never participated or made a move towards determining what had happened to Marcus Reno?" Charles replied:

> Having lived with the name of Reno for many, many years and having, shall we say, suffered a little bit in the sense of the rivalry between Custer and Reno in many, many discussions and arguments pro and con throughout the west, I rather found myself in the position that at times I would play down the role of Reno.... The family played it down.... I can say that insofar as actions in the case were concerned, I did not know of the Review Board or any of its facilities, any of the possibilities of carrying a case forward to its conclusion.

Charles discussed his chance meeting with Walton and reading *Faint the Trumpet Sounds* "with a little bit of emotion." He thought, "The book rather covers my views, and I would like to say that this file that was compiled by the staff of the board, I feel, is excellent and meets with my approval; and I can think of nothing further that I could say other than what is in this document that could be presented to the board. I respect it very much."

After Charles Reno's testimony, Counsel Borzilleri suggested to Esgain: "Mr. Chairman, I think there is an important question that must be put for the record to Mr. Reno, and that is: Assuming that this board clears him, would you want Marcus Reno's remains removed from the present site and buried in the National Cemetery?" Charles provided the answer: "I would say that is probably one of the prime objectives of my being here."[20]

The chairman then opened the meeting for questions from the other board members, but asked the first question himself: "Is there any evidence in the records that were available to you [Counsel Borzilleri] of any disciplinary action being taken against Major Reno subsequent to his graduation from West Point except for the two court martial actions that are reflected in this brief?" Walton provided the response: "There were no other disciplinary actions taken. As a matter of fact, his record is excellent, particularly during the Civil War, where he led a Brigade as a Captain in the Regular Army although breveted to Brigadier General of Volunteers."[21]

A board member asked whether prior to the establishment of the Correction Board a private bill had ever been introduced into Congress for Marcus Reno's reinstatement. Walton again handled the response: "During the last several years of Major Reno's life, while he was a clerk in the Pension Bureau, every year there would be a Bill introduced for his relief and restoration; but he being a quite controversial figure, it never came out of the then Military Affairs Committee."[22]

This was followed by another question: "On the Bills introduced in Congress during Reno's last years, did they ever ask the War Department for a report on those Bills?" Walton replied, "Yes, they did...the report would be generally his brevets, his military career, the battles he was in, and all that. Although I am not quite sure about this, I don't believe the War Department made any recommendations."[23]

A discussion followed about Reno's 1879 request for resignation and the 1880 subsequent withdrawal of his request. Secretary Williams asked Borzilleri, "What in your opinion would have happened if the resignation had been accepted? Would it have been a resignation with honor or without honor?" Borzilleri replied, "In my opinion it would have been a resignation with honor.... [T]hey would have let him withdraw, under honor, and then close the whole books on the subject."[24]

Examiner Foley provided more information on the subject to the board:

> [T]he second one [telegram] was sent in March of 1880, and this was after the recommendations of the Convening Authority, General Terry, and of the General of the Army, General Sherman, had been made; and it is reasonable to assume that those were of record and that he [Reno] was withdrawing his resignation in view of what apparently may have become a favorable outcome to this case.[25]

Walton was asked if he thought politics played a factor in President Hayes' decision to not follow the recommendations of clemency. Walton replied:

> [T]here had been many, many articles in the press over the years prior thereto, actually blaming Reno for the death of Custer and the death of the other troops of the command and charging him with cowardice; and the "big lie" had been told so often that a great many people were thoroughly convinced that that was true. So as far as the President was concerned there was certainly no political advantage and a great deal of political disadvantage in showing clemency as far as the Major was concerned.[26]

Several questions concerned the Little Big Horn battle and Reno's actions during the fight. Walton thought, "The steps he had taken during the Battle were quite proper and were absolutely necessary for his Command and actually resulted in saving the few lives that he did save."[27]

The board asked Walton about Mrs. Custer's role in blaming Reno for the disaster at the Little Big Horn. Walton replied:

> [T]here is a lot of evidence of this in correspondence, and in articles about lectures she has made, and that sort of thing. Originally she blamed General Terry. Then she blamed Reno and Benteen, as did Whittaker in his biography. Thereafter she dropped Benteen and concentrated on Reno. That is a matter of record. It is in her correspondence and it is in various lectures she has made. She almost made it a career.[28]

A brief discussion followed about the officers appointed to the 1879 court-martial and whether some may have been biased against a cavalry officer as the majority were infantry. Borzilleri said he did not think this was the case and that even Colonel Wood, an infantry officer, was one of the five officers who recommended clemency.[29]

Esgain closed the open proceedings with the statement:

> Mr. Reno, fine Counsels, and other Witnesses, we express our appreciation for your coming and giving us your story. We find it very interesting, and we will give it very careful and meticulous consideration, rest assured, and for the press and observers we appreciate your cooperation and your courtesy.[30]

The Army Correction Board went into closed session and evaluated the merits of the case for about a day. On May 5, 1967, the board issued its recommendations:

THE BOARD CONCLUDES:

1. That in the interest of justice and for good cause shown, the failure of the applicant to timely file within the period prescribed by law is excused.

2. That RENO had more than 20 years of active service at the time of his discharge, including combat duty on the Northwest Frontier prior to the Civil War and further combat service against hostile Indians in the West subsequent to the Civil War.

3. That during the Civil War RENO had extensive combat service and attained the brevet rank of Brigadier General as a result of gallant and exemplary service.

4. That there is no record, subsequent to his appointment, of any disciplinary or other adverse action against RENO until after his survival of the disastrous Battle of the Little Big Horn, an event which apparently led to widespread belief that through incompetence or cowardice, he may have been responsible for the loss of Colonel Custer and five companies of the 7th Cavalry Regiment; that this belief created intense hostility toward him which resulted in strained relationships and a defensive attitude, on his part, toward officers and others within the command, which ultimately led to his excessive use of alcohol and abnormal behavior.

5. That in addition to the foregoing, the recent loss of his wife, his state of bachelorhood in a desolate frontier fort and in the field, and the attendant primitive conditions, were not conducive to producing "plaster saints."

6. That the available historical records support the contention that RENO's survival of the Battle of the Little Big Horn, though cleared by a Court of Inquiry of allegations of cowardice and disobedience of orders, made him a very controversial and unpopular figure; that this experience had a traumatic effect on his personality and conduct, and the resulting stigma led to a rapid decline in his prior exemplary conduct and ultimately resulted in his dismissal from the service.

7. That the recommendations of the Department Commander and the General of the Army, both experienced field combat of-

ficers, to the effect that RENO was not unfit to serve as an officer, that the sentence of the General Court-Martial which adjudged dismissal was too severe and that he should be retained in the military service, should have been given more weight by the Approving Authority.

8. That it is reasonable to assume that RENO's tender of resignation from service while the proceedings of his court-martial were undergoing review would have been approved under honorable conditions, on the basis of his over-all record of service, had RENO not withdrawn his resignation on the erroneous belief that the recommendations for clemency on his behalf would be approved by the approving authority.

9. That the ultimately approved findings left RENO "Guilty" of offenses which did not require a mandatory sentence to dismissal; that the opinions and recommendations of the majority of the court, the Staff Judge Advocate, the Convening Authority and the General of the Army relative to the conviction and mitigation of the sentence, were based upon valid and compelling evidence; that the reason for the Approving Authority's action in approving the sentence to dismissal in apparent disregard of such recommendations for clemency, without a stated basis, raises a reasonable doubt as to the propriety of such a course of action.

10. That while subsequent to RENO's dismissal from the Army, several unsuccessful attempts were initiated in Congress to attempt relief thru legislative action, the relief sought related to his restoration to military status in the Army, a matter not under consideration in these proceedings, which are concerned solely with a request for recharacterization of the separation of a deceased former officer.

11. That while the board does not condone the course of conduct which led to RENO's conviction and dismissal, the board is nevertheless of the opinion that in consideration of the over-all records available to the board, the circumstances attendant at the time, RENO's many years of honorable and distinguished military service, and the recommendations of senior general officers, the execution of a sentence to dismissal was excessive and therefore, unjust.

THE BOARD RECOMMENDS:

That all of the Department of the Army records of MARCUS A. RENO be corrected to show that he was honorably discharged from the United States Army in the Grade of Major, United States Army (Brevet Colonel, United States Army and Brevet Brigadier General, United States Volunteers), on 1 April 1880.

It would not be until May 31, 1967, that Under Secretary of the Army David E. McGiffert signed a "Memorandum for the Adjutant General" directing the correction of all Army records to show Marcus A. Reno being honorably discharged as a major on April 1, 1880.[31] Army Board of Correction Executive Secretary Raymond J. Williams wrote to the American Legion's National Rehabilitation Commission in Washington, D.C., that same day enclosing copies of the proceedings and McGiffert's decision to correct Reno's records. Charles Reno, accepting the official document of the decision from the Army Board, said:

I am deeply grateful to the board, and the Secretary of the Army — and to The American Legion for their help in this case. It is vindication and a victory at last for Major Reno....88 (sic) years later justice comes to Major Marcus A. Reno, who will come to rest, recognized, and rewarded for 23 years faithful and loyal commissioned service to his country.[32]

On June 5, Williams sent a "Disposition Form" to the Adjutant General's Office requesting the "necessary administrative action be taken to effect the correction of the record indicated." Colonel C. A. Stanfiel, the acting adjutant general, sent a letter to Charles Reno, dated June 9, 1967, stating "in reference to your application for correction of the military records of Marcus A. Reno," and by direction of the "Secretary of the Army...appropriate action is now being taken to accomplish the correction of records indicated above."[33]

Charles had cleared the first, and most difficult, hurdle in getting the major's remains buried in the Custer Battlefield National Cemetery. Charles then had to give consideration to the expenses involved in the disinterment of the remains from the Glenwood Cemetery, transportation to Montana and reburial in the National Cemetery. The Montana American Legion offered to make the necessary arrangements for the burial and solicit its membership for donations to defray the costs. On July 8, 1967, Charles Reno signed the "Standard Interment Authorization Form of the Maryland-District of Columbia Cemetery Association," authorizing the disinterment of the remains of Marcus

367

Service at Custer Battlefield National Monument
(Charles Reno, center, dark suit, arms folded)
(John Popovich photo)

A. Reno from Site 8, Lot 98, Section O of the Glenwood Cemetery. As noted on the cemetery card, Reno's remains were disinterred Aug. 16, 1967, "to be interred in Custer Battlefield Natl. Cem., Crow Agency, Montana."[34]

Reno's remains were transported to a funeral home in Billings, Mont., where they remained until the morning of Sept. 9 when they were moved to the First Christian Church, 522 29th St. North. Services were held at the church starting at 9 a.m. and were conducted by the Rev. Gene Robinson, pastor. Included among the attendees were Charles Reno, his sisters Leora Skates and Mrs. Lavernia Bachman, and George Walton. Following the church service, a military funeral procession began at 9:30 a.m. at the First Christian Church, and, following Army regulations for honors due a general officer, moved south on 29th Street to 1st Avenue North and then turned east to 22nd Street North. The 163rd Armored Cavalry Regiment, Montana National Guard, furnished an escort and honor guard for the procession. Music was provided by the 46th Army Band, Bozeman, Montana National Guard and the color guard was from the Clark Stops Post No. 135, Crow Agency, with the Crows in tribal regalia. Representatives of the Sioux, Northern Cheyenne and Arikara tribes marched in the solemn procession. The Sheridan, Wyo., American Legion 7th Cavalry Drum and Bugle Corps furnished the muffled drum cadence and played the 7th Cavalry's regimental song, "Garry Owen." Following the horse-drawn artillery caisson bearing the flag-covered casket was a riderless horse, with boots reversed in the stirrups, led by Guy Sperry, commanding officer of Troop B, 7th Cavalry, Bozeman Parade Unit, dressed in a period cavalry uniform.

At 10:30 a.m., a motorcade with a hearse bearing Reno's remains, left Billings and headed to Hardin, Mont. American Legion Post No. 8, Hardin, was in charge of the short military funeral procession in Hardin which included elements of the 163rd Armored Cavalry Regiment, the 46th Army Band, the Sheridan American Legion Drum and Bugle Corps, and members of the Sioux, Northern Cheyenne, Arikara and Crow tribes. At 1 o'clock, the motorcade left Hardin for the final 15-mile drive to the Custer Battlefield National Monument.

Committal services with full military honors began at 2 o'clock at the National Cemetery and were conducted by the Rev. Chester A. Bentley, past department chaplain of the American Legion. The grave site was located near the cemetery's flagpole, less than 250 yards from the hill where Custer and all the soldiers with him were killed. Tributes were given by John Wooden Leg, grandson of a Cheyenne warrior in the battle, and Crow Chief Edison Real Bird. Other representatives of Indian tribes included Austin Two Moons, grandson of Cheyenne Chief Two Moon; Arlis Whiteman, grandson of White Man Runs Him, a Crow scout with Custer; and Ed Mcgaa, whose ancestors fought under Chief Crazy Horse.[35]

A tribute to the soldier Reno, restored to his Civil War rank of brevet brigadier general of volunteers, was an 11-gun salute by the 163rd Armored Cavalry Regiment. As the last of three volleys echoed over the hills, the casket was lowered slowly into its final resting place. The clear notes of "Taps" drifted into the Little Big Horn Valley and the long journey that had begun in a small Illinois town in 1834 was, at last, finished.

(Author's photo 1998)

Endnotes

[1] Kenneth E. Shiflet, *The Convenient Coward* (The Stackpole Company, Harrisburg, Pa., 1961).

[2] *Billings Gazette*, May 11, 1962, p. 13.

[3] John Upton Terrell and Colonel George Walton, *Faint the Trumpet Sounds* (David McKay Co., Inc., New York, 1966).

[4] Army Board For Correction of Military Records, Transcript of Hearing, May 3, 1967, pp. 47-49. In Reno's personal file.

[5] Correction Board Transcript, p. 56.

[6] Correction Board Transcript, p. 58.

[7] Letter dated Nov. 1, 1966, from Corcoran to the Army Board for Correction of Military Records. Copy in Reno's personal file.

[8] Application For Correction of Military or Naval Record, Form DD 149, dated Oct. 29, 1966, Docket Number 66-2215, in Reno's personal file.

[9] Letter (no date) to the Army Board for Correction of Military Records, signed by Charles Reno, and received on Nov. 18, 1966. Copy in Reno's personal file.

[10] Letter dated Dec. 5, 1966, from Charles Reno to the Army Correction Board, in Reno's personal file. Charles had talked to his sister, Leora Skates of Billings, Mont., and had learned that he was not Marcus' great-grandson but he was the great-grandson of Marcus' brother Henry, which made him Marcus' great-nephew.

[11] Letter dated Jan. 31, 1967, from Williams to Fraser, in Reno's personal file.

[12] Letter dated Jan. 31, 1967, from Williams to the U.S. Military Academy; and an undated letter, probably Jan. 31, to the assistant archivist for military archives. Both letters in Reno's personal file.

[13] Letter dated Feb. 7, 1967, to the executive secretary of the Correction Board (Williams) from John G. Connell, Jr., Administrative Assistant, "by order of the Secretary of the Army." In Reno's personal file.

[14] Notice of Case Hearing, dated April 13, 1967, from the Department of the Army (Williams) to Charles Reno, in Reno's personal file.

[15] Correction Board Transcript, p. 4.

[16] Correction Board Transcript, Borzilleri's testimony covers pages 6-30.

[17] Correction Board Transcript, Fattig's testimony covers pages 31-44.

[18] Correction Board Transcript, Shore's testimony covers pages 44-50.

[19] Correction Board Transcript, Walton's testimony covers pages 51-55.

[20] Correction Board Transcript, Charles Reno's testimony covers pages 55-62.

[21] Correction Board Transcript, p. 62-63.

[22] Correction Board Transcript, p. 64.

[23] Correction Board Transcript, p. 65.

[24] Correction Board Transcript, p. 67.

[25] Correction Board Transcript, p. 68.

[26] Correction Board Transcript, p. 69.

[27] Correction Board Transcript, p. 70.

[28] Correction Board Transcript, pp. 72-73.

[29] Correction Board Transcript, p. 79. In fact three of the five officers on the court-martial board who voted for clemency were infantry officers: Colonel Wood, and Majors Moore and Conrad. The other two were Major Irwin, Medical Department, and Lieutenant Colonel Alexander, 2nd Cavalry.

[30] Correction Board Transcript, p. 81.

[31] Department of the Army, Office of the Under Secretary, dated May 31, 1967, and signed by McGiffert. In a final note of irony, although the reinstatement memorandum was not signed by the Army Secretary Stanley Resor, he undoubtedly was aware of the proceedings and the final decision by his Under Secretary. Resor was married to Ella Jane Pillsbury — the granddaughter of Ella Marie Sturgis.

[32] News release issued by The American Legion's Washington Headquarters, dated May 31, 1967. In author's collection.

[33] Both the June 5 letter from Williams and the June 9 letter from Colonel Stanfiel to Charles Reno can be found in Barry C. Johnson's "The Case of Marcus A. Reno," (The English Westerners' Society, London, 1969), pp. 86-87. This pamphlet has the full text of the Correction Board's proceedings and a summary of both the 1877 and 1879 courts-martial.

[34] Interment Authorization Form, dated July 17, 1967, copy in author's collection.

[35] *The State Journal*, Lansing, Mich., Sept. 10, 1967.

• Postscript •

Robert Ross Reno (1864 - ?)

Unable to secure a burial site for Marcus in the Ross family plot, Robert Ross and Ittie Reno left Harrisburg on Friday, April 5, 1889, and returned to Nashville. Ross filed a "Letters of Administration" on the 9th which stated that "Marcus A. Reno has died, leaving no will, and the Court...having ordered that Letters of Administration be issued to you...the said R. R. Reno to take into your possession and control all the goods, chattels, and papers of the said intestate."[1] Ross said Marcus had transferred the Mutual Life Insurance Company of New York life insurance policy for $6,000 to him before he executed the assignment to Isabella. Being in physical position of the policy, Ross requested the money from the insurance company. Isabella, Marcus' widow, also wrote to the insurance company claiming to be the sole beneficiary. She cited the March 4, 1884, document that Marcus had signed which gave her "all my right, title, and interest in Policy #186142 issued by The Mutual Life Insurance Company of New York."[2]

The insurance company, having two claims against the policy, had no choice but to bring suit against both Ross and Isabella and let the courts decide who should get what. In a disposition taken by the court, Ross claimed that the policy had been pledged as collateral for his trust fund for $800 borrowed by Marcus in December 1878, and $1,000 borrowed in March 1880, and the total owed, with interest, was $3,000. The Court decreed: "that R. R. Reno shall be paid $1,600 and Mrs. Isabella Ray Reno shall be paid the sum of $3,784 and the remainder of the fund shall remain in court subject to its further orders."[3]

As noted earlier, several months after Ross married Ittie in May 1885, he purchased an one-fourth interest in Kinney, McLaughlin & Co. By mid-1888, the firm, now Kinney & Co., was in financial trouble and creditors were beginning to press the partners for payment of outstanding debts. When Marcus visited Ross and Ittie in Nashville in May 1888, he and Ross signed over to Ittie their interests in the New Cumberland farm and the Harrisburg house. These transactions prevented Ross' personal property being seized in the event Kinney & Co. ceased operations.

By the summer of 1889, Kinney & Co. needed immediate cash to fend off the creditors and Ittie provided the money. She sold the Harrisburg property for $12,000, less than three months after Marcus' death, and obtained a $15,000 mortgage against the New Cumberland farm in August 1889. During the next few months she loaned Kinney & Co. the $27,000.

The firm continued in business for the next two years and Ross traveled extensively in the North "selling goods." Finally, in August 1891, Kinney & Co. failed and George Kinney formed a new corporation, Kinney Distilling Company. On March 3, 1892, Ross appointed G. P. Lipscomb his "Attorney in Fact" to "execute and make all receipts, notes and bills in revenue or otherwise, that he and G. D. Kinney may deem proper or necessary to make and execute in the settlement, and winding up of the business and affairs of the late firm of Kinney & Co."[4] Ross did not have any ownership interest in the new Kinney Distilling Company. In anticipation of a lawsuit by the firm's creditors, George Kinney transferred the deed of his home at 605 Cedar Street, Nashville, to Ittie as collateral for her loans to Kinney & Co.

The creditors of the old Kinney & Co. brought suit against the partners, including Ross Reno, in early 1893. There was a question of whether, in 1888, Ross had transferred the two pieces of property he received from his mother's estate to Ittie only to prevent them from being seized by the creditors. Ross told the court why he did it: "Having contracted very convivial habits, I did it as a protection to myself, as sometimes under the influence of liquor I might have disposed of it very disadvantageously."[5]

In 1892, Ross, although no longer a partner in the firm, was employed as a salesman for the new Kinney Distilling Company of Nashville. This employment frequently took him away from Nashville for long periods of time. He was in New York in early March 1892, and did not return to Nashville until September of that year.[6] By the summer of 1893, it was apparent to both Ittie and Ross that their marriage was failing. Ittie would later testify in court about their marriage:

> For some years they lived happily together, and until he fell into evil ways and habits of extreme dissipation. After some years he became addicted to gambling, and drunkenness, and was exceedingly reckless during these periods of dissipation; and usually he absented himself and remained away from his home during such times. As a consequence she saw but little of him while intoxicated; and his conduct was decorous and polite while sober.[7]

In the fall of 1893, Ross left Nashville for what Ittie thought was another business trip. Ross went to Buffalo, N.Y., and, apparently having quit his job with the Kinney Distilling Company, took a position of employment with C. W. Frankel & Company of Buffalo under the name of John R. Cameron. Months passed before he informed Ittie where he was and that he was then working for the Hotel Iroquois in Buffalo. Ittie wrote to him "urging him to reform," and "he expressed a purpose to do so, but he neither expressed a willingness to return to [her], or a desire to have her with him."[8]

Ross would write from time to time asking Ittie for money which she refused to send. After two years he no longer wrote and she had no idea where he had gone. Finally in July 1897 he wrote to Ittie asking her to have her father write to "a certain firm in St. Louis, Missouri, that he had once been a member of the firm of Kinney & Co."[9] George apparently refused to write the letter for the next time Ittie heard from Ross was when she received a telegram in October 1897, from Atlanta, Ga. Ross asked her to meet him at the train depot in Nashville as he would "pass through" the next day, but she received the telegram after the time the train was scheduled to arrive.

Ittie did not hear from Ross again until February 1898 when she received a letter from Seattle, Wash., which stated "he was about to sail for Alaska, and that if [she] did not hear from him within a year, she might know that he was dead."[10] Ross sent a telegram to Ittie's brother-in-law, G. P. Lipscomb, on August 19, 1898, saying, "Make Ittie get a divorce or I will."[11] It was the last she was to hear of Ross and consequently filed for divorce on Oct. 15, 1898, stating Ross had "willfully and maliciously abandoned her...and...deserted her in 1893...and...refused to live with her ever since."[12]

In her divorce decree Ittie also stated that while Ross had lived in Buffalo "he lived with and introduced a woman as his wife...and in said city, committed adultery with a woman represented to be his wife, and that these adulterous acts were numerous and repeated." She also indicated Ross had "failed, refused and neglected to provide for her."[13] The divorce was granted on June 22, 1899.

There are no further records about what happened to Robert Ross Reno — he may have again changed his name, gone to Alaska, and met his demise in the great Klondike gold rush of 1898. Ittie Kinney Reno died on June 4, 1941, in Louisville, Ky., and was buried in the Cave Hill Cemetery.[14]

Endnotes

[1] State of Tennessee, Davidson County, Letters of Administration, signed April 9, 1889.

[2] Extract of Mid-Tennessee Supreme Court Record, Mutual Life Insurance Company of New York vs. Robert R. Reno and Isabella Reno, Tennessee State Library and Archives, Record Box 899.

[3] Extract, Final Decree.

[4] Power of Attorney, signed March 3, 1892, registered May 10, 1892, Robert Ross to G. P. Lipscomb, General Index to Deeds, April 15, 1871 to February 10, 1924, Davidson County Courthouse, Nashville, TN.

[5] Deposition of R. R. Reno, May 18, 1893, Tennessee State Library Archives Mid-Term, Supreme Court Records, Box 1006, !894.

[6] Deposition, May 18, 1893, p. 220.

[7] Davidson County, Tennessee, Chancery Court Records, Volume 55, Case #21116, p. 2.

[8] Case #21116, pp. 2-3.

[9] Case #21116, p. 3.

[10] Case #21116, p. 4.

[11] Case #21116, p. 4.

[12] Case #21116, p. 4.

[13] Case #21116, p. 5.

[14] *Nashville Banner*, June 5, 1941.

• Appendix A •

Military History
of

MAJOR MARCUS A. RENO,
7th U.S. CAVALRY

Cadet at U.S. Military Academy, West Point, N.Y., Sept. 1, 1851, to July 1, 1857. Appointed:

Brevet Second Lieutenant, 1st U.S. Dragoons, July 1, 1857

On duty Carlisle Barracks, Penna., Oct. 1, 1857, to Mar. 22, 1858; Jefferson Barracks, Mo, to April 24, 1858; Fort Leavenworth, Kan., to June 21, 1858. Promoted:

Second Lieutenant, 1st U.S. Dragoons, June 14, 1858

Enroute to Washington Territory to Oct. 5, 1858; on duty Fort Walla Walla, Washington Territory, 1858-59; Fort Dalles, Oregon Territory, 1859; Fort Walla Walla, Washington Territory, to Nov. 16, 1861. Promoted:

First Lieutenant, 1st U.S. Dragoons, April 25, 1861
First Lieutenant, 1st U.S. Cavalry, Aug. 3, 1861
Captain, 1st U.S. Cavalry, Nov. 12, 1861

Enroute to Washington, D.C., to March 10, 1862; in the field with the Army of the Potomac to March 25, 1863. Participated in the following engagements:

Siege of Yorktown, Va., April and May 1862
Williamsburg, Va., May 5, 1862
Mechanicsville, Va., June 26, 1862
Gaines Mill, Va., June 27, 1862
Glendale, Va., June 30, 1862
Malvern Hill, Va., July 1, 1862
Crampton's Gap, Md., Sept. 14, 1862
Antietam, Md., Sept. 17, 1862
Sharpsburg, Md., Sept. 19, 1862
Kelly's Ford, Va., March 17, 1863

For "Gallant and Meritorious Services" at Kelly's Ford, Va., appointed:

Brevet Major, U.S. Army, March 17, 1863

On leave to May 1863, for injury received at Kelly's Ford; on recruiting service, Harrisburg, Penna., to June 20, 1863; Acting Chief of Staff to General W. F. Smith, with Pennsylvania Militia, to July 12, 1863. Participated in the following engagement:

Hagerstown, Md., July 10, 1863

On recruiting service to October 8, 1863; with the Army of the Potomac (Rappahannock) to March 1864; Assistant in Cavalry Bureau to May 1864; Acting Assistant Inspector General, 1st Division Cavalry, Army of the Potomac, to August 1864. Participated in the following engagements:

Hawes Shop, Va., May 28, 1864
Cold Harbor, Va., May 31 - June 1, 1864
Trevillian Station, Va., June 11, 1864
Darbytown Road, Va., July 28, 1864

On duty as Acting Assistant Inspector General and Chief of Staff, Cavalry Corps, Middle Military Division, to Jan. 1, 1865. Participated in the following engagements:

Winchester, Va., Aug. 16, 1864
Kearnysville, Va., Aug. 25, 1864
Smithfield, Va., Aug. 29, 1864
Cedar Creek, Va., Oct. 19, 1864

For "Gallant and Meritorious Services" at Cedar Creek, Va., appointed:

Brevet Lieutenant Colonel, U.S. Army, Oct. 19, 1864

Mustered into Volunteer Service on January 1, 1865, and commissioned:

Colonel, 12th Pennsylvania Cavalry, Jan. 1, 1865

Served with the regiment to April 5, 1865; engaged in skirmish with Mosby's Guerrillas at Harmony, Va., March 20-25, 1865; commanded Provisional Brigade to July 20, 1865. For "Gallant and Meritorious Services" during the Rebellion, appointed:

Brevet Colonel, U.S. Army, March 13, 1865
Brevet Brigadier General, U.S. Volunteers, March 13, 1865

Mustered out of Volunteer service, July 20, 1865, and returned to duty as Captain, 1st U.S. Cavalry; on duty as Assistant Instructor of Infantry Tactics at West Point, N.Y., to Oct. 2, 1865; Judge Advocate, Military Commission at New Orleans, La., to Dec. 4, 1865; in Bureau of Refugees, Freedmen and Abandoned Lands at New Orleans, La., to Aug. 28, 1866; on leave to Feb. 8, 1867.

On duty as Acting Assistant Inspector General, Department of the Columbia to July 15, 1869; enroute and member of Board of Survey and Court-Martial duty to Nov. 28, 1869; at Fort Hays, Kan., to July 1871. Promoted:

Major, 7th U.S. Cavalry, Dec. 26, 1868

Commanding post at Spartansburg, S.C., July 21, 1871, to Aug. 22, 1872; member of Small Arms Board, New York, N.Y., to April 25, 1873; commanding escort to Northern Boundary Survey Commission 1873-74; on leave Sept. 14, 1874, to Oct. 24, 1875; on duty Fort Abraham Lincoln, Dakota Territory to May 11, 1876; commanded battalion of regiment to June 26, 1876; participated in the following engagement:

Little Big Horn River, Montana Territory, June 25-26, 1876

Commanded regiment June 26, 1876, to Sept. 22, 1876; on duty at Fort Lincoln to Dec. 15, 1876; commanding post at Fort Abercrombie, Dakota Territory, to Feb. 28, 1877; undergoing trial and awaiting sentence of General Court-Martial to May 8, 1877; suspended from rank and pay to May 8, 1879.

Before a Court of Inquiry at Chicago, Ill., January 13, 1879, to Feb. 11, 1879; commanding post of Fort Meade, Dakota Territory, from May 21, 1879, to July 17, 1879; on duty at that post to Oct. 28, 1879; undergoing trial and awaiting sentence of General Court-Martial to April 1, 1880; dismissed from service April 1, 1880.

Born Carrollton, Ill., Nov. 15, 1834; died Washington, D.C., March 30, 1889.

• Appendix B •

Terry's Instructions to Custer

Camp at Mouth of Rosebud River
Montana Territory, June 22nd, 1876

Lieut.-Col. Custer, 7th Cavalry
Colonel:

The Brigadier General commanding directs that, as soon as your regiment can be made ready for the march, you will proceed up the Rosebud in pursuit of the Indians whose trail was discovered by Major Reno a few days since. It is, of course, impossible to give you any definite instructions in regard to this movement; and were it not impossible to do so, the department commander places too much confidence in your zeal, energy and ability to wish to impose upon you precise orders, which might hamper your action when nearly in contact with the enemy.

He will, however, indicate to you his own views of what your action should be, and he desires that you should conform to them unless you shall see sufficient reason for departing from them. He thinks that you should proceed up the Rosebud until you ascertain definitely the direction in which the trail above spoken of leads. Should it be found (as it appears almost certain that it will be found) to turn towards the Little Horn, he thinks that you should still proceed southward, perhaps as far as the headwaters of the Tongue, and then turn towards the Little Horn, feeling constantly, however, to your left, so as to preclude the possibility of the escape of the Indians to the south or southeast passing around your left flank.

The column of Colonel Gibbon is now in motion for the mouth of the Big Horn. As soon as it reaches that point it will cross the Yellowstone and move up at least as far as the forks of the Big and Little Horns. Of course its future movements must be controlled by circumstances as they arise; but it is hoped that the Indians, if upon the Little Horn, may be so nearly inclosed (sic) by the two columns that their escape will be impossible.

The Department Commander desires that on your way up the Rosebud you should thoroughly examine the upper part of Tullock's Creek; and that you should endeavor to send a scout through to Colonel Gibbon's column with information of the result of your examination. The lower part of this creek will be examined by a detachment from Colonel Gibbon's command. The supply steamer will be pushed up the Big Horn as far as the forks if the river is found to be navigable for that distance, and the Department Commander, who will accompany the column of Colonel Gibbon, desires you to report to him there not later than the expiration of the time for which your troops are rationed, unless in the meantime you receive further orders.

Very respectfully,
Your obedient servant,
E. W. Smith, Captain, 18th Infantry
Acting Assistant Adjutant-General

• Appendix C •
Casualties in Valley & Hilltop Fights*
Valley Fight - June 25, 1876

Staff
Act. Asst. Surg. James M. DeWolf - killed   2nd Lt. Benjamin H. Hodgson - killed

Company A
1st. Sgt. William Heyn - wounded   Pvt. Francis M. Reeves - wounded
Cpl. James Dalious - killed   Pvt. Richard Rollins - killed
Pvt. John E. Armstrong - killed   Pvt. Elijah T. Strode - wounded
Pvt. James Drinan - killed   Pvt. John Sullivan - killed
Pvt. James McDonald - killed   Pvt. Thomas P. Sweetser - killed
Pvt. William Moodie - killed

Company G
1st Lt. Donald McIntosh - killed   Saddler Crawford Selby - killed
Sgt. Edward Botzer - killed   Pvt. John J. McGinniss - killed
Sgt. Martin Considine - killed   Pvt. John Rapp - killed
Cpl. Otto Hagemann - killed   Pvt. Henry Seafferman - killed
Cpl. James Martin - killed   Pvt. Edward Stanley - killed
Farrier Benjamin O. Wells - killed

Company K
Pvt. Elihu F. Clear - killed

Company M
Sgt. Miles F. O'Hara - killed   Pvt. William D. Meyer - killed
Sgt. H. Charles Weihe - wounded   Pvt. William E. Morris - wounded
Cpl. Henry M. Cody - killed   Pvt. Daniel J. Newell - wounded
Cpl. Frederick Stressinger - killed   Pvt. Edward D. Pigford - wounded
Pvt. Henry Gordon - killed   Pvt. George E. Smith - killed
Pvt. Henry Klotzbucher - killed   Pvt. David Summers - killed
Pvt. George Lorentz - killed   Pvt. Henry J. Turley - killed
Pvt. John H. Meier - wounded

Quartermaster
Interperter Isiah Dorman - killed

Guide
Charles A. Reynolds - killed

Interpreter
Bloody Knife - killed

Indian Scouts
BobTailed Bull - killed   Little Brave - killed
Goose - wounded   White Swan - wounded

Hilltop Fight - June 25, 1876

Company A

Cpl. George H. King - wounded (died July 2)   Pvt. Sameul Foster - wounded
Pvt. Jacob Deihle - wounded   Pvt. Frederick Holmstead - wounded

Company B

Sgt. Benjamin Criswell - wounded   Cpl. Charles Cunningham - wounded

Company D

Farrier Vincent Charley - killed   Pvt. Edward Housen - killed
Pvt. Jacob Hetler - wounded   Pvt. Patrick McDonnell - wounded

Company E

Pvt. Herod T. Liddiard - killed

Company G

Pvt. Benjamin F. Rogers - killed   Pvt. John McVay - wounded

Company H

Cpl. Alexander Bishop - wounded   Pvt. Wm. George - wounded (Died July 3)
Pvt. Charles H. Bishop - wounded   Pvt. Jan Moller - wounded
Pvt. Henry Black - wounded   Pvt. John Phillips - wounded
Pvt. John Cooper - wounded   Pvt. Samuel Severs - wounded
Pvt. William Farley - wounded   Pvt. Charles Windolph - wounded

Company K

1st. Sgt. DeWitt Winney - killed   Trumpeter Julius Helmer - killed

Company M

Pvt. Frank Braun - wounded (died Oct. 4)   Pvt. Roman Rutten - wounded

Quartermaster

Packer Frank C. Mann - killed

Hilltop Fight - June 26, 1876

Company B

Sgt. Thomas Murray - wounded   Pvt. George B. Mask - killed
Cpl. William M. Smith - wounded   Pvt. James Pym - wounded
Pvt. Richard B. Dorn - killed

Company C

Pvt. James Bennett - wounded (Died July 5)   Pvt. Peter Thompson - wounded
Pvt. John B., McGuire, Jr. - wounded   Pvt. Alfred Whitaker - wounded

Company D

Pvt. Patrick M. Golden - killed   Pvt. Joseph Kretchmer - wounded

Company E

Sgt. James T. Riley - wounded   Saddler William M. Shields - wounded

Hilltop Fight - June 26, 1876 (cont.)

Company G

Pvt. James P. Boyle - wounded
Pvt. Charles W. Campbell - wounded
Pvt. John Hackett - wounded

Pvt. Andrew J. Moore - killed
Pvt. John Morrison - wounded
Pvt. Henry Petring - wounded

Company H

Capt. Frederick W. Benteen - wounded
1st. Sgt. Joseph McCurry - wounded
Sgt. Patrick Connelly - wounded
Sgt. Thomas McLaughlin - wounded
Sgt. John Pehl - wounded
Trumpeter William Remell - wounded
Saddler Otto Voit - wounded

Cpl. George Lell - killed
Pvt. P. Henry Bishley - wounded
Pvt. Thomas Hughes - wounded
Pvt. Julien D. Jones - killed
Pvt. Thomas Meador - killed
Pvt. William C. Williams - wounded

Company I

Pvt. David Cooney - wounded (died July 20)

Company K

Saddler Michael P. Madden - wounded
Pvt. Patrick Corcoran - wounded

Pvt. Max Mielke - wounded

Company L

Pvt. Jasper Marshall - wounded

Company M

Sgt. Patrick Carey - wounded
Pvt. James W. Darcy - wounded
Pvt. Jacob H. Gebhart - killed

Pvt. Thomas B. Varner - wounded
Pvt. Henry C. Voight - killed
Pvt. Charles T. Wiedman - wounded

*This analysis is a compilation of information from three sources: Kenneth Hammer's *Men With Custer: Biographies of the 7th Cavalry*; Douglas W. Ellison's *Sole Survivor*; and Edward S. Luce's *Keogh, Comanche and Custer*. None of the three sources are in 100% agreement with the other.

• Appendix D •

Reno's Report - July 5, 1876

Headquarters Seventh United States Cavalry
Camp on Yellowstone River, July 5, 1876

Captain E. W. Smith
A.D.C. and A.A.A. Gen:

The command of the regiment having revolved upon me as the senior surviving officer from the battle of the 25th and 26th of June, between the Seventh Cavalry and Sitting Bull's band of hostile Sioux, on the Little Big Horn River, I have the honor to submit the following report of its operations from the time of leaving the main column until the command was united in the vicinity of the Indian village.

The regiment left the camp at the mouth of the Rosebud River, after passing in review before the department commander, under command of Bvt. Major General G. A. Custer, Lieutenant Colonel, on the afternoon of the 22nd of June, and marched up the Rosebud 12 miles and encamped; 23rd, marched up the Rosebud, passing many old Indian camps, and following a very large lodgepole trail, but not fresh, making 33 miles; 24th, the march was continued up the Rosebud, the trail and signs freshening with every mile, until we had made 28 miles, and we then encamped and waited for information from the scouts. At 9:25 p.m. Custer called the officers together and informed us that beyond a doubt the village was in the valley of the Little Big Horn, and in order to reach it it was necessary to cross the divide between the Rosebud and the Little Big Horn, and it would be impossible to do so in the daytime without discovering our march to the Indians, that we would prepare to march at 11 p.m. This was done, the line of march turning from the Rosebud to the right up one of its branches which headed near the summit of the divide. About 2 a.m. on the 25th the scouts told him that he could not cross the divide before daylight. We then made coffee and rested for three hours, at the expiration of which time the march was resumed, the divide crossed, and about 8 a.m. the command was in the valley of one of the branches of the Little Big Horn. By this time Indians had been seen and it was certain that we could not surprise them, and it was determined to move at once to the attack. Previous to this, no division of the regiment had been made since the order

387

had been issued on the Yellowstone annulling wing and battalion organizations, but Custer informed me that he would assign commands on the march.

I was ordered by Lieutenant W. W. Cooke, Adjutant, to assume command of Companies M, A, and G; Captain Benteen, of Companies H, D, and K; Custer retained C, E, F, I, and L under his immediate command, and Company B, Captain McDougall, in rear of the pack train.

I assumed command of the companies assigned to me, and without any definite orders, moved forward with the rest of the column and well to its left. I saw Benteen moving farther to the left and, as they passed, he told me he had orders to move well to the left and sweep everything before him. I did not see him again until about 2:30 p.m. The command moved down the creek toward the Little Big Horn Valley, Custer with five companies on the right bank, myself and three companies on the left bank, and Benteen farther to the left, and out of sight.

As we approached a deserted village, and in which was standing one tepee, about 11 a.m., Custer motioned me to cross to him, which I did, and moved nearer to his column, until about 12:30 a.m. (sic) when Lieutenant Cooke, Adjutant, came to me and said the village was only two miles ahead and running away; to move forward at as rapid a gait as prudent, and to charge afterward, and that the whole outfit would support me. I think those were his exact words. I at once took a fast trot, and moved down about two miles when I came to a ford of the river. I crossed immediately, and halted about ten minutes or less to gather the battalion, sending word to Custer that I had everything in front of me, and that they were strong. I deployed and, with the Ree scouts on my left, charged down the valley, driving the Indians with great ease for about two and a half miles. I, however, soon saw that I was being drawn into some trap, as they would certainly fight harder, and especially as we were nearing their village which was still standing, besides, I could not see Custer or any other support, and at the same time the very earth seemed to grow Indians, and they were running toward me in swarms, and from all directions. I saw I must defend myself and give up the attack mounted. This I did. Taking possession of a front of woods, and which furnished near its edge, a shelter for the horses, dismounted and fought them on foot, making headway through the woods. I soon found myself in the near vicinity of the village, saw that I was fighting odds of at least five to one, and that my only hope was to get out of the woods, where I would soon have been surrounded, and gain some high ground. I accomplished this by mounting and charging the Indians between me and the bluffs on the opposite side of the river. In this charge, First Lieutenant Donald McIntosh, Second Lieutenant Benjamin H. Hodgson, Seventh Cavalry, and Acting Surgeon J. M. DeWolf, were killed.

I succeeded in reaching the top of the bluff, with a loss of three officers and 29 enlisted men killed and seven wounded. Almost at the same time I reached the top, mounted men were seen to be coming toward us, and it proved to be Colonel Benteen's battalion, Companies H, D, and K. We joined forces, and in a short time the pack train came up. As senior, my command was then A, B, D, G, H, K, and M, about three hundred and eighty men, and the following officers; Captains Benteen, Weir, and French and McDougall; First Lieutenants Godfrey, Mathey, and Gibson; and Second Lieutenants Edgerly, Wallace, Varnum, and Hare, and Acting Assistant Surgeon Porter.

First Lieutenant DeRudio was in the dismounted fight in the woods but, having some trouble with his horse, did not join the command in the charge out, and hiding himself in the woods, joined the command after night fall on the 26th.

Still hearing nothing of Custer, and with this reinforcement, I moved down the river in the direction of the village, keeping on the bluffs. We had heard firing in that direction and knew it could only be Custer. I moved to the summit of the highest bluff, but seeing and hearing nothing sent Captain Weir with his company to open communications with him. He soon sent back word by Lieutenant Hare that he could go no further, and that the Indians were getting around him. At this time he was keeping up a heavy fire from his skirmish line. I at once turned everything back to the first position I had taken on the bluffs, and which seemed to me the best. I dismounted the men and had the horses and mules of the pack train driven together in a deep depression, put the men on the crests of the hills making the depression and had hardly done so when I was furiously attacked. This was about 6 p.m. We held our ground, with a loss of 18 enlisted men killed and 46 wounded, until the attack ceased about 9 p.m. As I knew by this time their overwhelming numbers, and had given up any support from that portion of the regiment with Custer, I had the men dig rifle pits, barricaded with dead horses and mules and boxes of hard bread the opening of the depression toward the Indians in which the animals were herded, and made every exertion to be ready for what I saw would be a terrific assault the next day. All this night the men were busy, and the Indians holding a scalp dance underneath us in the bottom and in our hearing. On the morning of the 26th I felt confident that I could hold my own, and was ready, as far as I could be, when at daylight, about 2:30 a.m., I heard the crack of two rifles. This was the signal for the beginning of a fire that I have never seen equaled. Every rifle was handled by an expert and skilled marksman, and with a range that exceeded our carbines and it was simply impossible to show any part of the body before it was struck. We could see, as the day brightened, countless hordes of them pouring up the valley from the village and scampering over the high points toward the places designated for them by their chiefs, and which entirely surrounded our position. They had sufficient numbers to completely encircle us, and men were struck from opposite sides of the lines from where the shots were fired. I think we were fighting all the Sioux nation, and also all the desperadoes, renegades, half-breeds and squaw-men between the Missouri and the Arkansas and east of the Rocky Mountains, and they must have numbered at least twenty-five hundred warriors.

The fire did not slacken until about 9:30 a.m. and then we found they were making a last desperate effort and which was directed against the lines held by Companies H and M. In this charge they came close enough to use their bows and arrows, and one man lying dead within our lines was touched with the coup stick of one of the foremost Indians. When I say the stick was only ten or twelve feet long, some idea of the desperate and reckless fighting of these people may be understood.

This charge of theirs was gallantly repulsed by the men on that line, led by Colonel Benteen. They also came close enough to send their arrows into the line held by Companies D and K, but were driven away by a like charge of the line, which I accompanied. We now had many wounded, and the question of water vital, as from 6 p.m. the previous evening until now, 10 a.m., about 16 hours, we had been without.

A skirmish line was formed under Colonel Benteen to protect the descent of volunteers down the hill in front of his position to reach the water. We succeeded in getting some canteens, although many of the men were hit in doing so. The fury of the attack was now over, and to our astonishment the Indians were seen going in parties toward the village. But two solutions occurred to us for this movement; that they were going for something to eat, more ammunition (as they had been throwing arrows), or that Custer was coming. We took advantage of this lull to fill all vessels with water, and soon had it by campkettle full. But they continued to withdraw, and all firing ceased save occasional shots from sharpshooters sent to annoy us about the water. About 2 p.m. the grass in the bottom was set on fire and followed up by Indians who encouraged its burning and it was evident to me it was done for a purpose, and which purpose I discovered later on to be the creation of a dense cloud of smoke behind which they were packing and preparing to move their village. It was between 6 and 7 p.m. that the village came out from behind the dense clouds of smoke and dust. We had a close and good view of them as they filed away in the direction of the Big Horn Mountains, moving in almost perfect military order. The length of the column was fully equal to that of a large division of the cavalry corps of the Army of the Potomac, as I have seen it in its march.

We now thought of Custer, of whom nothing had been seen and nothing heard since the firing in his direction about 6 p.m. on the eve of the 25th, and we concluded that the Indians had gotten between him and us and driven him toward the boat at the mouth of the Little Big Horn River. The awful fate that did befall him never occurred to any of us as within the limits of possibility.

During the night I changed my position in order to secure an unlimited supply of water, and was prepared for their return, feeling sure they would do so as they were in such numbers, but early in the morning of the 27th, and while we were in the qui vive for Indians, I saw with my glass a dust some distance down the valley. There was no certainty for some time what they were, but finally I satisfied myself they were cavalry and, if so, could only be Custer, as it was ahead of the time that I understood that General Terry could be expected. Before this time however, I had written a communication to General Terry and three volunteers were to try and reach him. (I had no confidence in the Indians with me and could not get them to do anything.) If this dust were Indians it was possible they would not expect anyone to leave. The men started, and were told to go as near as it was safe to determine whether the approaching column was white men, and to return at once in case they found it so, but if they were Indians to push on to General Terry. In a short time we saw them returning over the high bluffs already alluded to. They were accompanied by a scout, who had a note from Terry to Custer saying Crow scouts had come to camp saying he had been whipped, but that it was not believed. I think it was about 10:30 a.m. that General Terry rode into my lines, and the fate of Custer and his brave men was soon determined by Captain Benteen proceeding with his company to his battle ground, and where was recognized the following officers, who were surrounded by the dead bodies of many of their men; General G. A. Custer; Colonel W. W. Cooke, Adjutant; Captains M. W. Keogh, G. W. Yates, and T. W. Custer; First Lieutenants A. E. Smith, James Calhoun; Second Lieutenants W. V. Reily, of the Seventh Cavalry and J. J. Crittenden, of the 20th Infantry, temporarily attached to this regiment. The bodies of Lieutenant J. E. Porter and Second Lieutenants H. M. Harrington and J. G. Sturgis, Seventh Cavalry, and Asst. Surg. G. W. Lord, U.S.A., were not recognized but there is every reasonable probability they were killed. It was now certain that the column of five companies with Custer had been killed.

The wounded in my lines were, during the afternoon and evening of the 27th, moved to the camp of General Terry, and at 5 a.m. on the 28th, I proceeded with the regiment to the battleground of Custer, and buried 204 bodies, including the following named citizens; Mr. Boston Custer, Mr. Reed (a young nephew of General Custer) and Mr. Kellogg (a correspondent for the New York Herald). The following named citizens and Indians who were with my command were also killed; Charles Reynolds, guide and hunter; Isaiah Dorman (colored), interpreter; Bloody Knife, who fell from immediately by my side, Bob Tail Bull and Stab, of the Indian scouts.

After traveling over his trail, it was evident to me that Custer intended to support me by moving farther down the stream and attacking the village in flank; that he found the distance greater to the ford than he anticipated; that he did charge, but his march had taken so long, although his trail shows that he had moved rapidly; that they were ready for him; that Companies C and I, and perhaps part of E, crossed to the village, or attempted it; at the charge were met by a staggering fire, and that they fell back to find a position from which to defend themselves but they were followed too closely by the Indians to permit time to form any kind of a line.

I think had the regiment gone in as a body, and from the woods which I fought, advanced upon the village, its destruction was certain. But he was fully confident they were running away, or he would not have turned from me. I think (after the great number of Indians that were in the village) that the following reasons obtained for the misfortune; his rapid marching for two days and one night before the fight; attacking in the daytime at 12 p.m., and when they were on the qui vive, instead of early in the morning and lastly, his unfortunate division of the regiment into three command

During my fight with the Indians I had the heartiest support from officers and men, but the conspicuous services of Bvt. Colonel F. W. Benteen I desire to call attention to especially, for if ever a soldier deserved recognition by his government for distinguished services, he certainly does. I enclose herewith his report of the operations of his battalion from the time of leaving the regiment until we joined commands on the hill. I also enclose an accurate list of casualties, as far as it can be made at the present time, separating them into two lists; A, those killed in General Custer's command; B, those killed and wounded in the command I had.

The number of Indians killed can only be approximated until we hear through the agencies. I saw the bodies of eighteen and Captain Ball, Second Cavalry, who made a scout of thirteen miles over their trail, says that their graves were many along their line of march. It is simply impossible that numbers of them should not be hit in the several charges they made so close to my lines. They made their approaches through the deep gulches that led from the hill top to the river and, when the jealous care with which the Indian guards the bodies of killed and wounded is considered, it is not astonishing that their bodies were not found. It is probable that the stores left by them and destroyed the next two days was to make room for many of those on their travois. The harrowing sight of the dead bodies crowning the height on which Custer fell, and which will remain vividly in my memory until death, is too recent for me not to ask the good people of this country whether a policy that sets opposing parties in the field armed, clothed, and equipped by one and the same government should not be abolished.

> All of which is respectfully submitted.
> M. A. Reno
> Major, Seventh Cavalry,
> Commanding Regiment

• Index •